Metaphor and Metonymy at the Crossroads

D1392802

287-291

329.

155; 137   61; 88-97

110-115

285 +256

279-277

Metaphor and Metonymy at the Crossroads

A Cognitive Perspective

edited by
Antonio Barcelona

Mouton de Gruyter
Berlin · New York   2003

Mouton de Gruyter (formerly Mouton, The Hague)
is a Division of Walter de Gruyter GmbH & Co. KG, Berlin.

First published in 2000 as volume 30 of the series
Topics in English Linguistics.

♾ Printed on acid-free paper which falls within the guidelines
of the ANSI to ensure permanence and durability.

ISBN 3 11 017556 8

Bibliographic information published by Die Deutsche Bibliothek

Die Deutsche Bibliothek lists this publication in the Deutsche
Nationalbibliografie; detailed bibliographic data is available in the
Internet at <http://dnb.ddb.de>.

To Marta, the theme of every sweet metaphor

Preface to the paperback edition

This new edition will make the basic notions of the cognitive theory of metaphor and metonymy, and a sample of its applications, available to more students and scholars of English linguistics as well as other fields. I am grateful to the series editors of *Topics in English Linguistics*, Bernd Kortmann and Elizabeth Closs Traugott, for proposing to Mouton de Gruyter to re-issue the book in this format, and to Anke Beck, its editor-in-chief, for accepting the idea. My gratitude also goes to Birgit Sievert, the managing editor of the series, for her careful work, and for inviting me to write this preface.

With the exception of this preface, the present paperback edition does not constitute a revision of the contents of the book as it was published two years ago. Such a brief time span since its publication did not justify altering the contents of the book or adding some extra essays. On the other hand, having the various contributors revise their articles, or inviting and editing some additional ones, would have delayed the publication of this re-issue enormously, thus frustrating its main purpose, namely, to make the book immediately accessible to a larger potential readership. Another reason for keeping the contents unchanged is that the theoretical positions and the methodologies reflected in the book are still completely valid and fairly representative of the major trends in metaphor and metonymy research from a cognitive linguistic perspective. Finally, it would be very difficult in a collection of essays to cover *every* important topic or line of research in the field, and adding two or more essays would hardly bring us any closer to exhaustiveness. The book is still completely adequate for its purpose as it stands, and its references to other major books and articles remain relevant today, and will remain so for some time.

The Cognitive Theory of Metaphor and Metonymy is still at the three "crossroads" specified in the introductory chapter of this book, which will frame future research in the field for a number of years. The first crossroads concerns the important changes the theory is undergoing. Some of these are the attempts to provide more precise definitions of metaphor and metonymy, especially of the latter, the new proposals regarding the perennial issue of the distinction between metaphor and metonymy, and the attempts to account more precisely for the experiential motivation of metaphor. Concerning this last issue, two different but complementary proposals are the hypothesis of the metonymic motivation of metaphor, discussed in some detail in the present volume, and the theory of primary metaphor put forward by Grady (e. g. Grady 1999). All of these topics and proposals, and many others, are discussed at length in Dirven and Pörings (2002), a collection of essays in the series *Cognitive Linguistic Research*, published by Mouton de Gruyter. Another important theoretical departure is the continued development of the theory of conceptual integration, also known as "blending theory" (its most recent presentation being Fauconnier and Turner 2002), which regards metaphor and metonymy as subcases of a general mapping ability.

The second crossroads refers to the interaction between metaphor and metonymy. This issue is still the subject of lively discussion and investigation, and will continue to be so for a long time. Again, Dirven and Pörings' book contains a number of papers which supplement the information on the topic contained in the present book.

And the third crossroads concerns the new tendencies or results in the applications of the cognitive theory of metaphor and metonymy. Some of them are the development of operational techniques for metaphor identification in texts, the study of emotional and physiological responses to metaphor, and the continued investigation into the ubiquitous interaction of metaphor and metonymy with language structure (especially grammar) and discourse. With regard to this last area, the systematic investigation into the crucial role of metonymy at all linguistic levels, in particular in grammar and discourse pragmatics (Panther and Thornburg, forthcoming), and the cross-linguistic study of high-level metonymies will bring some interesting results in the near future.

Most of these future research results will be a continuation of the type of research represented in this paperback. Therefore, the user of this book will be perfectly equipped to assimilate those results quite easily.

References

Dirven, René and Ralf Pörings. eds.
2002   *Metaphor and Metonymy in Comparison and Contrast* (Cognitive Linguistic Research 20). Berlin/New York: Mouton de Gruyter.
Fauconnier, Gilles and Mark Turner
2002   *The Way We Think. Conceptual Blending and the Mind's Hidden Complexities.* New York: Basic Books.
Grady, Joseph
1999   A typology of motivation for conceptual metaphor. Correlation vs. resemblance. In: Gibbs Raymond and Gerard J. Steen (eds.), *Metaphor in Cognitive Linguistics*, 79–100. Amsterdam: John Benjamins.
Panther, Klaus-Uwe and Linda Thornburg. eds.
Forthc.   *Metonymy and Pragmatic Inferencing.* Amsterdam: John Benjamins.

Acknowledgments

Before beginning this brief section of acknowledgments, I would like to describe in a few words the various stages that were followed in the editing of this book. This has proved to be a most laborious, time-consuming task. After carefully studying the proposals received from various authors and deciding which ones to accept, and which additional contributions to invite, the second step was to revise again in very close detail each and every paper in terms of content and form (to ensure that all the articles conformed to the publisher's very detailed specifications of format and style, and that a common rule was followed in other aspects of form*). During the third phase, all the contributions were carefully revised again, and a pre-final printout was sent to the publisher. The final stage included writing the introduction, completing the indexes and other ancillary parts of the book, and doing the final proofreading of the whole book. The whole process has taken a very long time, much longer than I would have liked, and an immense expenditure of energy: book editing is by no means an easy job, as I have learnt. Yet this experience has been a very rewarding one. I have learnt a lot through it, and the final result has been worth the effort. Since I have been granted the privilege of being the only editor of a book in this excellent series, it is only fair that I alone should be held responsible for any editing errors that may have gone unnoticed despite my many revisions.

The difficulty of my work has been mitigated by the generous support and cooperation received from a number of people and institutions. I want to express my most heartfelt gratitude, therefore, to:

The other authors in the volume, for their cooperation at each stage of my editorial work, and for their willingness to consider, and usually accept, my suggestions and those offered by the anonymous reviewers;

Bernd Kortmann, the series director, for his excellent guidance and advice, particularly in the initial stages of the project;

The anonymous reviewers of the various papers, whose careful work was of great assistance in the selection and revision of the papers;

My student assistants, Mike Rueter and Francisco Abril Portero, especially the latter, for their most invaluable collaboration in the complex process of checking the style and format of all the articles;

Dr. David Walton, my colleague in the English Department of the University of Murcia, Spain, for his careful, appreciative revision of the English language proficiency of every text in the book written by a non-native speaker of English;

---

* But I have striven to respect as far as possible the authors' original manuscript. For example, when two authors have used two different versions of a forthcoming work, differing, among other aspects, in the title. I have maintained the title of the version used by each author.

Mouton de Gruyter, particularly its Editor-in-Chief, Dr. Anke Beck, and Ms Katja Huder, of the editorial team, for their useful, professional advice and their cooperation throughout this protracted editorial work;

Finally, I want to thank most particularly my wife, Marta, for her loving support and encouragement, and for understanding my frequent periods of unavailability throughout the completion of this project.

Contents

Acknowledgments ix

Introduction. The cognitive theory of metaphor and metonymy 1
Antonio Barcelona

**The interaction of metaphor and metonymy, and other
theoretical issues**

On the plausibility of claiming a metonymic motivation for conceptual
metaphor 31
Antonio Barcelona

Refining the Inheritance Hypothesis: Interaction between metaphoric
and metonymic hierarchies 59
Kurt Feyaerts

The scope of metaphor 79
Zoltán Kövecses

How metonymic are metaphors? 93
Günter Radden

The role of mappings and domains in understanding metonymy 109
Francisco José Ruiz de Mendoza Ibáñez

Metaphor, metonymy, and binding
Mark Turner and Gilles Fauconnier 133

Metaphor and metonymy in language structure and discourse

Metaphor and metonymy in language structure

Patterns of meaning extension, "parallel chaining", subjectification, and
modal shifts 149
Louis Goossens

Metaphor in semantic change 171
Verena Haser

• Straight from the heart — metonymic and metaphorical explorations .. 195
Susanne Niemeier

The EFFECT FOR CAUSE metonymy in English grammar 215
Klaus-Uwe Panther and Linda Thornburg

Metaphorical extension of *may* and *must* into the epistemic domain ... 233
Péter Pelyvás

Metaphor and metonymy in discourse

Poetry and the scope of metaphor: Toward a cognitive theory
of literature 253
Margaret H. Freeman

The cohesive role of cognitive metaphor in discourse and conversation   283
Diane Ponterotto

More metaphorical warfare in the Gulf: Orientalist frames in
news coverage 299
Esra Sandikcioglu

Muted metaphors and the activation of metonymies in advertising 321
Friedrich Ungerer

Author index 341
Subject index 345

Introduction
The cognitive theory of metaphor and metonymy[1]

Antonio Barcelona

1. Preliminary remarks

The present volume includes a selection of the papers presented at two scholarly meetings which I organized in 1997. One of them was a theme session on the metonymic motivation of metaphor included in the 5th International Cognitive Linguistics Conference at the Free University of Amsterdam (July, 1997). The other was a seminar on the cognitive theory of metaphor and metonymy and its application to English studies, included in the Fourth Conference of the European Society for the Study of English, held at Lajos Kossuth University, Debrecen, Hungary (September, 1997). In addition to these papers, the book includes several specially invited contributions.

The volume addresses a number of important topics in the cognitive theory of metaphor and metonymy (henceforth, abbreviated as CTMM) and is an excellent example of its application. Metaphor and metonymy are described by the title of the book as being *at the crossroads* in three senses. One of them alludes to the fact that the CTMM is at present at a turning-point in its evolution as a theory. This is reflected by the articles dealing with or applying the new theory of "blending", by the paper suggesting the existence of "simple" abstract metaphors, and by the articles concerned with the nature of metonymy, a topic which had been relatively neglected in earlier stages of the CTMM. The second sense alludes to another important current theoretical issue, namely the interaction between metaphor and metonymy: metaphor and metonymy often "meet" at conceptual and linguistic crossroads. The issue of interaction is the focus of some of the articles; and of the various kinds of interaction, the metonymic basis of metaphor receives particular attention. The third sense in which the CTMM is claimed to be at a crossroads is by noting the emergence of new tendencies, new ways, in its application. Some of them are represented in the book: the study of the metaphorical motivation of crosslinguistic patterns of lexical semantic change; the study of the metonymic motivation of grammar; the study of the role of metaphor and metonymy in conversation and advertising. With these relatively new applications, new appraisals or new instances of earlier applications of the CTMM are also represented in the volume (applications to the investigation of the semantic and grammatical shifts of English modals, to the study of cognitive models, and to the analysis of literary and journalistic discourse).

As will become apparent to the reader as (s)he progresses through the book, the fact that all of the contributors accept the basic principles of this theory does not necessarily mean that they agree on each or most of the controversial issues. My own views on some of these are stated in this introduction and in my own contribution, but they are not necessarily shared by all the other authors, nor do I necessarily agree with every contributor on all of his/her proposals. I have preferred to reflect in the book some of the healthy diversity of views which keep cognitive linguistics alive, rather than choosing a list of papers that, by providing exactly the same answers to the same questions, would create in the reader the quite misleading notion that students of cognitive metaphor constitute a uniform group.

The cognitive theory of metaphor and metonymy is a fundamental aspect of the enterprise of cognitive linguistics. Since not all of the readers for whom the *Topics in English Linguistics* series is intended are likely to be familiar with the CTMM or with the main principles of cognitive linguistics, it may be necessary to describe them briefly before actually introducing the articles included in this volume.

2. A cognitive approach

The general approach to the study of language known today as cognitive linguistics has evolved as an essential part of a broader quest for a more satisfying account of the nature of human cognition in general and of linguistic meaning in particular; a quest in which a sizable group of cognitive scientists (i.e. linguists, psychologists, anthropologists, philosophers, computer scientists, even literary critics) has been engaged since the mid-seventies, initially in the United States and shortly afterwards in Europe and, to a lesser extent, in other parts of the world. The linguistic "side" of this wide-ranging effort is cognitive linguistics.

I cannot discuss here in detail the main principles and methodologies that are followed by this group of linguists (which is far from being homogeneous). A brief summary can be found in Barcelona (1997b). Longer introductions to cognitive linguistics are Taylor (1995) and Ungerer and Schmid (1996). It should suffice here to enunciate the overriding assumption shared by all of these researchers, i.e. that the so-called "language faculty" is just a reflection, in some cases a specialization, of general-purpose cognitive abilities, and is governed by general neural processes. Thus, in their view, there is a continuum between all sorts of cognition (especially body-based cognition, but also cognition acquired on the basis of social and cultural experience) and language, there being little ground for claiming that language, let alone syntax, is a separate "module" in the mind or in the brain. They adduce as evidence recent research in neurology (see, e.g. Edelman 1992) and cognitive psychology, especially the work of Eleanor Rosch (see e.g. Rosch and Lloyd eds., 1978). One of the major general cognitive abilities is imagination, or in more technical terms, the ability to project concepts onto other concepts. And this is why such imaginative devices as metaphor and metonymy have become an object of prime interest for cognitive scientists (see Johnson 1987, especially chapter 6, Lakoff and Johnson 1999, or Barnden and Holyoak 1994).

An important result of this movement is that the study of all the aspects and manifestations of language, including literature, becomes again a central part of the enterprise of cognitive science (Turner 1991, 1996).

3. Metaphor

Metaphor is the cognitive mechanism whereby one experiential domain is partially 'mapped', i.e. projected, onto a different experiential domain, so that the second domain is partially understood in terms of the first one. The domain that is mapped is called the *source* or *donor domain*, and the domain onto which the source is mapped is called the *target* or *recipient* domain. Both domains have to belong to different superordinate domains. This is basically the cognitive concept of metaphor propounded by George Lakoff, Mark Johnson and Mark Turner and by other cognitive linguists that have been investigating the field for the past nineteen years.

In the well-known metaphor LOVE IS A JOURNEY (cf. Lakoff and Johnson 1980; Lakoff 1987), the domain of journeys, itself a subdomain in the domain of movement, is mapped, that is, superimposed, onto the domain of love, itself a subdomain of the domain of emotions:

(1)   *Look how* far *we've* come.
(2)   *Our relationship is* off the track.
(3)   *We're* spinning our wheels.

This mapping transfers a large number of aspects (attributes, entities and propositions) from the experiential domain of journeys to the experiential domain of emotions, and specifically to the domain of love (Lakoff 1993: 206-209). Among them we can single out the following correspondences:

–   The lovers correspond to the travelers.
–   The love relationship corresponds to the vehicle in the journey.
–   The lovers' common goals correspond to their common destinations on the journey.
–   Difficulties in the relationship correspond to impediments to travel

These are *ontological submappings or correspondences*: that is, the entities (people, objects, etc.), actions or states in the source are mapped onto their counterparts in the target domain. There are also *knowledge* (or *epistemic*) *submappings / correspondences*. For example, the journey situation in which the vehicle gets stuck and the travelers try to set it in motion again, either by fixing it or getting it past the impediments that prevent its progress, corresponds to the love situation in which the love relationship becomes unsatisfactory and the lovers try to make it satisfactory again either by improving it or by solving the difficulty that prevented it from functioning properly. An important aspect of metaphor is that its elaboration is typically open-ended (Lakoff and Turner 1989: 106-110; Barcelona 1997a), and can be creatively exploited in text and conversation, as is shown convincingly by Diane Ponterotto's or Margaret Freeman's contributions to this book.

The main constraint on metaphorical mappings seems to be the so-called Invariance Hypothesis (Lakoff and Turner 1989: 82-83; Lakoff 1990, 1993). Its main thrust is that the mapping cannot violate the basic structure of the target domain. It seems to explain why most metaphors are only partial. For instance, the well known metaphor TIME IS MONEY, allows us to think and talk about time as a valuable commodity that can be spent, which is limited in supply, etc., but not as a commodity which one can get back (I give you my money and it is perfectly possible that, if asked to do so, you will give me back exactly the same money, not only the same amount of money, but also the same notes and coins; however, if I give you my time you cannot give me back exactly the very minutes, hours or days I spent on you; you can, however, give me back the same amount of time). This limitation comes from the inherent structure of the target domain, in which time goes on and cannot be recovered.

4. Metonymy

Metonymy has received much less attention from cognitive linguists than metaphor, although it is probably even more basic to language and cognition. Metonymy is a conceptual projection whereby one experiential domain (the target) is partially understood in terms of another experiential domain (the source) included *in the same common experiential domain*. Metonymy is, in my view, a special case of what Langacker (1987: 385-386) calls *activation*. The metonymic mapping causes the mental activation of the target domain (Kövecses and Radden 1998: 39), often with a limited discourse purpose (Lakoff 1987: 78-80). See examples (4)-(9):

(4)   *She's just a pretty* face. (FACE FOR PERSON)
(5)   *The* ham sandwich *is waiting for his check.* (CONSUMED GOODS FOR CUSTOMER)
(6)   *There are a lot of good* heads *at the University.*
         (BODY PART FOR PERSON and BODY PART FOR INTELLECTUAL ATTRIBUTES CONVENTIONALLY ASSOCIATED WITH IT)
(7)   *I'll have a* Löwenbrau. (PRODUCER FOR PRODUCT)
(8)   *He walked with* drooping shoulders. *He had lost his wife.* (DROOPING BODILY POSTURE FOR SADNESS) (EFFECT FOR CAUSE)

(9)   *John has* a long face (DROOPING FACIAL MUSCLES FOR SADNESS) (EFFECT FOR CAUSE)

Examples (4)-(7) have been borrowed from Lakoff and Johnson (1980: chapter 8). (8) and (9) come from Barcelona (1986). In all of them, the mapping occurs within one common domain. Take example (4): The domain of people includes the subdomain of the face, which is mapped onto the whole matrix domain of people. In other words, we have a part-for-whole metonymy in which the face is mapped onto the person. In the other examples, the mapping also occurs within one common superordinate domain. In (5), this is the restaurant domain, which includes customer and food as parts; in (6), this is the domain of the person (the whole), which includes the head as a part; the head, in turn, includes the intellectual attributes connected with it. In (7), the common domain is the production domain, which includes producer and product as parts; and in (8) and (9), the common domain is that of sadness, which includes as parts the emotion-cause and its effects.[2]

5. Some basic common traits of metaphor and metonymy

From what has been said so far, it should be clear that both metaphor and metonymy are regarded in cognitive linguistics as *conventional mental mechanisms*, not to be confused with their expression, linguistic or otherwise. Metaphors and metonymies are often not verbalized, but can be expressed through gestures or other non-verbal communicative devices, or not be communicated at all and simply motivate our behavior (Lakoff and Johnson 1980: 156-158).

An important distinction exists, then, between metaphorical and metonymic *conceptual projections*, on the one hand, and metaphorical or metonymic *expressions*, linguistic or otherwise, on the other. A conceptual metaphor or metonymy may conventionally be activated by or instantiated in, a morpheme, a word, a phrase, a clause, a sentence, a whole text, gestures and other types of behavior, reasoning processes, etc. A linguistic expression may eventually cease to be used metaphorically or metonymically but the corresponding conceptual projection may still be alive and be reflected in other linguistic expressions. And the more entrenched conceptual metaphors or metonymies, those with a more direct bodily basis seldom, if ever, die (Lakoff and Turner 1989: 49-67).

Cognitive linguistics also stresses the fact that conventional metaphors and metonymies are usually *automatic*, *unconscious* mappings, *pervasive* in everyday language, as some of the examples above demonstrate. Literary metaphors and metonymies are normally just creative extensions and elaborations of these conventional mappings (Lakoff and Turner 1989: 67-72).

Cognitive linguistics has insisted upon the *systematicity* of metaphor and metonymy. Complex hierarchical networks of conceptual metaphors and metonymies have been discovered in English and other languages, which reveals that a given metaphor or metonymy is often just a particular manifestation of a more abstract superordinate metaphor or metonymy. The metaphor LOVE IS A JOURNEY can ultimately be shown to be a specification of a more abstract metaphor, LIFE IS A JOURNEY, which is, in turn, a manifestation of a yet more abstract one, the EVENT STRUCTURE metaphor (Lakoff 1993). The metonymy FACE FOR PERSON is a manifestation of the superordinate metonymy BODY PART FOR PERSON (*We need more* hands *for our factory*), and this metonymy, in turn, is a manifestation of the overarching metonymy PART FOR WHOLE. The systematicity of metaphor and metonymy is also apparent in the construction of conceptual domains through the combination of a large number of metaphors and metonymies. These complex combinations have been analyzed in great detail in the domain of emotions; see Barcelona (1986), Lakoff and Kövecses as reported in Lakoff (1987: 380-415), and most particularly, Kövecses (1990).

Metaphors and metonymies are to a large extent culture-specific, because the domains of experience are not necessarily the same in all cultures, but the most abstract, overarching metaphors and metonymies seem to have as input or "source" domains universal physical notions like "verticality", "container", etc., known as "image schemas", which are acquired on the basis of our earliest bodily experiences (Johnson 1987; Lakoff 1990, 1993; Taylor 1995: 127-130).

Both metaphor and metonymy are fundamental types of cognitive models (Lakoff 1987: 68-90), both are experientially motivated (Lakoff and Johnson 1980: 61-68), and both can be used for an immediate pragmatic purpose (Ruiz de Mendoza, 1997: 171-176). Their characterization as "models" also underscores their stability as part of our "cognitive equipment": conceptual metaphors and metonymies are supposed to be stable elements of our system of categories. And in this respect the CTMM is in opposition to theories of metaphor like Searle's, which does not grant metaphor (or metonymy for that matter) the status of a cognitive model which can be directly activated in the process of language understanding and production. Searle (1979:76-116) regards metaphorical expressions as special uses of language which have to be reduced to literal meaning through the application of pragmatic rules, and whose interpretation necessarily requires extra cognitive effort. Searle would have said that the use of *come* in (1) above is just a conventional special sense of the verb, synchronically unconnected with other manifestations of the metaphor, like (2) and (3). Other modern theories, like Davidson's or Grice's, also stress the primary role of the literal meaning of the linguistic expression in metaphor interpretation (for a discussion of these and other theories, see Johnson 1981). In the CTMM, metaphors consist of fixed multiple simultaneous projections (mappings) from the so-called "source" domain onto the so-called "target" domain, and metaphorical meaning is claimed to be irreducible to literal meaning.

According to the standard CTMM, the mapping in metaphor is always *unidirectional*: only the source is projected onto the target domain, and the target domain is not at the same time mapped onto the source domain. Therefore, simultaneous *bidirectional* metaphorical projections do not exist, according to this theory. This is an important difference between the CTMM and other theories, like Black's interaction theory (Black 1962). For example, there seems to exist a conventional metaphor PEOPLE AS ANIMALS. If we say *Don't* snap *at me*, or *Their love* nest *has been discovered*, we project an aspect (aggressive behavior, living place) of some animals (dogs or birds) on some aspects of people (anger, lovers' meeting point), but no aspect of people is mapped onto animals by virtue of the existence of *this* metaphor. However this claim does not mean that there cannot exist a different metaphor, ANIMALS AS PEOPLE, which maps aspects of people onto aspects of animals, as in the sentence *Lions are courageous*, in which a human moral attribute is projected onto an animal instinct (but nothing is mapped from animals onto people). They are not two variants of the same metaphor, because what is mapped is different in each case (cf. Lakoff and Turner 1989: 132).

6. Some recent new trends

A recent tendency in cognitive linguistics which subsumes metaphor and metonymy as special cases of more general mental mapping mechanisms is the theory of "blending" or conceptual integration, which is an extension of Gilles Fauconnier's earlier work on mental spaces (Fauconnier 1994) and has been developed by him and Mark Turner (Fauconnier 1997, Turner and Fauconnier 1995). This new theory seeks to explain how speakers and hearers keep track of referential values and build new inferences throughout discourse, often by constructing provisional conceptual domains or "blends".

This new approach is not incompatible with the standard two-domain theory of metaphor and metonymy that has been outlined above, because it presupposes it. However, it seems to explain more precisely the functioning of metaphor and metonymy in discourse. This new approach basically claims that in conceptual mapping, as it proceeds in discourse, the source and the target domains (or "input spaces", as they are called) are mapped onto a "blended space" or "blend", whose conceptual structure is not wholly derivable from both input spaces. There is also a fourth "generic space", which contains skeletal conceptual structure taken to apply to both source and target. The theory of blending, or the "many-space model", as it is also called, is designed to account, not only for metaphor and metonymy, but also for irony, counterfactuals, and grammar.

Turner and Fauconnier's work places in a new perspective the common claim in the CTMM that metaphorical mappings are unidirectional, i.e. that they move only from the source to the target domain, and points to the existence of multiple projections. Turner and Fauconnier do not argue for a return to interaction theories of metaphor. Although projections go from both inputs to the blend, the principal inferences project from the blend to the target, not to the source. To be sure, possibilities may arise for projecting some inferences back to the source, but those are special cases. Therefore, where the theory of conceptual integration touches on metaphor, it offers a refined version of the unidirectionality thesis in the standard theory of metaphor and metonymy.

The paper by Turner and Fauconnier in this volume is an excellent illustration of the nature and functioning of this new theory. The papers by Margaret Freeman and by Ruiz de Mendoza also apply it and explore some of its aspects.

7. Some problems in the cognitive notions of metaphor and metonymy

There are a sizable number of issues in the CTMM that require clarification. Many of them have to do with the distinction between metaphor and metonymy; sometimes it is not easy to say with certainty whether an observed mapping is to be regarded as metaphorical or metonymic. Closely linked to the problems of distinction are those presented by the frequent interaction between metaphor and metonymy. Other problems affect specifically the nature of metonymy. Yet another type of problem is how to account for the effect of general discourse-pragmatic principles on the exploitation of a metaphor or a metonymy in a text (which submappings are foregrounded, which ones are backgrounded, how they are elaborated or extended etc.). All of these groups of problems are, in fact, closely related.

Something else that the CTMM still has to do is compile a systematic typology of the major metaphors and metonymies in English and other languages with a specification of their systematic connections with each other and their hierarchical relationships. Kövecses and Radden (1998) is an initial attempt at a systematic typology for metonymy.

In the rest of this section, I will briefly suggest a possible answer to at least some of these problems. Despite these problem areas, I think that the CTMM is, compared with other approaches to metaphor and metonymy developed in linguistics, rhetorics or philosophy, the theory that can best account for these conceptual mechanisms.

7.1 The distinction between metaphor and metonymy

A fundamental problem, which lies at the heart of the cognitive theory of metaphor and metonymy, is the one created by the very notion of a cognitive, experiential domain. The cognitive domain is characterized by Langacker (1987: 154-158), Taylor (1995: 83-87), and most other cognitive linguists, as an "encyclopedic" domain (i.e. it includes all the entrenched knowledge that a speaker has about an area of experience). Thus it will normally vary in breadth from person to person, and in many cases, it has no precise boundaries. How can, then, the neat distinction between two domains be used to distinguish metonymy from metaphor?

Let us illustrate this problem with an example belonging to one of the first domains whose metaphorical structure was uncovered by cognitive linguistics, namely, that of emotions. The effects of emotions can plausibly be supposed to be a subdomain in the domain of emotions; that is, the effects of an emotion on our body or on our behavior[3] are obviously a part of our experience of that emotion. One of the behavioral effects of sadness consists in displaying a drooping bodily posture (drooping shoulders, head, or facial muscles). Remember (8) and (9) above. Now the experiential subdomain constituted by this specific effect includes as a part of it the subdomain of verticality ("drooping"), and with it, that of three-dimensional space. If the definitions of metaphor and metonymy offered earlier were applied blindly, we would have to conclude that verticality and three-dimensional space are included in the conceptual domain of sadness, and that expressions like those in (10) would actually be *metonymic* and not metaphorical, because a part of a domain (verticality and three-dimensional space) would be standing for that domain (sadness):

(10)   *She is* in the pits.
         I'm in low *spirits.*
         Cheer up.
         Pete is down in the dumps.

In other words, the sentences in (10), like those in (8) and (9), would all be metonymic, and not metaphorical. This process of inclusion in the domain of sadness of presupposed domains might continue *ad infinitum*, and, if applied to other known metaphors, would result in most of them having to be regarded as metonymies, and not as metaphors.

However, most cognitive linguists would say that the sentences in (10) are linguistic manifestations of the SADNESS IS DOWN / HAPPINESS IS UP metaphor. How can we solve this paradox? We should note that a sort of reasoning like the one we have just sketched would reach a conclusion that seems to be at odds with the actual psychological facts. It seems that, at least on a conscious conventional level, no speaker of English categorizes verticality as a part of sadness or happiness, although on an unconscious level verticality seems to enter the construction of both notions via metonymy and metaphor. Therefore when we say that metaphor is a mapping across two *separate* domains, we mean that they must be *consciously* regarded as separate. The definition of metaphor given a few pages earlier should then contain this specification: metaphor is a mapping of a domain onto another domain, both being conventionally and consciously classified as separate domains, i.e. not included in the same superordinate domain. With this addition to the definition, the sentences in (10) can be regarded as expressions of a metaphor, rather than of a metonymy. This addition does *not* mean that every time a speaker utters a metaphorical expression, (s)he has to be conscious of the separation between source and target. As I said above, metaphor and metonymy are mostly used unconsciously. The additional specification of the definition of metaphor suggested here is simply that source and target have to be treated as being in separate domains by the conventional conscious classification of domains prevailing in a given culture: Speakers of English do not consciously and conventionally categorize sadness as a type of spatial location, or verticality as a part of emotion.

The above addition to the definition of metaphor does not mean that we cannot postulate a metonymic *motivation* for the SADNESS IS DOWN / HAPPINESS IS UP metaphor, or indeed for many other metaphors. This issue will be discussed briefly below, as one of the types of metaphor-metonymy interaction.

Examples like (10) lead some cognitive linguists (e.g. Goossens, Niemeier, Radden, all in this volume) to suggest that the distinction between metaphor and metonymy should be regarded as scalar, rather than as absolute.

7.2. Metaphor-metonymy interaction

It is well known that metaphor and metonymy often interact with each other, sometimes in fairly intricate ways (see Lakoff and Turner 1989:104-106; Goossens 1990; Gibbs 1994: 449-451; Goossens et al. 1995). In my view, the patterns of interaction or combination could be reduced to two general types:

1) Interaction at the purely conceptual level.
2) Purely textual co-instantiation of a metaphor and a metonymy in the same linguistic expression.

The most important of these is interaction at the purely conceptual level. We discuss it in the first place. In my view, there are two main subtypes of metaphor-metonymy interaction at this level:

a) The metonymic conceptual motivation of metaphor.
b) The metaphorical conceptual motivation of metonymy.

The metonymic conceptual motivation of metaphor is fairly problematic, and it constitutes a real challenge for the theory of metaphor. It has long been noticed that a great many metaphors are motivated conceptually by a metonymy, which is closer to their experiential basis. The metaphor SADNESS IS DOWN / HAPPY IS UP is conceptually motivated by the metonymy, discussed above, in which a behavioral effect of sadness stands for this emotion (see Barcelona, this volume). Another case is the ANGER IS THE HEAT OF A FLUID metaphor, as investigated by Lakoff and Kövecses (Lakoff 1987: 380-415). Taylor (1995: 139) suggests some other cases. These are some of Lakoff and Kövecses' examples of the metaphor:

(11)   *I had reached* boiling point.
        She got all steamed up.
        When I told him, he just exploded.

According to Lakoff and Kövecses, this metaphor is motivated by a group of metonymies in which certain physiological effects of anger stand for this emotion. These are some of their examples of these metonymies, preceded by the kind of physiological effects of anger that stand for the emotion:

(12)   Body heat: *Don't get* hot under the collar.
          Internal pressure: *When I found out, I almost* burst a blood vessel.
          Agitation: *I was* hopping mad.

A very interesting area of research is, thus, the study of the extent to which the whole metaphorical network of a language is motivated by the metonymic one. A great deal of careful research has to be done before reaching safe conclusions. Two of the articles in this book (those by Radden and by Barcelona) explore this issue in detail.

The metaphorical conceptual motivation of metonymies can be discovered in metonymic interpretations of a linguistic expression that only seem possible *within* a co-occurring metaphorical mapping, as in (13):

(13)   *She caught the Minister's ear and persuaded him to accept her plan.*
          (example borrowed from Goossens, 1990).

The metaphor here is ATTENTION IS A (TYPICALLY MOVING) PHYSICAL ENTITY (that one has to get hold of, attract, or "call"). At the same time we find in this sentence a specific version of the conventional metonymy BODY PART FOR (MANNER OF) FUNCTION. In this conventional metonymy, a body part stands for its function and / or for the manner in which its function is performed (cf. *He has a* good hand, *She has* a good head).

The specific version of the conventional metonymy in this example is EAR FOR ATTENTION; or, to put it differently, we have a body part whose function (hearing) is characterized as being performed in a highly specific manner: "with attention". This body part stands for *this* manner of its function. This specific version of the metonymy only takes place in metaphorical mappings involving attention as the target domain (this is my interpretation of Goossens' (1990: 333) discussion of this and similar examples of "metonymy within metaphor"). That is, only when attention has been made the target domain in a metaphorical mapping is it possible, within the target domain, to carry out a metonymic mapping in which the ear stands for a specific attribute (attention) of its typical function (hearing). In fact if we look at cases where EAR stands for ATTENTION, we find that this is indeed the case:

(14)   *She* won his ear.
(15)   *She* lent *me* her ear.

Again, in these two cases, as in (13), attention is understood as an entity (usually a moving one) that has to be attracted or obtained in some way, and it is metonymically represented by the ears.

The fact that a certain metonymy is only possible within a matrix metaphor does not mean that one cannot argue that the latter is motivated conceptually by a different metonymy.[4]

The second general type of interaction is the purely textual co-instantiation of a metaphor and a metonymy by the same linguistic expression. This happens, for instance, when a metonymy co-occurs in the same linguistic expression with a certain metaphorical mapping, from which it is conceptually independent. Their co-occurrence is not owing to the fact that they conceptually motivate each other, but to the fact that they are *compatible*. See (16):

(16)   *The* ham sandwich *started* snarling.

The metaphor in this example is a special version of the PEOPLE ARE ANIMALS metaphor. The special version is ANGRY BEHAVIOR IS AGGRESSIVE ANIMAL BEHAVIOR (Lakoff 1987: 393). This sentence would refer, in a restaurant situation, to the angry behavior of the customer who bought the ham sandwich.The metonymy is, as in example (5) above (*The ham sandwich is waiting for his check*), CON-SUMED GOODS FOR CUSTOMER.

The metaphor and the metonymy in (16) are compatible with each other because both have (a class of) people as target. But they are conceptually independent from each other. It is easy to see this fact, as regards the metonymy, by noting that example (5) can occur without the metaphor. As for the metaphor, it is enough to replace the subject in (16) to realize that the metaphor does not depend conceptually on *this* metonymy:

(17)   John *started* snarling.

7.3. Specific problems with the notion of metonymy

Some of the main problems that specifically concern the notion of metonymy are: Is it really a conceptual mapping or rather a type of conceptual activation of certain aspects of a domain? Does it have to be referential? Is there any fundamental difference between metonymy and lexical (or grammatical) ambi-guities due to the special activation or "highlighting" (Croft 1993: 349-350) of a domain? How does a metonymy become conventional?

Kövecses and Radden (1998) do not seem to regard metonymy as a sort of mapping; at least, they do not use the term *mapping* in their definition of me-tonymy. They say that metonymy is a "cognitive process in which one concep-tual entity, the vehicle, provides mental access to another conceptual entity, the target, within the same domain, or ICM" (Kövecses and Radden 1998: 39). Their conception of metonymy is, in part, based on Langacker's notion of con-ceptual "reference-point" (Langacker 1993). Langacker (1993: 29-35), on the other hand, seems to regard metonymies at the same time as "active zone" phenomena, in which an aspect or an entity of an "abstract domain" is mentally "active"; again, the notion of mapping does not seem to be relevant. However, Lakoff and Turner (1989:103) regard both metaphor and metonymy as conceptual mappings. The issue is addressed in this volume by Ruiz de Mendoza. To him, the fact that metonymy is a type of mapping is not incompatible with the fact that it often consists of the "highlighting" or the "activation" of the target domain. This position is correct, in my opinion. A mapping is the projection of a domain or subdomain onto another domain or subdomain. In metonymy, the projection of the source simultaneously causes the mental activation of the target; but the mapping does take place. In example (18), borrowed from Croft (1993),

(18)   Proust *is tough to read.*

the whole domain PROUST is mapped onto one of its subdomains – PROUST'S LITERARY WORK. We are invited to understand Proust's work *from* the author, and the further inference is suggested that his literary work is an extension of his personality. That is, the general domain of the author is projected onto that of his work.

Although some writers seem to have a referential notion of metonymy, metonymy need not be referential. As Ruiz de Mendoza says in his article in this volume, predicative metonymies like *John is a Picasso* (implying that John is a genius in painting) are not referential (at least according to the traditional concept of reference). Stereotype-based metonymic prototypes like the "housewife-mother" prototype or the "stereotypical bachelor" (Lakoff 1987: 79-86) prototype can operate independently from any acts of reference, as shown by this example of reasoning in terms of a model of motherhood with the "housewife-mother" as metonymic center:

(19)   *Mary is an excellent mother, even though she has a demanding job.*

There often occur mappings and phenomena of activation or highlighting that seem to be quite akin to typical metonymies. Croft (1993: 349) discusses, in this connection, several examples, among them (20) and (21):

(20)   This book *is heavy.*
(21)   This book *is a history of Iraq.*

In the reading of (20) that Croft is concerned with, *heavy* is used (non-metaphorically) in the domain of physical objects; he is not concerned here with its (metaphorical) use in the domain of semantic content, i.e. as equivalent to "tedious". Croft contends that, by contrast with (18) above, neither (20) nor (21) are clear cases of metonymy, although a subdomain within the general BOOK domain, namely the PHYSICAL OBJECT domain, is highlighted in (20) by the adjective *heavy*, and another subdomain within BOOK, namely SEMANTIC CONTENT, is activated in (21) by the NP *a history of Iraq.* The reason Croft gives is that both of these subdomains are highly "intrinsic" (Langacker 1987:159-161) in the conceptualization of a book. Thus, they are not "extrinsic" enough to be regarded as distinct conceptual entities from a book, with the result that no shift in reference is possible. Hence no metonymy really occurs in (20) and (21). Croft has a fundamentally referential notion of metonymy. The metonymic target, in Croft's view, has to be extrinsic within the source domain matrix. This is what happens in (18) above, in which the LITERARY WORK subdomain is highly extrinsic by comparison with the PERSON subdomain in the conceptual matrix for PROUST.

This issue certainly requires careful discussion among researchers interested in metonymy. On the one hand, examples like (20) and (21) do seem to satisfy the basic requirement for all metonymies: in both of them, the whole domain BOOK is mapped onto one of its subdomains, which is thus mentally activated. In this respect, they are not essentially different from (18). In my view, even these examples should be regarded as metonymic at least in a broad sense. Examples like (18) are certainly more typical. In typical metonymies, the source and the target are neatly distinct subdomains. This sometimes happens in WHOLE FOR PART metonymies like (18), and it always happens in PART FOR WHOLE metonymies, like those in (4) or (6) above, and in PART FOR PART metonymies like those in (5), (7), (8) or (9).[5]

The factors favoring the conventionalization of metonymy can be quite varied. They could, perhaps, be summed up by saying that a metonymy becomes conventional if it satisfies these requirements (Taylor 1995: 122-123):

(a) It must follow one of the "natural" patterns or types of conceptual metonymic relationships (types like PART FOR WHOLE, WHOLE FOR PART, PRODUCER FOR PRODUCT, PATH FOR GOAL, etc.). Kövecses and Radden (1998) provide a systematic list of these "default" patterns.

(b) It must be socially sanctioned. This is, obviously, the most important requirement for conventionalization. Social sanction depends, in turn, on:

(b1) The number of general cognitive and communicative principles favoring "natural" cases of metonymy that apply in the case in question. Kövecses and Radden (1998: 62-71) have proposed a number of general cognitive and communicative principles favoring the conventionalization of a metonymy. The larger the number of these principles licensing a specific metonymy, the more motivated it will be and the more likelihood there will for it to become conventional.

(b2) The existence of a specific cultural principle favoring the conventionalization of that metonymy (Taylor 1995: 123), or conversely, the lack of a specific principle blocking the conventionalization.

Let us briefly illustrate requirement (b). One of the general types of metonymy is AUTHOR FOR WORK (a subcase of PRODUCER FOR PRODUCT), as in (22):

(22) *I have just bought a* Picasso.

The metonymy PICASSO FOR HIS WORK is a conventional specific realization of AUTHOR FOR WORK. The expression *a Picasso* activates the subdomain of Picasso's artistic work, and in this example, it refers to a particular painting by this artist. Kövecses and Radden (1998:71) say that a metonymy like that in (22) is motivated by the cognitive principles that they call HUMAN OVER NON HUMAN, CONCRETE OVER ABSTRACT, and GOOD GESTALT OVER POOR GESTALT. That is, it satisfies requirement (b1). Perhaps another principle that could be added to their list and that also seems to motivate this metonymy is SALIENT OVER NON SALIENT, because in the domain of artists, their works are a naturally salient subdomain. The metonymy in (22) also gets conventionalized because there exists a cultural principle whereby works of art are regarded as unique products of the creative genius of artists, as an extension of their personality. Thus, the metonymy also meets requirement (b2).

However, if my sister Jane paints what I take to be wonderful landscapes, which are, however, only bought by our family and a few friends, the specific realization of AUTHOR FOR WORK intended in (23)

(23)   *I have just bought a* Jane.

certainly responds to the general pattern – requirement (a) – and is motivated by the same cognitive-communicative principles as in (22) – requirement (b1) – but it is not socially conventionalized according to requirement (b2), except perhaps within my small family circle (see Taylor 1995: 123).

For a waitress, the kind of food consumed by her customers is a naturally relevant domain in her "restaurant ICM", which explains the conventionality of example (5), in which the food consumed is metonymically mapped onto the customer. As regards (b1), what applies here is the general communicative principle RELEVANT OVER IRRELEVANT, which overrides the cognitive principle HUMAN OVER NON HUMAN (Kövecses and Radden 1998: 70). As for (b2), no additional specific cognitive-cultural principle seems to contribute to, or to block, the conventionalization of this metonymy.

8. The articles in this volume

The contributions in the book can be loosely arranged into two main groups, which are reflected in the table of contents: a) those whose main focus is a general theoretical discussion of the nature of metaphor or metonymy, or their interaction; b) those which consist of a case study, or a series of case studies, aimed at investigating the effect of conceptual metaphor or metonymy on some aspect of language structure and language use (polysemy, grammar, discourse). But, in fact, it is impossible to fit all the papers neatly into these categories. On the one hand, most of the papers assigned to the first group also include one or more detailed case studies, and, on the other hand, most of the authors in the second group also make some general claims about metaphor and / or metonymy on the basis of their research.

8.1. Theoretical issues

The papers by Barcelona, Feyaerts, Kövecses, Radden, Ruiz de Mendoza, and Turner and Fauconnier have been included in the first general group. One of the issues that was mentioned in an earlier section of this introduction with respect to metaphor-metonymy interaction was the fact that metonymy often seems to motivate metaphor. The papers by Antonio Barcelona and by Günter Radden directly address this issue. Other essays in the book, particularly Niemeier's or Ungerer's, also touch upon this topic. Another important view held by most of the authors in this group (Barcelona, Radden, Ruiz de Mendoza), and by some others (notably Goossens and Niemeier) included in the second group, is the claim that the distinction between metaphor and metonymy is scalar, rather than discrete: they seem to be points on a continuum of mapping processes. But these are just two of the issues treated by the contributors in this first group. As the ensuing presentations show, they also deal with many other important topics in the CTMM.

The article by *Antonio Barcelona* is an exploration of the plausibility of a radical hypothesis, namely, the hypothesis that *every* metaphor is motivated by conceptual metonymy. The notion of metonymy assumed in his essay is a broad conceptual notion; that is, metonymy is a conceptual mapping of one domain onto another domain within the same superordinate domain, so that the former mentally activates the latter. The author surveys some important recent research that offers numerous examples of metonymy-motivated metaphors. Then he examines some examples, like *Loud color*, or *The high notes on a piano* that, according to Taylor (1995), cannot reasonably be claimed to have a metonymic basis. On the basis of the analysis of these and other examples, Barcelona identifies two different general types of metonymic motivation for metaphor. In one of them, as in *loud color*, an experience-based metonymic model of the metaphoric target seems to motivate and constrain the choice of the metaphoric source; "deviant", gaudy colors seem to be understood primarily as "attention-getting" colors, which motivates the choice of loud sounds as source. In the other type, as in MORE IS UP, or SADNESS IS DOWN, the metaphor comes about as the generalization of a metonymy which encapsulates experiential knowledge. The author then explores the connections between the hypothesis under examination and the Invariance Principle; his main (tentative) conclusion is that invariance can be regarded as a consequence of the frequent metonymic motivation of metaphor. Emotional domains are particularly interesting in this respect, as their image-schematic structure seems to arise metonymically. After offering a possible reply to some objections against the hypothesis, the article ends with a comparison between this hypothesis and the proposals by Kövecses (this volume) and Grady to treat specific metaphors as reducible to "simple" or "primitive" ones.

Kurt Feyaerts presents a proposal for refining Lakoff's "Inheritance Hypothesis" (Lakoff 1993), i.e. the claim that metaphorical mappings are organized in complex hierarchies, so that subordinate mappings "inherit" all the details of superordinate mappings. Feyaerts claims that metonymic mappings are likewise organized as hierarchies which interact with metaphorical hierarchies to determine the meaning of a linguistic expression. In the first section of the paper he rejects the standard view of metonymy and metaphor in cognitive linguistics as mappings across or within domains, due to the unreliability of the notion of domain. He views metaphor as a mapping that achieves conceptual similarity, and metonymy as a "relationship" of conceptual contiguity. In the second part, the author illustrates the operation of a metonymic hierarchy in a cultural model. Then he contrasts metaphoric and metonymic hierarchies. In the latter type, subordinate metonymies do not inherit from more schematic ones any domain-internal structures, as in metaphoric hierarchies, but only their contiguity relationship. Feyaerts then contends that in the German folk model of stupidity, there is a systematic "metaphtonymic" interaction between two metonymies and one submapping of the EVENT STRUCTURE metaphor (Lakoff 1993). On the basis of his data, Feyaerts suggests that "metaphtonymic" interaction can take place at the more specific level of the hierarchy, right above the level of linguistic instantiation, but not at the more schematic levels.

Zoltán Kövecses' essay develops and amply illustrates his notion of the "scope of metaphor", i.e. the mapping potential of a given source domain. Allied to this notion are those of "main meaning focus" and of "central mapping". The main meaning focus (there can, in fact, be more than one main meaning focus) is the central knowledge ("central knowledge" in Langacker's sense) about the source domain. The existence of one or more main meaning focus / foci can be seen as a kind of metonymic basis for metaphor. The main meaning focus of the source is inherited, according to Kövecses, by the target. A central mapping is a submapping in a metaphor that projects the main meaning focus / foci of the source. Central mappings motivate the emergence of other submappings, are strongly motivated experientially and culturally, and are linguistically most productive. Kövecses illustrates his proposals with a detailed analysis of the generic metaphors COMPLEX SYSTEMS ARE BUILDINGS (which includes, among others, THEORIES ARE BUILDINGS), and A SITUATION IS HEAT (OF FIRE). He identifies one or more main meaning focus / foci in their source domains, and consequently, one or more central mappings. For example, in A SITUATION IS HEAT (OF FIRE), the main meaning focus is "intensity", and the central mapping links "heat of fire" with "intensity of a situation", whereas in COMPLEX SYSTEMS ARE BUILDINGS, there are three meaning foci and three central (sub)mappings: "making the building" → "creating or developing the system"; "strength of the building" → "stability or strength of the system"; and "physical structure" → "abstract structure". He proposes to use the term "simple metaphors" for those that capture central submappings (i.e. ABSTRACT STABILITY IS PHYSICAL STRENGTH) and the term "complex metaphors" for metaphors like THEORIES ARE BUILDINGS, which result from the combination of simple metaphors.

Günter Radden's essay is a lucid survey of what he calls "metonymy-based metaphors". Radden does not claim that every metaphor is necessarily based on a metonymy. However, his paper argues in favor of the acceptance of metonymy-based metaphor as an analytical category, which is needed to account for the experiential basis of a great number of metaphors. Metonymy-based metaphors are also evidence of the metaphor-metonymy continuum, with prototypical cases of metaphor and prototypical cases of metonymy at both ends of the continuum, and with metonymy-based metaphors in the middle area. Radden surveys a sample of metonymy-based metaphors drawn from Lakoff's *Master Metaphor List* and Lakoff and Johnson (1999), classifying his material into four main groups. In the first group, both source and target have a common experiential basis. An example is ACTIVE IS ALIVE / INACTIVE IS DEAD. This metaphor is based on the experiential correlation between life and activity, on the one hand, and death and inactivity, on the other hand. Correlation, in the author's opinion, is a metonymic relationship that is involved in a great many metaphorical mappings. Other metaphors in this group are based on such metonymic relationships as complementarity and comparison, both of which also imply a strong, experientially grasped, conceptual interdependence between two entities or counterparts. The second group is based on conversational implicature, which is likewise presented as a metonymic relationship. For example, the relationship of contiguity between two sequential events underlies such metaphors as KNOWING IS SEEING. We take what we see to be true; that is, we tend to establish an automatic metonymic connection between seeing and knowing, which underlies the metaphor. The third group is based on category structure, i.e. metaphors based on such metonymic relationships as member-for-category (which motivates ACTION IS MOTION). Finally the fourth group contains metaphors based on metonymies arising on the basis of cultural models (e.g. ANGER IS HEAT, based on metonymies arising in the folk model of emotions).

The long, complex article by *Francisco Ruiz de Mendoza* also favors the metonymy-metaphor continuum hypothesis. The author claims that there exist two main types of metaphors: "one-correspondence" metaphors, with just one "central correspondence" (similar to Kövecses' notion of "central mapping") between source and target, and just one "central implication" (similar to Kövecses' notion of "main meaning focus"), and "many-correspondence" metaphors, with several central mappings and central implications. Of them, "one-correspondence" metaphors occupy the middle ground on the continuum, together with predicative (non-referential) metonymies. The bulk of the paper concentrates on metonymy. Ruiz de Mendoza proposes to distinguish only two general types of metonymy: "source-in-target" (i.e. part-for-whole), and "target-in-source" (i.e. whole-for-part) metonymies, excluding part-for-part metonymies. This proposal runs counter to established tradition. He substantiates this claim on the basis of these facts: the tendency for one of the domains to be conventionally included in the other, the functioning of anaphoric reference with conjoined predicates (particularly in cases of what Nunberg calls "predicate transfer" and "deferred indexical reference"), and metaphor-metonymy interaction. His suggestion that in their interaction with metaphor, source-in-target metonymies signal the central inference for the metaphoric mapping, whereas target-in-source ones highlight some aspects of the target, can be regarded, in my view, as types of metonymic constraints on metaphor, and can be related to Barcelona's paper and to Radden's. Ruiz de Mendoza also suggests that source-in-target metonymy has a fundamental role in the creation of a generic space, in Turner and Fauconnier's "many-space" model. He then examines the requirement for metonymy, set by Croft (1993), that its target be a secondary subdomain in the domain matrix for the source, and suggests that the ranking of subdomains in a domain matrix depends on their "centrality" (in Langacker's sense), not just on their intrinsicness, as Croft claims. Ruiz de Mendoza finally uses his basic binary typology and the distinction between primary and secondary subdomains to provide a new definition of metonymy.

The article by *Mark Turner* and *Gilles Fauconnier* is an illustration of their recent theory of "blending" or conceptual integration and a demonstration of the crucial role of metonymic connections in the construction of "blended spaces". It consists of five case studies. It has been included in this group because of its theoretical concern with the role of metonymy in blending. The first study concerns a joke conceptual blend that was popular for some time in some circles, with President Clinton and American politics as the target mental space, on the one hand, and the movie "Titanic", on the other, as the source space ("If Clinton were the Titanic, the iceberg would sink"). The authors show that a re-framing of both the source and the target occurs in the blended space, in which, counter to normal expectations derived from the source input (i.e. that the ship would be sunk by the iceberg), the metaphorical fusion of Clinton and the Titanic is made to look superior to the entity resulting from the figurative fusion between special prosecutor Starr and the iceberg. This re-framing is then mapped back onto the target (Clinton, politics), which is regarded as capable of surviving even the worst threats. In the second study they explain how a well-studied metaphor like ANGER IS HEAT can be analyzed in terms of the interaction of metaphor, metonymy and blending, in a way that explains how physiological reactions to anger can be connected to heat and fire. They show that the metonymic correspondences in the blend are mapped onto those in the target on the basis of their "metonymy projection constraint", one of their "optimality principles on integration networks", which consists in shortening the metonymic distance between elements in the blend. The same constraint is illustrated in the remaining three studies, aimed at showing that blends can combine non-counterparts if the right metonymic connections are in place. This is particularly clear in the study of the conventional Grim Reaper image: for example, the skeleton after decomposition of the body normally has a distant, indirect metonymic relationship to death, but this relationship is shortened in the blend. The fourth and the fifth studies describe how the same metonymic principle operates in a cartoon and in a passage of the *Divine Comedy*. An important feature of conceptual integration that can be observed in the five studies is that the blend has emergent structure and inferences of its own, not present or possible in the input source or the target. This was not quite evident, they claim, in earlier research on metaphor.

8.2. Metaphor and metonymy in language structure and discourse

The articles by Freeman, Goossens, Haser, Niemeier, Panther and Thornburg, Pelyvás, Ponterotto, Sandikcioglu, and Ungerer have been included in the second general group of papers, namely, the articles that investigate the influence of metaphor and metonymy on a particular aspect of language structure and use. This second group can be subdivided into two subgroups. The first subgroup studies the effect of metaphorical and / or metonymic mappings on two aspects of linguistic structure, namely, polysemy / semantic change and grammar. The second subgroup is concerned with the operation of metaphor and metonymy in discourse, including conversation, literary (poetic) discourse, journalism, and advertising.

8.2.1. Metaphor and metonymy in language structure

The goal of the article by *Louis Goossens* is to identify the general extension patterns which give rise to the shifts in the meaning of English modals, from what he calls (following Van der Auwera and Plungian) "participant-internal" to "participant-external modality", and from participant-external to epistemic modality and beyond modality. In Goossens' view, the data for *may* and *will* cannot be sufficiently accounted for just in terms of metaphor or metonymy, but in terms of a chaining of uses motivated by what Langacker calls the "partial sanction" of certain uses with respect to a prototypical use. The relevant type of partial sanction in these shifts is "parallel chaining", i.e., a chaining of parallel uses of the modals moving in the same direction. In a detailed study devoted to *must* Goossens attempts to show that, in addition to parallel chaining, increased subjectification taking place in the deontic area paved the way for the development of the epistemic sense. (Subjectification is the general tendency for meanings to become increasingly situated in the area of the speaker's belief or attitude toward the proposition.) Among his conclusions he surmises the idea that a merely metaphorical or metonymic interpretation of the polysemy of English modals does not reflect the cognitive processing by the speakers of present-day English. The author's claims are based on a detailed study of numerous data drawn from various corpora, both of present-day English and of various historical stages of the language.

Verena Haser's paper is a very amply documented inquiry into the metaphorical shifts that account for the polysemy of a wide range of lexemes in languages belonging to very different language families around the globe. Haser offers several case studies of some of these possibly universal shifts. Before presenting the studies, she lays out clearly her own notions of lexical semantic change, metaphor and metonymy, and describes the methodology followed in her research and the scope of her results. The number and range of sources used by the author is impressive. To Haser, metaphor and metonymy are the foremost agent of semantic change, yet earlier applications of metaphor theory to the study of semantic change have mostly concentrated on grammaticalization, to the neglect of the study of lexical-semantic change. The various studies in the article focus on the regularities in lexically encoded extensions to other domains from the domains of vision, hearing, physical manipulation, searching, counting, and from certain spatial domains. Cross-linguistic surveys like Haser's are of prime importance when trying to decide which metaphorical mappings – and to what extent – are universal, and to characterize in a more precise way seemingly universal patterns in lexical semantic change and in human cognition in general. Her research, in my view, can also be related to Kövecses' (this volume), as it displays the cross-linguistic scope of a number of source domains. The author finally points out what she deems to be some shortcomings of the notion of "image schema", as developed by Mark Johnson.

Susanne Niemeier analyzes the metaphorico-metonymic folk model of the heart in English. She shows how the various metaphors involving the heart have a metonymic basis, and how the language user's understanding, as a metaphor or as a metonymy, of a given linguistic expression including vocabulary from the heart domain, depends upon the degree of his/her awareness of the subtle intermediate conceptual steps linking the source to the target. So her paper is also relevant for three of the main theoretical foci of the volume, namely, the interaction between metaphor and metonymy, the metaphor-metonymy continuum, and, most particularly, the metonymic basis of metaphor. The article analyzes in great detail a large corpus of linguistic expressions involving the heart as a domain in metaphor and / or metonymy. The material is arranged into four overlapping categories, established on the basis of the strength of the metonymic motivation of the corresponding metaphors. This metonymic motivation becomes increasingly less obvious as one moves from the first category, in which it is clearly perceivable, to the fourth one, in which it is quite remote. An important fact highlighted by the article is that the various metaphors focus on different aspects of the folk model of the heart. This, in my view, is another type of metonymic basis for metaphor, which is also reminiscent of Kövecses' notion of "main meaning focus", or of Ruiz de Mendoza's notion of "central implication". Niemeier also claims that, in many cases, metaphor results from the generalization of a metonymy, an idea also present in Barcelona's paper.

The article by *Klaus-Uwe Panther* and *Linda Thornburg* presents groundbreaking research on the systematic interaction between conceptual metonymy, on the one hand, and grammar and / or meaning, on the other hand. In the first part of the paper, they study the grammaticalization in English of a specific subcategory of the general EFFECT FOR CAUSE metonymy, namely RESULT FOR ACTION. The authors first construct a number of test frames, which they call "action constructions", and which typically admit only action predicates and do not accept stative predicates. Then they note that certain stative predicates can enter these frames. One of them, the imperative construction, sometimes accepts stative predicates, as in *Stand behind the yellow line*. Other frames are infinitive complement sentences requiring action verbs, and constructions like *What about VP_{ing}?*, *How to VP* and *Why not VP?*. The authors note that some instances of typically stative constructions, like *Be + Adj / NP* constructions and passive sentences, and certain non-actional verbs, can be inserted or combined with action constructions, as shown by such examples as *What about being quiet?* or *Don't be deceived by his looks*. Yet in some other instances this is not possible (**How to be tall in five weeks*). The explanation is that, in the acceptable cases, the predicate denotes a "resultant state" which is metonymically related to its cause, an unmentioned previous action. *What about being quiet?* can be paraphrased as "What about acting in such a way so as to become quiet?". In the unacceptable cases, the stative predicate just denotes a state not resulting from a previous action. English contrasts in this respect with German, which normally requires an explicit causative verb like *lassen* in the translation equivalent of acceptable English passives inserted in action constructions. In the authors' view, there is no need to claim, in an *ad hoc* manner, that these English stative predicates acquire a special dynamic sense in these constructions. Metonymy affords a more elegant explanation. The second part of the paper is devoted to a general study of the impact of EFFECT FOR CAUSE on the *What's that N?* construction. This construction does not encode a metonymy, but its meaning, and the type of responses that it can elicit, are metonymically motivated. The authors identify two main metonymy-based senses of this construction, the "taxonomic" sense and the "causal" sense. The taxonomic reading (as in *What's that bird? It's a titmouse*) is motivated by the GENERIC FOR SPECIFIC METONYMY. The causal reading, activated by certain noun classes, typically those denoting sense impressions (as in *What's that noise? It's a squirrel*) is based on the EFFECT FOR CAUSE metonymy. Again, English is compared with German in this respect. This article coincides with several others in the volume (e.g. Barcelona, Radden, Ruiz de Mendoza) in the view of metonymy as a conceptual mapping not necessarily restricted to the act of reference, and in the recognition of its pervasiveness in language.

The paper by *Péter Pelyvás* is a careful attempt at characterizing the metaphorical projection of root modal meanings onto the epistemic domain. His article can, thus, be interestingly contrasted with Goossens'. Sweetser's force-dynamics analysis of *may* is criticized by Pelyvás, because, in his view, she ignores the fact that in the image-schematic structure of the epistemic target domain, not only one barrier, but two barriers (simultaneously lifted or imposed), must be postulated. To the author, the crucial difference between deontic and epistemic *may* is that whereas deontic *may* and *may not* are contradictory, their epistemic counterparts can be entertained together. Another reason for his criticism is that Sweetser's analysis of the extension of this modal from the deontic into the epistemic domain violates the Invariance Principle. Furthermore, he observes that diachronic evidence strongly suggests that the deontic sense of *may* appeared later than the epistemic one. Pelyvás' alternative is based on the concept of "counteracting forces", rather than on the concept of rigid barriers. The author attempts to relate both deontic and epistemic meanings of *may* to its original (now extinct) ability meaning ("be strong enough"). In this original meaning, only the doer and the potential action are in the "objective scene" (in Langacker's terms), whereas the speaker/conceptualizer remains in the "ground", and does not make any epistemic commitment. Although in deontic *may* the speaker often enters the objective scene as permission giver, (s)he exerts a weak counterforce to oppose the force exerted by the doer, as (s)he just relinquishes authority. In the epistemic sense, the speaker again exerts a weak force, as (s)he relinquishes epistemic commitment. This account, the author contends, satisfies invariance, because the roles and relations remain constant in the mapping, even though increasing subjectification takes place in the epistemic domain. Pelyvás criticizes Sweetser's and Talmy's analyses of *must* in similar terms. His alternative analysis introduces into Sweetser's model for deontic *must* a new, relatively weak, force, i.e. the doer's reluctance to perform, which is mapped, in the epistemic extension, onto "forces of unknown reality". His account of this extension is also accompanied by subjectification and satisfies invariance, as the structural relations between forces and roles are preserved. Pelyvás also suggests an explanation, in terms of his model, for the external negation of epistemic *must* by means of *cannot*.

8.2.2. Metaphor and metonymy in discourse

Margaret Freeman puts forward a theory of literature – "cognitive poetics" – grounded in cognitive linguistics and in cognitive science at large, and outlines its main features. Freeman sees both literary texts and their interpretation as the product of cognizing minds. She then demonstrates the power and usefulness of cognitive poetics by means of four brilliant case studies. The first two are devoted to a poem of E. Dickinson each (The "Cocoon" and the "Loaded Gun" poems), in which she shows how analogical reasoning and "blending" underlie the possible interpretations of the poem. Freeman contrasts partial readings based just on "attribute" mappings (e.g. THE GUN IS THE SELF), and readings based just on "relational" mappings (which just map relations onto relations), on the one hand, with "system" or "structural" readings, on the other hand, which provide a holistic interpretation of a poem. System readings generate all the partial readings that have been provided by other critics. Freeman also rigorously connects the semantics of the "Cocoon" poem with its form. In the third case study, she applies cognitive poetics to the issue of authorship by comparing

Emily Dickinson's "cognitive style" with that of a forged poem wrongly attributed to her. And the fourth study is an analysis of Sylvia Plath's poem "The Applicant", through which Freeman discusses the compatibility of cognitive poetics with, and its advantages over, other cognitive theories of literature like discourse theory, possible worlds theory, and schema theory.

Diane Ponterotto claims that metaphor has a central role in the structuring of conversation and proposes to regard conceptual metaphor as a fundamental part of cognitive theories of discourse. The model of discourse analysis used by the author (the "blueprint" model proposed by Tomlin et al.), requires that the interlocutors achieve "knowledge integration" and "information management" if the conversation is to be successful. Ponterotto claims that metaphor is the conceptual device that guarantees the satisfaction of this requirement. Then she briefly discusses the complexity of the factors intervening in the coherence underlying the apparent formlessness of a conversation and emphasizes the role of memory and storage in our ability to hold a conversation. She claims that metaphor also facilitates the storage and retrieval of information. Her two brief case studies – one on the script of a film scene and another on a recorded authentic conversation – show that a major metaphor normally provides the *heuristic frame*, as she calls it, for the rest of the conversation, which then calls up a complex web of thematically related conceptual metaphors that are used to explore and elaborate the major theme in the conversation. Metaphor networks often constitute the backbone of conversation and give it cohesion. The pivotal role of metaphor in conversation, Ponterotto says, is a consequence of the brevity, conciseness and vividness of metaphor, and of the multiplicity, open-endedness and flexibility of metaphor networks.

Esra Sandikcioglu's essay applies her personal interpretation of the cognitive theory of metaphor to her own analysis of the coverage of the Gulf War by two prominent American magazines. She claims that other analyses, like Ann Pancake's, or like Lakoff's, are insufficient insofar as they fail to take into account the powerful cultural cognitive model that at the same time motivates and is implemented by the metaphors the media used. This cultural frame is called "Orientalism" by Edward Said, and it is described, in the first part of the article, as an unfair schematization and oversimplification of the Orient and its people by conventional Western thought. Sandikcioglu breaks down this model into a set of "frames of Self-presentation" (of the West to itself), which systematically contrast with a corresponding set of "frames of Other-representation" (of the East by the West). The author claims that each of these frames is structured by a number of conceptual metaphors and metonymies. She presents an ample subset of her corpus of data to illustrate her claims. The paper is, then, both a conceptual analysis of a collection of texts, and at the same time, a critique of the way in which these magazines and other media used, in the author's opinion, this cultural cognitive model to assist the Bush administration and the Pentagon in their "psychological" strategy against Iraq.

Friedrich Ungerer deals in his article with the interesting textual device which he brands "the muting of metaphor", as employed in advertising and trade names. This device consists in the use of certain carefully contrived strategies that artificially filter out the "undesirable" (i.e. negatively valued) submappings in a metaphor. Ungerer also studies how these muted metaphors activate what he calls the "GRABBING" metonymy, whereby grabbing an object stands for desiring it, a metonymy that often also motivates these metaphors conceptually. Throughout the paper the author uses the basic distinction between conceptual motivation and (textual, situational) activation. Ungerer first argues for the existence of the GRABBING metonymy as a conceptual physiological metonymy, and for its status as an essential component of every advert. Then he deals with what he calls the VALUE metaphor, i.e. THE DESIRED OBJECT IS A VALUABLE OBJECT (like a jewel), and explains how it interacts with the metonymy in advertising. But, as advertisers know, the VALUE metaphor has no longer enough attention-getting potential. This metaphor is an instance of an overarching metaphor family, THE DESIRED OBJECT IS AN INTERESTING OBJECT, a subset of which, "SHOCK" metaphors (e.g. THE DESIRED OBJECT IS A REVOLTING OBJECT), are better eye-catchers. Yet advertisers must avoid the negative reflection of the source domain of these metaphors (e.g. a snake) on the object advertised. This goal is achieved by constraining or "muting" the mapping potential of the "shocking" source, so that its "negative" aspects will not be transferred to the target i.e. the advertised object. The author carefully describes these strategies and the complex patterns of muted metaphors and of metonymies used in advertising. He finally devotes a brief section to metaphor, metonymy and muting in trade names.

As I hope to have shown in this final section of the introduction, the contributions gathered in this book are a fair reflection of the current state of the cognitive theory of metaphor and metonymy. They are also an excellent sample of the many areas of English, and of English-language, literature and culture, whose study can benefit enormously from an insightful application of this theory.

Notes

1.   I thank the Spanish Ministry of Education and Culture (Dirección General de Investigación Científica y Enseñanza Superior), for funding with grant no. PR95-441 a five-month stay (September 1996-February 1997) at the University of Cambridge, United Kingdom, during which I did some of the research reflected in this introductory article and in my other article in this volume.

2.   EFFECT FOR CAUSE is considered by Kövecses and Radden (1998) as a PART FOR PART metonymy, within the ICM of CAUSATION. Emotions can be said to incorporate this ICM, so that two different subdomains (i.e. parts) of each emotional domain would be its physiological or behavioral *effects*, on the one hand, and the emotion itself in its role as *cause*, on the other hand.

3.   The linguistically encoded identification and understanding of such effects is mediated by a folk theory of the effects of emotions (Kövecses 1990).
4.   ATTENTION IS A MOVING PHYSICAL ENTITY seems to be motivated by the understanding of attention primarily in terms of one of its aspects, namely the fact that, in actual experience, there are normally several competing foci of our attention; attention is, thus, metonymically understood for the purpose of this metaphor as "fleeting, wandering attention", rather as "rapt, undivided attention", "meticulous attention", or any other kind of attention. Now one can correlate the *variability in the focus* (i.e. the mental reference point) of fleeting attention, with the *variability in the location* (i.e. the spatial reference point) of a moving physical entity. The concept of a moving physical entity is, therefore, an excellent metaphorical source to be mapped onto the concept of attention. Another possible metonymic basis, fully compatible with the one just suggested, is the fact that when something attracts our attention, we tend to *move* to the location of the attention-getting entity. Thus, the event of paying attention which is followed by such a change in location would stand metonymically for all the other ways in which the event of paying attention can take place, including those cases in which we do not actually move towards the attention center.
5.   In Barcelona (n.d.) I have recently proposed to consider, for various research purposes, four classes of metonymies which progressively constrain their range of membership. *Schematic* metonymies are those that satisfy the minimal requirements for every conceptual metonymy: intra-domain mapping and activation of target by source. *Typical* metonymies are those schematic metonymies in which the source and the target remain clearly distinct (within the superordinate overall domain) from each other. *Prototypical metonymies* are those typical metonymies with individuals as targets and as referents (they are the "classical" instances of metonymy). *Conventional metonymies* are typical metonymies which are socially sanctioned in virtue of a number of parameters (see below).

References

Barcelona, Antonio
    1986   "On the concept of depression in American English: A cognitive approach", *Revista Canaria de Estudios Ingleses*, 12:7-33.
    1997a   "Clarifying and applying the notions of metaphor and metonymy within cognitive linguistics", *Atlantis* 19-1 (21-48).
    1997b   "Cognitive linguistics: A usable approach", in: Antonio Barcelona (ed.), 7-32.
    this volume "On the plausibility of claiming a metonymic motivation for conceptual metaphor."
    n.d.   "Problems in the cognitive definition of metonymy". [Unpublished MS. University of Murcia.]
Barcelona, Antonio (ed.)
    1997   *Cognitive linguistics in the study of the English language and literature in English*. Monograph issue of *Cuadernos de Filología Inglesa*, volume 6:2.

Barnden, John A. and Keith Holyoak (eds.)
1994   *Analogy, metaphor and reminding*. Norwood, New Jersey: Ablex.
Black, Max
1962   *Models and metaphors*. Ithaca, N.Y.: Cornell University Press.
Croft, William
1993   "The role of domains in the interpretation of metaphors and metony-
           mies", *Cognitive Linguistics*, 4-4: 335-371.
Edelman, Gerald
1992   *Bright air, brilliant fire: On the matter of mind*. New York: Basic Books
Fauconnier, Gilles
1994   *Mental spaces: Aspects of meaning construction in natural language*.
           Cambridge, England: Cambridge University Press.
1997   *Mappings in thought and language*. Cambridge, England: Cambridge
           University Press.
Gibbs, Raymond W. jr.
1994   *The poetics of mind. Figurative thought, language, and understanding*.
           Cambridge, England: Cambridge University Press.
Goossens, Louis
1990   "Metaphtonymy: The interaction of metaphor and metonymy in expres-
           sions for linguistic action", *Cognitive Linguistics* 1-3: 323-340 (also
           reproduced in Goossens et al. 1995, 159-174).
Goossens, Louis – Paul Pauwels – Brygida Rudzka-Ostyn – Anne-Marie Simon-
Vanderbergen – Johan Vanparys.
1995   *By word of mouth. Metaphor, metonymy and linguistic action in a cog-
           nitive perspective*. Amsterdam/ Philadelphia: John Benjamins.
Johnson, Mark
1981   *Philosophical perspectives on metaphor*. Minneapolis: Minnesota Uni-
           versity Press.
1987   *The body in the mind: the bodily basis of meaning, imagination, and
           reason*. Chicago: University of Chicago Press.
Kövecses, Zoltán
1990   *Emotion concepts*. New York: Springer Verlag.
Kövecses, Zoltán – Günter Radden
1998   "Metonymy: Developing a cognitive linguistic view", *Cognitive Lin-
           guistics*, 9-1: 37-77.
Lakoff, George
1987   *Women, fire and dangerous things. What categories reveal about the
           mind*. Chicago: Chicago University Press.
1990   "The Invariance Hypothesis: Is abstract reason based on image-sche-
           mas?", *Cognitive Linguistics* 1-1: 39-75.
1993   "The contemporary theory of metaphor", in: Andrew Ortony (ed.),
           Metaphor and thought. (2nd edition.). Cambridge: Cambridge Univer-
           sity Press, 202-251.
Lakoff, George – Mark Johnson
1980   *Metaphors we live by*. Chicago: University of Chicago Press.
1999   *Philosophy in the flesh. The embodied mind and its challenge to western
           thought*. New York: Basic Books.

Lakoff, George – Mark Turner
  1989   *More than cool reason: A field guide to poetic metaphor.* Chicago: University of Chicago Press.
Langacker, Ronald
  1987   *Foundations of cognitive grammar. Vol. 1: Theoretical prerequisites.* Stanford, California: Stanford University Press.
  1993   "Reference-point constructions", *Cognitive Linguistics* 4: 1-38.
Rosch, Eleanor and Barbara B. Lloyd (eds.)
  1978   *Cognition and categorization.* Hillsdale, New Jersey: Lawrence Erlbaum.
Ruiz de Mendoza, Francisco
  1997   "Cognitive and pragmatic aspects of metonymy", in: Antonio Barcelona (ed.), 161-178.
Searle, John R.
  1979   *Expression and meaning.* Cambridge: Cambridge University Press.
Taylor, John
  1995   *Linguistic categorization. Prototypes in linguistic theory.* (2nd. edition.) Oxford: Clarendon.
Turner, Mark
  1991   *Reading minds. The study of English in the age of cognitive science.* Princeton, N.J.: Princeton University Press.
  1996   *The literary mind.* Oxford: Oxford University Press.
Turner, Mark and Gilles Fauconnier
  1995   "Conceptual integration and formal expression", *Metaphor and Symbolic Activity.* 10:3, 183-203.
Ungerer, Friedrich, and Hans-Jörg Schmid
  1996   *An introduction to cognitive linguistics.* London: Longman.

The interaction of metaphor and metonymy, and other theoretical issues

On the plausibility of claiming a metonymic motivation for conceptual metaphor

Antonio Barcelona

1. Introduction

The goal of this paper[1] is to examine the empirical evidence and the theoretical soundness of the hypothesis according to which conceptual metaphor is necessarily motivated by metonymy. It has long been realized that a great many metaphorical mappings seem to have an ultimately metonymic basis (see section 3 below). The hypothesis that I want to examine is, in other words, that every metaphorical mapping presupposes a conceptually prior metonymic mapping, or to put it differently, that the seeds for *any* metaphorical transfer are to be found in a metonymic projection.

This hypothesis does not deny that a specific metonymy can often be conceptually motivated by a metaphor, as Goossens (1990) has demonstrated – he calls these situations "metonymy within metaphor". In a great many cases, some specific metonymies seem to be only possible within the conceptual network created by a conventional metaphor. The patterns of interaction between metaphor and metonymy can sometimes be fairly intricate, although they could perhaps be reduced to just a few types (see my introduction to this volume). The hypothesis that is examined here, however, states that even in these cases a different metonymy would underlie the existence of the metaphor.

Therefore, the expression "motivate (metaphor)" in the context of this hypothesis is to be understood in the sense of "being a conceptual prerequisite for (metaphor)".

The motivation is not necessarily tied up with a sequential ordering of the mappings. They may be simultaneous; the hypothesis does not make any claims in this respect. The metonymic understanding of the source or the target domain in a metaphor need not have become conventionalized (i.e. as a new sense of a lexical item) *chronologically* prior to the conventionalization of the metaphor, although this has often been the case historically, as shown in section 3. What is claimed by this hypothesis is simply that the target and/or the source must be *understood* or *perspectivized* metonymically for the metaphor to be possible. After all, it is not at all common for a single metaphor to structure a whole target domain, but only some aspects or substructures of it. This is so because we seize on these aspects and metaphorically "make sense" of them by finding another domain whose abstract image-schematic structure at least contains the same substructures (see below).

The precise formulation of the hypothesis requires a clarification of what is meant by metonymy and by metaphor. To this we turn in the following section.

2. The notions of metaphor and metonymy

Metaphor has been defined, within cognitive linguistics, as a conceptual mapping in which the source and the target domain belong to two different superordinate experiential domains (Lakoff – Turner 1989: 103-104; Lakoff 1993: 245). This raises the additional problem of stating precisely what an experiential domain is, when two domains are different, and when a domain is superordinate to another domain. There are no easy answers to these questions. The reader is referred to my introductory article in this volume, where my position on these problems is laid out in greater detail. It can be summed up by saying that we have to assume that the boundaries and membership of experiential domains (structured blocks of knowledge and experience which constitute the background for linguistic meaning) are established by a conscious folk taxonomy of experiential domains.

As for *metonymy*, there is no definition yet on which cognitive linguists agree in every detail. There is consensus, though, in stating that it consists of a mapping within the same experiential domain or conceptual structure (Lakoff – Turner 1989: 103-104; Ruiz de Mendoza, this volume; Taylor 1995: 123-124). The main points of divergence revolve around the issue of the referential character of metonymy, and around the question of the (sub)domains which can be the target of a metonymic mapping. Again these problems are addressed in greater depth in my introduction to this volume (Barcelona, this volume). Therefore, I also refer the reader to that part of the volume and here I will only summarize my own position.

The notion of metonymy that is most congenial to me is the one recently put forward by Zoltán Kövecses and Günter Radden (Kövecses – Radden 1998: 39): "Metonymy is a cognitive process in which one conceptual entity, the vehicle, provides mental access to another conceptual entity, the target, within the same domain, or ICM." See also Radden – Kövecses (forthcoming). By talking of "providing mental access" (an idea borrowed from Langacker 1993: 30), Kövecses and Radden stress the fundamental cognitive role of metonymy and free it (as an intradomain mapping) from necessarily having a referential function. In this respect they would depart from Croft's position (1993:349), but not from Taylor's (1995:124).

However, since metonymy is no less a mapping than metaphor (see Lakoff – Turner 1989: 103), since mappings take place between domains, rather than between conceptual entities,[2] and since mappings involve a source and a target, I propose the following broad definition of metonymy, which incorporates these three aspects to Kövecses and Radden's definition: "Metonymy is the conceptual mapping of a cognitive domain onto another domain, both domains being included in the same domain or ICM, so that the source provides mental access to the target".[3]

In my view, broader definitions like this or like Kövecses and Radden's, insofar as they stress the cognitive role of metonymy, have the advantage of stressing the *cognitive commonality* between "prototypical" (i.e. referential) metonymy and other types of "within-domain" mappings, which, according to such definitions, would also be treated as metonymies.[4]

Finally, as regards the typology of metonymies to be used in discussing the hypothesis of the metonymic basis of metaphor, I will basically follow the one proposed by Kövecses and Radden (1998), which besides being rigorously systematic, has been elaborated on the basis of a series of principles commonly held in cognitive linguistics.[5]

3. A brief survey of metonymy-based metaphors in the literature

Some of the papers in this volume offer examples of metonymy-based metaphors, and some discuss this type of interaction (see the introduction to this volume).[6] In this section I enumerate and briefly comment on other books and articles which contain examples of metonymy-based metaphors. In quite a few of them the authors also point out that metaphor is typically motivated by metonymy. None of them, however, claims that this happens with *every* metaphor. The following is just a small sample, confined to recent writings, of the large mass of references I have been able to collect.

Kövecses (1986, 1988, 1990, 1991), Barcelona (1986), Lakoff and Kövecses (as reported in Lakoff 1987: 380-415) and other linguists, have uncovered the metonymic motivation of most metaphors for emotion (anger, happiness, sadness, love, pride, fear, etc.) on the basis of physiological or behavioral responses to emotions. For example, a physiological effect of emotion that is often metonymized, according to all of these studies, is what might be called AFFECTED HEART RATE (the heartbeat rate, which is believed to change as a result of a strong emotional impact, stands for the emotion): *His heart stopped when he saw her.* This metonymy is at least part of the motivation of a metaphor like THE HEART IS A LOCUS FOR EMOTIONS: *Her heart was filled with sorrow.* An instance of the metonymic mapping of a behavioral effect of an emotion (sadness) functioning as the conceptual motivation of a metaphor (SADNESS IS DOWN) is discussed in a later section in this article.

Kövecses (1995) is a cross-linguistic study of emotional metaphors (in English, Chinese, Japanese, Hungarian, Tahitian and Wolof), which seem to be constrained by physiological responses to anger. Apresjan (1997) studies cases in English and Russian of direct physiological correlation between sensations such as cold and emotions such as fear (which underlie metaphors like FEAR IS

COLD). She contrasts them with culturally mediated correlations, like that between light and happiness, which underlies HAPPINESS IS LIGHT. These correlations depend, in my view, on metonymic perspectivizations of both source and target.

Dirven (1985) studied 24 senses of the English word *cup*, which developed over time from the original sense, i.e. that of a prototypical cup with its typical shape and function (drinking). In most cases the extensions due to metonymy and synecdoche preceded those due to metaphor. The important thing is that, as Dirven (1985: 103) noticed, in *all* the metaphorical extensions (12 meanings out of the 24) "some characteristic features of the concept *cup* are in their entirety or partial aspects transferred to other domains". All of the metaphorical extensions consisted of a transfer of some aspect of the cup, that is, they presupposed a metonymic understanding of the cup.[7] For instance, in *acorn cup*, the domain of cups is mapped onto the domain of "natural formations"; the "overall shape" subdomain of prototypical cups is the one seized upon in this metaphorical mapping. That is, other aspects or subdomains of cups are not transferred to acorns: for instance, the fact that cups are conventionally used for drinking. This choice is imposed by the shape subdomain of acorns, which evokes that of a cup.

He also discussed "synesthetic" examples like *loud perfume, warm colors* and others, saying that what is transferred to smell or sight from, respectively, sound or heat is not the percept itself, but "some other experience that co-occurs with" it (p. 99).

Goossens (1990) coins the expression "metaphtonymy" to refer to two frequent patterns of interaction between metaphor and metonymy: "metaphor from metonymy" and "metonymy within metaphor". The first pattern is actually the development of a metaphor on the basis of a metonymy. Goossens (1995) does a diachronic study of metonymic extensions, many of them preceding metaphorical ones. Pauwels (1995) also emphasizes the metonymic motivation of metaphor in a number of instances. Like Goossens (1995), he insists that the distinction "literal-metonymic-metaphorical" is scalar.

In a very insightful paper, the late Brygida Rudzka-Ostyn (1995) did a historical analysis of the metaphorical semantic extension of English verbs of answering to other semantic domains, arriving at the conclusion that under an extended (i.e. not necessarily referential) notion of metonymy "any extension affected by abstraction, metaphoric or not, can be seen as involving a metonymic dissociation" (p. 241).

Taylor (1995: 138-141) gives some examples of metonymy-based metaphors, noting that this seems to be a typical, rather than an exceptional pattern. Wildgen (1994: 122-24), a semiotician working within the framework of catastrophe theory, says that "certain objects or processes *stand for* complex situations and can thus be used as generalized metaphors" (p. 124) [my italics]. Allan (1995) claims that the semantic extensions of *back* occur on the basis of just one aspect, namely "that part of the body opposite the interactive side" in the "anthropomorphic model of the prototypical human being in upright stance confronting the world". This type of extension, according to the hypothesis that is being examined, presupposes a metonymic understanding of the concept BACK as fundamentally "non-interactive". Heine, Claudi and Hünnemeyer (1991: 70-71) proposed that the mapping of space onto time and modality, as manifested in the semantic extension of *going to* as a marker of futurity and intention, was mediated by metonymic perspectivization (see Goossens, this volume, for an alternative view).

4. Some apparent counterexamples

In his excellent survey of cognitive linguistics, John Taylor (1995) observes, as we stated above, that metaphor is often motivated by metonymy, a fact which, as he himself acknowledges (p. 139), prompts him to say that metonymy "turns out to be one of the most fundamental processes of meaning extension, more basic, perhaps, even than metaphor" (p. 124). Taylor says that the hypothesis examined in the present article is not at all new. He quotes Eco and Skinner as some of its previous defenders. But he later apparently rejects the hypothesis, because there are "numerous instances of metaphor which cannot reasonably be reduced to contiguity" (p. 139) [8] and that, therefore, "the theoretical puzzle of similarity remains" (p. 140). He adduces three counterexamples involving synesthesia, and another two involving pitch and smell. I will be claiming below that a metonymic grounding can also be found for the metaphors realized in these examples.

4.1. Synesthesia

Below are laid out Taylor's counterexamples, which (according to him) involve synesthesia. I have added before each of them a nonmetaphorical variant, followed by a slant; in the metaphorical expressions, the term corresponding to the target domain appears in regular font style:

(1)   *Loud music* / *Loud* color.
(2)   *Sweet cake* / *Sweet* music.
(3)   *Black cloth* / *Black* mood.

4.1.1. LOUD COLOR

Taylor says that in example (1) the metaphor in question is one in which "an attribute of the auditory domain is mapped on to the visual domain" (p. 139). I am not quite happy with this description of the metaphor at work in the example.

    A good way to improve on it might be to begin by citing the relevant parts of the entry for *loud* in a standard dictionary like the *Oxford English Dictionary*, henceforth O.E.D. (Sampson – Weiner, eds., 1989). First, the definition of the basic, nonmetaphorical, sense of *loud*: "1. a. Of sounds or voices: strongly audible; making a powerful impression on the sense of hearing. Hence with agent-noun: That (speaks, sings, etc.) with a loud voice." (By the way, the extension of its meaning with an agent-noun is obviously a metonymic extension.)

Now the definition of the same lexeme in metaphorical uses with a visual target domain: "4. Of colours, patterns, dress, etc.: Vulgarly obtrusive, flashy. Opposed to *quiet*."

In the light of these definitions, I would suggest that a more fine-grained analysis of example (1) has to recognize the fact that the metaphorical mapping illustrated by it takes place between a highly specific auditory domain, i.e. the domain of "DEVIANT" SOUNDS, and a highly specific visual domain, i.e. the domain of "DEVIANT" COLORS.[9] The metaphor in (1), therefore, can be mnemonically formulated as DEVIANT COLORS ARE DEVIANT SOUNDS.

Since most colors can be construed as scalar in some dimension (we can, for instance, talk about degrees in luminosity – *dark red*, *light blue*), the domain of color has a built-in norm for the corresponding scale, i.e. a "normal point" on the scale. This leads people to experience some colors as "breaking the norm" in some dimension (normally brightness or luminosity) and others as "normal" along that dimension. In this metaphor, then, the target domain is not the whole domain of color, but only one of its subdomains: the subdomain of those colors which violate the norm in some respect. This specific target domain is itself metonymically understood from one of its own subdomains: the subdomain of the main effect caused on the perceivers by the percept, that is, by these (gaudy, eye-catching, often vulgar) colors. This effect is that of *forcing themselves on their attention* (note the term "obtrusive" in the O.E.D. definition of this sense of *loud*). Deviant colors are thus understood primarily as attention-getting deviant colors.

Now the sensory domain of sound is likewise susceptible of a scalar construal, thus also admitting of a distinction between the subdomain of "deviant" sounds and that of "normal" sounds. And the same kind of main effect on perceivers is also frequently present in this type of sounds, i.e. they also typically force themselves on the attention of perceivers, which leads to metonymically categorizing the whole auditory experience in terms of this specific subdomain: deviant sounds are primarily understood as attention-getting deviant sounds.[10] The domain of deviant loud, strident sounds is thus ideally suited as a source domain to *metaphorically* describe and understand our experiential notion of a color which violates a social norm.

My claim of the metonymic motivation of the metaphor in example (1) is represented synoptically in table 1, where the whole of the first column should be read before the second column:

Table 1. The metonymic motivation of the metaphor in example (1):

Target domain in the metaphor	Source domain in the metaphor
"Deviant" colors	"Deviant" sounds
Metonymic understanding in terms of typical salient subdomain (attraction of involuntary attention), determines choice of metaphorical source →→→→	Also metonymically understood in terms of the same typical salient subdomain (attraction of involuntary attention)

The thesis presented in the preceding paragraphs will be more easily understood by recalling the definition of metonymy that was put forward in section 2: Metonymy is a conceptual projection (or mapping) occurring inside a domain that includes source and target, whereby the target is mentally accessed from the source. In other words, the source causes the mental activation of the target. For example, the general domain of the HAND can activate one of its subdomains, namely that of MANUAL SKILL, in virtue of the conventional metonymy – BODY PART FOR AN ATTRIBUTE CONNECTED WITH ITS TYPICAL FUNCTION – instanced in an example like (4)[11]

(4)   *To keep my* hand *in I practice the piano on a regular basis.*

From my point of view, the only possible explanation for the existence of the metaphor represented in example (1) is the fact that one of the aspects (that is, one of the experiential subdomains) of color which are normally most important for the average viewer is her/his reaction to it. The fact that colors are actually often categorized in terms of the effects they cause on perceivers is a demonstration that their effects are part of the (folk) experiential domain of color. Apart from categorizing colors in terms of their hue (as *red, gray, blue,* etc.), their lightness or brightness (*light* (red), *dark* (green)), or their saturation (*deep, suffused,* etc.), the average speaker categorizes them, in virtue of his/her reaction to them, as *pleasant* or *unpleasant, loud* or *quiet, relaxing* or *disturbing, boring* or *exciting,* etc. Much the same happens with sounds: besides classifying them in terms of the means with which they are produced (*percussion, clap, shout, peal,* etc.), the manner of their production (*knock, thud, tap, scrape, rattle* etc.), their pitch (a *sharp / low/ flat* sound, etc.), or their intensity (*a loud* sound, *a bang, a din,* etc.), the folk model of sound uses the effect on hearers as a major categorizing factor: sounds can be *unpleasant (racket, din), pleasant (soft, sweet, melodious), attention-getting (insistent, loud, ear-piercing, shrill),* etc. (As usual, different categories are sometimes realized by the same polysemous lexemes.)

The mere fact of classifying a given domain of experience – a sensory one in this case – from a specific perspective (the effect it causes) can be regarded legitimately as a metonymic operation, because the domain in question is accessed mentally from one of its subdomains. In examples like (1) there exists implicitly a basic metonymy that categorizes colors and sounds in terms of one of their possible effects (an effect for cause metonymy). A conceptual metaphor like the one represented by example (1) is possible because:

a. There exists a natural tendency to categorize kinds of colors and other sensory stimuli (like sounds) in terms of their effects on perceivers.

b. That natural tendency is a metonymic operation; that is, it consists of the projection onto the whole domain constituted by a given sensory stimulus (in example (1), a deviant color and sound), of a subdomain included in it (a specific effect caused by the stimulus).

c. The specific subdomain mapped onto deviant colors and sounds in example (1) is the effect consisting of the irresistible (perhaps also unpleasant) attraction of the perceiver's attention.

It may be argued that the only metonymically highlighted subdomain motivating this metaphor is in fact the violation of the built-in norm by a gaudy color, rather than its effect on attention.[12] A "long-distance" metonymic motivation for the existence of the metaphor in example (1) is doubtless the categorization of colors and other sensory stimuli in terms of their degree of conformity to an implicit social norm (this is why we talk about "deviant" colors or sounds above). It is an indisputable fact that gaudy colors attract our attention precisely because they break that norm, whatever it is in each culture. However, this metonymy does not directly motivate the specific metaphor in example (1). If it did, then the description of the metaphorical sense of *loud* registered by the O.E.D. would probably be phrased differently, perhaps "obtrusively vulgar", instead of "vulgarly obtrusive"; that is, it would highlight the deviance aspect ("vulgar") at the expense of the "attention-getting" one ("obtrusively"). Another dictionary, the Oxford Advanced Learner's Dictionary of Current English, henceforth OALDCE (Hornby 1974) offers the following definition of this metaphorical sense of *loud*: "2 (of a person's behavior; of colors) of the kind that *forces itself on the attention*" (my italics).

The kind of metonymic motivation that has just been discussed consists, then, in achieving similarity between a domain (i.e. the target domain of the metaphorical mapping) which is metonymically understood from one of its subdomains, and another domain (i.e. the source domain in the metaphorical mapping) which is also metonymically understood from one of its subdomains. The main basis of the similarity achieved lies in the fact that the metonymically highlighted subdomain is the same both in the metaphorical source and in the metaphorical target. This achievement of similarity is ultimately stimulated by the experiential-semantic structure of the metaphorical target domain of deviant colors, in which the aspect of involuntary attention is metonymically highlighted, thus leading to the search for a metaphorical source with the same metonymically highlighted subdomain. The driving force in the establishment of the metaphor in (1) thus lies in the target domain.

The other counterexamples offered by Taylor will be discussed more briefly, due to lack of space.

4.1.2. BLACK MOOD

Example (2) is discussed later, as it is very similar in metonymic motivation to example (1). Example (3) is different from (1) in this respect. The metaphor underlying the idiomatic expression in (3) – *black mood* – , which can be found in such sentences as (5),

(5)   *Jane is in a black mood today.*

also has a metonymic basis, but it appears to be different.

In the more strict sense attributed by Ullmann (1957: 233) to the term "synesthesia" as a technical term in semantics (i.e. as denoting the semantic association between two sensations, between the impressions or between the feelings they produce), it is highly doubtful that examples (3) and (5) are really synesthetic metaphors at all. In fact, Ullmann explicitly removes similar examples from the class of synesthesias altogether (p. 225).

It is not easy to decide which and how many metaphors motivate these two examples. According to the OALDCE, *be in a black mood* means "be silent and bad tempered". And according to the Oxford Dictionary of Current Idiomatic English (Cowie *et al.* 1983), it means "[to have] a fit of depression, bad temper, etc., usually temporary, though perhaps recurring". The Webster's Dictionary (McKechnie, ed., 1978) offers a number of emotional figurative senses of *black*, which can apply to these examples: "dismal, gloomy, sullen, forbidding, or the like; destitute of moral light or goodness; mournful, calamitous; evil; wicked, atrocious; thus Shakespeare speaks of *black* deeds, envy, tidings, despair, etc.". The O.E.D. gives a similar list of figurative emotional or moral senses of *black*.

The aspects of the meaning of examples (3) and (5) which are common to the more specific dictionary descriptions above are "silence + intense anger or sadness"; and the aspects which are common to the more general descriptions of the figurative emotional senses of *black* are "negativeness + extreme intensity of an emotion". That is, *a black mood* can be regarded either as silent and intense anger or sadness (or both at the same time), or more generally, as any intensely felt negative emotional state.

On the basis of all of these common aspects, at least the following general metaphor can be claimed to motivate this idiom: NEGATIVE IS DARK (AND EX-TREMELY NEGATIVE IS BLACK). Other metaphors probably also contribute to the meaning of the expression. This general metaphor motivates both the more general and the more specific sense of the expression, because both sadness and anger are "negative" emotions, an intense degree of which is designated by the idiom. As for the "silence" aspect (mentioned by the OALDCE), it is implicit in the folk model of an intense emotion, since impairment of social functioning is one of its usual effects, which is thus not necessarily mentioned in all of the dictionary descriptions. This is, then, the metaphor whose metonymic motivation will be discussed here.

This general metaphor, in this application to emotions, becomes the specific submetaphor A NEGATIVE EMOTION IS DARK (AND AN EXTREMELY NEGATIVE EMOTION IS BLACK), which is the one apparently at work in examples (3) and (5). It is not clear whether *black*, as a designator of the color area with the lowest degree of luminosity, should be regarded as literally included both in the folk model of the color domain *and* in that of the light domain, or literally just in the folk model of color, and metaphorically in the folk domain of light. Whatever the case, the fact is that *black* commonly functions as a term designating an extreme lack of light, as well as a type of color.

There exists a (probably universal) experiential association between (relative) lack of light (e.g. the dark experienced at night, or the relative dark experienced on an overcast day) and certain physiological and psychological reactions. Light is likely to arouse a feeling of confidence, safety, liveliness or happiness, etc. and physical well-being, which is positively valued, whereas dark tends to bring about a feeling of insecurity, melancholy and physical unease, which is negatively valued. There is thus a metonymic connection between darkness (as source) and negatively-valued physical and psychological states (as target), which we might call DARK FOR NEGATIVE STATES CAUSED BY DARK. This association in turn leads to the association of darkness with a culturally sanctioned negative value judgment, whereas the (relative) presence of light is positively valued. We might say, then, that in the domain of light there exists a built-in value judgment, which sanctions the further metonymy DARK (source) FOR NEGATIVE VALUE JUDGMENT OF DARK (target).

The metaphor NEGATIVE IS DARK (AND EXTREMELY NEGATIVE IS BLACK) arises as the further generalization of this metonymy (which is still necessarily connected to real physical experiences of light or dark), so that every negative event or state (even an abstract or invisible one), irrespective of the lighting conditions under which it occurs, is regarded as dark or black.

Another specific metaphor which is subordinate to NEGATIVE IS DARK is SADNESS IS DARK. This metaphor also probably contributes the nuance of intense sadness in the more specific reading of the idiom as silent intense sadness. I showed long ago (Barcelona 1986), that, besides the general metonymic basis of the superordinate metaphor, which it also inherits, this metaphor has a specific metonymic motivation arising in the subdomain of the behavioral effects of sadness.[13]

4.1.3. SWEET MUSIC

Example (2) above (*Sweet music*) and the rest of Taylor's counterexamples will be discussed even more briefly. It appears that the metaphor at work in example (2) is EXPERIENCES ARE FOOD, under its manifestation PLEASURABLE EXPERIENCES (SENSATIONS, PEOPLE, EVENTS) ARE SWEET FOOD.[14] More specifically what we find in the example is its submetaphor PLEASURABLE MUSIC IS SWEET FOOD. The motivation for the choice of this type of "positive" gustative sensation as the source domain metaphorically mapped onto the auditory domain of pleasant music is to be sought, as in the LOUD example, in this target domain. The domain of pleasurable music (like the domain of pleasurable experiences) is metonymically understood, for the purposes of this metaphorical mapping, primarily as music causing at least two positive effects on perceivers: pleasure and well-being. These effects are positively valued in our culture, and so is the music producing them. The same effects, among others, are typically caused by sweet items of food (chocolate, cakes, sugar), with the same culturally-attached positive value judgments.

This metonymic understanding of pleasurable music explains why SWEET FOOD is selected as the source domain for this synesthetic metaphor.[15]

4.2. The other counterexamples

Taylor's remaining two counterexamples are (Taylor 1995: 139):

(6)   *The high notes on a piano.*
(7)   *The meat smells high.*

Taylor wrongly assumes that the metaphors at work here consist of a mapping of verticality onto, respectively, pitch and smell, and this leads him to deny a metonymic basis for the metaphors underlying these examples. But the metaphors that operate here are different.

4.2.1. HIGH NOTES ON A PIANO

The metaphor operating both in examples (6) and (7) is MORE IS UP.

In examples (6) and (7) MORE IS UP is allied to (or rather implies) SPATIAL MEASUREMENT SCALES ARE PATHS (see Lakoff 1993: 214).[16] In its specific application to musical pitch, this second metaphor is allied to another general metaphor that maps spatial measurement (e.g. like that performed by means of a rule or a yardstick) onto any kind of measurement (in this case, a measurement of a sensory perception like musical pitch), thus yielding the composite specific metaphor PITCH SCALES ARE PATHS.[17] That is, a notion like "high pitch" ultimately reflects a type of quantitative measurement.

I only have space to describe here the metonymic basis of MORE IS UP, which is the most relevant metaphor at work in the example. Quantitative measurements are often metaphorically understood as positions on a vertical path (see Lakoff – Johnson 1980: 15-16). The experiential basis of MORE IS UP is, according to Lakoff and Johnson (1980: 16-20), the causal link between the act of piling objects onto one another and the rise in height of the pile.

The conceptual metonymy motivating the metaphor arises in this experiential situation. The "piling frame"[18] implies, among others, two aspects, i.e. two subdomains: a) quantity: there occurs an increase in the quantity of the objects or the substance added up to the pile; b) verticality: as quantity increases, there results an increase in the height of the pile. There exists a "natural" metonymic relationship between causes and effects, with effects normally functioning as mental vehicles for causes (Kövecses – Radden, 1998).[19] Therefore "increase in height" (UP) in the specific piling situation comes to be metonymically mapped onto "increase in quantity" (MORE); that is, it provides mental access to it. Further metonymic generalization to the whole domain of quantity and to the whole domain of verticality (freed now from any concrete reference to piling-up events) leads to the abstract metaphor MORE IS UP, which can be applied to a host of domains (music, inflation, wages and prices, smell, etc.) in which quantitative measurement is relevant.

4.2.2. HIGH SMELL

Example (7) is likewise motivated by the same metaphor, MORE IS UP, whose metonymic motivation has just been described. This idiomatic example points to a "high" degree in the intensity with which a given (bad) smell is perceived. Again the notion of quantitative measurement is relevant here. The basic metaphor is also here allied to SPATIAL MEASUREMENT SCALES ARE PATHS. This second metaphor is likewise allied to the generalized mapping of spatial measurement scales onto any type of measurement (again that of a sensory perception like smell), also yielding the composite metaphor SMELL SCALES ARE PATHS.

4.3. A provisional summary

We have identified two main kinds of metonymic motivation for metaphor in the preceding analysis of examples (1)-(7). In one of them, a metonymic model of the target domain of the metaphorical mapping has been claimed to motivate and constrain the choice of the source domain in the metaphor. This is apparent in our study of LOUD COLOR and SWEET MUSIC: the metaphor does not really develop "out of" the metonymy. It is simply motivated and constrained by the metonymic model of the target.

In the other kind, as revealed in our study of BLACK MOOD, HIGH NOTES, or HIGH SMELL, the metaphor comes into existence as a generalization (see also Niemeier, this volume) of a metonymy. This hypothetical process of generalization is described in greater detail below, in connection with SADNESS IS DOWN.

5. SADNESS IS DOWN

Following the example of Lakoff and Kövecses (as reported in Lakoff 1987: 377-417), and of Kövecses (e.g., 1986, 1990), I studied long ago (Barcelona 1986) the effect for cause metonymy in which a typical behavioral effect of sadness, namely a droopy bodily posture, stands for this emotion. See examples (8) and (9):

(8)   *John's head* drooped *(sadly)*.
(9)   *Mrs. Johnson's face* fell *(on hearing sad news)*.

Similar examples can be found in many other languages. The downward bodily orientation assumed by the folk model of the effects of sadness can affect not only the shoulders, but also the head – example (8) – or even some facial muscles – example (9).

Now by means of a process of generalization or abstraction, itself metonymic, the source domain in the metonymy (i.e. the bodily behavior) gets reduced to the purely spatial domain, which now becomes the source domain of the metaphor SADNESS IS DOWN. See examples (10) and (11):

(10)   *I am in* low *spirits*.
(11)   *Her attitude has really* got *me* down.

Let us see how that abstraction process works. It is laid out in table 2:

Table 2.   Development of SADNESS IS DOWN from an effect-for-cause metonymy within SADNESS

Domain of SADNESS		
	Source Domain	Target domain
Basic metonymy ⇓	Downward oriented bodily posture (effect)	Sadness (cause)
Metonymy within metonymic source ⇓	"Downward spatial orientation" for "Downward bodily posture"	
Metaphor	DOWN	SADNESS

First of all, in my view it is undeniable that there is an experiential association between sadness or other emotions and certain behavioral patterns. It is debatable whether this association is one of cause and effect, or just of cooccurrence (see Radden, this volume, Ungerer, this volume). I have made the working assumption, here and in previous sections of this paper, that the association is one of cause and effect. The important thing is, however, that emotions and their associated behavioral patterns constitute an experiential block, i.e. a domain, and that each behavioral pattern can provide mental access to the corresponding emotion; in other words, that there can be metonymic connections between them in the various domains of the emotions.

One of these built-in metonymies is the one connecting SADNESS to one of its typical behavioral effects. The source domain in the metonymy is "downward oriented bodily posture". The most salient subdomain within that source domain is "downward spatial orientation". Therefore, downward oriented bodily posture is metonymically understood as downward spatial orientation, which, thus, mentally "stands for it". This "pruning" of the source domain in the built-in effect-for-cause metonymy yields the purely spatial source domain of what now becomes the metaphor SADNESS IS DOWN.

As we can see, the generating metonymy takes place within what eventually becomes the target domain in the metaphor (SADNESS). But it is developed into a metaphor thanks to a further metonymy taking place within the metonymic source domain (the downward bodily posture). In NEGATIVE IS DARK, the generating metonymy takes place within what eventually becomes the source domain in the metaphor (DARK), and it is probably the result of a further metonymic "pruning" of the DARK FOR NEGATIVE STATES CAUSED BY DARK metonymy, by metonymically replacing NEGATIVE STATES CAUSED BY DARK with NEGATIVE VALUE JUDGMENT OF DARK, and NEGATIVE VALUE JUDGMENT OF DARK with NEGATIVE VALUE JUDGMENT IN GENERAL. In MORE IS UP, the generating metonymy takes place in a domain that includes both source and target (i.e. the "piling" frame) and it is also probably developed by means of two further metonymies within both the metonymic source and the metonymic target: VERTICALITY IN GENERAL FOR VERTICALITY IN A PILING FRAME, and QUANTITY IN GENERAL FOR QUANTITY IN A PILING FRAME.

In the three cases in which a metonymy develops into a metaphor, the metonymic source becomes the metaphorical source, and the metonymic target becomes the metaphorical target. That is, the metonymy UP (IN PILING) FOR MORE becomes the metaphor MORE IS UP, the metonymy DARK FOR NEGATIVE STATES ... becomes NEGATIVE IS DARK, and DOWN(WARD BODILY POSTURE) FOR SADNESS develops into SADNESS IS DOWN. Thus in this generalization process the source and target roles seem to remain constant.

6. Invariance

In the preceding discussion, the idea that metonymy "constrains" metaphorical mappings has been occasionally expressed. The main constraint on metaphorical mappings proposed so far in cognitive linguistics is the so-called Invariance Hypothesis or Invariance Principle, henceforth "invariance" (Lakoff – Turner

1989: 82-83; Lakoff 1990; Lakoff 1993: 215-217). It is worthwhile, then, to examine this hypothesis and compare it with the one under scrutiny in this article, in order to find out what they have in common. If invariance is ultimately found to be correct, and if it can be shown to be in fact a metonymic (or metonymy-related) constraint on metaphorical mappings (Rudzka-Ostyn 1995), this would be an additional type of metonymic basis for metaphor. However, the argumentation presented in this section is only tentative and is just put forward as a means to provoke further debate on this issue.

Invariance has been criticized from several points of view (Brugman 1990; Jäkel 1997). However, despite the refinements that it may require, I think this principle has managed to elucidate two fundamental characteristics of metaphorical mappings:

(1) The fact that there has to be a degree of structural correlation, on some semantic dimension, between the semantic structure of the source and that of the target, which allows the former to be projected onto the latter; this correlation is either discovered or created on the basis of experience.

(2) The fact that the semantic structure of the target domain constrains the mapping (this fact is referred to by Lakoff (1993: 216) as "target domain overrides").

Invariance is formulated in these terms: "Metaphorical mappings preserve the cognitive topology (that is, the inherent image-schematic structure) of the source domain, in a way consistent with the inherent structure of the target domain." (Lakoff 1993: 215) As a result, the "image-schematic structure inherent in the target domain cannot be violated" (Lakoff 1993: 216). The principle, under different names and in the context of different technical conventions, plays an important role in more recent theories of mapping and metaphor developed in cognitive science. Invariance is eliminated as a separate principle in Lakoff's recent Neural Theory of Language (see Lakoff – Johnson 1999), because that theory stipulates that all metaphorical inferences must be carried out in the source domain, and that those inferences must be neurally inhibited that contradict the inherent structure of the target domain, like any other contradictory inferences. Such inferences would have been "overridden" by the target domain structure, in the earlier formulation of invariance quoted above. However, invariance inspires those stipulations themselves. And in Fauconnier and Turner's work on integration networks (see Turner – Fauconnier, this volume), invariance survives under two of their "optimality principles on integration networks" known as Web and Topology, especially the latter (see also Fauconnier – Turner, 1998).

Invariance, in its "classical" formulation, can be interpreted as a metonymic constraint on metaphor. The principle means, in fact, that a prerequisite for a metaphorical mapping is an internal metonymic mapping in the target domain, whereby (a part of) the abstract image-schematic structure of the target is projected onto the whole of the target; that is, the target is understood *as* (part of) its image-schematic structure. It also means that (part of) the image-schematic structure of the source has to be metonymically mapped onto the whole of the source domain to check its degree of structural similarity to the target domain. If a metaphorical mapping requires the abstraction of a common schema for both source and target, this abstraction is surely a metonymic understanding of both (Rudzka-Ostyn 1995: 239-242). This metonymic understanding, by the way, was already implicit in Lakoff's earlier notion of the (experientially perceived) *structural correlation* between source and target (Lakoff 1987: 277-78), which is, according to him, what makes a metaphor possible.

The kinds of metonymic motivation for metaphor identified in sections 4 and 5 can easily be related to invariance. This relationship is more easily perceivable in the first kind, in which the metonymic understanding of the target (as in *loud color, sweet music*) both motivates and constrains the choice of a suitable source. The relationship lies in the search for correlation between two domains, and in the dominant role taken by the semantic structure of the target, both in invariance and in this type of metonymic motivation. And if the elucidation of some (metonymically highlighted) aspect of the inherent structure of the target is the driving force in the metaphorical mapping, then "target domain overrides" are a natural consequence of this kind of metonymic motivation.

In the examples of this kind examined above – take *loud color* – , the satisfaction of invariance could be said to be a *consequence* of the metonymic motivation of metaphor:

– The target ("deviant" colors) is metonymically understood from its image-schematic structure. There is a percept, and the percept has certain features that violate a social norm; there is a perceiver; the features of the percept have certain effects on the perceiver. But in this special case, the image-schematic structure of "deviant colors" is itself metonymically understood as additionally including one of its possible subdomains: the specific effect of irresistibly drawing the perceiver's attention. That is, in the *loud color* example (just as in the *sweet music* one), the metonymic motivation is twofold: besides the abstraction of its inherent image schematic stucture, this image-schematic structure is itself constructed metonymically.

– The source ("deviant" sounds) is also metonymically understood from its image-schematic structure. Again, we have a percept with certain features, a perceiver, and the effects of these features on the perceiver, with attention being likewise metonymically highlighted. Not everything we know about disturbing sounds is considered for the mapping. For example, the instrument used to produce the sound is not considered for the mapping: *It was a fife color* (to mean a gaudy color). Only those subschemas that correlate with the inherent image-schema of gaudy colors are mapped.

The metaphorical mapping is possible because the metonymically understood source structure is able to match the metonymically understood target structure.

The other kind of metonymic motivation which was discussed in earlier sections, namely the development of a metonymy into a metaphor by means of further metonymies (as in SADNESS IS DOWN, MORE IS UP or NEGATIVE IS DARK), is apparently not so similar to invariance. But closer scrutiny of these metaphors uncovers the connection between their metonymic motivation and invariance.

The inherent semantic structure of emotions is perhaps less obvious than that of the domain of perception. In fact, the various emotional domains are almost wholly structured by complex networks of metaphors and metonymies (Kövecses 1990), and this creates a problem for invariance, as Brugman (1990) pointed out. However, as Kövecses demonstrated long ago (1986), most metaphors for emotion are, to a very large extent, based on metonymies, which encapsulate the conventional beliefs (folk models) about the effects – physiological or behavioral – of emotions on people (people are believed to go red if they are angry, walk erect if they are proud, etc.). These metonymies provide an array of inherent dynamic image-schematic structures for the target domains of emotions. A large part of their inherent image-schematic structure seems to have been built on the basis of EMOTION-DRIVEN BEHAVIOR/PHYSIOLOGY and other experientially accessible and contiguous (sub)domains. As a result, the inherent abstract image-schematic structure of emotions contains – besides an emotional cause, an experiencer and a number of physiological and behavioral effects – other metonymically mapped elements like measurement scales, limits, etc. These elements constitute minimal scenarios,[20] which are enriched by the various metaphors arising from the metonymies and converging on a richer prototype scenario, like those proposed in Barcelona (1986), Kövecses (1986), Lakoff (1987: 397-401).

In the case of sadness, a part of its image-schematic structure is provided by one of the conventional bodily-behavioral patterns of the sad person: a droopy bodily posture. Other parts of its image-schematic structure would be provided by lack of brightness in the eyes, by the shedding of tears, or other effects caused by sadness (see Barcelona 1986). In order to satisfy invariance, the image-schematic structure of the source domain must be mapped onto the target, provided it does not violate the image-schematic structure of the target. The source domain in the metaphor SADNESS IS DOWN is the domain of verticality, in fact only one of its subdomains (DOWN) and its associated knowledge. The image-schematic structure of sadness as structured by the metonymy DOWNWARD BODILY POSTURE FOR SADNESS consists of a cause (the emotion itself) and the droopy bodily posture effect (which presupposes implicitly the notion of verticality). In the metaphorical schema SADNESS IS DOWN, as in examples (10) and (11) above, the source (VERTICALITY, UP-DOWN) is no longer understood as a subschema of a bodily posture. The metaphorical mapping of DOWN onto SADNESS is possible because the metaphorical source domain structure has a structural element which also appears in the metaphorical target, as structured by the metonymy: the DOWN point on the vertical axis, and its associated knowledge, namely, that DOWN presupposes the full image-schema of the vertical PATH, and that the latter can be mapped onto the notion of measurement.[21] The structure of the target is thus preserved.

The metonymic understanding of SADNESS as one of its subdomains (DOWN-WARD BODILY POSTURE), therefore, provides this emotion with another element included in the knowledge network associated with this part of its inherent image-schematic structure, namely, the notion of MEASUREMENT SCALE, which places SADNESS at one end and HAPPINESS at the other. The metaphorical mapping is possible because, thanks to the "mother" metonymy, the metaphorical source, DOWN, also shares with the metaphorical target, SADNESS, this element of its associated knowledge. The notion of measurement (of emotional intensity) is the subdomain of sadness most forcefully highlighted by the metaphor.[22]

In MORE IS UP, the metonymic cause-effect link between quantity and the verticality dimension occurring in concrete piling-up events provides quantity with two of its abstract image-schemas and their associated knowledge. The image schemas are VERTICALITY (UP-DOWN) and PATH, which is regularly associated to VERTICALITY (the compound image-schematic structure of quantity, like that of sadness, includes a vertical path). PATH includes, as a part of its associated knowledge, the notion of measurement scale, as stated above. The measurement subdomain is a nuclear aspect of quantity, and it is provided by the metaphor on the basis of the metonymy UP FOR DOWN. This metonymic basis, thus, makes the metaphor possible, because the image-schematic structure of the metaphoric source (UP) which is mapped onto the target (MORE) is shared by the latter, whose inherent image-schematic structure is thus preserved.

In NEGATIVE IS DARK, motivated by the metonymy DARK FOR NEGATIVE STATES …, the metonymic source (DARK) also provides the metonymic target with part of its image-schematic structure: the opposition between light and dark. Part of the knowledge associated to this image-schematic opposition is that of a measurement scale. The scale from extreme dark – as denoted by *black* – to extreme light – as denoted by, say, *radiant* – is metonymically imposed onto the opposition NEGATIVE STATES-POSITIVE STATES, implying that there can be intermediate degrees between both poles. The metaphor NEGATIVE IS DARK is possible because the image-schematic structure imposed by the metaphorical source, DARK, correlates with the (metonymically imposed) image-schematic structure of the metaphorical target, NEGATIVE; this structure is thus not overridden.[23]

In these three cases of generalization of a metonymy, the *metonymic* source imposes its image-schematic structure onto what eventually becomes the *metaphorical* target. If the latter is a complex abstract concept, as in these three cases, its image-schematic structure is normally richer, as it often receives its other components from other source domains on the basis of other metonymies. For instance, the domains of SADNESS and HAPPINESS are provided with such image-schemas as verticality, container, light, path, etc. We tend to conceptualize "elusive" domains like EMOTION, QUANTITY, or NEGATIVENESS via experientially accessible and contiguous domains like EMOTION-DRIVEN BEHAVIOR/PHYSIOLOGY, VERTICALITY IN PILING UP, or DARKNESS (AS A CAUSE FOR NEGATIVE STATES). The important thing, as regards invariance, is that in each of the metaphors resulting from a generalized metonymy which construct a complex concept, the target domain structure cannot be violated precisely because this structure has first been imposed metonymically by the source: the satisfaction of invariance seems to be a consequence of their metonymic genesis.[24]

In sum, invariance can be interpreted as a consequence of the metonymic precomprehension of domains which both motivates and constrains metaphorical mappings.

7. A paradox and other objections

Rudzka-Ostyn (1995: 242) says that the hypothesis which we have been discussing above is sort of fallacious, since our understanding of domains as having a part-whole structure, which is the basis of our metonymic understanding of them, presupposes in itself a pervasive conceptual metaphor mapping *physical* part-whole configurations onto *conceptual* domains. If one wants to maintain the hypothesis of the metonymic motivation of *every* metaphor, then which is the underlying metonymy for *that* general metaphor? Or, I might add, for such complex, pervasive metaphors as EVENT STRUCTURE or CLASSICAL CATEGORIES ARE CONTAINERS (Lakoff 1990, 1993)?

Rudzka-Ostyn's is a serious objection, as it amounts to claiming that the very notion of metonymy presupposes a conceptual metaphor. The entrenched metaphor that treats concepts and conceptual domains as physical entities with a part-whole structure results in metonymy being technically described as a matter of connections between parts and wholes, wholes and parts, or parts and parts. But this could turn out to be a false paradox: The fact that metonymy is *described* by linguists on the basis of that conventional metaphor does not automatically entail that the human metonymic *capacity* is motivated by that metaphor. This is at best a hypothesis that would have to be empirically tested.

Metonymic mapping simply consists in the activation of one conceptual domain by means of an experientially related domain. (This is why cognitive linguists talk of them as belonging to the same domain.) This does not necessarily mean that, for metonymy to be possible, people have to conceive both domains as parts of a metaphorical abstract object with a part-whole structure. Take this example of the metonymy ACTION FOR OBJECT INVOLVED IN THE ACTION, adapted from Kövecses and Radden (1998: 55):

(12)   *Give me a bite.*

In it, the speaker does not have to conceptualize an action as an object with a part-whole structure. All (s)he may be aware of is that actions and the objects involved in them are closely related in experience. Of course, they may choose to use the metaphor that regards an action as a "thing" and the object involved in it as one of its parts, as reflected in examples like (13),

(13)   *The object bitten is* a part of *the act of biting.*

which, incidentally, seems quite a contrived expression. But it is not at all clear that this metaphor necessarily underlies a metonymic mapping like the one in (12).

Let us examine the other two possible objections. The EVENT STRUCTURE metaphor maps space (including spatial movement) and physical forces onto events (including actions). It would take another article to investigate the metonymic basis of all the submappings making up this complex metaphor. However, Radden (this volume) has shown that some of the key ones, like ACTION IS MOTION, PURPOSES ARE DESTINATIONS, CHANGE IS MOTION, or CAUSE IS FORCE, have a metonymic basis; the others might be shown to have a similar basis. As for CLASSICAL CATEGORIES ARE CONTAINERS, as in example (14),

(14)   *The category of "living beings" contains the concepts "animal" and "plant".*

the metonymic motivation can be found in the fact that objects that are known to be located in a container are both physically and conceptually accessible without a strong cognitive effort, because the visual perception of the inside of the container, or our recollection of it, can easily bring about the mental activation of all or some of the concepts corresponding to the objects. This "mental coactivation subdomain" in our experiential domain of containers is also present in the series of concepts which can activate each other, due to the fact that they enter a well-defined (i.e. classical) category or, for that matter, a well-defined experiential domain. The concepts ANIMALS and PLANTS are more likely to activate each other than, say STONE and AIR, because the former, unlike the latter pair, is part of the conceptual-experiential set LIVING BEINGS.[25]

8. Two similar approaches

Kövecses (this volume) claims that it is the central knowledge (i.e. the set of central subdomains) of the source that primarily participates in metaphor by imposing one or several "meaning foci" on the target, and that this central knowledge is captured by decomposing a metaphor into simpler metaphors.[26] These simple metaphors constitute the "central mappings" in complex metaphors. He acknowledges in a note that this fact can be regarded as a kind of metonymic motivation for metaphor. In his conclusions, he also seems to acknowledge a fundamental role to the target domain in the selection of the meaning focus or foci, when he says: "... when we use the concept of building as a source domain, we do so because we are primarily concerned with the creation of stable abstract complex systems and when we use fire, we do so because we are primarily concerned with issues of intensity of a situation".

Kövecses explicitly recognizes the similarity of his distinction between simple and complex metaphors to Grady's (1997) proposal to decompose what he calls "compound" metaphors like THEORIES ARE BUILDINGS into "primitive" metaphors, which pick out the *relevant* parts of the metaphor and are closer to its experiential motivation. For instance, THEORIES ARE BUILDINGS, he suggests, should be decomposed into ABSTRACT ORGANIZATION IS PHYSICAL STRUCTURE and PERSISTING IS REMAINING ERECT, whose experiential motivation is based on experiential correlations. Complex physical objects, like abstract structures, also involve logical, causal relationships; physical entities and structures like poles, buildings, active people, trees, etc., are in a standing position while they are in a canonical, functioning state, which correlates with another salient element in abstract structures: their functionality, i.e. their relevance in some context (Grady, 1997: 278). As Radden (this volume) demonstrates, and as I have claimed in the section on invariance, correlations are a sort of metonymic operation. In my view, correlation is metonymic because it entails the metonymic abstraction of the image-schematic structure of both the source and the target to check their similarity. Grady's "primitive metaphors", therefore, are motivated by metonymically captured experiential correlations.

These two approaches to the structure of metaphor are perfectly compatible with the hypothesis that has been examined here. A large number of metaphors studied by cognitive linguists can be shown to be, in fact, a compound of other independent metaphors, whose direct experiential motivation requires metonymic abstraction.

9. Conclusion

The hypothesis examined in this article depends for its viability on the acceptance of the broad concept of metonymy proposed at the beginning. The range of metonymy-motivated metaphors would be drastically reduced, and the hypothesis could not even be entertained, if we required that every metonymy be referential or involve a mapping onto an *entity* rather than onto a conceptual *domain*. The common thread in all the definitions of metonymy presented at the beginning of the paper is the cognitive activation of a conceptual complex by another with which it has strong cognitive-experiential links. This is why I proposed the broadest definition, as it highlights the basic cognitive operation which gives rise to *any* metonymy.

Evidence has been provided that, at least *typically*, metaphor is based on one or more metonymic mappings. Our brief survey of the literature clearly points in this direction. We have examined some apparent counterexamples and shown that a metonymic motivation can also be discovered for the metaphors instantiated in them.

We have noted that some metaphors seem to develop out of a metonymy which encapsulates part of the experiential motivation of the mapping, through a process of generalization, itself metonymic. Other metaphors, like DEVIANT COLORS ARE DEVIANT SOUNDS or PLEASURABLE MUSIC IS SWEET FOOD, seem to be motivated by a metonymic precomprehension of the target domain, which constrains the choice, both of the source and of the subdomain(s) of the latter to be mapped (i.e. the "focus/foci", in Kövecses' terminology).[27]

The invariance principle has been compared with the metonymic motivation hypothesis. It has been claimed, tentatively, that it is a metonymic constraint on metaphor, whose satisfaction is a consequence of the metonymic motivation of metaphor.

We have offered a possible answer to the fundamental objection presented by Rudzka-Ostyn, although the issue remains unresolved, and a metonymic basis has been suggested for two very abstract general metaphors.

Finally, it has been pointed out that the hypothesis is compatible with proposals to decompose conventional metaphors into more primitive or basic ones.

In view of the above results, we can conclude that there seem to be quite serious grounds for the claim that metaphorical mappings are necessarily based on metonymy:

(1) The number of metonymy-based metaphors has been shown to be very high indeed. This cannot be a casual fact.[28]

(2) Metaphors are normally "partial" i.e. they focus on just one or a few aspects of the target. In many cases, as in DEVIANT COLORS ARE DEVIANT SOUNDS, each of these aspects is selected by a "metonymic model" of the metaphorical target. In others, as in MORE IS UP or SADNESS IS DOWN, these aspects are provided by the "mother" metonymy whose generalization leads to the metaphor.

(3) Metaphors are based on experience. Experience-based connections between two different domains are often encapsulated by means of metonymic abstraction. This is particularly obvious in cases in which a conventionalized metonymy generalizes to a metaphor, but it occurs in the other cases, too. The metonymic connection between deviant colors and sounds on the basis of their common effects on perceivers also depends on our sensory experience in both domains.

(4) A possible, more fundamental reason (but this requires further investigation) is that both perception and mental activation are normally "partial": just as we cannot possibly perceive *every* detail of a percept at the same time (Gregory 1998), we probably cannot activate *every* subdomain of a domain at the same time in our minds. This parallel between bodily perception and mental activation probably makes it inevitable to select metonymically both the aspects of the target domain to be "elucidated" by means of a metaphor, and the main subdomains of the source to be mapped onto the target.

The hypothesis also lends support to the view, voiced in this volume by several contributors and by other cognitive linguists (e.g. Dirven 1993, who recovers the Jakobsonian notion of the metonymic and metaphorical poles) that metonymy and metaphor should be regarded as two poles in a continuum, rather than as separate categories.

A substantial amount of detailed research into the motivation of the various metaphor systems uncovered so far in English and other languages ought to be carried out to verify the hypothesis that *all* metaphors are ultimately motivated by metonymy. I hope, though, to have presented enough evidence and arguments in support of its plausibility and of the need to pursue its careful examination.

Notes

1. An initial version of this paper (Barcelona, n.d.) was presented as a contribution to the theme session ("Metonymy as a conceptual motivation for metaphorical mappings") which I organized in Amsterdam in July 1997 as part of the 5th International Cognitive Linguistics Conference.
2. Unless by a "conceptual entity" in a domain Kövecses and Radden actually mean what I mean by a "subdomain" in it. This appears to be the case with most of the metonymies they discuss, e.g. in INSTRUMENT / ORGAN OF PERCEPTION FOR THE PERCEPTION (Kövecses – Radden 1998: 56) a subdomain within the domain of perception (the organ) is mapped onto the whole of a given perceptual domain, as in *to eye someone*.
3. See example (4) below, as an illustration.
4. Ruiz de Mendoza (this volume) offers a more constrained non-referential definition of metonymy as occurring within one domain, and involving, like Croft's definition (Croft 1993), Langacker's (1987: 165) notions of primary and secondary domains.
5. Ruiz de Mendoza (this volume) just recognizes two general types of metonymies (whole for part and part for whole). I prefer Kövecses and Radden's global classification into three types (whole for part, part for whole, part for part) because it is done against the background of a series of ICMs (Idealized Cognitive Models; see Lakoff, 1987), which makes it easy to know which is the superordinate domain within which the metonymic mapping takes place. Ruiz de Mendoza's proposal deserves further examination, though, and may eventually prove to be correct.
6. Radden's paper (Radden, this volume), which has been written on the basis of an exploratory analysis and classification of the metonymy-based metaphors in Lakoff's *Master Metaphor List*, offers the largest number of examples in the volume, with several references to examples found in other recent cognitive linguistic publications.
7. But Dirven himself did not classify this selection of aspects as a metonymic operation.
8. Taylor means here conceptual, not purely spatial, contiguity.
9. That this is a systematic conceptual metaphor, not just a nonce usage of *loud*, is

attested by other expressions like *Those two reds* jar, *She was wearing a skirt that cried aloud to heaven, These colors grate, That color really screams*.

10.   This may not be a linguistically conventionalized metonymy for deviant colors or sounds, but it certainly underlies reasoning processes, as the following examples show: *It was a loud color/sound even though it did not force itself on my attention*, or *It was a loud color/ sound because it drew my attention*. In this respect, this metonymy is similar to other metonymic models, like the *housewife mother* discussed by Lakoff (1987: 79-85).

11.   Other examples would be (Barcelona 1997): *John has a good* head ("head" for "intelligence", an attribute connected with the folk theoretical main function of the head, i.e. thinking); *John has good legs. He can walk five miles without stopping* ("leg" for "walking / running capacity", an attribute of the function of the legs, i.e. walking); *They have good* eyes ("eyes" for "sharpness of vision", an attribute of the main function of the eyes, i.e. seeing).

12.   I became aware of this alternative view thanks to Joseph Hilferty (personal communication).

13.   The folk model of sadness predicts lack of "brightness" in the look of sad people (in this case the metonymy itself is metaphorically motivated), so that an expression like *Her eyes no longer* glowed *as they had before* can be read as a metonymic reference to sadness. Both the general and the specific metonymy motivate the specific metaphor SADNESS IS DARK. The metaphor is attested by numerous expressions: *He is a bit* gloomy, *A somber demeanor, He is in a* dark *mood*.

14.   *A sweet smell, A sweet little girl, A sweet singer, It was sweet* to hear them praise my work, etc. Note that another possible manifestation of the same general metaphor is UNPLEASANT EXPERIENCES ARE SOUR OR BITTER FOOD (*She has as a* sour *temper*, *What a* sour *face he has!*, *They had a* bitter *argument*).

15.   Dirven (1985: 106) notices that in some synesthetic expressions with *sweet* as source domain, like *sweet air* (defined by the Collins' dictionary as "free from unpleasant odours"), or *sweet soil* (defined by the same dictionary as "containing no corrosive substances"), what is mapped is the negation of a negatively evaluated attribute like "unpleasant" or "corrosive", rather than a positively evaluated attribute like "pleasant". These cases may represent a specialization of the metaphor PLEASURABLE EXPERIENCES ARE SWEET FOOD, which comes about as a result of a metaphorical entailment: if what is pleasant is sweet, what is not unpleasant is also sweet. The rather neutral sense ("polarized", as Dirven calls it) of *sweet* in these examples, in which it has come to mean the opposite of a negatively-valued attribute, is probably due to metonymic abstraction, leading from "pleasant" to "not unpleasant" and to "not negative in general". This metonymic abstraction would also account for the non-metaphorical extensions of *sweet* in which this lexeme acquires a polarized meaning: *sweet water* (i.e. "not salty"), *sweet milk* ("not sour"), *sweet butter* ("not rancid"), etc.

16.   Johnson (1987: 122-23) prefers to treat SCALE as a basic image-schema, and not as a concept metaphorically structured in terms of the PATH schema. But scales are better regarded as paths. One of the reasons he uses is that, by contrast with paths, scales are cumulative and typically given a normative character.

17.   We tend to measure spatially perceivable entities by mapping onto them the path image-schema. The frequent mapping of spatial onto nonspatial concepts leads to

measuring nonspatial phenomena (like intelligence or pitch) in spatial terms, too, as when we say *She is* miles *above you* (in intelligence), *You should try and sing higher*. In these examples, as in (6), the three metaphors work together.

18. This piling frame has to be conceived in very general terms, including the act of pouring a fluid into a container (see Radden, this volume).

19. The connection between increase in quantity and rise in verticality may also be conceived as one of simultaneity; but in fact, it is the act of addition that results in the level rising.

20. For instance, the elementary image-schematic structure of sadness, as structured by the DOWNWARD POSTURE metonymy (see below).

21. Via the associated metaphors SPATIAL SCALES ARE PATHS and MEASUREMENT SCALES ARE SPATIAL SCALES.

22. And this is reflected by the fact that linguistic expressions of SADNESS IS DOWN are mainly used to express various degrees of emotional intensity: *She's a bit crest-fallen* (weak intensity); *I am in* low *spirits* (medium intensity); *I have* touched bottom, *I am* in the pits (strong intensity).

23. In the light of the preceding remarks, it seems that MORE IS UP is indirectly present in the construction of SADNESS/HAPPINESS and BADNESS/GOODNESS, as the notion of measurement, implicit in the oppositions UP-DOWN and GOOD-BAD, evokes the notion of quantity, which is understood metaphorically by means of MORE IS UP.

24. The preceding section should not be understood as claiming that all the metonymi-cally imposed subdomains of the target necessarily become *conventional* sub-domains of it. For instance, verticality is not a conventional subdomain of sadness. Verticality is not consciously regarded by speakers as a "part" of happiness or sadness, and this is why SADNESS IS DOWN is a metaphor and not just a metonymy. The metonymy UP FOR SADNESS simply includes verticality as an unconscious ele-ment in the image-schematic structure of happiness/sadness, and this makes it possible for DOWN to be re-mapped metaphorically in a way that satisfies invari-ance.

25. The metonymic basis for this metaphor can also apply to the overarching metaphor that Rudzka-Ostyn claims to lie at the basis of every metonymy.

26. See his discussion of metaphors with BUILDINGS and HEAT as "wide-scope" source domains for COMPLEX SYSTEMS (e.g. a theory) or SITUATIONS (e.g. an emotional state or a political crisis).

27. In the cases of metonymy-to-metaphor generalization discussed above, a similar metonymic perspectivization of the metaphorical target domain might be shown to motivate the generalization. For instance, once sadness is (metonymically) endowed with a measurement scale, further metonymic highlighting of this element seems to stimulate the metonymic transition from DOWNWARD-ORIENTED BODILY POSTURE to DOWN and the emergence of the metaphor. The metaphor would arise to elucidate a metonymically imposed aspect of the target, that is, measurement. The driving force for the generalization to a metaphorical mapping would be located in the target domain in these cases, too. However, this idea requires further examination.

28. Another instance of metonymic motivation, not only for metaphor, but also for "blending" (see Turner – Fauconnier, this volume), can be discovered in the ab-straction of a generic space, as Ruiz de Mendoza (this volume) suggests. He states that only "source-in-target" metonymies (approximately "part-for-whole" ones)

are the basis for such an abstraction. But, even in the cases (like his example 34) where he denies metonymy a role in the construction of the generic space, this space is built, I believe, by correlating the abstract image-schemas (doer, action and affected, in his example) of the two input spaces. Abstracting the image-schema in each space implies, as we said above, a metonymic mapping within each of them.

References

Allan, Keith
    1995   "The anthropocentricity of the English word(s) *back*", *Cognitive Linguistics*, 6-1: 11-31.
Apresjan, Valentina
    1997   "Emotion metaphors and cross-linguistic conceptualization of emotion". In: Antonio Barcelona (ed.), *Cognitive linguistics in the study of the English language and literature in English*. Monograph issue of *Cuadernos de Filología Inglesa*, 6:2, 179-213.
Barcelona, Antonio
    1986   "On the concept of depression in American English: A cognitive approach", *Revista Canaria de Estudios Ingleses*, 12:7-35.
    1997   "Clarifying and applying the notions of metaphor and metonymy within cognitive linguistics", *Atlantis* 19-1 (21-48).
  this volume "Introduction".
    n.d   Types of arguments for the metonymic motivation of conceptual metaphor [Unpublished M.S.]
Brugman, Claudia
    1990   "What is the Invariance Hypothesis?", *Cognitive Linguistics*, 1-2, 257-67.
Cowie, Anthony P., Ronald Mackin, and Ian R. McCaig
    1983   *Oxford dictionary of current idiomatic English*. Oxford: Oxford University Press.
Croft, William
    1993   "The role of domains in the interpretation of metaphors and metonymies", *Cognitive Linguistics*, 4-4: 335-371.
Dirven, René
    1985   "Metaphor as a basic means of extending the lexicon". In: Wolf Paprotté and René Dirven, (eds.), *The ubiquity of metaphor. Metaphor in language and thought*. Amsterdam/Philadelphia: John Benjamins, 85-120.
    1993   "Metaphor and metonymy: Different mental strategies of conceptualisation", *Leuvense Bijdragen* 82:1-28.
Fauconnier, Gilles – Mark Turner
    1998   "Conceptual integration networks", *Cognitive Science* 22: 2, 133-187.
Goossens, Louis
    1990   "Metaphtonymy: The interaction of metaphor and metonymy in expressions for linguistic action", *Cognitive Linguistics* 1-3: 323-340 (also reproduced in Goossens et al. 1995, 159-174).

1995   "From three respectable horses' mouth. Metonymy and conventionalization in a diachronically differentiated data base". In: Goossens et al. (1995), 175-204.

this volume   "Patterns of meaning extension, 'parallel chaining', subjectification, and modal shifts".

Goossens, Louis – Paul Pauwels – Brygida Rudzka-Ostyn – Anne-Marie Simon-Vanderbergen – Johan Vanparys

1995   *By word of mouth. Metaphor, metonymy and linguistic action in a cognitive perspective.* Amsterdam/ Philadelphia: John Benjamins.

Grady, Joseph

1997   "THEORIES ARE BUILDINGS revisited", *Cognitive Linguistics* 8-4, 267-291.

Gregory, Richard

1998   *Eye and brain.* (5th edition.) Oxford: Oxford University Press.

Heine, Bernd – Ulrike Claudi – Friederike Hünnemeyer

1991   *Grammaticalization: A conceptual framework.* Chicago and London: University of Chicago Press.

Hornby, A.S.

1974   *Oxford advanced learner's dictionary of current English.* Oxford: Oxford University Press.

Jäkel, Olaf

1997   *Metaphern in abstrakten Diskurs-Domänen: eine Kognitiv-linguistische Untersuchung anhand der Bereiche Geistestigkeit, Wirtschaft und Wissenschaft.* Frankfurt a.M. etc.: Peter Lang.

Johnson, Mark

1987   *The body in the mind: the bodily basis of meaning, imagination, and reason.* Chicago: University of Chicago Press.

Kövecses, Zoltán

1986   *Metaphors of anger, pride and love.* Amsterdam: John Benjamins.

1988   *Language of love. Semantics of passion in conversational English.* Lewisburg: Bucknell University Press.

1990   *Emotion concepts.* New York: Springer Verlag.

1991   "Happiness: A definitional effort", *Metaphor and Symbolic Activity* 6-1: 29-46.

1995   "Anger: Its language, conceptualization and physiology in the light of cross-cultural evidence". In: John Taylor and Robert E. MacLaury (eds.), *Language and the cognitive construal of the world.* Berlin / New York: Mouton de Gruyter.

this volume   "The scope of metaphor".

Kövecses, Zoltán – Günter Radden

1998   "Metonymy: Developing a cognitive linguistic view", *Cognitive Linguistics,* 9-1: 37-77.

Lakoff, George

1987   *Women, fire and dangerous things. What categories reveal about the mind.* Chicago: Chicago University Press.

1990   "The Invariance Hypothesis: Is abstract reason based on image-schemas?", *Cognitive Linguistics* 1-1: 39-75.

1993   "The contemporary theory of metaphor". In: Andrew Ortony (ed.),
              Metaphor and thought. (2nd edition.) Cambridge: Cambridge University Press, 202-251.
Lakoff, George – Mark Johnson
1980   *Metaphors we live by.* Chicago: University of Chicago Press.
1999   *Philosophy in the flesh. The embodied mind and its challenge to western thought.* New York: Basic Books.
Lakoff, George – Mark Turner
1989   *More than cool reason: A field guide to poetic metaphor.* Chicago: University of Chicago Press.
Langacker Ronald
1987   *Foundations of cognitive grammar. Vol. 1: Theoretical prerequisites.* Stanford, California: Stanford University Press.
1993   "Reference-point constructions", *Cognitive Linguistics* 4: 1-38.
McKechnie, Jean L. (ed.)
1978   *Webster's new twentieth century dictionary of the English language.* (2nd. edition.) [No indication of place]: Collins World.
Niemeier, Susanne
this volume   "Straight from the heart – Metonymic and metaphorical explorations".
Pauwels, Paul
1995   "Levels of metaphorization". In: Goossens et al., 125-159.
Radden, Günter
this volume   "How metonymic are metaphors?"
Radden, Günter – Zoltán Kövecses
forthcoming   "Towards a theory of metonymy". In: Klaus-Uwe Panther and Günter Radden (eds), *Metonymy in cognition and language.* Amsterdam/Philadelphia: John Benjamins.
Rudzka-Ostyn, Brygida.
1995   "Metaphor, schema, invariance. The case of verbs of answering". In: Goossens et al, 205-243.
Ruiz de Mendoza, Francisco
this volume   "The role of mappings and domains in understanding metonymy".
Sampson, J.A. – E.C.C. Weiner (eds.)
1989   *The Oxford English dictionary.* (Second edition.) Oxford: Clarendon Press.
Taylor, John
1995   *Linguistic categorization. Prototypes in linguistic theory.* (2nd. edition.) Oxford: Clarendon.
Turner, Mark – Gilles Fauconnier
this volume   "Metaphor, metonymy, and binding".
Ullmann, Stephen
1957   *The principles of semantics.* Oxford: Basil Blackwell.
Ungerer, Friedrich
this volume   "Muted metaphors and the activation of metonymies in advertising".
Wildgen, Wolfgang
1994.   *Process, image and meaning. A realistic model of the meaning of sentences and narrative texts.* Amsterdam / Philadelphia: John Benjamins.

Refining the Inheritance Hypothesis: Interaction between metaphoric and metonymic hierarchies

Kurt Feyaerts

0. Introduction[1]

Within a cognitive semantic framework, this paper focuses on the role conceptual hierarchies play in an in-depth analysis of any semantic structure. More specifically, I want to demonstrate that the meaning of a linguistic expression may be determined by several conceptual hierarchies which might be of a different nature: metaphoric as well as metonymic. I will argue that the Inheritance Hypothesis, as it was originally formulated by George Lakoff (1993), requires a more *refined* interpretation than a first reading and the first studies written so far might indicate.

Up until now, the field of cognitive semantics has produced overwhelming evidence for the prominent role metaphor plays in structuring large parts of our knowledge. Although the notion of metonymy was never entirely absent, it was mostly treated as a secondary phenomenon in an essentially metaphorical context. However, recent years have witnessed an increasing interest in the role of metonymy as a pervasive conceptual mechanism. In recognizing the importance of metonymy for the Inheritance Principle, this contribution forms part of this renewed interest in metonymy.

This paper is structured as follows. First, I will situate this study in the context of my research project with, additionally, some basic information about the material of my database (1.1) as well as my definition of the categories metaphor and metonymy (1.2). In the second part, I will concentrate on the notion of conceptual hierarchies both in a metaphoric (2.1) and a metonymic (2.2) elaboration. The third part is devoted to conceptual-semantic structures situated at the intersection of metaphoric and metonymic hierarchies. The relevance of our observations to the Inheritance Hypothesis is illustrated in two detailed examples.

1. Preliminary remarks

1.1 Background and material

Within the overall cognitive semantic framework, as it appears in the writings of Lakoff (and his associates) and Langacker,[2] this article links up with broader research that I have been doing on the role of metonymy as a conceptual mechanism (Feyaerts 1997). The empirical basis for this investigation consisted of German idiomatic expressions (about 500) which all profile the schematic target concept STUPID (e.g. DUMM).[3] The analysis of these expressions revealed that this conceptual domain is primarily metonymically structured. This is the kind of material that I will be using throughout this contribution. These expressions constitute a single category in that they elaborate a common schematic concept, STUPID, which I define as "a negatively valued, non-pathological deviance from the norm in the domain of mental abilities". For present purposes, I abstract from several kinds of stupidity like ignorance, credulity, narrow-mindedness, etc., which all represent different elaborations of this schematic notion.

The database consists of more or less fixed expressions, most of which are collected from phraseological dictionaries. As a consequence of this methodological approach, it does not come as a surprise if native speakers of German appear to be unfamiliar with some of the material presented here. However, from a cognitive semantic, usage-based point of view, it is important not to restrict the material to an arbitrary set of familiar, well-established expressions. Instead, an adequate description of the structure of a particular concept requires that as many relevant expressions as possible be taken into account.[4]

1.2 Metaphor and metonymy

In this contribution it is not my aim to discuss in great detail the different views of metaphor and metonymy that have developed in the last 20 years. Instead, I devote this entire subsection to a general description of my own view of both phenomena. The reason for doing so is that, although this study adopts an overall cognitive semantic perspective, I cannot fully subscribe to the definitions of both phenomena as they are commonly accepted within this linguistic paradigm.

In accordance with cognitive semantic theory, I define both metaphor and metonymy as fundamentally *conceptual* phenomena, which can be studied through their appearance in language. An important implication of this claim is that concepts are not *represented* as metaphoric/metonymic, but that they essentially *are* metaphoric/metonymic. From the rich cognitive semantic literature on metaphor it has become clear that conceptual metaphors (henceforth just "metaphors") are typically instantiated by more than just one linguistic expression.[5] The same observation holds for (conceptual) metonymies.

1.2.1 Metaphor

Metaphor can further be defined as the (partial) mapping of two concepts belonging to different knowledge domains onto each other.[6] As a result of this linking, one concept (the *target*) is structured (understood) in terms of the other (the *source*).[7] Concepts or aspects of concepts that can be characterized in terms of their own conceptual domain – these are said to be *semantically autono-*

mous[8] – typically function as source concepts. This structural projection from source to target domain takes place on three different conceptual levels. The first type of mapping consists of a correspondence between ontological entities[9] in both domains. The second type of mapping is situated on a highly abstract level of our knowledge system. It takes the form of a *topological* projection whereby the image-schematic structure from the source is mapped onto the target. Image schemata are very abstract structures, which according to Johnson (1987) emerge directly at the level of our bodily interaction with the world. They are relatively simple structures, which play an important role in the structuring of our experience and our conceptual system.[10] Examples of image schemata are structures like CONTAINER, BALANCE, BLOCKAGE, PART-WHOLE, PATH etc., but also spatial orientations like UP-DOWN, CLOSE-FAR etc. A good illustration of how an image schematic structure can be mapped onto a target is the conceptualization of the mind as a container in expressions like *What do you have* in *mind?*, *It slipped* out of *my mind* etc. Most importantly, both these (ontological and topological) mappings allow us to apply the *logical* knowledge structures of the source domain to the target domain (third type of mapping). This means that a semantically non-autonomous concept obtains (parts of) its internal structure through the rationality that shows up in inference patterns and logical entailments related to a source domain.[11] As Lakoff and Johnson (1980: 193) put it: "Metaphor is one of our most important tools for trying to comprehend partially what cannot be comprehended totally: our feelings, aesthetic experiences, moral practices, and spiritual awareness." The examples in (1), which all instantiate the conceptual metaphor LIFE IS A JOURNEY, illustrate what is meant by these multi-level projections from source to target.[12]

(1) a. *We are at a crossroads in our life.*
     b. *You're off the track.*
     c. *There is no way back!*
     d. *Our relationship is a dead-end street.*
     e. *We may have to go our separate ways.*
     f. *She gave her life a new direction.*

More than just describing aspects of life in terms of a journey, the examples in (1) project our knowledge about traveling onto different aspects of life. The mapping consists more specifically of the structuring of LIFE according to the PATH image schema. This schema implies that life is generally conceived as a movement from a starting-point (SOURCE) in a specific direction towards a specific destination (GOAL). Apart from this global structural mapping between life and a journey, there are also more specific ontological correspondences occurring between both domains. A traveler corresponds with a living person, traveling destinations structure goals in life, decisive moments in life are understood in terms of crossroads, the road already covered corresponds to past periods of our life etc. However, the mapping does not consist of these static correspondences alone. Its conceptual strength lies in the entire logic of journeys being implemented in the domain of life. Consequently, it is no problem for the hearer to infer from these basic correspondences which concepts are profiled in the target domain, when we use source domain images like hitting a long and bumpy road, choosing a wrong direction, a train getting off the track, a car that goes too fast and then breaks down, etc.

1.2.2 Metonymy

In the relevant contemporary literature, two major approaches to metonymy can be distinguished depending on whether the nature of the conceptual relationship between two entities or the range of the semantic extension between them is used as the main criterion. What both views have in common is the schematic representation of a metonymic relationship as "A *stands for* B". A first approach describes metonymy in terms of "contiguity" and thus focuses on the nature of the relationship between the concepts involved. It finds its origin in traditional structuralist theories in which linguistic meaning is seen as applying to an objective reality. In this view, the notion of contiguity appears to be limited to an observable, real-world relationship between two referents. The second approach was developed in cognitive semantics and describes metonymy in terms of the conceptual range of the extension involved. More specifically, it defines metonymy as a conceptual extension taking place within the boundaries of a single domain matrix[13] and bringing about a referential shift (compare among others Lakoff 1987, Croft 1993, Langacker 1993, Goossens 1995). A domain matrix is defined as the totality of knowledge structures which are activated in multiple domains as the conceptual background of a particular meaning. Consistent with this definition, metaphor is then characterized in terms of an extension taking place between *different* domain matrices.

What makes this second approach to metonymy somewhat problematic is the use of the notion "domain matrix" as the key element in the distinction between metaphor and metonymy. Drawing distinct boundaries around a domain (matrix) always reflects an arbitrary intervention by an external observer (a linguist). *Per se*, this observation does not pose such a big problem since no linguistic research can ever escape this kind of subjective interference. However, it does raise a methodological problem when the distinction between two important conceptual phenomena is based on the arbitrary delimitation of a domain matrix without the addition of any independent support.

According to this theoretical model, metaphors never occur within a single domain matrix. Consider, however, the conceptual relationship between the concepts KNOWING and SEEING, which is traditionally described as a metaphoric one (KNOWING IS SEEING as in *I see what you mean*). The question, then, is how can it be demonstrated in a convincing and objective way that a concept like VISUAL or, more schematically, SENSORY PERCEPTION does *not* belong to the domain matrix of an expression that profiles a concept like MENTAL PERCEPTION/

KNOWING? An adequate answer to this question would have to explain that one *does not* experience sensory/visual perception as being causally or conditionally linked to knowledge. Intuitively, it does not seem very likely that such an explanation can ever be found. The same problem arises for the relationship between LINGUISTIC ACTION and (HUMAN) SOUND (see Goossens (1995), example (1): "*Oh dear*", *she giggled, "I'd quite forgotten*"). For both source concepts, SEEING and (HUMAN) SOUND, it is not unreasonable to claim that they belong to the same domain matrix as their respective target concepts.

Let us consider again the relationship between KNOWING and SEEING. Although both concepts can be systematically mapped onto each other, involving ontological, image schematic as well as logical structures, I claim that this metaphoric characterization does not exhaust the conceptual relationship between both concepts. Another important aspect of this relationship which cannot be ignored, is the causal-conditional contiguity of both experiences, which indicates that a metonymic extension (PERCEPTION FOR RESULT OF PERCEPTION) can be identified as well.[14] This observation seriously questions the hypothesis of two *different* domain matrices being involved in this extension pattern. As for the second example, I do not see any reason to conclude that in the metaphoric interpretation of Goossens' example ("to say something *as if* giggling"), the domain (HUMAN) SOUND does not belong to the domain matrix of the profiled concept LINGUISTIC ACTION. In my opinion, this auditory experience represents an essential aspect of every linguistic utterance. Again, the question remains, how can a decision be motivated in a convincing and possibly objective way as to which conceptual structures belong to a particular domain and which structures do not?

Methodologically speaking, it appears that the notion of domain border is too malleable to serve as an adequate criterion in the discussion about the distinction between metaphor and metonymy. As an ultimate consequence, the feature indicating the range of a conceptual extension cannot maintain its categorial status: it fails to identify a metonymic (or metaphoric) extension. Although it seems to be true – speaking from my own intuition – that metonymy takes place within a single domain matrix, the involvement of a single domain matrix is not restricted to metonymic extensions alone; it turns out that also metaphoric mappings (mostly when metonymy is involved as well) can occur within a domain matrix.

In light of these observations I subscribe to the view that metonymy can be characterized in terms of a contiguity relationship between two entities (meanings, concepts). In this approach, which developed from structuralist, rhetoric-oriented semantics, the categorization of an extension as metaphoric or metonymic resides in the nature of the relationship which is involved. With Ullmann (1962) I define contiguity in a negative way as a relationship of association that does not involve similarity. In the relevant literature on metonymy many attempts have been made to present a typology of different contiguity relationships. Some of the most frequently cited illustrations of contiguous relationships include associative-functional relationships as cause-effect, container-contained, producer-product, part-whole, substance-object etc.[15] In this diversity, metonymy differs from metaphor, in which the structural mapping between domains basically reduces to a relation of (conceptually embedded) similarity (A is like B). Adopted in a cognitive semantic framework, contiguity is radically interpreted as *conceptual* contiguity, as Dirven (1993: 14) argues:

> Contiguity cannot be based on any form of objective or natural contiguity. This has the far-reaching implication that contiguity must be taken to mean conceptual contiguity and that we can have contiguity when we just "see" contiguity between domains.

So far, three features have been identified in the attempt to distinguish between metaphor and metonymy. Metaphor, on the one hand, consists of a systematic projection of ontological, image schematic as well as logical structures from a source domain onto a target domain, whereby in addition to this primary feature the relationship between both domains can be characterized in terms of similarity. Metonymy, on the other hand, involves a contiguity relationship, which can be expressed by several specific associative relationships. As a fourth characteristic, the function of metonymy is traditionally determined as causing a referential shift, through which a salient conceptual structure is used to access a less prominent concept.[16] Compare in this respect Langacker (1993: 30) about the function of metonymic expressions:

> The entity that is normally designated by a metonymic expression serves as a reference point affording mental access to the desired target (i.e. the entity actually being referred to). (...) By virtue of our reference-point ability, a well chosen metonymic expression lets us mention one entity that is salient and easily coded, and thereby evoke – essentially automatically – a target that is either of lesser interest or harder to name.

We are now able to present the difference between metaphor and metonymy in a schematic way. Figure 1 shows the four characteristics mentioned above situated on two dimensions, namely function and nature of the conceptual relation. Heavy lines indicate the relatively higher prominence of a particular feature. For metaphor, its function of establishing "imagistic reasoning" is the most important one, whereas for metonymy, the nature of the conceptual relation is the dominant one.

	metaphor	metonymy
function of conceptual relationship	"imagistic reasoning"	referential shift
nature of conceptual relationship	similarity	contiguity

Figure 1. Metaphor and metonymy

2. Conceptual hierarchies

A conceptual hierarchy can generally be described as a cluster of concepts linked to each other by a relationship of elaboration or schematization. Both relations represent opposite "movements" on a vertical scale, indicating the level of abstraction (degree of schematicity) of a particular concept, whereby schematic concepts are ranked higher than more specific ones. This is illustrated in figure 2, where the following concepts/meanings are ordered on a vertical scale: THING – OBJECT – PIECE OF WOOD – PIECE OF FURNITURE – TABLE – "table". A concept like PIECE OF FURNITURE is schematized by the concept PIECE OF WOOD and elaborated by a concept like TABLE (among others). The form "table" in double quotes at the bottom of this hierarchy stands for the semantic pole of the symbolic linguistic structure in which the concept TABLE is *instantiated*.[17]

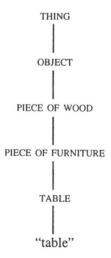

THING

OBJECT

PIECE OF WOOD

PIECE OF FURNITURE

TABLE

"table"

Figure 2. Conceptual hierarchy

2.1 Metaphoric hierarchies

In his 1993 article, Lakoff argues that most metaphoric mappings, similar to simple concepts, do not occur in isolation, but that they are integrated in larger hierarchically organized structures. Lakoff demonstrates this with the so-called *Event Structure Metaphor* (henceforth "ES-metaphor"), a schematic, large-scale metaphor, which encompasses several specific metaphors, all pertaining to notions that, in one way or another, belong to the global conceptual structure of an *event* (taken in a broad sense). For instance, for English, German and certainly also for other languages, it can be shown that concepts like EVENT, ACTION, STATE, CHANGE OF STATE, PROPERTY, CAUSE etc. receive their internal structure from domains like SPACE, MOVEMENT and PHYSICAL POWER.

I will here focus on just one aspect of this complex ES-metaphor, which is the schematic metaphor ATTRIBUTES (PROPERTIES) ARE POSSESSIBLE OBJECTS. To illustrate this mapping, look at the examples in (2):

(2)   a.   *He* has *troubles*
      b.   *I don't* have *any luck*

Metonymically related to this particular mapping are the following metaphors pertaining to two other event structures (events and actions): CHANGES (EVENTS) ARE MOVEMENTS (TRANSFERS) OF OBJECTS and CAUSES OF CHANGE (ACTIONS) ARE CONTROLLED MOVEMENTS (TRANSFERS) OF OBJECTS. Both metaphors are illustrated by the examples in (3) and (4) respectively.

(3)   a.   *He lost his luck*
      b.   *Sie hat den Verstand verloren*
           'She has lost her mind'
(4)   a.   *She threw her troubles away*
      b.   *Er hat den Verstand in der Garderobe abgegeben*
           'He has left his mind in the wardrobe'
      c.   *Als die Dummheit ausgeteilt wurde, ist sie zweimal hingegangen*
           'When stupidity was handed out, she went for it twice'

With respect to the many elaborations of these schematic metaphors, Lakoff draws attention to the hierarchic structure of the ES-metaphor. He uses the LIFE/ LOVE IS A JOURNEY metaphor to illustrate his point (Lakoff 1993: 222). Figure 3 represents the hierarchic structure of this mapping. The source concepts LOVE and CAREER are elaborations of the more schematic notion PURPOSEFUL LIFE, which in its turn elaborates the highly schematic concept of an EVENT.

Regarding the internal structure of hierarchic metaphoric constructs, Lakoff observes that specific mappings preserve the basic structure of schematic metaphors and thus he formulates the *Inheritance Hypothesis*, according to which "lower mappings in the hierarchy inherit the structures of the 'higher' mappings" (Lakoff 1993: 222). With respect to metaphoric structures, this means that the internal structure of a particular metaphor is determined by the logical structure the source concept displays on a higher, more generic level. Focusing on the target structure, Kövecses (1995: 341) already observed that "a target seems to borrow its source domains from target domains that are above it in various conceptual hierarchies."

The idea of a concept being structurally determined by a large conceptual hierarchy is further elaborated by Kövecses (1995) in his analysis of the concept FRIENDSHIP as it occurs in American culture. In comparison to Lakoff, who in his analysis sticks to one single hierarchy, Kövecses describes the conceptual structure of FRIENDSHIP against the background of six large metaphor systems (hierarchies), which are all of structural relevance for the concept FRIENDSHIP: 1. communication metaphors, 2. emotion metaphors, 3. state metaphors, 4. complex systems metaphors, 5. event structure metaphors, and 6. positive/negative evaluation metaphors (ibid.: 344). Accordingly, Kövecses (1995: 317) argues that "the concept FRIENDSHIP lies at the intersection of several systems of metaphors, the relevant parts of which make up the abstract domain that is called friendship".

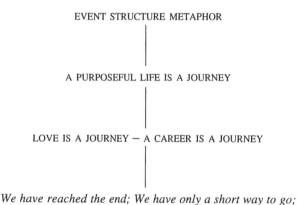

EVENT STRUCTURE METAPHOR

A PURPOSEFUL LIFE IS A JOURNEY

LOVE IS A JOURNEY — A CAREER IS A JOURNEY

We have reached the end; We have only a short way to go; he is climbing the ladder rapidly

Figure 3. Metaphoric hierarchy (event structure metaphor)

2.2 Metonymic hierarchies

It appears that metonymic extensions display basically the same hierarchic structures as metaphors do (see also Feyaerts forthcoming). Just like metaphors, conceptual metonymies can be described on different levels of abstraction, involving relationships of schematization and elaboration/instantiation. Unlike metaphors, however, where the object of the inheritance process consists of the logical structure of the source domain, metonymies inherit no domain-internal structures. Instead, highly elaborated metonymies inherit their contiguity relationship – together with their function of causing a referential shift – from schematic metonymic patterns.

A nice illustration of this structural characteristic is the *Mantafahrer* model ("Manta-driver model") in which stupidity plays a central role (Feyaerts forthcoming). This metonymic model gets its name from a particular kind of car (Opel Manta) which can be characterized as having a sporty look, a low and aerodynamic profile, a powerful engine, etc. Moreover, it is a relatively cheap car, which made it a big commercial success. At the same time, however, this popularity has "degraded" it to an ordinary car everyone can afford. To (re)gain some exclusiveness many people used to equip their Opel Manta with fancy, aggressive-looking accessories like chrome spoilers, muscle tires, rally seat belts, high-beam headlamps, racing colors, etc. All these elements contribute to the typical image of this car as an "ordinary car dressed up with kitschy gadgets".

Of particular interest for the present purpose is the cultural (German) model in which this car is associated with the typical kind of person owning and driving it. This social stereotype characterizes a Manta-driver as being macho, having a blond girlfriend or wife, belonging to a lower social class, driving fast and aggressively, and also as not very intelligent. Calling somebody a *Mantafahrer* can thus be interpreted in a particular context as "he is stupid". This conceptual extension is clearly metonymic since salient properties like deviant behavior, appearance and possession (in this case the car itself) are construed as manifestations of stupidity.[18] Accordingly, these concepts all take part in the source domain structure which serves as the conceptual base for profiling the target STUPID. To put it another way, these source concepts overlap in any stupidity expression that instantiates this *Mantafahrer*-model. This model is represented schematically in figure 4. This type of schema differs from the previous representations in that the extension (in this case, a metonymic one) is symbolized only once: the broken arrow at the bottom of the figure stands for the metonymic extension from source to target (BEING STUPID). The main part of the figure focuses on the complex structure of the source domain. It shows how the *Mantafahrer*-concept in its metonymic extension onto the target concept STUPID elaborates (unbroken lines) several schematic concepts. Essentially, the schematic structure SALIENT DEVIANT HUMAN PROPERTY reduces to universal principles of relative cognitive salience, according to which a feature like VISIBLE is more salient than INVISIBLE, CONCRETE more salient than ABSTRACT, HUMAN more salient than NOT HUMAN, MOVING more salient than NOT MOVING etc. (see also, among others Langacker 1993: 30).

In comparing metaphorically and metonymically organized conceptual hierarchies, it appears that both systems have three major structural characteristics in common (Feyaerts forthcoming). According to the first – and most obvious – characteristic, a conceptual hierarchy is situated on different levels of schematicity. According to the second feature, there is a certain degree of overlap (interaction) between structures belonging to one or more hierarchies. To put it another way, a particular concept may elaborate several schematic structures; compare, for instance, the source concept MANTAFAHRER which elaborates at least three schematic structures like DEVIANT BEHAVIOR, DEVIANT APPEARANCE and DEVIANT POSSESSION. As to the third characteristic, low-level conceptual structures, like the German Mantafahrer-model, tend to be culturally more specific with a correspondingly restricted use. Higher-level structures are more widespread in their usage because of their general cognitive, culturally unspecified nature (see, among others, Lakoff 1993 and Kövecses 1995).

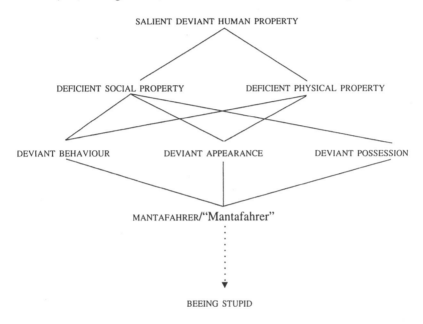

Figure 4. Hierarchical structure of the Mantafahrer-model

2.3 Metaphtonymic hierarchies

In the cognitive semantic literature on conceptual structure, it has already been demonstrated that metaphor and metonymy are not to be seen as two isolated conceptual mechanisms that exist independently from one another without any mutual interaction (see especially, among others, Goossens 1990, Warren 1992, and also the rapidly growing literature on conceptual blending: Fauconnier – Turner 1994, Turner – Fauconnier 1995). In his pioneering 1990 article, Goossens used the term *metaphtonymy* to refer to several forms of interaction between both phenomena.

From my analysis of German idiomatic expressions which all refer to the target concept STUPID (Feyaerts 1997), it has become evident that in some cases, the source concept can be described as an elaboration of both metaphoric and metonymic patterns, i.e. two different conceptual systems. I will illustrate my point with two examples from my material. What I want to demonstrate is the interaction between the metonymies LACKING SENSES FOR BEING STUPID and OWN-ING/DRIVING A MANTA FOR BEING STUPID on the one hand and one aspect of the ES-metaphor, namely A PROPERTY IS A POSSESSIBLE OBJECT on the other hand.

The first structure is illustrated by the examples in (5):

(5)   a.   *Sie hat nicht alle beisammen.*
            'She does not have them all together.'
       b.   *Er hat drei Sinne wie ein Bär.*
            'He has three senses like a bear.'
       c.   *Sie hat ihre fünf Sinne alle drei.*
            'She has her five senses, all three of them'

The part of the ES-metaphor which is relevant for these expressions can be paraphrased as "a mental property is structured in terms of one or more possessed objects (senses[19]) or the lack thereof". More specifically, it is the quantitative dimension of the notion POSSESSION which is relevant: a deviant property like STUPIDITY is conceptualized in terms of having an insufficient number of possessions. According to the logic of this model, having all your possessions together is mapped onto a (positive) property of mental equilibrium. Losing some of your goods or not getting enough of them initially, is projected onto a property of mental norm deviance.

Apart from this metaphoric structure, there is also a clear metonymic pattern involved: in most cultural models of the internal structure of human beings, body and mind are conceptualized in a dual structure as two contingent entities. The body is seen as the expression of what can be found inside it (the mind, emotions, etc.) and thus its properties are believed to tell us something about the mental, emotional and intellectual condition of a person. Accordingly, a physical deviation is interpreted as an indication or the cause of a mental deviation. The general cognitive mechanism in which these cultural models are grounded is the principle of relative salience, according to which we use a salient, easily accessible concept as a reference point in order to reach another, less accessible and thus less salient concept. Viewed from a broader perspective, (the semantic structure of) the examples in (5) instantiate two different conceptual systems. Figure 5 represents the interaction between the metaphoric and the metonymic hierarchy in these examples. Please note the specific representation of metaphor and metonymy: source concepts are placed above, target concepts underneath the lines. Asterisks represent a metaphor whereas a single line stands for a metonymic extension. The broken double line refers to the metaphtonymic nature of the conceptual relationship between the source concept LACKING SENSES and the target BEING STUPID.

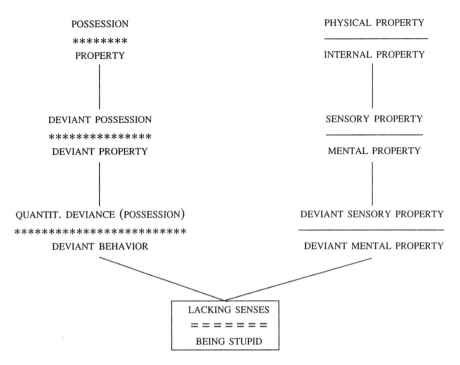

Figure 5. Metaphtonymic structure of LACKING SENSES FOR BEING STUPID

In the second example, the same target BEING STUPID is conceptualized in terms of a deviant content of the head. This conceptual pattern is instantiated by many expressions, of which I mention only a few in (6).

(6) a. *Sie hat Scheiße/einen Furz ... im Kopf*
         'She has shit/a fart ... inside her head'
     b. *Er hat Stroh/Häcksel/Sägemehl/Wasser ... im Kopf*
         'He has straw/chaff/sawdust/water/ ... inside his head'

In this case, the ES-metaphor PROPERTIES ARE POSSESSIONS is elaborated consecutively as DEVIANT PROPERTIES ARE DEVIANT POSSESSIONS, DEVIANT LOCATED POSSESSIONS and, on the next level, as DEVIANT CONTENT OF A CONTAINER. Just above the level of the linguistic instantiation, this concept is further elaborated as DEVIANT CONTENT OF THE HEAD. This source structure is of particular interest, because the concept HEAD is not just an elaboration of the image schematic CONTAINER structure, which further specifies the metaphoric structure. At this specific level, the relationship between source and target is also clearly metonymic, since the mind, intellectual capacities etc. are commonly considered to be the result or the product of the human brain, which, of course, is situated inside the head. Hence, the contiguity relationship which is involved here, is of the PRODUCER FOR PRODUCT, CAUSE FOR EFFECT kind. Figure (6) represents a schematic overview of this metaphtonymic interaction. Here also, asterisks indicate a metaphor, whereas a single line represents a metonymic extension.

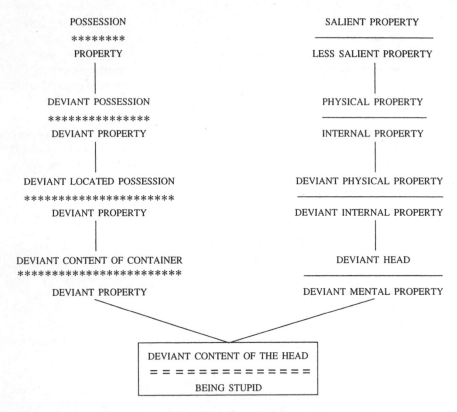

Figure 6. Metaphtonymic structure of DEVIANT CONTENT OF HEAD FOR BEING STUPID

From both examples it appears that the elaboration of a schematic conceptual structure onto a more specific level of abstraction can "bring in" a new kind of relationship between the source and target concept. This means that throughout a conceptual hierarchy, the relation between source and target cannot be described as being constant. In the examples mentioned above, it is only on a level with a relatively high degree of image specificity, i.e. right above the level of linguistic instantiation, that metaphoric and metonymic conceptual patterns start to interact. In the first case, it is through the elaboration of DEVIANT SENSORY PROPERTY and QUANTITATIVE DEVIANCE OF POSSESSIONS as LACKING SENSES that both metaphor and metonymy can be identified. As for the second example, it is not until the specification of two schematic concepts (CONTAINER in the metaphorical hierarchy and PHYSICAL PROPERTY in the metonymic one) that the interaction occurs.

With respect to the Inheritance Hypothesis, these observations lead to an additional refinement. The hypothesis as it was formulated by Lakoff (1993: 222) (see 2.1) can be interpreted too strictly, whereby any metaphtonymic interaction is neglected; according to such an interpretation, one could argue that schematic metaphors automatically generate specific metaphors just like schematic metonymies always generate specific metonymies. From that point of view, metaphor inherits metaphor and metonymy inherits metonymy, regardless of the level of abstraction which is involved. What I have tried to show is that the interaction between metaphor and metonymy can occur at a specific level of description, but remain absent on another – likely a more schematic one – in a conceptual hierarchy.

Another point which needs to be raised, is the different degree of salience by which the components of a metaphtonymic structure may be characterized. The examples in (7) nicely illustrate this phenomenon.

(7)   a.   *Er besitzt ein Spatzenhirn*
         'He possesses the brain of a sparrow'
     b.   *Du hast wohl den Verstand verloren?*
         'Surely, you must have lost your mind?'
     c.   *Ihm haben sie wohl einen Nerv geklaut?*
         'Surely, they must have stolen one of his nerves?'
     d.   *Bei ihr haben sie wohl eingebrochen?*
         'Surely, she must have been burgled?'
     e.   *Sie hat einen Wurm*
         'She has a worm'
     f.   *Wasserkopf!*
         'Waterhead!'

Although these expressions, in addition to the ones in (6), all instantiate more or less directly the conceptual extension DEVIANT CONTENT OF THE HEAD FOR BEING STUPID, they highlight[20] different aspects of this schematic image. Accordingly, in some expressions, the metonymic structure is more prominent whereas in others the metaphoric pattern seems to be the primary one.

With respect to a possibly different degree of salience, the expressions in (6) are relatively neutral. Both the metonymic and metaphoric structure are symbolized by one or more components of the idiom. Whereas in the components *X im Kopf* the metonymic relation with the target concept is being explicated, the verb *haben* ('to have') symbolizes the metaphoric structure of POSSESSION, and thus also the schematic ES-metaphor. Although in these expressions the concept POSSESSION is formally present, its salience is still rather low because of the relatively flat and schematic meaning of the verb "haben".[21] Through the strong contiguous relationship between the concepts CONTENT OF THE HEAD and BEING

STUPID, the metonymic structure is the dominant one. In view of the weak semantic value of the verb *haben*, one could argue that the identification of a metaphoric POSSESSION structure in these expressions is a rather artificial construct. This objection is rejected by expressions like (7a), in which this metaphoric meaning is put forward in a much stronger way: the verb *besitzen* ('to possess') does not leave much doubt regarding its primary meaning. In the same respect, the examples in (7b-d) also represent interesting cases. Regardless of the absence of a locative complement such as *im Kopf*, as a result of which the metonymic structure already loses some of its explicitness, the respective verbs in these expressions also refer to the conceptual reality of the metaphoric POSSESSION structure. It appears that in each of these expressions the source concept DEVIANT CONTENT OF THE HEAD is conceptualized in causal-metonymic terms of a (controlled) transfer of the head's content. In (7b), the absence of the head's proper content, which is the dominant but implicit source concept behind this expression, is construed in terms of an *event* ("losing one's mind"). A similar causal relationship underlies the expressions in (7c) and (7d), but in these cases it holds between the implicit concept DEVIANT CONTENT OF THE HEAD and the profiled *action* ("stealing" and "breaking in"[22]). Despite the fact that in (7e) *haben* is used as a verb (cf. the examples in (6)), the metaphoric POSSESSION structure is clearly present. An indication of this relative prominence lies in the absence of a locative complement like *im Kopf*. Finally, in a term of abuse like (7f), only the concept HEAD – without the image schematic structure of CONTAINMENT – is formally explicated, so that compared to the equivalent expression in (6b) (*Wasser im Kopf haben*), in which the same image is used, the metonymic structure is the most prominent one.

3. Conclusion

This contribution is based on a differentiated view of metaphor and metonymy, whereby both conceptual phenomena are characterized on two dimensions: their respective function and the type of the conceptual relationship which is established between two entities. Accordingly, metaphor basically consists of a systematic projection of logical structures from the source onto the target domain. The relation between source and target reduces to a (conceptually embedded) similarity structure. As for metonymy, the type of relationship turns out to be its most prominent feature. Metonymic extensions bring about a referential shift from a prominent, easily accessible entity to a less salient, more abstract one. Their essential characteristic, however, lies in the contiguous nature of the conceptual relationship. It turns out that metonymies can elaborate several kinds of contiguity relationships. This view of metonymy deviates from the common cognitive semantic approach in that the range of the semantic extension with regard to the borders of a domain matrix, is considered to be not of central importance. Accordingly, the feature of only one single domain matrix being involved in a metonymic extension is seen as an effect of the contiguity between two conceptual entities.

With respect to the Inheritance Hypothesis as it was developed by Lakoff (1993), the analysis of the conceptual structure of some expressions from my material suggests a double refinement of this hypothesis, which has been commonly interpreted with respect to the internal structure of metaphoric hierarchies only. First, it appears that this hypothesis applies to metonymic structures, i.e. contiguity relationships, as well. Unlike metaphors, it is not the internal logical structure of the source domain which is inherited, but instead low level metonymic structures appear to elaborate highly schematic contiguous relationships of relative salience. The second refinement concerns the overlap between metaphoric and metonymic hierarchies in a particular conceptual or semantic structure (metaphtonymic hierarchy). This observation leads to the conclusion that the nature of a conceptual relationship between two entities may be different according to the level of specification on which the entities are being looked at. In other words, the elaboration of a schematic concept into a more specific one may bring in an additional relationship between the source and target concept.

These observations are made on the basis of a relatively small corpus of German expressions. Further research on a much broader scale including other languages is now needed in order to determine the specific types of metaphtonymic interaction between conceptual hierarchies.[23] Compared to an outspoken *linguistic* investigation of metaphtonymic structures such as Goossens (1990), this future research will have to enlarge the linguistic component with an analysis of the more general conceptual background as well. This will allow us to get a more systematic picture of not only the complex phenomenon of metaphtonymic interaction itself, but also of its relation to the "vertical" dimension of schematization and/or elaboration.

Notes

1. I am very grateful to Bert Cappelle for proofreading and discussing an earlier version of this paper.
2. This article presupposes a certain acquaintance with the basic theses and terminology of cognitive semantics and of the Lakovian theory of metaphor in particular.
3. In correspondence with conventional cognitive semantic typography, conceptual structures are represented as small capitals (TREE), linguistic (symbolic) structures in italics (*tree*), whereas mere semantic structures (meanings) are represented between double quotes ("tree").
4. Compare Kövecses (1990: 44) who claims that "each and every expression related to a concept has to be examined if we wish to uncover the minute details of the concept", but see in this respect also Geeraerts & Grondelaers (1995: 174ff).
5. Accordingly, conceptual metaphors are also named *generalized metaphors*.

6.   The relevant knowledge structures that function as the broad conceptual background for a meaning are called *domains*.

7.   As a matter of convention, conceptual metaphors are represented with the form TARGET CONCEPT IS SOURCE CONCEPT.

8.   I borrow this term from Lakoff & Turner (1989: 113).

9.   Although *ontology* refers to an experienced, conceptually embedded reality, the use of this terminology might be confusing with regard to the traditional philosophical use of this category.

10.   Johnson (1987: 29) defines an image schema as "a recurrent pattern, shape, and regularity in, or of, [our] ongoing ordering activities. These patterns emerge as meaningful structures for us chiefly at the level of our bodily movements through space, our manipulation of objects, and our perceptual interactions. ... I conceive of them as structures for organizing our experience and comprehension."

11.   Lakoff and Johnson (1980: 193) speak of *imagistic reasoning*.

12.   These examples are taken from, or at least inspired by, Lakoff and Johnson (1980).

13.   Croft (1993: 348) speaks of *domain highlighting*.

14.   Compare in this respect Turner (1987: 17): "Cognition and vision are different, *though related* [my emphasis, KF], domains of experience".

15.   It is not my intention to present an extensive overview of the different kinds of contiguity relations. The examples which are mentioned here represent an arbitrary selection; for a more detailed list I refer to, among others, Ullmann (1962: 32-35), Lakoff & Johnson (1980: 35-40), Schmid (1993: 92) and Radden & Kövecses (forthcoming).

16.   In a certain way, this also applies to metaphor, where the referential shift is much bigger.

17.   Both elaboration and instantiation refer to a process of specification. I speak of elaboration when this process is entirely situated on the conceptual level (compare PIECE OF FURNITURE – TABLE), whereas instantiation refers to the specificaion of a conceptual structure in a linguistically symbolized, semantic structure (as in TABLE – "table").

18.   An extensive analysis of my database (Feyaerts 1997) reveals that the concepts DEVIANT APPEARANCE and DEVIANT BEHAVIOR also function as "autonomous" source concepts (i.e. without any schematic relation to the Mantafahrer model) of metonymic extensions onto the target BEING STUPID.

19.   I realize that the conceptualization of senses as possessible objects already represents a metaphor on its own, but this is not at stake here.

20.   I do not use the term "highlight" in the same restricted sense as Croft (1993: 348) and Goossens (1995: 179) do. They preserve the term, as well as "domain highlighting", to characterize the nature of a metonymic extension. In the present context, I use the term as a kind of synonym for "focus on".

21.   Originally, German *haben*, just like English *to have*, was a verb indicating physical control ("to hold, to grasp"); see also Langacker 1993: 13-14.

22.   The use of the verb *einbrechen* ('to break in') activates the conceptual metaphor HUMAN BODIES ARE BUILDINGS as a conceptual background.

23.   A first survey of English expressions for stupidity (e.g. *to be weak in the head*, etc.) indicates that similar patterns of metaphtonymic interaction can be found for English as well.

References

Croft, William
    1993   "The role of domains in the interpretation of metaphors and metonymies", *Cognitive Linguistics* 4: 335-370.
Dirven, René
    1993   "Metonymy and metaphor: Different mental strategies of conceptualisation" *Leuvense Bijdragen* 82: 1-28.
Fauconnier, Gilles – Mark Turner
    1994   *Conceptual projection and middle spaces.* [Unpublished UCSD Cognitive Science Technical Report 9401. San Diego.] (Available from the WWW at http://cogsci.ucsd.edu at http://www. wam.umd.edu/~mturn.)
Feyaerts, Kurt
    1997   *Die Bedeutung der Metonymie als konzeptuellen Strukturprinzips. Eine kognitiv-semantische Analyse deutscher Dummheitsausdrücke.* [Unpublished Ph.D. dissertation, Katholieke Universiteit Leuven.]
    forthcoming   "Metonymic hierarchies: The conceptualization of stupidity in German idiomatic expressions", in: Klaus-Uwe Panther – Günter Radden (eds.). Amsterdam – Philadelphia: John Benjamins.
Geeraerts, Dirk – Stefan Grondelaers
    1995   "Looking back at anger: Cultural traditions and metaphorical patterns" in: John Taylor – Robert E. MacLaury (eds.), *Language and the cognitive construal of the world.* Berlin: Mouton de Gruyter, 153-179.
Goossens, Louis
    1990   "Metaphtonymy: the interaction of metaphor and metonymy in expressions for linguistic action", *Cognitive Linguistics* 1: 323-340.
    [1995]   in: Louis Goossens – Paul Pauwels – Brigida Rudzka-Ostyn – Anne-Marie Simon-Vandenbergen – Johan Vanparys, 159-174.
Goossens, Louis – Paul Pauwels – Brigida Rudzka-Ostyn – Anne-Marie Simon-Vandenbergen – Johan Vanparys (eds.)
    1995   *By word of mouth: metaphor, metonymy, and linguistic action in a cognitive perspective.* Amsterdam: Benjamins
Johnson, Mark
    1987   *The body in the mind. The bodily basis of meaning, imagination, and reason.* Chicago: University of Chicago Press.
Kövecses, Zoltán
    1990   *Emotion concepts.* New York: Springer.
    1995   "American friendship and the scope of metaphor", *Cognitive Linguistics* 6: 315-346.
Lakoff, George
    1987   *Women, fire, and dangerous things. What categories reveal about the mind.* Chicago: University of Chicago Press.
    1993   "The contemporary theory of metaphor" in: Andrew Ortony (ed), *Metaphor and thought.* (2nd edition.) Cambridge: Cambridge University Press, 202-251.
Lakoff, George – Mark Johnson
    1980   *Metaphors we live by.* Chicago: University of Chicago Press.

Lakoff, George – Mark Turner
    1989   *More than cool reason. A field guide to poetic metaphor.* Chicago: University of Chicago Press.
Langacker, Ronald W.
    1993   "Reference-point constructions", *Cognitive Linguistics* 4: 1-38.
Klaus-Uwe Panther – Günter Radden (eds.)
    forthcoming *Metonymy in thought and language.* Amsterdam – Philadelphia: John Benjamins.
Radden, Günter. – Zoltàn Kövecses
    forthcoming "Towards a theory of metonymy" in: Klaus-Uwe Panther – Günter Radden (eds.).
Schmid, Hans-Jörg
    1993   *Cottage und Co., idea, start vs. begin. Die Kategorisierung als Grundprinzip einer differenzierten Bedeutungsbeschreibung.* Tübingen: Niemeyer.
Turner, Mark
    1987   *Death is the mother of beauty: mind, metaphor, criticism.* Chicago: Chicago University Press.
Turner, Mark – Gilles Fauconnier
    1995   "Conceptual integration and formal expression", *Metaphor and Symbolic Activity* 10: 183-203.
Ullmann, Stephen
    1962   *Semantics. An introduction to the science of meaning.* Oxford: Basil Blackwell.
Warren, Beatrice
    1992   *Sense developments.* Stockholm: Almqvist & Wiksell International.

The scope of metaphor

Zoltán Kövecses

1. Introduction

In the cognitive linguistic literature on metaphor, we often find analyses of cases in which a target domain is characterized by a number of source domains. For example, in Lakoff & Johnson (1980) the concept of argument is shown as being understood in terms of metaphors such as:

AN ARGUMENT IS A JOURNEY

AN ARGUMENT IS A BUILDING

AN ARGUMENT IS A CONTAINER

AN ARGUMENT IS WAR.

Furthermore, Lakoff & Johnson pointed out that there is a good reason why a single target concept is understood via several source concepts: one source just cannot do the job because our concepts have a number of distinct aspects to them and the metaphors address these distinct aspects. This process was shown in detail for the concept of anger by Lakoff & Kövecses (1987) and for happiness by Kövecses (1991), the latter being characterized by means of metaphors such as the following:

HAPPINESS IS UP

HAPPINESS IS LIGHT

HAPPINESS IS VITALITY

HAPPINESS IS A FLUID IN A CONTAINER

HAPPINESS IS AN OPPONENT

HAPPINESS IS RAPTURE

HAPPINESS IS INSANITY

HAPPINESS IS A NATURAL FORCE

etc.

Similarly, many additional abstract concepts have been shown to be characterized by a large number of distinct source domains. These abstract target domains include time, love, life, ideas, theories, morality, mind, anger, fear, politics, society, communication, God and religion, and many more.

However, what has not been observed, or at least not made an empirical and theoretical issue, is that a single source concept can characterize many distinct target domains (Kövecses n.d. a). In fact, most of the typical specific source domains appear to characterize not just one target concept but several. For instance, the concept of war applies not just to argument but also to love, the concept of building not only to theories but also to societies, fire not only to love but also to anger, etc.

2. The scope of metaphor

This raises an interesting empirical and theoretical question: How many and what kind of target domains does a single source concept apply to? I will call this issue the question of the *scope of metaphor*, which can be defined in the following way:

> The scope of metaphor is simply the full range of cases, that is, all the possible target domains, to which a given specific source concept (such as war, building, fire) applies.

To throw some light on this issue and to see why it is important, it seems best to go through a number of examples, where it is the case that a single source characterizes a number of distinct targets. In the remainder of this paper, I will attempt to develop further some ideas first described in Kövecses (1995).

Consider, for instance, the source domain of buildings, as it applies to several targets. The following examples of metaphorical linguistic expressions are taken from or are based on *Cobuild's English Guide 7, Metaphor* (Deignan 1995):

THEORIES ARE BUILDINGS
- The truth is that standard economic models *constructed* on the evidence of past experience are of little use.
- In an attempt to overcome that, the city is actually *constructing* an environmental protection plan.
- Increasingly, scientific knowledge *is constructed* by small numbers of specialized workers.
- McCarthy *demolishes* the romantic myth of the Wild West.
- She lay back for a few moments contemplating the *ruins* of her idealism and her innocence.
- ... providing a *foundation* for developmental planning and action.
- Don't be tempted to skip the first sections of your programme, because they are the *foundations on which* the second half *will be built.*
- ... the advance that *laid the foundations* for modern science.
- In support of the theory, she is forced to resort to statements which are entirely *without foundation.*
- Our view, he said, is that these claims are entirely *without foundation.*
- My faith was *rocked to its foundations.*
- The second half of the chapter *builds on* previous discussion of change and differentiation in home ownership.

RELATIONSHIPS ARE BUILDINGS
- Since then the two have *built a solid* relationship.
- You can help *lay the foundations* for a good relationship between your children by preparing your older child in advance for the new baby.

A CAREER IS A BUILDING
- Government grants have enabled a number of the top names in British sport *to build* a successful career.
- Her career was *in ruins.*

A COMPANY IS A BUILDING
- Ten years ago, he and a partner set up on their own and *built up* a successful fashion company.
- The following year he borrowed enough money to buy his first hotel and spent three years *building up* a hotel empire.

ECONOMIC SYSTEMS ARE BUILDINGS
- ... citizens fleeing their country's economic *ruins.*
- With its economy *in ruins*, it can't afford to involve itself in military action.
- There is no painless way to get inflation down. We now have an excellent *foundation on which to build.*

SOCIAL GROUPS ARE BUILDINGS
- He's about *to rock the foundations* of the literary establishment with his novel.
- By early afternoon queues *were already building up.*

A LIFE IS A BUILDING
- Now another young woman's life is *in ruins* after an appalling attack.

As these cases indicate, the specific source domain of buildings applies to a variety of distinct targets. However, we can note that the target domains of theory, relationships, careers, economic systems, companies, social groups, and life all appear to be what can be called *complex abstract systems* of one kind or another. We conceive of a complex abstract system as a nonphysical domain which has many parts that interact with each other in complex ways. We can generalize these observations by suggesting that the overarching metaphor that includes all the special metaphorical subcases above (such as THEORIES ARE BUILDINGS, RELATIONSHIPS ARE BUILDINGS, etc.) is a generic-level metaphor that I will call COMPLEX ABSTRACT SYSTEMS ARE BUILDINGS.

3. The main meaning focus of conceptual metaphors

The common thread that runs through these specific conceptual metaphors is that they are all concerned with a limited number of features of complex systems; namely, the creation of a strong and stable complex system. Most of the metaphorical expressions capture these two interrelated features of complex systems – their creation and their stability. This is clear from the preponderance of such expressions as *build, construct, strong foundation, without foundation, rock the foundation, in ruins, solid, lay the foundation* in the examples above.

We will say that these conceptual metaphors have a *main meaning focus*, a major theme, so to speak. This is simply the idea that each source domain highlights one or a limited number of aspects of a target.

What determines the main meaning orientation of a given source-to-target pairing, such as COMPLEX SYSTEMS ARE BUILDINGS? I will suggest that each source domain is designated to play a specific role in characterizing a set of targets to which it applies. This role can be stated as follows:

> Each source is associated with a particular meaning focus (or foci) that is (or are) mapped onto the target. This meaning focus (or foci) is (are) constituted by the central knowledge that pertains to a particular entity or event within a speech community. The target inherits the main meaning focus (or foci) of the source.

What this statement says is that a source domain contributes not randomly selected but predetermined conceptual materials agreed upon by a community of speakers to the range of target domains to which it applies.

Obviously, in order for the above statement to gain more substance, we have to define the notion of *central knowledge*. Langacker (1987: 158-161) characterizes this in the following way. Central knowledge is knowledge (about an entity or event) that is conventional, generic, intrinsic, and characteristic, given the class of entities or events designated by a particular linguistic expression. Conventionality of knowledge means that some meaning specification (like a property or feature) associated with an entity is shared by a linguistic community. Genericness of a meaning specification implies that the specification applies to not just one or some instances of an entity but to many, most, or all of them. A meaning specification is intrinsic if it does not make reference to entities external to the entity that it is evoked to describe. Finally, a meaning specification is characteristic of a class of entities if it is unique to this class only. As can be seen, all four factors are graded notions. Any given meaning specification can be *more* or *less* conventional, generic, intrinsic, and characteristic. The higher it scores on the four factors, the more central the piece of knowledge (a property or feature) will be.[1]

In the present case of the complex systems-as-buildings metaphor, the main meaning focus (based on knowledge that is regarded as central) is the creation of a stable complex system. These are also the mappings that predominate in Lakoff & Johnson's metaphor AN ARGUMENT IS A BUILDING:

AN ARGUMENT IS A BUILDING
- We've got the *framework* for a *solid* argument.
- If you don't *support* your argument with *solid* facts, the whole thing will *collapse*.
- He is trying to *buttress* his argument with a lot of irrelevant facts, but it is still so *shaky* that it will easily *fall apart* under criticism.
- With the *groundwork* you've got, you can *construct* a pretty *strong* argument.

Most of these examples have to do with the strength, (strong) structure, and the creation of an argument. This is not surprising since the concept of argument is closely related to that of theory (or more generally, a set of structured ideas) and hence, to complex systems.

4. Central mappings

Given the generic metaphor COMPLEX SYSTEMS ARE BUILDINGS, we can capture the main meaning focus of the metaphor with the help of three additional metaphors: CREATION IS BUILDING, ABSTRACT STRUCTURE IS PHYSICAL STRUCTURE, and ABSTRACT STABILITY (OR STRENGTH) IS PHYSICAL STRENGTH (OF A BUILDING). We can ask what the relationship is between COMPLEX SYSTEMS ARE BUILDINGS, on the one hand and CREATION IS BUILDING, ABSTRACT STRUCTURE IS PHYSICAL STRUCTURE and ABSTRACT STABILITY (OR STRENGTH) IS PHYSICAL STRENGTH, on the other. It seems reasonable to suggest that the CREATION IS BUILDING, ABSTRACT STRUCTURE IS PHYSICAL STRUC-TURE, and the ABSTRACT STABILITY (OR STRENGTH) IS PHYSICAL STRENGTH metaphors are submappings (or submetaphors) of COMPLEX SYSTEMS ARE BUILDINGS. This notion could be spelled out in the following way:

COMPLEX SYSTEMS ARE BUILDINGS
    Source: *Target:*

(a) building   → complex system
(b) making the building   → creating or developing the system
(c) the foundation of the building   → the basis of the system
(d) the maker of the building   → the creator of the system
(e) the strength of the building   → the stability or strength of the system
(f) physical structure   → abstract structure

Since the main socially agreed-upon meaning focus of the concept of build-ing as a source is the making of a strong building, this will be mapped onto the target. Technically, this process takes place by means of basic constituent map-pings. Of these, one or some are more important than others. Now the mappings that seem to be central in the COMPLEX SYSTEMS ARE BUILDINGS metaphor, that is, the ones without which we could not easily imagine the others, are (b), (e), and (f) above: making a building corresponding to creating a complex system, the strength of a building corresponding to the stability (or strength) of a complex system, and physical structure corresponding to abstract structure. Let us call mappings like these *central mappings*. Mappings are central if they map what we have called the main meaning focus of the source (i.e. central knowledge) onto the target.

Characteristic of central mappings are the following: (1) Conceptually, cen-tral mappings lead to the emergence of other mappings, either constituent basic mappings or metaphorical entailments. (2) Culturally, central mappings reflect major human concerns relative to the source in question (e.g. building a strong house). (3) Motivationally, they are the mappings that are most motivated experientially – either culturally or physically. (4) Linguistically, they give rise to metaphorical linguistic expressions that dominate a metaphor. This last property of central mappings is especially clear in the case of another COMPLEX SYSTEMS metaphor that was discussed by Kövecses elsewhere (Kövecses, n.d. b): COMPLEX SYSTEMS ARE PLANTS. Most of the metaphorical linguistic expressions dominating that metaphor can be seen as being related to the notion of "abstract development (or progress)" of a complex system in one way or another.

The notion of the role of specific source domains in conceptual metaphors as stated above resembles superficially what has become known as the *invariance principle* (see Lakoff 1990, 1993; Turner 1990; Brugman 1990). However, it is a very different notion. The invariance principle states that all the image-schematic structure of the source that is consistent with the image-schematic structure of the target is mapped onto the target. By contrast, the main meaning focus of a source involves a particular assembly of meanings that is associated by speakers with any given source domain within a cultural-linguistic community. In our example, the source domain of building may have a large number of different meanings associated with it, but for the purposes of metaphor (such as COMPLEX SYSTEMS ARE BUILDINGS) it carries a small but coherent assembly of specific meanings: the construction of a strong and lasting building.

5. The case of FIRE

Now let us see in another example how the three theoretical concepts – metaphorical *scope, main meaning focus,* and *central mapping* – developed above operate jointly. To do this, let us take the concept of fire, which is a common source domain for many target concepts (Kövecses n.d. a; Kövecses – Szabó 1996). Again, the particular metaphorical linguistic examples that demonstrate the application of fire as a source domain to a variety of target domains will be derived from *Cobuild's English Guides 7: Metaphor* (Deignan 1995).

For most people, the related concepts of fire and heat are primarily associated with the metaphorical comprehension of emotions, such as anger, love, desire, and so on. We can generalize this by assuming the metaphor EMOTION IS HEAT OF FIRE. Here's a list of fire-related metaphorical expressions for these and other emotions (we indicate the emotion involved in square brackets):

EMOTION IS HEAT (OF FIRE)
- Behind his soft-spoken manner, *the fires* of ambition *burned.* [AMBITION-DESIRE]
- Forstmann was a deeply angry man, *burning* with resentment. [RESENTMENT-ANGER]

- Marianne and I are both *fiery* people. [EMOTION]
- The young boy *was burning with* a fierce emotion. [EMOTION]
- Dan *burned* to know what the reason could be. [CURIOSITY-DESIRE]
- He gave his son a look of *burning* anger. [ANGER]
- The trial left him with a *burning* sense of injustice. [INDIGNATION-ANGER]
- As a boy my *burning* ambition was to become either a priest or a family doctor. [AMBITION-DESIRE]
- ... the *burning* desire to break free and express himself on his own terms. [DESIRE]
- And the *burning* question will be: is he still the player he was? [CURIOSITY-DESIRE]
- The lady was ten years his senior. It was a *fiery* relationship. [RELATIONSHIP-LOVE]
- As a child I had real *hot* temper. [ANGER]

The emotion concepts of anger, love, curiosity, desire, ambition, can all take heat-fire as their source domain. Other examples reflect the many metaphorical entailments that are mapped from this source to the target of emotion:

THE HIGHEST DEGREE OF EMOTIONAL INTENSITY IS THE HIGHEST DEGREE OF FIRE
- He got to his feet and his dark eyes *were blazing with* anger. [ANGER]
- He *was blazing* with rage. [ANGER]
- Eva stood up and indignation *blazed* in her eyes. [ANGER]

MAINTAINING THE INTENSITY OF THE EMOTION IS MAINTAINING THE FIRE
- ... *keeping the flames* of love *alive*. [LOVE]
- ... *fuelling the flames* of hatred. [HATRED]

CONTROLLING THE INTENSITY OF THE EMOTION IS CONTROLLING THE FIRE
- He'll have *to keep his fiery* temper *under control*. [ANGER]

LOW INTENSITY OF EMOTION IS A SMALL AMOUNT OF FIRE
- Though we knew our army had been defeated, hope still *flickered* in our hearts. [HOPE]
- For the first time she felt a *tiny spark* of hope. [HOPE]

A SUDDEN INCREASE IN EMOTION INTENSITY IS A SUDDEN INCREASE IN THE INTENSITY OF FIRE
- Tempers *flared* and harsh words were exchanged. [ANGER]
- At this I *flared up*. 'What difference does it make?' I demanded. [ANGER]
- Just occasionally he *did flare up*; not at me of course. [ANGER]
- He thought from the change in her face that she was going *to flare up* in anger. [ANGER]
- It wasn't like Alex *to flare up* over something he had said about her looks. [ANGER]

CAUSATION IS LIGHTING AN OBJECT
- Nicholas travelled to India which helped *spark* his passion for people and paintings. [PASSION-EMOTION]
- By drawing attention to the political and social situation of their communities, they *sparked off* a renewed interest in Aboriginal culture. [INTEREST]

MOTIVATION TO DO SOMETHING AT A HIGH INTENSITY IS A SPARK THAT CAN START AN INTENSE FIRE
- Jimmy was so enthusiastic and motivated when he was in high school. But some *spark has gone out of* him at college. [ENTHUSIASM]
- The *spark had gone* and it was time for me to leave the club. [ENTHUSIASM]
- Her eyes were like her mother's but lacked the *spark* of humour and the warmth. [HUMOR-JOY]

LATENT INTENSITY IS POTENTIAL OPEN FIRE
- There is a *smouldering* anger in the black community throughout the country. [ANGER]
- The atmosphere *smouldered* with resentment. [ANGER]
- Baxter *smouldered* as he drove home for lunch. [ANGER]
- Melanie Griffith seems *to smoulder* with sexuality. [SEXUALITY-LUST]
- ... Isabella Rossellini, the *smouldering* daughter of actress Ingrid Bergman. [SEXUALITY-LUST]

CHANGE IN INTENSITY IS A CHANGE IN THE DEGREE OF HEAT
- Tempers *have cooled down* a bit and I hope we could sort things out between us. [ANGER]
- She should leave the room when her anger gets the best of her and not come back until she's *cooled down*. [ANGER]
- You should each make your own lives, and when emotions *have cooled*, see if there's a possibility of friendship. [EMOTION]
- You're angry, Wade, that's all. You ought to let yourself *cool off* for a few days. [ANGER]

LACK OF INTENSITY IS LACK OF HEAT
- 'Look here,' I said, without *heat*, 'all I did was to walk down a street and sit down.' [ANGER]

As these entailments show, the main meaning focus of the metaphor is emotional intensity. Most of the entailments center around this particular aspect of the emotion concepts involved.

But the heat-fire source is not limited to the emotions, as indicated by the examples below. In other words, the scope of the metaphorical source of heat-fire extends well beyond the emotions. Consider the additional examples that follow:

- They directed the full *heat* of their rhetoric against Mr. Bush. [ARGUMENT]
- He took a girl into the studio and *in the heat* of an argument, she threw a glass

of gin and tonic over the mixing desk. [ARGUMENT]
– The trouble with arguments is that things get said *in the heat* of the moment that are regretted afterwards. [ARGUMENT]
– You need to perform well when the *heat is on*. [PRESSURE-EVENT]
– We kept going just that little bit better than our rivals when *the heat was on*. [PRESSURE-EVENT]
– Behind the next door a more *heated* discussion was taking place. [ARGUMENT]
– It was a very *heated* argument and they were shouting at each other. [ARGUMENT]
– One of the councillors attacked a fellow member during a *heated* debate. [ARGUMENT]
– Some members argued *heatedly* that they had not supported the emergency committee. [ARGUMENT]
– ... one of the most *heatedly* debated aspects of the theory. [ARGUMENT]
– This problem has been *hotly* debated. [ARGUMENT]
– The book has been *hotly* disputed by experts in the various fields that it touches on. [ARGUMENT]
– 'How many times have I told you,' I responded *hotly*, 'No surprises in meetings.' [ARGUMENT]
– This year's final will be as *hotly* contested as ever. [ARGUMENT]
– The figures are being *hotly* debated by the Minister of the Interior,... [ARGUMENT]

As can be seen, the fire-heat metaphorical source domain applies to actions (argument) and events (pressure). It also applies to states of various kinds. In general, we can claim that the source domain has as its scope any intense situation (actions, events, states). The following examples given and arranged as metaphorical entailments amply illustrate this:

THE HIGHEST DEGREE OF INTENSITY IS THE HIGHEST DEGREE OF HEAT (FIRE)
– His eyes *blazed* intently into mine. [LOOKING-ACTION]
– The President launched his anti-drugs campaign *in a blaze* of publicity. [PUBLICITY-ACTION]
– The career that began *in a blaze* of glory has ended in his forced retirement. [GLORY-STATE]
– Vivien Richards bowed out of country cricket *in a blaze* of glory last week. [GLORY-STATE]
– My husband had just had a *blazing* row with his boss. [ARGUMENT]
– As soon as he walked in there was a *blazing* row. [ARGUMENT]

CHANGE IN INTENSITY IS A CHANGE IN HEAT
– The President will be bombarded with criticism as the election campaign *heats up*. [ARGUMENT]
– Then, in the last couple of years, the movement for democracy began *to heat up*. [POLITICAL MOVEMENT-ACTIVITY]

- The battle for the Formula One Championship *hotted up*. [BATTLE-CONFLICT]
- The debate *is hotting up* in Germany on the timing of elections. [ARGUMENT]
- In a clear bid *to take the heat out of* the rebellion he authorised an interest rate cut. [REBELLION-CONFLICT]
- *Some of the heat could be taken out of* Cabinet disputes if Ministers went on a course in basic team work. [ARGUMENT]
- He has been advised to take a long family holiday *to take the heat off* the scandal. [SCANDAL-CONFLICT]
- He's hoping that this will *take the heat off* criticism of his economic policy. [CRITICISM-ARGUMENT]
- I think that the Scottish problem might *cool off*. [PROBLEM-CONFLICT]
- The hope must be that the economy *has cooled* sufficiently to relieve inflationary pressures. [ECONOMIC ACTIVITY]

The metaphorical entailment CAUSATION IS LIGHTING AN OBJECT that we saw in the EMOTION IS HEAT (OF FIRE) metaphor can be given as the next entailment: CAUSE OF A SITUATION IS CAUSE OF HEAT (FIRE)

- About twenty thousand people heard a *fiery* speech from the Secretary General. [ARGUMENT/CONFLICT]
- … a *fiery* magazine article. [ARGUMENT/CONFLICT]
- She's a *fiery* political figure. [CONFLICT]
- Many commentators believe that his resignation speech *ignited* the leadership battle. [CONFLICT]
- Books can *ignite* the imagination in a way films can't. [IMAGINATION]
- She has failed *to ignite* what could have been a lively debate. [ARGUMENT]
- The strike was *sparked* by a demand for higher pay. [CONFLICT]
- An interesting detail might *spark off* an idea. [THOUGHT]

MOTIVATION TO DO SOMETHING INTENSELY IS A CAUSE OF HEAT (FIRE)
- He said they were looking for someone with a bit of *spark* as the new technical director. [AGILITY IN ACTION]

CONTROLLING THE SITUATION IS CONTROLLING THE HEAT
- This proved insufficient *to dampen the fires* of controversy. [ARGUMENT]

MAINTAINING INTENSITY IS MAINTAINING HEAT (FIRE)
- The fact is that the very lack of evidence seems *to fan the flames* of suspicion. [SUSPICION-THOUGHT]
- The President warned that this *will fuel the fires* of nationalism. [CONFLICT]
- He accused the president of *fanning the flames* of violence. [CONFLICT]

A SUDDEN INCREASE IN INTENSITY IS A SUDDEN INCREASE IN THE DEGREE OF HEAT (FIRE)
- Even as the President appealed for calm, trouble *flared up* in several American cities. [CONFLICT]
- Trouble *flared up* a year ago when David had an affair. [CONFLICT]
- Dozens of people were injured as fighting *flared up*. [CONFLICT]

- There's a risk of civil war *flaring up.* [CONFLICT]
- 23 people have died in the new *flare-up* of violence in the townships. [CON-FLICT]
- ... this latest *flare-up* in fighting. [CONFLICT]
- It is very difficult for two people to live in these circumstances without tension and we do have *flare-ups.* [CONFLICT]
- Dale stayed clear of the disease for six years until it *flared up* last summer. [DISEASE-STATE]
- I felt good but then this injury *flared up.* [INJURY-STATE]

LATENT INTENSITY IS POTENTIAL HEAT (FIRE)
- The government was foundering on an issue that *had smouldered* for years. [SOCIAL PROBLEM]
- ... the *smouldering* civil war. [WAR-CONFLICT]

INTENSITY CEASING IS THE HEAT (FIRE) GOING OUT
- Some were simply *burnt out*, exhausted. [AGILITY IN ACTION]
- ... a *burnt-out* business executive. [AGILITY IN ACTION]

Thus, it appears that fire-metaphors have a wide scope; they apply to a variety of situations or states of affairs (many kinds of actions, events, and states). The main meaning focus of this source domain appears to be the intensity of a situation. We can show the basic constituent mappings for this metaphor as follows:

A SITUATION IS FIRE

Source:		*Target:*
the thing burning	→	the entity involved in the situation
the fire	→	the situation (action, event, state)
the heat of the fire	→	the intensity of the situation
the cause of the fire	→	the cause of the situation

These basic mappings account for the majority of the linguistic expressions above (see also Kövecses – Szabó 1996). Among them, it is "the heat of fire → the intensity of the situation" mapping that is central. The reason is that most of the metaphorical entailments of this metaphor follow from or are based on this particular mapping (e.g., maintaining intensity, sudden increase in intensity, latent intensity). Second, a major human concern with fire is its intensity; that is, we ask whether or not we have a fire that is appropriate for the purpose at hand. Third, the linguistic examples that dominate the various applications of this source domain consist of metaphors that reflect intensity as a main meaning focus. Finally, there is very clear experiential basis for this mapping. When we engage in intense situations (actions, events, states), we produce body heat. This is especially clear in the case of such emotion concepts as anger and love, where many linguistic expressions capture this kind of bodily experience associated with intense emotion.

6. Simple and complex metaphors

This account makes use of two distinct kinds of metaphor: *simple* and *complex*. It should be recalled that we have characterized the metaphors in which the source concepts of building and heat-fire participate as COMPLEX SYSTEMS ARE BUILDINGS and A SITUATION IS HEAT (OF FIRE), respectively. But we have also noted that given the central mappings of these metaphors, it is reasonable to suggest that the same data can be accounted for by postulating four other metaphors: ABSTRACT CREATION IS PHYSICAL BUILDING, ABSTRACT STABILITY IS PHYSICAL STRENGTH, and ABSTRACT STRUCTURE IS PHYSICAL STRUCTURE for complex systems, as well as INTENSITY IS HEAT for various states of affairs.

Abstract complex systems include theories, relationships, society, social groups, economic and political systems, life, and others. All of these can be individually conceived as buildings. The resulting metaphors THEORIES ARE BUILD-INGS, SOCIETY IS A BUILDING, ECONOMIC SYSTEMS ARE BUILDINGS, RELATIONSHIPS ARE BUILDINGS, LIFE IS A BUILDING, etc. are *complex metaphors*, in that they are constituted by the corresponding submetaphors ABSTRACT CREATION IS PHYSICAL BUILD-ING, ABSTRACT STRUCTURE IS PHYSICAL STRUCTURE, and ABSTRACT STABILITY IS PHYSI-CAL STRENGTH. By contrast, these submetaphors will be said to be *simple*, in that they are the ones that make up complex ones and they characterize an entire range of specific-level target concepts. One such case is the range of target concepts under the overarching concept of complex systems. We can also call these two kinds of metaphor "primitive" vs. "compound", corresponding to simple vs. complex metaphors, respectively.[2]

Similarly, a large number of target concepts are characterized by the source concept of (heat of) fire. Various specific kinds of actions, events, and states are understood as fire. Correspondingly, there is a simple metaphor INTENSITY IS HEAT (OF FIRE). This simple metaphor is a mapping in such complex metaphors as ANGER IS FIRE, LOVE IS FIRE, CONFLICT IS FIRE, ARGUMENT IS FIRE, and several others. In all of these, it is a central mapping (INTENSITY IS HEAT) on which several other mappings and metaphorical entailments depend.

In sum, simple metaphors constitute mappings in complex ones. The reverse of this does not hold; complex metaphors like THEORIES ARE BUILDINGS or ANGER IS FIRE do not constitute mappings in simple ones like ABSTRACT STABILITY IS PHYSICAL STRENGTH or INTENSITY IS HEAT. It is the simple metaphors (i.e. sub-mappings) that provide the major theme of complex metaphors by means of the process of mapping. Thus, the various complex fire-metaphors, like ANGER IS FIRE, LOVE IS FIRE, ENTHUSIASM IS FIRE, IMAGINATION IS FIRE, CONFLICT IS FIRE, etc. will all be characterized by the mapping "intensity of fire → intensity of a state or action" (see Kövecses – Szabó 1996). This mapping can be restated as a simple metaphor: INTENSITY (OF A SITUATION) IS THE INTENSITY OF HEAT (OF FIRE). The complex metaphors contain as a mapping this simple metaphor.

7. Conclusion

I have attempted here to develop three interlocking notions for the analysis of metaphorical language and thought: the scope of metaphor, main meaning focus, and central mapping. Metaphorical source domains seem to have a certain range of application: some have a wide scope (like fire), some have a narrow scope, and obviously, there are many in-between cases. Each source domain imposes a certain meaning focus, or orientation on its target domain(s). For example, when we use the concept of building as a source domain, we do so because we are primarily concerned with the creation of stable abstract complex systems and when we use fire, we do so because we are primarily concerned with issues of intensity of a situation. The transfer of the main meaning focus of metaphorical source domains is enabled by central mappings. These are mappings on which the existence of other mappings depends. The primary cognitive significance of the notion of the scope of metaphor is that it allows us to make maximal generalizations about the use of particular source domains, thus making it possible to discover new systems of metaphors. In the same way as, for instance, we have found that physical movement as a source domain has within its scope events in general as a target domain and complex physical objects (e.g., buildings) have within their scope complex abstract systems, we can find further similar systems of metaphor. In addition, as Freeman (this volume) showed, the notion of metaphorical scope also has relevance to the study of poetry. Judging by the size of the phenomena, however, most of the work trying to figure out the general patterns lies before us.

Notes

1. Incidentally, if the knowledge that primarily participates in metaphor is central, i.e., partial, knowledge, then we can see in this one kind of metonymic basis for metaphor. See Barcelona, this volume. For another kind of metonymic basis, see Kövecses – Radden (1998).
2. The terms "primitive" and "compound metaphors" are used by Grady 1998, in an approach to conceptual metaphor that bears some resemblance to the present view.

References

Barcelona, Antonio
    this volume   "On the plausibility of claiming a metonymic motivation for conceptual metaphor."
Brugman, Claudia
    1990   "What is the Invariance Hypothesis?", *Cognitive Linguistics* 1-2: 257-266.

Deignan, Alice
  1995   *Cobuild English guides 7: Metaphor.* London: HarperCollins Publishers.
Freeman, Margaret
  this volume "Poetry and the scope of metaphor: Toward a cognitive theory of literature."
Grady, Joseph E.
  1998   "THEORIES ARE BUILDINGS revisited", *Cognitive linguistics* 8-4: 267-290.
Kövecses, Zoltán
  1991   "Happiness: A definitional effort", *Metaphor and Symbolic Activity* 6-1: 29-46.
  1995   "American friendship and the scope of metaphor", *Cognitive Linguistics* 6-4: 315-346.
  n.d. a   The FIRE metaphor. [Unpublished plenary lecture. Second International Cognitive Linguistics Association Conference, Santa Cruz, 1991.]
  n.d. b   A student's guide to metaphor. [Unpublished MS.]
Kövecses, Zoltán – Günter Radden
  1998   "Metonymy: Developing a cognitive linguistic view", *Cognitive Linguistics* 37-98.
Kövecses, Zoltán – Péter Szabó
  1996   "Idioms: a view from cognitive semantics", *Applied Linguistics* 17-3: 326-355.
Lakoff, George
  1990   "The Invariance Hypothesis: Is abstract reason based on image-schemas?", *Cognitive Linguistics* 1-1: 39-74.
  1993   "The contemporary theory of metaphor", in: Andrew Ortony (ed.), *Metaphor and thought.* Cambridge: Cambridge University Press, 202-251.
Lakoff, George – Mark Johnson
  1980   *Metaphors we live by.* Chicago: The University of Chicago Press.
Lakoff, George – Zoltán Kövecses
  1987   "The cognitive model of anger inherent in American English", in: Dorothy Holland – Naomi Quinn (eds.), *Cultural models in language and thought.* Cambridge: Cambridge University Press, 195-221.
Langacker, Ronald W.
  1987   *Foundations of cognitive grammar.* Vol. 1. Stanford: Stanford University Press.
Turner, Mark
  1990   "Aspects of the Invariance Hypothesis", *Cognitive Linguistics* 1-2: 247-255.

How metonymic are metaphors?

Günter Radden

> *Natura non facit saltus.* 'Nature makes no leaps'
> (Leibnitz, quoted in Ullmann 1962: 211)

1. Introduction*

The grounding of metonymic concepts is, according to Lakoff and Johnson (1980: 39), "in general more obvious than is the case with metaphoric concepts, since it usually involves physical or causal association". Hence, metaphors which are grounded in metonymy are more basic and natural than those which do not have a metonymic basis: with these, metonymy provides an associative and motivated link between the two conceptual domains involved in metaphor.

The distinction between the notions of *metonymy* and *metaphor* is notoriously difficult, both as theoretical terms and in their application. Thus, it is often difficult to tell whether a given linguistic instance is metonymic or metaphoric. For example, the sentence *Suddenly the pilot comes over the intercom* may be interpreted metonymically in the sense that the pilot's voice comes over the intercom or it may be interpreted metaphorically in the sense that the pilot announces something over the intercom. Both interpretations are well-founded: A whole may metonymically stand for an "active zone" part, and an action may be metaphorized as motion. Maybe the sentence should be analyzed as both metonymic and metaphoric.

The intermediate notion of *metonymy-based metaphor* overcomes at least part of the problem created by limiting one's study to either particular category. Instead of always separating the two we may much rather think of a metonymy-metaphor continuum with unclear or fuzzy cases in between. Metonymy and metaphor may be seen as prototypical categories at the endpoints of this continuum. Metonymy-based metaphors take care of much of the fuzzy middle range of the continuum. They may either be closer to the metonymy end or the metaphor end of the metonymy-metaphor continuum.

Given the purpose of this paper, metonymy, metaphor and metonymy-based metaphor shall be defined as follows: *Metonymy* is a mapping within the same conceptual domain. *Metaphor* is a mapping of one conceptual domain onto another. *Metonymy-based metaphor* is a mapping involving two conceptual domains which are grounded in, or can be traced back to, one conceptual domain.

Four types of metonymy-based metaphor which may co-occur in particular cases can be distinguished: metonymy-based metaphors whose conceptual domains have a common experiential basis (Section 2), metonymy-based metaphors whose conceptual domains are related by implicature (Section 3), metonymy-based metaphors whose conceptual domains involve category structure (Section 4) and metonymy-based metaphors whose conceptual domains are interrelated by a cultural model (Section 5).

Most of the conceptual metaphors analyzed in this paper were drawn from Lakoff et al (1994) *Master Metaphor List* and Lakoff and Johnson (forthcoming); most of the conceptual metonymies referred to are described in Kövecses and Radden (1998) and Radden and Kövecses (1999). This study mainly aims to show that the notion of *metonymy-based metaphor* is needed in order to account for the experiential basis of a great number of metaphors. It neither claims that all metaphors have a metonymic basis nor that the metaphors analyzed here as being grounded in metonymy represent more than a cross-section of metonymy-based metaphors.

2. Common experiential basis

In pointing out the experiential basis of metaphor, Lakoff (1993) presents arguments for a metonymic basis of metaphor although he does not explicitly refer to it as *metonymy.* One of his examples is the following: "the MORE IS UP metaphor is *grounded in experience* – in the common experiences of pouring more fluid into a container and seeing the level go up, or adding more things to a pile and seeing the pile get higher." (p. 240) Taylor (1995: 138) takes up this issue and argues that height is literally correlated with quantity and that this natural association between quantity and vertical extent is one of metonymy. When more abstract instances of addition are involved, metaphor is assumed to take over as, for example, when one speaks of *high prices.* Taylor also cautions us that there are "numerous instances of metaphor which cannot reasonably be reduced to contiguity" such as the use of the verticality dimension in *the high notes on a piano* (p. 139).[1]

2.1. The metonymy-metaphor continuum

Let us look at various situations involving height and quantity and arrange them along a metonymy-metaphor continuum. The situation of pouring more fluid into a container and seeing the level go up illustrates literalness: the situation involves a single event which manifests itself in two ways. These two manifestations, more quantity and rising level, occur simultaneously and are so intimately correlated in our experience that most people probably do not conceive of them as different aspects of the situation.[2] We may indicate their common experiential basis by introducing as a notation X PLUS Y, i.e., in this case, QUANTITY PLUS VERTICALITY. The two manifestations may, however, also be imagined as separate parts of the same conceptual domain. In this case, we may have a metonymic mapping. For example, if my wife asked me *How much gas did you buy?* and I answered by saying *I filled her up*, my response would be metonymic. I answered her question about a quantity by naming a level of height; my answer might therefore be interpreted as 'I bought the quantity of gas that fits into the tank.' This metonymic situation might be described as UP FOR MORE.

Next, let us consider the expressions *high prices* and *rising prices*. Most people would probably not understand these expressions to be metaphoric usages but may, for example, envision a graph with a rising line as used in stock reports. The graphic representation of prices belongs to the same conceptual domain as the prices themselves but is a different facet of it. This understanding is metonymic and may be described as THING FOR ITS REPRESENTATION. Other people, in particular linguists interested in metaphorical systematicity, tend to view 'height' and 'prices' as belonging to two different conceptual domains and analyze *high prices* and *rising prices* as instances of the MORE IS UP metaphor. Since a common experiential basis is unmistakably present in most people's interpretation, however, this situation is best captured by analyzing it as an instance of metonymy-based metaphor.

Let us now look at descriptions of prices as in *soaring prices, sky-rocketing prices* and *exploding prices*. Unlike the fairly neutral words *high* and *rising*, these modifying expressions are semantically linked to specific domains and are therefore much more likely to evoke a domain of their own. They may evoke the image of a bird, an airplane or a rocket flying upward or of an upward-bursting explosion. These expressions are understood metaphorically due to our recognition of different conceptual domains. The metaphors involved might be described as PRICES ARE FLYING OBJECTS or PRICES ARE EVENTS. At the same time, the overall metaphor MORE IS UP applies so that we get complex submetaphors: for *soaring prices* we could formulate the conceptual metaphor MORE OF A PRICE IS HIGHER IN A BIRD'S FLIGHT. With respect to vertical orientation, the metaphor may still be said to be grounded in metonymy but is certainly more at the metaphorical end.

The discussion of the experiential basis of the MORE IS UP metaphor distinguished between the stages of literalness, metonymy, metonymy-based metaphor and metaphor. All of these stages involve the relationship of correlation. Correlation possibly best illustrates the transition from metonymy to metaphor. Other relationships which also manifest a metonymic basis are those of complementarity and comparison. These three relationships will be discussed below.

2.2. Correlation

Two events are said to correlate when changes in one event are accompanied by changes in another event. Correlations are mainly based on observation and, in order to compare the changes in the two events, they have to be in proximity. Correlation is thus a fundamentally metonymic relationship. It is also common in our view of the world to observe correlations between contiguous phenomena, often with a tinge of causality superimposed upon them (see Section 3.1). Proverbs provide a wealth of such correlated observations: *When it rains it pours; Rain before seven, fine before eleven; The nearer the church, the farther from God; Like master, like man; Short visits make long friends; What's good for General Motors is good for America*, etc.

Not surprisingly, we also find correlation as a metonymic basis in many metaphors. Apart from MORE IS UP/LESS IS DOWN, we have correlational metaphors such as HAPPY IS UP/SAD IS DOWN, FUNCTIONAL IS UP/DYSFUNCTIONAL IS DOWN (*The computer systems are down*), IMPORTANT IS BIG (*He is a big man*)/UNIMPORTANT IS SMALL (*The little guy always has to pay*), etc. The common experiential basis of the two domains is more obvious in some metaphors than in others. We witness the physical expression of HAPPY IS UP when a football player, after scoring a goal, throws up his arms and jumps for joy. Physical counterparts of FUNCTIONAL IS UP may be seen in levers that are flipped up to start an engine, an antenna that has to be put up to work or an umbrella that is put up to be used. The physical situation which underlies IMPORTANT IS BIG applies to the spacious environment that important persons tend to reserve for themselves, e.g., traditionally the most important person at the table has the biggest chair or the boss has the biggest office. Also a metaphor such as ACTIVE IS ALIVE/INACTIVE IS DEAD as in *The party was dead* is inherently correlational: the more alive someone or something is, the more active he, she or it is. The common experiential basis of 'active' and 'alive' is also reflected in the present-day meaning of *lively* and in the polysemy of the Old English adjective *cwicu*, which is related to Latin *vivus* and Greek *bios* and meant both 'active' and 'lively' and, as a particular form of liveliness, developed the present-day sense of 'quick'.[3]

Many metaphors involve correlations as part of the mappings between source and target domain. These correspondences are usually referred to as entailments but are, in fact, based on correlational relationships. For example, the metaphor ACTION IS MOTION has as one of its entailments SPEED OF ACTION IS SPEED OF MOTION as in *He flew through his work* and STARTING AN ACTION IS STARTING OUT ON A PATH as in *We have taken the first step*. Both entailments involve correlations: the former involves correlations which are measured by a scale – the faster the action the faster the motion, the latter involves the correlation of a once-only change. Once a conceptual metaphor is established, many structural correspondences and entailments derived from them turn out to be based on the metonymic relationship of correlation.

2.3. Complementarity

The notion of *complementarity* shall be understood here, not just in the narrow sense of semantic opposition, but in the everyday sense of two mutually completing parts. The relationship of complementarity provides a strong conceptual link between such counterparts. We therefore tend to think of a pair of complementary parts as a unity. This applies, amongst others, to "lovers," "married couples" and "body and mind." Lovers spend their time together, share their thoughts and feelings and are sometimes even physically united: hence, metaphors such as LOVE IS A UNITY and EMOTIONAL INTIMACY IS PHYSICAL CLOSENESS are direct reflections of our experience of love relationships.[4] The same applies to our concept of marriage, which, according to Quinn (1987), is described by words such as *cemented together, bound together, tied to each other,* etc. Hence, the metaphor MARRIAGE IS A DURABLE BOND BETWEEN TWO PEOPLE is firmly grounded in our experience and even institutionalized by a marital contract.

Body and mind, or body and soul, constitute, in our folk view, the two parts which constitute a human.[5] The close interdependence of body and mind is reflected in proverbial expressions such as *mens sana in corpore sano* or *keep body and soul together.* Unlike lovers and married couples, however, body and mind are not conceptualized as jointly forming a unity or bond, but we understand one complementary part in terms of the other: THE MIND IS A BODY. Thus, we have metaphorical expressions such as *to have a strong will, to handle a situation, to turn one's back on an issue, to swallow an idea,* etc. Many of these metaphorical expressions may be related to a common experiential basis: We commonly associate mental phenomena with physical phenomena or use body language to illustrate our thoughts. Thus, we might clench our fist in talking or thinking about a "strong will", literally use our hands in "handling" a situation, turn our back when we don't want to get involved, etc. Not surprisingly, complementary parts of a situation are often exploited metonymically.[6] For example, clenching one's fist or turning away evoke the person's mental attitudes that commonly go with these bodily gestures. Specific elaborations such as *swallow an idea* are only closer to the metaphor end on the metonymy-metaphor continuum. It is, of course, much harder to detect a common experiential basis between *swallowing food* and *accepting an unpleasant idea.* This is, however, not the decisive point. The conceptual metaphor THE MIND IS THE BODY is claimed to be based on our common complementary experience of BODY PLUS MIND.

2.4. Comparison

Like correlation and complementarity, the relationship of comparison involves the close interdependence of two entities. Acts of comparison may metaphorically be understood in terms of spatial distance: COMPARISON OF A AND B IS DISTANCE BETWEEN A AND B. The entities compared may be judged as being similar or different. Similar entities are metaphorized as being, or coming, close to each other, while different entities are metaphorized as being distant, or being distanced, from each other. Hence, we have the submetaphors SIMILARITY IS CLOSENESS (*This is close to the truth*) and DIFFERENCE IS REMOTENESS (*This is far from the truth*). As shown in Radden and Mathis (forthcoming), these metaphors are grounded in our folk understanding of similarity and difference: similar things are put together as reflected in the proverbial expression *Birds of a feather flock together*, whereas different things are put apart as expressed in *Oil and water don't mix.*

3. Implicature

A second metonymic source of metaphor is conversational implicature. The area of grammaticalization provides a good illustration of metaphor developed from the pragmatics of a situation. Grammatical categories tend to develop gradually rather than abruptly. Thus, the use of the spatial expression *be going to* as a future marker is in line with the ubiquitous metaphor TIME IS SPACE but, as shown by Heine, Claudi and Hünnemeyer (1991: 70-72), is more likely to have evolved along a continuum of metonymically related senses. The literal sense of "spatial movement" as in *Henry is going to town* may lead to the implicature of "intention" as in *Are you going to the library?* and "intention without spatial movement" as in *No, I am going to eat*, and, further, may invite the conversational implicature of "prediction" as in *I am going to do my very best to make you happy* and "prediction without intention" as in *The rain is going to come.*[7] These "context-induced reinterpretations" became conventionalized by pragmatic strengthening. Heine, Claudi and Hünnemeyer (1991: 60-61) refer to this type of pragmatically motivated metaphor as "emerging metaphors", as opposed to "creative metaphors", which involve "a willful violation of conceptual/semantic rules".

The conceptual relationships between a named and an implicated entity are based on contiguity, or metonymy. Metonymic relationships which are particularly prone to evoking conversational implicatures and lead to emerging metaphor include the following: sequential events, event and result, and place and activity.

3.1. Sequential events

In illustrating the experiential basis of metaphor, Lakoff (1993) gives as a further example the metaphor KNOWING IS SEEING: "The experiential basis in this case is the fact that most of what we know comes through vision, and in the overwhelming majority of cases, if we see something, then we know it is true." (p. 240) This situation in fact describes an inferencing process. We see many phenomena differently from what we know they "really" are: we might, for example, cancel the implicature in *I saw the sunset* by adding: *but I know that this is an illusion.* As observed by Lakoff, however, in the overwhelming majority of cases we take something we see to be true, i.e., "seeing something" invites the implicature "knowing it". This is reflected in the proverbial expression *seeing is believing* and the tautology in *I saw it with my own eyes* to indicate certainty (Sweetser 1990: 33). Visual information is assumed to be more reliable than information gained through other sources: This is nicely illustrated in the greater veracity we place on an eyewitness report than on one based on hearsay.

Instances of seeing and knowing may occur simultaneously or successively. The metaphor KNOWING IS SEEING blends the two experiences into one simultaneous event which may, however, still be conceptually split up into SEE PLUS KNOW. Thus, in *I see the solution,* I may at the same time both mentally visualize the solution to a problem and know it. It is, therefore, no contradiction to speak of *seeing things in my mind's eye.* As a rule, however, we think of "seeing" and "knowing" as occurring at successive stages. This is also the pattern that led to the development of the Germanic preterit present verbs. Thus, the Old English meaning of *witan* 'know' from an Indo-European root **weid-* 'see' is usually explained as derived from a perfect form as in Latin *vidi* 'I have seen', which readily invites the conversational implicature 'I know'.[8] The implicature became pragmatically strengthened and has in English completely superseded the old meaning of "see".

The sequential ordering of the two events may also give rise to an element of causality, which allows people to say *I know it because I saw it.* The causal interpretation of purely temporally linked events is also a matter of implicature and has long been known by the principle *post hoc ergo propter hoc.*[9] The two domains of "time" and "causality" thus have a common experiential basis which may, more specifically, be described as PRECEDENCE PLUS CAUSE and SUBSEQUENCE PLUS RESULT. The sentence *He started the fight* may therefore be interpreted in different ways along the metonymy-metaphor cline: The literal interpretation assigns the sentence a purely temporal sense, "He was the first to start the fight". The sentence may also invite a causal implicature resulting in a "temporal cum causal" interpretation, "He was the first to start the fight and was responsible for it". The sentence may only be understood in the implicated sense of "He is responsible for the fight" according to the metonymy PRECEDENCE FOR CAUSE. The sentence may be interpreted as a metonymy-based metaphor, in which the metaphor CAUSAL PRECEDENCE IS TEMPORAL PRECEDENCE is related to its metonymic basis, and it may lastly be interpreted as purely metaphorical with causation being understood in terms of time.

Our tendency to impose a causal interpretation on sequential events shows most clearly in correlational relationships, which, by definition, do not involve a causal relationship. Thus, *First come, first served* expresses a correlation between coming and being served but, due to the temporal sequence of the two events, invites a conditional or causal implicature: "If you come first, you will be served first" or "Since you came first you will be served first". Likewise, the correlative relationship expressed by *Once bitten, twice shy* gives rise to the causal implicature "because I was bitten once, I'll be twice as careful."

Invited causal implicatures may also account for the metaphors WELL-BEING IS WEALTH (*He has a rich life*) and STATES ARE SHAPES (*You are in good shape*). Wealth and a good physical shape are certainly understood by most people to be causally related to the states of well-being and health. They may, however, also be seen as preconditions to these states.

3.2. Event and result

As shown in the preceding section, we tend to see a causal connection between two sequential events. If we look at such a complex situation from the later event, the earlier one may be seen as its cause or precondition, which may be used to stand metonymically for the whole scenario. Lakoff (1987: 79) illustrated this case in transferring Rhodes' Ojibwa examples into the American context: a question such as *How did you get to the party?* may be metonymically answered by naming the precondition, *I have a car.*

Conversely, a given event may contextually induce us to anticipate a later event as its result. If I said that I have a car, the relevance of this utterance may be interpreted to be to drive someplace. The power of such conversational implicatures may be illustrated in the grammaticalization processes leading to the notion of "possession". In his crosslinguistic study, Heine (1997: 83-108) found that languages make use of six main event schemas as templates for expressing predicative possession, i.e., possession which, in English, is expressed by the *"have*-construction": the Action Schema, the Location Schema, the Companion Schema, the Goal Schema, the Genitive Schema and the Topic Schema. At least the first four event schemas can be analyzed as situations from which a resulting state of possession may be implicated – the latter two schemas are also syntactically determined.

The Action Schema denotes possession by means of verbs such as "seize", "take", "get" and "hold". An utterance such as "The man has taken the car" (from Nama, a Khoisan language; Heine 1997: 92) readily invites the implicature that the man now possesses the car. Although the Action Schema is "exotic" typologically in that it is not the source which is most widely employed to express possession, it is the pattern commonly found in European languages: English *have* probably originates from the Indo-European root **kap-* 'seize' as in Latin *capere* and Spanish *tener* goes back to Latin *tenere* 'hold'. English makes use of the idea of holding in describing possession as in *to hold a driver's license, to hold power, to hold a belief* and *stock holder.* It is probably fair to conclude that the metaphor POSSESSION IS HOLDING has a strong metonymic basis in our common experience of HOLDING PLUS POSSESSION.

The event schemas of Location (Y is located at X), Companion (X is with Y) and Goal (Y exists for/to X) provide good conceptual sources for implicating resulting possession and have also developed this sense in various languages, but they have, at least in English, apparently not further developed to larger conceptual metaphors of possession. Heine (1997: 95) notes one area where the Goal Schema is found to express possession in English: the use of the Goal preposition *to* in the expression *secretary to the president.* This directional-possessive usage of *to* is, in fact, fairly widespread in English: *the preface to a book, the prelude to war* and possibly also *essential to life.* If these cases can be said to establish a metaphor POSSESSION IS REACHING A GOAL, it is undoubtedly based on metonymy.

3.3. Place and activity

Places are often associated with events which typically occur at that place. Many spatial areas are specifically designed to be used as the setting for certain kinds of activities: playgrounds are designed for children to play on, hospitals are for ill people to be medically treated in, beds are made for us to sleep in, etc. The association between such man-designed spaces and the activities typically performed there is so tight that the mention of the place suffices to evoke the implicature of a special activity. Thus, the use of *but* confirms our expectation about PLACE PLUS ACTIVITY in *I am in my study but can't concentrate,* but not in *?I am in the bathroom but can't concentrate.* We understand *The children are on the playground* in the sense of "they are playing there" and *They are in bed* in the sense of "they are sleeping or getting ready to sleep" unless, of course, we have some other contextually relevant information, for example that they are lovers. The same applies to motion towards places: *The children are going to the playground* implicates that "they are going to play there" just like *They are going to bed* implicates that "they are going to sleep". In both the static and dynamic situations we are dealing with one domain and the metonymic relationship PLACE FOR ACTIVITY.

In addition to the activity performed at the place, mention of the destination of a motion also invites the implicature of a purpose. This implicature derives from our every experience: "to achieve most of our everyday purposes, we [...] have to move to some destination" (Lakoff 1993: 240). Since purposes belong to a different domain from destinations, this situation assumes a metaphorical quality. Thus, we have the metonymically-based metaphor PURPOSES ARE DESTINATIONS, which accounts for metaphorical expressions such as *We've reached the end* or *It took him hours to reach a state of perfect concentration.*

4. Category structure

A third type of metonymy-based metaphor relates to the structure of categories. The relation between a category and its members is widely exploited in metonymy: a category as a whole (genus) may stand for one of its members (species) and a member of a category (species) may stand for the category as a whole (genus). Thus, the category "pill" may be used to stand for one of its salient members, "birth control pill", and, conversely, the salient subcategory "aspirin" may stand for the category "pain-relieving tablets" as a whole.

The metonymic, or synecdochic,[10] relationships between categories and salient members may also be exploited in metaphor. Thus, the metaphor (PSYCHIC) HARM IS PHYSICAL INJURY as found in *You are hurting my feelings* is based on the relationship between the category "harm" and a salient member of this category, namely "physical injury". The relationship between "harm" and "physical injury" may be seen as involving one conceptual domain. PHYSICAL INJURY PLUS HARM also has a common experiential basis since physical injury and psychic harm are often experienced together. It is due to the fundamental distinction which we tend to make between the concrete and the abstract that we feel that physical injury belongs to a different conceptual domain than harm in general.

The distinction between the physical and abstract also accounts for the following metonymy-based metaphors: PROPERTIES ARE PHYSICAL PROPERTIES (*big discovery*), A PROBLEM IS A TANGLE (*a knotty problem*) and COMMUNICATION IS LINGUISTIC COMMUNICATION (*People should have a say on the treaty*). Perhaps less obvious instances of category-based metaphors are ACTION IS MOTION (*What's your next move?*) and CHANGE IS MOTION (*She fell in love*). Motion is probably the most salient type of action and forms part of a great many actions: writing a letter involves moving the pen over the paper, opening a door involves going to the door, turning the handle or knob and pulling or pushing the door open, etc. In elaborating the metonymy-based metaphor, we may then speak of *journeying through a book* or *sailing into a marriage*. Also changes which are not brought about by intentionally acting humans may involve motion: dark clouds drawing near go hand in hand with the setting in of rain, a vase "goes" to pieces when dropped, etc. Not surprisingly, therefore, changes of state are typically expressed by motion verbs, in particular *come* and *go* (cf. Radden 1996).

The metaphor CAUSE IS FORCE as in *The study sparked a controversy*, lastly, may also be seen as based on category inclusion. Causes are most immediately experienced in the shape of physical forces and typically also involve the exertion of physical force. Physical force is needed to start up the engine of a car by either turning the ignition key or pushing the car. We also transfer this experience onto abstract domains and speak of *being convinced by the force of his argument*. Since changes are understood as motion, caused changes are metaphorized as caused motion and, therefore, typically expressed by caused-motion verbs such as *send* and *leave*: *The explosion sent me into a tailspin* and *The fire left 200 people homeless* (cf. also Lakoff and Johnson, 1999).

5. Cultural models

Quinn and Holland (1987: 4) define cultural models as "presupposed, taken-for-granted models of the world that are widely shared [...] by the members of a society and that play an enormous role in their understanding of that world and their behavior in it". This definition shall also subsume folk models as naive theories of the world. Cultural models can only play this "enormous" cognitive role if they are internally coherent, stable and entrenched, i.e., if their elements are closely interconnected and seen as belonging to the same domain of experience. Such folk and cultural models account for conceptual metaphors in the areas of physics, communication and emotion, which will be discussed below. They probably also provide the experiential basis for metaphors in the fields of perception, morality and life, which, however, will not be gone into here.

5.1. Physical forces

McCloskey (1983) has shown that people hold a naive theory of motion, which they refer to as *impetus theory*. According to our folk model, objects are set in motion by imparting to them an internal force, or "impetus", which maintains the object's motion until gradually dissipating. In this model, forces are "literally" contained in the moving objects themselves and propel them in a certain direction. Hence, metaphors such as FORCE IS A SUBSTANCE CONTAINED IN AFFECTING CAUSES (*His punches carry a lot of force*) and FORCE IS A SUBSTANCE DIRECTED AT AN AFFECTED PARTY (*Use more force in driving the nail*) follow naturally from the impetus theory.

5.2. Communication and language

According to Reddy's (1979 [1993]) seminal study on the CONDUIT metaphor, seventy percent of the expressions used to describe communication in English are based on this metaphor. Reddy's main concern was the impact the metaphor has on our thinking – a view which already assumes that the metaphor leads a life of its own but does not ask how it originated. The CONDUIT metaphor is so successful precisely because it reflects what most people take for reality. In particular the aspect of transmission of information through a channel has always been present in traditional modes of communication and is even more omnipresent in modern information theory and communication technology. Thus, the metaphor COMMUNICATION IS TRANSFER (*I didn't get my point across*) has an immediate experiential basis and is certainly felt to be non-metaphorical to most people.

We also firmly believe that meanings reside in words and other linguistic "containers". This objectivist view of language makes it possible that the form of a word can metonymically stand for its content. The metonymy WORD-FORM FOR CONTENT applies to individual expressions as in *four-letter words, ugly words* or *using bad language* and to language at large, whose forms evoke, and stand for, meanings associated with them (Lakoff and Turner 1989:108; Kövecses and Radden 1998). The CONDUIT metaphor also provides the possibility for the sender to put meanings into words – which is inconsistent within the objectivist model because the meanings are already in the words – and for the

receiver to recover the meanings from the message. This whole complex establishes, not just a folk model of a few people, but an overall cultural model shared
by scholars of such diverse disciplines as information theory, who speak of
"encoding" and "decoding", and literary critics when analyzing poetry.[11]

5.3. Ideas and emotions

The container image schema also serves to structure part of our understanding
of the mind and emotions: THE MIND IS A CONTAINER FOR OBJECTS as in *to have
something in mind* and THE BODY IS A CONTAINER FOR THE EMOTIONS as in *to be
filled with hatred* (Kövecses 1990: 53). The grammar of English makes a fundamental distinction between the kind of contents typically mapped by each of
these metaphors: "ideas" in the "mind container" are typically coded as count
nouns, i.e., are seen as objects, while "emotions" are typically coded as mass
nouns, i.e., are seen as substances. Is there an experiential explanation for these
different conceptualizations? Objects are, amongst other things, conceptually
characterized as being externally bounded and having internal structure, while
substances are unbounded and unstructured (cf. Langacker 1991: 18-19). We
experience mental processes such as thoughts, judgments, guesses, doubts, etc.
as something we are in control of – we can sit down and start thinking about a
problem and stop when we are done, i.e., mental processes are bounded in time.
Emotions, by contrast, are experienced as being beyond our control – we cannot
willfully start or stop feeling love, hatred or anger, i.e., emotions are unbounded
in time. We also experience mental processes as being subject to our reasoning –
we may, for example, ask a person to justify his ideas: if someone said "That's
a stupid idea", I might reasonably ask "What's stupid about it?" and expect to
be given a detailed explanation, i.e., we assume that thoughts consist of structured rational parts. Emotions, by contrast, appear to us as being unstructured –
we cannot generally ask people to explain their emotions.

What people are concerned with in dealing with emotions are their causes
and their effects. The causes leading to a particular emotion are manifold, but
their effects are fairly consistent, in particular those that show up in people's
physiological reactions. As is well-known from Kövecses' studies on emotion,
the physiological effects of an emotion are commonly used to stand for the
emotion. In his case study of "anger", Lakoff (1987: 382) suggested that this
folk theory of physiological effects forms the basis of the metaphor ANGER IS
HEAT. Thus, one of the physiological effects of anger is increased body heat. This
metonymic relationship is further elaborated in two metaphorical versions:
ANGER IS THE HEAT OF A FLUID IN A CONTAINER as in *You make my blood boil* and
ANGER IS FIRE as in *He was breathing fire*. In a similar way, the metaphor ANGER
IS INSANITY as in *You're driving me nuts* is grounded in the metonymy INSANE
BEHAVIOR FOR ANGER as in *He is about to throw a tantrum*. The metonymic folk
model of physiological effects probably accounts for some more emotion meta-

phors, e.g., LUST IS HEAT, AFFECTION IS WARMTH, LOVE IS MADNESS and LOVE IS FIRE. Some emotions are closely associated with certain types of behavior and may give rise to metonymy-based metaphors. Thus, the experiential bases of the metaphors EMOTIONAL INTIMACY IS PHYSICAL CLOSENESS (*He is very near and dear to her*; cf. also *Out of sight, out of mind*) and GAINING PHYSICAL INTIMACY IS A COMPETITION (*Did you get to homebase with her?*) are self-explanatory.

6. Conclusion

The primary goal of the paper was to provide evidence for the assumption that at least some metaphors are grounded in metonymy. The great number of meta-phors which could be traced back to a metonymic basis in this investigation unequivocally confirm this assumption – it is very likely that a closer inspection of conceptual metaphors will reveal many more metonymy-based metaphors. The metonymic driving forces behind metaphors which were distinguished here are: (i) a common experiential basis of the two metaphorical domains, (ii) the operation of implicature, (iii) category structure, and (iv) cultural models.

In view of these findings, the traditional distinction between metonymy and metaphor can no longer be maintained. The classical notions of metonymy and metaphor are to be seen as prototypical categories at the end points of a con-tinuum of mapping processes. The range in the middle of the metonymy-meta-phor continuum is made up of metonymy-based metaphors, which also account for the transition of metonymy to metaphor by providing an experiential moti-vation of a metaphor. This approach may also contribute to reconciling the conflicting views that laymen and experts, i.e., cognitive linguists, have about metaphor. Anybody who has ever taught a course on metaphor, or talked to colleagues about metaphor, has, in all likelihood, come into a situation where their students or colleagues were very skeptical about accepting something as an instance of metaphor which they insist is literal speech. Both are right in their way. To repeat an example used at the beginning: to the layman, or the linguist outside the cognitive paradigm, *high* in *high prices* is literal (or metonymic) because height and quantity are not seen as incompatible with prices but, on the contrary, are part of the same domain. To the cognitive linguist, *high* in *high prices* is metaphorical because of the systematicity and ubiquity of the MORE IS UP metaphor. The notion of the metonymy-based metaphor retains the linguistic notion of conceptual metaphor and at the same time relates it to the view of naive speakers of the language who were the ones who developed metaphors in the first place.

Notes

*   I wish to thank Elizabeth Mathis and Karol Janicki for valuable comments and suggestions and Antonio Barcelona for first bringing up the topic "Metonymy as a conceptual motivation of metaphorical mapping" to be discussed in his session at the 5th International Cognitive Linguistics Conference at Amsterdam in 1997 (see Barcelona, this volume).

1.   Elizabeth Mathis drew my attention to usages such as *small voice* 'high, soft voice', in which more of a size apparently correlates inversely with height. Thus, with sizes, SMALL IS UP and BIG IS DOWN (as in *deep voice*). Physical analogs of this metaphor might be seen in the construction of mountains and trees, where the upper part is smaller than the lower part. Yet, since we also correlate size with quantity, i.e., BIGGER IS MORE, we are faced with the puzzling situation of positioning both more in quantity and less in size at the same end of a scale. Maybe this is also why we are often surprised when a small person has a loud deep voice and a big person has a soft or high voice.

2.   As is known from Piaget's experiments, children in the preoperational stage consistently judge the quantity of the fluid in a glass by the height of its level, ignoring other dimensions such as the glass's width. To them, quantity is literally height. Even adults may have preserved some of this preoperational thought.

3.   Cf. also the words *quicksilver* from *argentum vivum* 'living silver', *quicksand* 'mobile sand' and the meaning of the German word *keck* 'lively, sprightly'.

4.   See Kövecses (1986: 62ff) on the LOVE IS UNITY metaphor. I would not, however, subscribe to his claim that our "view of love [perfect harmony, idyllic state, one part is incomplete and cannot really function without the other one] is mainly the result of the metaphor [...]". It is much more likely that we developed the metaphor on the basis of our real or idealized experience of love.

5.   The fact that the metaphysical issue of body and mind has been so vigorously debated by philosophers confirms the well-established complementary status of these notions. The particular stance taken by philosophers – dualism of body and mind or single unit – is irrelevant for the folk understanding of the pair BODY AND MIND or BODY AND SOUL.

6.   The metonymic relationship between complementary pairs is also attested in the etymology of a word. For example, "bow" and "arrow" constitute a complementary pair, but *arrow* is related to Latin *arcus* ('arc, bow',) i.e., it originally meant "bow" as well.

7.   Heine, Claudi and Hünnemeyer explain the metonymic steps by context-induced reinterpretation. Cf. also Nicolle's (1998) relevance theory perspective on the grammaticalization of *be going to*. Langacker (1991: 219-220) describes the process as increasing subjectification by mental scanning.

8.   The English verb *witan* has given way to *know*, but derivates are still preserved in the English words *wise, witness, wit, wot, wis* archaic 'know'.

9.   Cf. the well-known grammaticalization processes from temporal meanings to causal meanings via an intermediate stage (A, B), in which the preceding and succeeding entities coexist side by side (see e.g., Heine, Claudi and Hünnemeyer 1991: 74).

10.   Seto (forthcoming) argues convincingly that relationships between entities in the world (called E-relations) need to be distinguished from those between conceptual

categories (called C-relations). The former relationships are at the basis of metonymy, while the latter are at the basis of synecdoche. The issue is, however, of no relevance here.

11. The use of metaphorical language in poem analysis by literary critics was investigated by Barbara Hott in her MA thesis (Hott 1994). The language used by literary critics is thoroughly metaphorical and particularly characterized by the CONDUIT metaphor. Metaphors such as *The passage is loaded with a special meaning* and *The magic and everything else are in the words* abound.

References

Barcelona, Antonio
    this volume "On the plausibility of claiming a metonymic motivation for conceptual metaphor."

Heine, Bernd
    1997   *Cognitive foundation of grammar.* New York, Oxford: Oxford University Press.

Heine, Bernd – Ulrike Claudi – Friederike Hünnemeyer
    1991   *Grammaticalization: A conceptual framework.* Chicago, London: University of Chicago Press.

Holland, Dorothy – Naomi Quinn (eds.)
    1987   *Cultural models in language and thought.* Cambridge: Cambridge University Press.

Hott, Barbara
    1994   "Ploughing into the poem: An empirical investigation of conceptual metaphors in poem analyses". Hamburg: C.L.E.A.R. No. 4

Kövecses, Zoltán
    1986   *Metaphors of anger, pride and love.* Amsterdam, Philadelphia: Benjamins.
    1990   *Emotion Concepts.* New York: Springer Verlag.

Kövecses, Zoltán – Günter Radden
    1998   "Metonymy: Developing a cognitive linguistic view", *Cognitive Linguistics* 9.1: 37-77.

Lakoff, George
    1987   *Women, fire and dangerous things. What categories reveal about the mind.* Chicago: Chicago University Press.
    1993   "The contemporary theory of metaphor", in: Andrew Ortony (ed.), 202-251.

Lakoff, George – et al.
    1994   *Master metaphor list.* Available on the WWW at http://cogsci.berkeley.edu/.

Lakoff, George – Mark Johnson
    1980   *Metaphors we live by.* Chicago: Chicago University Press.
    1999   *Philosophy in the flesh. The embodied mind and its challenge to western thought.* New York: Basic Books.

Lakoff, George – Mark Turner
1989   *More than cool reason: A field guide to poetic metaphor.* Chicago: Chicago University Press.
Langacker, Ronald W.
1991   *Foundations of cognitive grammar. Vol. II. Descriptive application.* Stanford: Stanford University Press.
McCloskey, Michael
1983   "Naive theories of motion", in: Dedre Gentner – Albert R. Stevens (eds.), *Mental models.* Hillsdale, NJ: Erlbaum, 299-324.
Nicolle, Steve
1998   "A relevance theory perspective on grammaticalization", *Cognitive Linguistics* 9: 1-35.
Ortony, Andrew (ed.)
1993   *Metaphor and thought.* (2nd edition.) Cambridge: Cambridge University Press.
Panther, Klaus-Uwe – Günter Radden (eds.)
forthcoming *Metonymy in language and thought.* Amsterdam, Philadelphia: Benjamins.
Quinn, Naomi
1987   "Convergent evidence for a cultural model of American marriage", in: Dorothy Holland – Naomi Quinn (eds.), 173-192.
Quinn, Naomi – Dorothy Holland
1987   "Culture and cognition", in: Dorothy Holland–Naomi Quinn (eds.), 3-40.
Radden, Günter
1996   "Motion metaphorized: The case of *coming* and *going*", in: Eugene H. Casad (ed.) *Cognitive linguistics in the redwoods: The expansion of a new paradigm in linguistics.* Berlin, New York: Mouton de Gruyter, 423-458.
Radden, Günter – Zoltán Kövecses
forthcoming "Towards a theory of metonymy", in: Klaus-Uwe Panther – Günter Radden (eds.).
Radden, Günter – Elizabeth Mathis
forthcoming "Prepositional construal of similarity".
Reddy, Michael
1979 [1993] "The conduit metaphor – a case of frame conflict in our language about language", in: Andrew Ortony (ed.), 164-210.
Seto, Ken-ichi
forthcoming "Distinguishing metonymy from synecdoche", in: Klaus-Uwe Panther – Günter Radden (eds.).
Sweetser, Eve
1990   *From etymology to pragmatics: Metaphorical and cultural aspects of semantic structure.* Cambridge: Cambridge University Press.
Taylor, John R.
1995   *Linguistic categorization. Prototypes in linguistic theory.* (2nd edition.) Oxford: Clarendon Press.
Ullmann, Stephen
1962   *Semantics: An introduction to the science of meaning.* Oxford: Blackwell.

The role of mappings and domains in understanding metonymy[1]

Francisco José Ruiz de Mendoza Ibáñez

1. Introduction

For well over a decade Cognitive Linguistics has been paying a great deal of attention to the study of metaphor (see, for example, the seminal work in Lakoff – Johnson, 1980; Lakoff – Turner, 1989; Lakoff, 1987, 1993, 1996). From the cognitive perspective, metaphor is seen as the partial mapping of a source domain onto a target domain, with a set of correspondences between the source and the target. As a result of this process, we talk and reason about the target in terms of the conceptual (and inferential) structure of the source.

Metonymy has received much less attention even though it is explicitly acknowledged that it is "one of the basic characteristics of cognition" (Lakoff, 1987: 77). As a result of this, there is much less certainty as to its status than with metaphor. For example, while Lakoff and Turner (1989: 103-4) see metonymy as a conventionalized conceptual mapping where – contrary to what happens with metaphor – only one domain is involved, Croft (1993) tries to capture the contrast between metaphor and metonymy in terms of "domain mapping" versus "domain highlighting"; from his point of view, metonymy involves "domain highlighting", which consists in making primary a secondary domain, an idea which shall be discussed later.

The position defended in this paper is slightly different. First, our analysis points to a continuum from metaphor to metonymy, a point which is substantiated by a distinction between two metaphor types: one in which the metaphor structures a relevant part of a domain as it brings some of its aspects to the foreground; the other in which the metaphor serves primarily to give special prominence to part of a domain but without structuring it. Metonymy is more related to this second type of metaphor. Second, we shall contend that metonymic mappings may be of two types: one, in which the source is a subdomain of the target ("source-in-target" metonymies); another in which the target is a subdomain of the source ("target-in-source" metonymies). We therefore exclude, for interpretation purposes, the traditional idea of mappings where a subdomain stands for another subdomain within the same domain. We shall give evidence for the relevance of this distinction between two metonymy types by examining correlations – where metonymy plays an important role – between each of them and cases of anaphoric reference in relation to the conjoining of predicates, on the one hand, and cases of conceptual interaction involving metaphor and metonymy, on the other hand. Third, we have the question – raised by Croft (1993) – of the role of the primary or secondary nature of the domains which take part in metonymy. Our conclusions here, in combination with the insights gained from the previous discussion, will allow us to spell out a full definition of metonymy which will take into consideration (i) the nature of the mappings, (ii) the type of relation between the domains involved, (iii) the nature of the domains in terms of centrality.

2. Metaphoric mappings

A metaphor has been defined as a set of correspondences (or conceptual mappings) between two conceptual domains where one of the domains (called the source) helps us to structure, understand and reason about the other (called the target) (see Lakoff, 1993: 206-207). One essential feature of metaphorical concepts is their systematicity. Consider Lakoff and Johnson's account of the metaphors ARGUMENT IS WAR and TIME IS MONEY (Lakoff – Johnson, 1980: 4-9). In the first metaphor, we see the person we are arguing with as an opponent, we attack his positions and defend our own, we gain or lose ground, we plan strategies, and we ultimately win or lose. In the second one, time is seen as a limited resource and a valuable commodity: in general, like many other physical entities, it can be given or taken; more particularly, it can be saved, spent, wasted, and invested. According to Lakoff and Johnson, the metaphorical concepts TIME IS MONEY, TIME IS A RESOURCE, and TIME IS A VALUABLE COMMODITY form a single system based on subcategorization relationships which characterize entailment between the metaphors (i.e. TIME IS MONEY entails that TIME IS A RESOURCE, which entails that TIME IS A VALUABLE COMMODITY). The following examples will help us understand the importance of systematicity in metaphor interpretation:

(1)   *The senator's proposals were attacked in the newspapers.*
(2) a. *I can't waste my time on your project.*
     b. *I haven't got enough time for your project.*
     c. *I can't give any more of my (valuable) time to your project.*

In (1) the senator and the journalists are seen as enemies at war. The senator's proposals are the target for the journalists' attacks (which is the negative criticism). These are the correspondences exploited by the metaphorical expression. However, there are also other latent correspondences, which belong to the ARGUMENT IS WAR system, but which are not explicitly invoked by (1). Thus, we know the senator may or may not have determined how to defend himself (i.e. we cannot be sure that he has "devised a strategy"); we further know that he may or may not respond to criticism (i.e. "counterattack"), and that success or failure in defending his proposals may be partial (i.e. he may "win or lose a battle") or complete (i.e. he may "win or lose the war").

It is these latent correspondences that create coherent stretches, as in:

(3)   *The senator's proposals were attacked in the newspapers, but he eventually outsmarted his opponents with devastating wit.*

The three examples in (2) are alternative ways of expressing lack of time. Each is based on one of the metaphors of the system: (2a) is based on TIME IS MONEY; (2b) on TIME IS A (LIMITED) RESOURCE; and (2c) on TIME IS A (VALUABLE) COMMODITY. Furthermore, as with ARGUMENT IS WAR, we may set up a number of correspondences which characterize the system: in the source domain, we have a person who has some commodity, resource, or simply money, which he is only willing to use for certain purposes; in the target domain, a person is involved in some activity which does not allow him or her to become engaged in any other activity. Although all of the correspondences are necessary to understand the metaphor, only one becomes central, namely, that between the type of commodity or resource and time. It is this correspondence that supplies what we may call the central implications of the metaphor: for example, we may reason for (2a) that since time is money and money is a limited resource, the speaker may have already set up his list of priorities to deal with them in a particular order; the addressee's project is obviously not among the speaker's priorities.

Consider now the following metaphorical expression, which has been explained in some detail in Lakoff – Turner (1989: 196):

(4)   *Achilles is a lion.*

According to Lakoff and Turner, the metaphor in this expression, which we may label PEOPLE ARE ANIMALS, results from an interaction between the commonsense theory of things called the GREAT CHAIN and the GENERIC IS SPECIFIC metaphor. The GREAT CHAIN is a cultural model defined by attributes and behavior which typically apply to each form of being (humans, animals, plants, complex objects, and natural physical things) in a hierarchy. For example, animals are characterized by having instinctual attributes and behavior; to these, humans add higher-order attributes and behavior (see Lakoff – Turner, 1989: 170-171). The GENERIC IS SPECIFIC metaphor singles out common generic structure from specific concepts. The combination of the two models allows us to understand animal behavior in terms of human character. For example, we believe that lions, like humans, are courageous. The PEOPLE ARE ANIMALS mapping, on the other hand, makes us understand human character in terms of animal behavior. Thus, in *Achilles is a lion*, we see Achilles' courage in terms of a lion's attributed courage. Finally, Lakoff and Turner (1989: 196) also point out that in (4) we not only map the lion's "courage" onto Achilles' courage, but also we map the lion onto Achilles, and the structural relation between the lion and his "courage" onto the relation between Achilles and his courage. This observation would seem to imply that there are three correspondences. However, this is not actually the case, since the mapping from the lion onto Achilles subsumes the other mappings, which are based on subdomains, and saying that the structural relations between a subdomain and the matrix domain are also mapped only means that an attribute is never mapped in dissociation from the conceptual structure to which it belongs. So, it may safely be asserted that the metaphor in (4) is based only on one correspondence. In order to contrast metaphors of this type with others where there is a fully-fledged system of correspondences, we shall refer to the former as "one-correspondence metaphors" and to the latter as "many-correspondence metaphors" (cf. Ruiz de Mendoza, 1997: 169-171).

Observe that saying that PEOPLE ARE ANIMALS is a case of one-correspondence metaphor does not entail that there is not a conventionalized system underlying the mapping. In fact, there is a system according to which non-physical behavioral attributes are mapped when the metaphorical expression takes the predicative "A is a B" form (e.g. *He is a pig, She is a dragon, He is a chicken, She is a cow, He is a shark*, and so on, where A is formally identified as a member of the class designated by B), and when the name of an animal or of part of an animal is used as a verb (e.g. *He dogged me all day, He has clawed his way through life*) or as an adjective (e.g. *She's rather catty*). In other constructions, like *John has an eagle eye*, the animal metaphor may refer to abilities. In general, physical appearance plays a small role in these metaphors, except when it helps us to understand a behavioral feature. For example, in *Her husband is a bull of a man*, we focus our attention on the person's clumsy, inconsiderate behavior, which is of course related to the person's physical appearance. Also, we have cases of situational metaphors involving animal behavior, as in the expressions *He got up on his hind legs*, and *He left with his tail between his legs*. In these cases it is the (aggressive or humiliated) reaction of an animal in a certain situation which maps onto a person's behavior also in connection to a certain situation. The elements of the situation are only relevant in the sense that they provide a background of similarities to make the mapping from animal to human behavior possible. We shall deal with this kind of metaphor in more detail later.

It is interesting to observe that in one-correspondence metaphors the target domain has a non-abstract nature. In many-correspondence metaphors, on the other hand, the target domain is abstract, which is why we need to make use of more concrete experience to deal with them. As a further example of a one-correspondence metaphor, think of PEOPLE ARE MACHINES (e.g. *He ran out of steam just before the end of the race*). Contrast it with LOVE IS A JOURNEY, where we identify lovers with travelers, goals with destinations, the love relationship with a vehicle, difficulties in the relationship with impediments to travel, and so on (Lakoff, 1993: 207-208). In LOVE IS A JOURNEY, each of the correspondences is used to come to terms with a different aspect of the concept of love on the basis of concrete experience, which is enough to justify the mapping. However, in PEOPLE ARE MACHINES what we do is rather different: we think of a person's attributes and behavior in terms of specific attributes and behavior which machines have. Thus, we say that a person is a machine when the person routinely works without thinking about it, perhaps untiringly. We say that someone has run out of steam when he no longer has energy or enthusiasm to go on doing something. We say that a person is rusty when he has partially lost his ability to perform a certain task because of lack of practice. So what we map is the way machines perform under certain circumstances onto the way humans behave when they work. As with the one-correspondence metaphor PEOPLE ARE ANIMALS, this attribute is not mapped independently of its overall domain of reference (i.e. the type of machine or the conditions in which the machine works).

One-correspondence metaphors make use of the GREAT CHAIN and the GENERIC IS SPECIFIC cognitive models. This should come as no surprise since the GREAT CHAIN defines attributes and behavior for non-abstract entities, and the GENERIC IS SPECIFIC metaphor allows us to abstract away quintessential characteristics of such entities which thus become available for correlation. Thus, the correspondences are established on a fairly abstract level (behavior or way of performing correlate with human behavior).

The GENERIC IS SPECIFIC metaphor works differently in the case of many-correspondence metaphors, where we have some aspects of an abstract target domain which are correlated with a concrete source domain. Here, the function of this metaphor is exclusively to derive, from source and target, generic structure which shares enough properties to make the correlation between both domains possible. Its function is not to find any quintessential property of the source which will be mapped onto the target. We shall take up this point later in relation to work carried out by Mark Turner and Gilles Fauconnier in the field of conceptual interaction (see especially Turner – Fauconnier, 1995; Fauconnier – Turner, 1996).

3. Metonymic mappings

Lakoff and his collaborators have sketched the differences between metaphor and metonymy as follows (see Lakoff – Johnson, 1980: 36; Lakoff – Turner, 1989: 103):

– Metaphors involve two conceptual domains; metonymies only one.
– In metaphor the structure and logic of the source domain is mapped onto the structure and logic of the target domain; this means that the primary function of a metaphor is understanding, while metonymies are mainly used for reference.
– The relationship between the source and target of a metaphor is of the "is-a" kind; in metonymies there is a "stand-for" relationship.

These criteria apply well to most metonymies. However, only the first one is truly definitional. Consider the following oft-quoted metonymies (see Lakoff – Johnson, 1980: 35, 38):

(5)   *The ham sandwich is waiting for his check.*
(6)   *Nixon bombed Hanoi.*

In (5) "the ham sandwich" stands for and refers to the customer who has ordered a ham sandwich. In (6) "Nixon" stands for and refers to the army which he controlled and which actually did the bombing.

But in these examples, the stand-for relationship between source and target which apparently characterizes metonymy is only a by-product of its referential use. We may, occasionally, have non-referential uses of metonymy, where there is no such clear relationship as in *John is a brain, I'm all ears, She's just a pretty face, Jim is the fastest gun*. Also, in the appropriate contexts we may have others. For example, a choir director who is really impressed by the beauty of the voice of one the members of the choir might say *He is a fine bass*. Conversely, it is possible to make a referential use of a metaphor. For example, *The pig is waiting for his check* might be an appropriate expression to be used by a waitress to refer to a particularly unpleasant customer who keeps harassing her. In this case, "the pig" both refers to and stands for the customer.

In fact, the false impression that metonymies necessarily involve a stand-for relationship derives from the common failure to make a difference between referential and predicative uses of both metaphoric and metonymic mappings. Nevertheless, metonymies seem more apt for referential than for predicative use. This is a consequence of the fact that metonymies are constructed on the basis of just one conceptual domain, which makes it difficult to map the structural relation between source and target onto the target since one of the domains is already part of the other.

It is only when it is possible for a metonymic relationship to bring out a quintessential characteristic of the source to map to the target that a predicative use of a metonymy is possible. This is often achieved by explicitly parametrizing the source domain by means of an adjective as in *John is a fine bass*, where "fine" allows us to know what aspect of John's voice is to be considered. However, parametrization may not be necessary as in *John is a brain*, whose interpretation has been established by convention. Furthermore, predicative uses of metonymy may only occur in cases where the source is clearly a subdomain of the target since only a subdomain may provide a relevant feature – which thus becomes available to be brought into focus – of the domain to which it belongs, but not the other way around. In this connection, consider:

(7)   *John is the ham sandwich.*
(8)   *?John is a ham sandwich.*

Even in the restaurant context, the expression "ham sandwich" may only be used referentially, as in (7), but not predicatively, as in (8). The reason for this is that it is difficult to find out a quintessential characteristic of a ham sandwich which will map onto John. We could even think of (8) as a rather infelicitous metaphor since it is not even clear in what sense the notion of ham sandwich is connected to John. This is not the case with the referential use, in which the hearer is not required to find a relevant feature of the source that will map onto the target, but rather to identify an entity which is a subdomain of the target domain, an activity which is facilitated by the appropriate framing of the utterance. Thus, a ham sandwich may stand for a customer in a restaurant more easily than in a doctor's surgery.

From the examples given, it is apparent that metonymies are cases of one-correspondence mappings within a domain; that is to say, either a whole domain maps onto one of its subdomains or viceversa. Since the predominantly referential use of metonymy and the stand-for relationship are not really definitional criteria, being a one-correspondence mapping combines with its domain-internal nature to characterize metonymy. If this is correct, we may think of a continuum from metaphor to metonymy where many-correspondence metaphors would be at one end and clear cases of referential metonymy would be at the other, with one-correspondence metaphors and predicative uses of metonymy in the middle.

4. Domains and subdomains

The difference between one-correspondence and many-correspondence mappings concerns the nature of the mapping process itself. Now we need to look into the nature of the relationship between the domains involved. Let us go back to the ham sandwich metonymy above. In our interpretation, for the purpose of the mapping, we have treated "ham sandwich" as a subdomain of "customer" rather than of "restaurant". This does not deny that "sandwich" is a subdomain of "restaurant". What it does is simplify the number of domain relationships which have a role in metonymy from the traditional three (i.e. part to whole, whole to part, and part to part) to only two (i.e. part to whole, whole to part)[2]. There are several reasons why this should be so. In general, if a mapping between two independent, discrete entities within a given conceptual structure were possible, this mapping would have more in common with metaphor than with metonymy. Also, we would have the problem of determining why not any two entities in a conceptual structure could be mapped metonymically. For example, it would be very difficult to refer to a customer by mentioning the wallpaper, the carpeting on the stairs to the second floor, the restrooms, or simply another customer. There must be some particularly relevant connection between the customer and the entity which is named to refer to him, but once the connection has been made – aided by our conventional encyclopedic knowledge about what people do at restaurants – the entity becomes part of the conceptual domain for customer in the context given. This means that the restaurant serves to license the inclusion of one domain within the other.

A second reason for rejecting the relevance of postulating part-for-part metonymies is related to questions of anaphoric reference in connection to the conjoining of predicates. First of all, consider the following metonymies:

(9)   *In* Goldfinger *Sean Connery saves the world from a nuclear disaster.*
(10)   *James Bond was really convincing in* Goldfinger.

In the part-for-part view, these two sentences could be explained as involving similar metonymies where a part of the film-making domain is mapped onto another part. Thus, in (9) the actor stands for the role, and in (10) the role stands for the actor. However, we may think of an actor's role in a film or play as part of what we know about him, which thereby becomes the full domain. We may refer to this full domain as the "matrix domain" in the sense that it provides a framework of reference for other domains which are part of it. If this view is correct, (9) would be explained as a mapping from the matrix domain to one of its relevant subdomains, while (10) would map a relevant subdomain to the matrix domain. This explanation has some advantages to account for anaphoric reference to expressions which involve a metonymic mapping. Compare:

(11)   *In* Goldfinger *Sean Connery* (= James Bond) *saves the world from a nuclear disaster, but* he (= James Bond) *had real trouble achieving it.*
(12)   *?In* Goldfinger *Sean Connery* (= James Bond) *saves the world from a nuclear disaster, but I don't understand why* he (= Sean Connery) *sometimes tends to overact.*
(13)   *James Bond* (= Sean Connery) *was fairly convincing in* Goldfinger, *but sometimes* he (= Sean Connery) *tends to overact.*
(14)   *?James Bond* (= Sean Connery) *was fairly convincing in* Goldfinger, *but I don't understand why* he (= James Bond) *took so long to save the world.*

In (11), where we have a target-in-source metonymy, "he" is grammatically anaphoric to Sean Connery, the source domain of the metonymy (although it refers conceptually to James Bond, the character). In (13), with a source-in-target metonymy, anaphoric "he" may only refer to Sean Connery, the metonymic target. Since, as shown by examples (12) and (14), it is not possible to break these correlations, it may be suggested that anaphoric reference makes use of the source domain of target-in-source metonymies, and of the target domain of source-in-target metonymies. In either case, it is the matrix domain (i.e. Sean Connery), rather than one of the subdomains, that is selected for reference. The reason for this probably lies in the fact that for anaphoric reference to be more workable, it is preferable to have a clear, unambiguous domain, and matrix domains usually qualify better in this respect than subdomains. Thus, the source of a metonymy of the source-in-target type needs to be developed into its matrix domain – as in the "ham sandwich" example – to be available for reference, while the target of a target-in-source metonymy, which is itself a subdomain of the source, is usually too vague to be an adequate candidate for anaphoric reference – as in *Nixon bombed Hanoi*, where "Nixon" refers rather imprecisely to some part of the army under Nixon's command.[3] And even though sometimes subdomains may be unambiguous, like "James Bond" in the examples above, a matrix domain is more likely to qualify for the requirements of anaphoric reference, if only because it contains more information. These observations become all the more evident if we consider the following extensions of examples (5) and (6) above (cf. Ruiz de Mendoza, 1997):

(15)   *The ham sandwich is waiting for his check, and* he *is getting restless.*
(16)   *?The ham sandwich is waiting for his check, and* it *looks rather stale.*
(17)   *Nixon bombed Hanoi, and* he *knew what* he *was doing.*
(18)   *?Nixon bombed Hanoi, but* they *were under orders* (where "they" refers to the soldiers who did the bombing).

In the ham sandwich examples, only the target of the metonymy, which is the matrix domain for "customer", is available for anaphoric reference. That is why (15) is correct while (16) is semantically anomalous. In (17) and (18), "Nixon", which is the source of the metonymy, is referred to by anaphoric "he" but not by "they", since "Nixon" is the matrix domain.

Our observations about anaphoric reference in relation to metonymy are capable of providing a more elegant, alternative explanation for two related linguistic phenomena which Nunberg (1995) has called "predicate transfer" and "deferred indexical reference". Nunberg (1995: 110) illustrates the distinction with the following examples:

(19)   *This is parked out back.*
(20)   *I am parked out back.*

Both (19) and (20) are uttered by a customer as he hands his key over to a parking lot attendant. Sentence (19) is a case of deferred indexical reference, and (20) of predicate transfer. In Nunberg's own words, deferred reference occurs when a demonstrative or indexical is allowed "to refer to an object that corresponds in a certain way to the contextual element picked out by a demonstration or by the semantic character of the expression". In a predicate transfer, on the other hand, "the name of a property that applies to something in one domain [is] used as the name of a property that applies to things in another domain, provided the two properties correspond in a certain way" (Nunberg 1995: 111). So, in (19) the demonstrative "this" refers to the customer's car in virtue of the semantic representation of the sentence (a key cannot be parked). In (20) the property of "being parked out back" is transferred from the domain of cars to the domain of people in such a way that the predicate "parked out back" contributes the property that a person possesses in virtue of the location of his car. In order to lend more support to his argument, Nunberg further notes that although both the demonstrative in (19) and the personal pronoun in (20) refer to the car, in (19) it is only possible to conjoin another predicate provided it describes the car, while a conjoined predicate in (20) can only describe the speaker, but not the car:

(21)   *This is parked out back and may not start.*
(22)   **This fits only the left front door and is parked out back.*
(23)   *I am parked out back and have been waiting for 15 minutes.*
(24)   **I am parked out back and may not start.*

According to Nunberg these examples are evidence that in (20), but not in (19), there is a transfer which involves the predicate and which is subject to two constraints: one is that there must be some sort of correspondence between the property denoted by the derived predicate (which is a characteristic of people) and the one designated by the original predicate (which is a feature of cars) (Nunberg, 1995: 112); the other is that the property contributed by the new predicate is to be "noteworthy" (Nunberg, 1995: 114). While this account is strong enough to rule out cases of deferred ostension as involving predicate transfer (probably because it is difficult to think of demonstratives and indexicals as either having or acquiring properties), it still falls short of accounting for why examples which strongly parallel the interpretation process in (19) do not involve predicate transfer. For example, the sentence *The ham sandwich is waiting for his check*, as we saw in (16) above, cannot take a conjoined predicate which describes the ham sandwich, in the same way as (21) cannot take a conjoined predicate that describes a property of the key, as is evident from (22). However, on the basis of the constraints on transfers described by Nunberg there is nothing that prevents "the ham sandwich" from acquiring the property designated by "is waiting for his check" since the property is noteworthy in the restaurant context and there is a functional correspondence between the ham sandwich and the property of the customer having ordered a ham sandwich.

This problem is sorted out by considering deferred reference and predicate transfer as subsidiary phenomena inside the framework of a broader theory of metonymy which takes into account its structural properties. Thus, in (19) the demonstrative refers to the key which the customer is holding up in his hand, which is a subdomain of the car to which it belongs. The metonymic mapping needed to interpret the sentence is no different from the one in the ham sandwich example. Predicate transfers, on the other hand, are explained as metonymies of the target-in-source type, as with *Nixon bombed Hanoi*. In (20) the personal pronoun is the source domain of a metonymy whose target ("the car") becomes, for the purpose of interpretation – and as cued by the predicate "parked out back" – a subdomain of the source. Then, the impossibility (or strong oddity) of examples (22) and (24) is accounted for by our more general observation that it is the matrix domain of a metonymic mapping that is used for semantic operations like anaphoric reference and conjoining. Finally, it is worth noting that our interpretation has the advantage of finding a motivation for transfer processes to take place or not in terms of the structural relationship between the conceptual domains involved. Thus, a predicate transfer occurs when the speaker is prompted by the predicate to perform a metonymic mapping in which the target is a subdomain of the source. Deferred indexical reference takes place when (i) the predicate demands a metonymic mapping in which it is the source that is a subdomain of the target, and (ii) the source domain is referred to by a demonstrative or indexical.

Nunberg has further noted – but not given the reason why – deferred reference is not possible when a description is used rather than a demonstrative, as in the following incorrect sentence:

(25)   *The key I'm holding is parked out back.*

However, since the expression "the key I'm holding" is evidently a subdomain of the car domain, we need to explain not only why deferred ostension is impossible in (25) but also why the metonymic mapping from key to car cannot be performed. One evident reason is that descriptions are intended to provide information about the referent in order to allow the hearer to identify it. In this process, the context plays a secondary role since the hearer only needs to match the features supplied by the expression with contextual information. Indexicals, on the other hand, have no descriptive content and their function is to draw the hearer's attention directly to the most accessible referent in a given context, which now plays a primary role. In the case of (25), the expression "the key I'm holding" leads the hearer to focus on the content of the description and then to find a referent which matches the description. Since the referent is the actual key the speaker has in his hand and the key cannot be parked, there is a strong semantic incompatibility between the subject and the predicate. In contrast to what happens with the ham sandwich example, this incompatibility cannot be solved metonymically since the hearer has first performed the referential operation which uniquely identifies the referent. Compare the similar oddity of a waitress holding up a ham sandwich and saying:

(26)   *The ham sandwich I'm holding is waiting for his check.*

In (26) the expression "the ham sandwich" may not stand for the customer who has ordered it because the expression uniquely identifies a specific ham sandwich which may hardly be associated with any of the customers. This hinders the mapping from ham sandwich to customer.

In the case of *This is parked out back* there is no internal incompatibility between subject and predicate since the subject has no descriptive content. There is only an external contextual incompatibility when the hearer understands that there is a mismatch between the object the speaker is holding and the content of the predicate (a key cannot be parked). Since a key is part of a car and a car may be parked, given the appropriate context (i.e. the parking lot), the key may metonymically become a token of the car.

Finally, in order to appreciate better the strength of our account, let us consider some examples which, being apparently similar to Nunberg's, cannot be explained adequately in terms of the distinction between deferred ostension and transfer mechanisms; but they do fit in well within our distinction between two metonymy types. Think of the following sentence, uttered by someone as he holds up a picture of the Coliseum in Rome in order to show it to a friend:

(27)   *This is Rome.*

In spite of its apparent similarity to the sentence *This is parked out back*, (27) presents a somewhat different situation. To begin with, there is a double metonymic mapping. Thus, there is a metonymy in which the source is the picture referred to by the demonstrative and the target – which is a subdomain of the source – is whatever is seen in the picture. The target is in turn the source of another metonymy whose target is Rome itself. In this second mapping, it is the source that is a subdomain of the target. Observe, also, that in (27) there is no "deferred" indexical reference since "this" simply refers to the picture which the speaker is holding in the presence of the hearer. The differences noted may account for why a sentence like (28) below, although certainly odd, would not necessarily be completely unacceptable like example (25):

(28)   ? *This picture (I'm holding) is Rome.*

In (28), the description "this picture I'm holding" as was the case with the description "the key I'm holding" in (25) above, provides information about the referent for the purpose of making identification possible. The hearer is, again, led to focus on the content of the description and then find a referent which satisfies the description. In (25) there was a strong semantic incompatibility between the description and the predicate "is parked out back", a situation which could not be solved metonymically once the best possible referent had already been identified in the immediate context. However, in (28), the incompatibility between the description and the predicate "is Rome" can be solved, to some extent, since it is contextually evident to the hearer that whatever is seen in the picture is part of it and, at the same time, part of Rome; which makes the metonymic operation feasible.

The existence of a double metonymy also explains the appropriateness of the following conjoined predicates:

(29)   *This is Rome, but* it*'s a bit blurred.*
(30)   *This is Rome, and* it*'s a really beautiful place.*

In (29) the anaphoric pronoun refers to the source matrix domain "picture" (i.e. the picture as an image[4]), while in (30) it refers to the target matrix domain "Rome" (i.e. the city). Since in both cases it is a matrix domain that is used for reference, the acceptability of (29) and (30) is in full accord with our previous observations in this respect. Note, in contrast, that anaphoric reference to the subdomain "the Coliseum" (which is the target of the first metonymy and the source of the second) is not possible, something also predicted according to our account:

(31)   *This is Rome, and* it*'s a really nice building.*

5. Conceptual interaction

The problem of the interaction between metaphor and metonymy has been discussed in Cognitive Linguistics (see, for example, Goossens, 1990, Barcelona, this volume, and Barcelona 1997). In this section it will be argued that the distinction between part-for-whole and whole-for-part metonymies is also helpful to understand some aspects of the interaction between metaphor and metonymy. We may observe two basic interactional possibilities: one, in which a metonymic mapping provides the source for a metaphor – as will be seen in our analysis of example (32) below – and another in which the output of a metaphoric mapping becomes the source of a metonymy, as in (33). There is still a third possibility, which is but a variation of the latter, where a metonymy determines in what sense a specific correspondence within a metaphoric mapping has to be interpreted, as in example (34). It should be noted, however, that these possibilities are less consequential for the ultimate interpretation of the interaction than the mapping type in terms of our distinction between target-in-source and source-in-target metonymies. Consider the following examples:

(32)   *He got up on his hind legs to defend his views.*
(33)   *He kept his eyes peeled for pickpockets.*
(34)   *She could read my mind.*

Goossens (1990: 335) has treated the expression "get up on one's hind legs" as a case of metaphor within a metonymy. In it, a person stands up to argue in public. So, the action of standing up is used metonymically for the whole scene. The addition of "hind" introduces the metaphorical element thereby forcing the hearer to reinterpret the expression in terms of an animal standing up, which suggests greater effort. This explanation contains the essential ingredients for the interpretation of (32). However, it may be argued that rather than a metaphor within a metonymy, what we have in (32) is a metonymy within the source of a metaphoric mapping in which animal behavior is mapped onto human behavior. From this point of view, we first have access through metonymy to the overall scene of an animal (typically a horse) suddenly moving (out of fear) the front part of its body upwards, its forelegs adopting an attacking position. This scene is metaphorically mapped onto another scene in which a person briskly stands up and moves his arms or hands in a threatening way in order to argue in public. Note that the target of this metaphor could in turn become the source of another metaphoric mapping in a situation in which the person who argues in public does not actually stand up. In this case, the overall energetic behavior of a person standing up and making vigorous gestures would be mapped onto the particular energetic behavior which the actual person displays in stating his views. As we noted in a previous section, the metaphor maps animal behavior onto human behavior in relation to a whole scene or situation which provides a common background of similarities for the correspondence to be possible. This does not mean, however, that this is a case of many-correspondence metaphor, since the elements of the scene are subsidiary to the mapping from animal behavior to human behavior and both the source and target scenes are non-abstract, well structured domains. A simplified version of the whole process is given in figure 1:

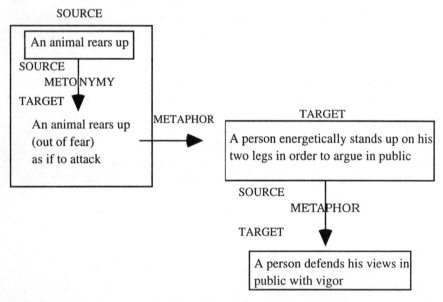

Figure 1. Source-in-target metonymy within the metaphoric source.

It may be observed that the metonymy is one of the source-in-target type and that its main function is to develop the source of the metaphor for full interpretation to be possible. The role of this kind of metonymy is the same independently of whether it acts on the source or on the target of the metaphoric mapping. This is readily appreciated if we examine example (33). In it, a person is described as performing the counterfactual action of "peeling" his eyes as the only way of keeping them wide open. The target of this metaphor then maps onto a more general situation in which a person keeps his eyes open in order to be alert to the dangers around him. Again, there is a source-in-target metonymy whose function this time is to develop the target of the metaphoric mapping, as can be seen in figure 2.

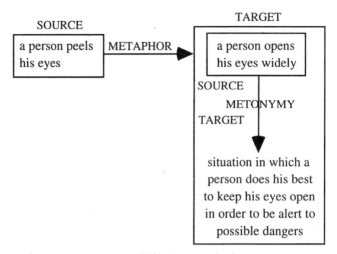

Figure 2. Source-in-target metonymy within the metaphoric target.

Finally, take example (34). In it, the mind is seen as a text which can be read and understood, and the person's thoughts, which are part of the mind, become readable. Here, the metonymy is – unlike the ones in examples (32) and (33) – one of the target-in-source type. Its function is to highlight that part of its source domain (the thoughts) which is relevant for the understanding of the metaphoric correspondence on which it operates, thus focusing on one possible meaning of *mind*. The process is diagrammed in figure 3.

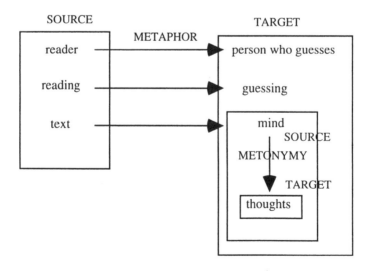

Figure 3. Target-in-source metonymy within the metaphoric target.

The functions of source-in-target and target-in-source metonymies in cases of metaphor-metonymy interaction are, in principle, no different from their functions outside an interaction: the former develop a conceptual domain, while the latter highlight some relevant aspect of it. However, in the interaction, source-in-target metonymies serve the additional purpose of signaling to the hearer where to find the central inference from the metaphoric mapping. Thus, both in (32) and (33) the metonymic source draws our attention specially to a specific key action within the whole scene (the person energetically standing up and the person opening up his eyes, respectively). Target-in-source metonymies, on the other hand, only allow us to understand the nature of one of the meta-phoric correspondences (for example, what is meant by "mind" in (34) above), independently of the central inference (i.e. the idea that a certain person is capable of doing a surprisingly accurate type of guesswork), which is cued by the predicate of the metaphoric expression.

6. Generic spaces

Part of our observations so far have allowed us to understand better the impor-tant role of metonymy in some cases of conceptual interaction where both metaphor and metonymy are involved. So far, we have dealt with metaphor and metonymy, following the tradition originated by the work of Lakoff and his collaborators, as involving two domains. However, fairly recently Mark Turner and Gilles Fauconnier have revised the traditional two-domain model in a very interesting way (see especially, Turner – Fauconnier, 1995; Fauconnier – Turner, 1996; and Ruiz de Mendoza, 1998 for discussion and refinement of some aspects of their model). They have proposed what they called the "many-space model" of metaphor and conceptual projection. This model is based on the notion of "mental space", which they define as "a (relatively small) conceptual packet built for purposes of local understanding and action" (Turner – Fau-connier, 1995: 184). A mental space typically recruits information from more than one conceptual domain to develop its own structure, always smaller than the structure of the input domains. In this account, the source and the target of a mapping are mental spaces. Other spaces are the "blend", a rich conceptual structure which integrates part of the structure from input spaces like the source and target of metaphors, and the generic space, which contains skeletal structure that applies to the input spaces and allows their correlation. For example, in sentence (1) above, *The senator's proposals were attacked in the newspapers*, the attacks may be mapped onto negative criticism since both elements share the general property of causing harmful effects; similarly, the enemy may be mapped onto the journalists since both are the instigators of certain damaging activities.

Turner and Fauconnier's analysis revealingly applies to all the types of con-ceptual interaction which we have examined in the previous section, as reflected in examples (32)-(34), but in different ways. As will be seen, when the metonymy involved in the interaction is one of the source-in-target type, its role is to provide all the elements of conceptual structure necessary for the creation of a generic space which will license the basic metaphoric mapping. On the other hand, a target-in-source metonymy cannot perform that function since it serves the purpose of highlighting part of a domain in order to determine the exact nature of a correspondence within a metaphor. In this latter case, the generic space which licenses the correlation between the source and target spaces has to be abstracted away from both, as in example (34). In the former, the generic space is constructed exclusively on the basis of the space which has been acted upon by the metonymy, as in examples (32) and (33). To give just one example of the way the full interaction takes place, we detail below how this may work for example (32). We need to bear in mind that our previous diagram for (32) was an out-of-context idealization. However, imagine that (32) had been uttered in connection to a student's angry and threatening attitude of standing up to argue as he shakes his right fist when taking part in a debate between two contending teams (for the sake of simplicity we do not take into account the possibility of a second metaphoric mapping for the case in which the person might not stand up):

Table 1. Full interaction process for example (32) in a context

SOURCE (INPUT SPACE 1)	GENERIC SPACE	TARGET (INPUT SPACE 2)
– An animal,	– An animate entity,	– An angry student,
– in an apparently dangerous situation,	– in a stressful situation,	– taking part in a difficult debate with his team,
– rears up,	– performs a sudden, upward energetic movement,	– stands up to argue,
– out of fear or anger,	– emotionally driven,	– in anger,
– behaving aggressively	– behaving in a potentially harmful way,	– shaking his fist and generally behaving in an aggressive way,
– and without control,	– and without control,	– and without control,
– as if to attack an enemy.	– against an enemy.	– against (attacks from) the other contending team.

BLENDED SPACE

An angry student, taking part in a difficult and stressing debate with his team, suddenly and energetically stands up to argue, moved by anger, shaking his fist very aggressively and threateningly, without control, with the intention of frightening the contending team.
The student cannot be calmed down easily, he might be dangerous to others, etc.

Note that we regard the blend as the mental space where the language user interprets information in terms of the metaphoric correspondences and also where reasoning by implication takes place. The generic space, on the other hand, is the result of a mental operation of abstraction. It is created in order to control the mapping process, and its structure depends fully on the metonymic development of the source of the metaphor. Much the same may be said about example (33), *He kept his eyes peeled for pickpockets*, where the metonymy, which develops the target of the metaphor, allows the generic space to be constructed. Such a space will contain a person who performs an action (opening the eyes), in a certain way (so that they may not be closed) and for a specific purpose (being alert to danger). Note that most of this information is not derivable from the underspecified source, but it is the source that provides us with the clue to access the most central information (i.e. that the person will keep his eyes wide open) which may be later developed metonymically. In contrast, the metonymy in (34), *She could read my mind*, which is of the target-in-source type, has no role in the construction of the generic space which will license the metaphoric mapping. This space is derived from the correlation between the metaphoric source and target independently of the metonymy. Thus, in both source and target there is a doer, an action, and an affected entity. It is these elements that make up the generic space.

7. Primary and secondary domains

We shall finally examine the question of the centrality of domains in metonymy. This is a question which evidently does not affect metaphor, where the mapping is carried out across domains. However, in metonymy there is a domain-subdomain relationship in which a given subdomain may have either primary or secondary status, i.e. may be more or less central. We shall show that there is an important correlation between the nature of subdomains in terms of centrality and the nature of the relationship between source and target in terms of inclusion.

Here, it may prove useful to discuss what Croft (1993) has called "domain highlighting", a process which, in his view, is characteristic, though not exclusive, of metonymic mappings. Consider one of his examples (Croft, 1993: 348):

(35)   *Proust is tough to read.*

According to Croft, in this sentence, there is a metonymic shift from Proust to Proust's literary work. In the encyclopedic view of semantics – which Croft, with other cognitive linguists, upholds – the works of Proust are part of the concept of "Proust", although a less central part than the fact that he was a person. An encyclopedic characterization of "Proust" will include the domain of creative activity; since Proust was famous for being a writer, and the work produced is a salient element in the domain of creativity, there is nothing strange in the metonymic shift, which has the effect of giving primary status to what is otherwise (in its literal meaning) secondary in nature. Such an effect is called "domain highlighting".

Croft further argues that domain highlighting is typical of metonymy (not of metaphor) although it may also occur in other types of lexical ambiguity. In relation to this, he gives the following two examples:

(36)   *This book is heavy.*
(37)   *This book is a history of Iraq.*

The concept "book" may be used at least with reference to its physical characteristics, as in (36), or to its semantic content, as in (37). In Croft's terminology (which is largely Langacker's), the concept "book" may be "profiled" in the domain of physical objects or in the domain of semantic content. Croft points out that neither of these uses is metonymic since the elements profiled in each domain are highly intrinsic. The concept of intrinsicness is borrowed from Langacker (1987), who argues that a property is intrinsic to the extent that it makes no reference to external entities, as is the case with shape; size, on the other hand, would be extrinsic since it may only be understood by comparison with other objects (see Langacker, 1987: 160). As an example of the application of this concept, Croft gives another two examples:

(38)   *I broke the window.*
(39)   *She came in through the bathroom window.*

In Croft's view, these two uses of "window" highlight respectively the physical object and shape domains of the concept, but while the interpretation of a window as an opening in the shape domain makes reference to what is around it, which makes it extrinsic,[5] being a physical object is intrinsic to the concept. But – he goes on to argue – the shape domain for "window" seems to be less extrinsic than Proust's writings for "Proust", which makes (35) a clearer case of metonymy than (38) and shows that there is "a continuum between clear cases of metonymy and the highlighting of highly intrinsic facets of a concept" (Croft, 1993: 350).

While the process of domain highlighting is relevant for a description of metonymy, there are several problems with Croft's analysis. First, he assumes that a secondary domain is defined exclusively in terms of intrinsicness, which is only one of several criteria of centrality. In fact, in Langacker's account, centrality also correlates with the extent to which a semantic specification is conventional (i.e. shared by a community), generic (not idiosyncratic with a particular item), and characteristic (unique to the class of items concerned). If we apply the centrality criteria to (37) above, we will observe that all of them, except intrinsicness, are violated: books are not conventionally histories; being a history is not unique to the class of items designated by "book"; and it is not

generic knowledge that books are histories. Furthermore, the intrinsicness criterion is not a relevant measure of centrality in (37) since this sentence deals with
a non-physical property of books which cannot be defined in terms of external
entities. In contrast, all of the centrality criteria, except uniqueness (since other
classes of items share this property), are satisfied in (36): on the one hand, it is
generic and conventional knowledge that books have weight; on the other,
having weight is also an intrinsic property of books as physical entities. Having
weight is a fairly central characterization of "book" and therefore there is no
metonymy in (36). The situation in (37) is altogether different, since being a
history is not an essential but rather a peripheral characteristic of books. This
would allow the metonymic shift to take place. However, there are intuitively
clearer cases of metonymy, like (35), which is probably due to the higher degree
of lexicalization of the metonymic shift in (37).

Now, consider Croft's analysis of examples (38) and (39) as outlined above.
He argues that (39) is a metonymy but (38) is not, since being a physical object
is intrinsic to the concept window, while shape is extrinsic because it makes
reference to what is around it. However, this analysis is problematic. If we say
that someone has broken a window, we only think of a relevant part of it, i.e. the
window pane (not the window frame), that has actually been damaged. So, (38)
is a target-in-source metonymy where the whole domain stands for a subdomain.
On the other hand, (39) cannot be a metonymy since the central idea about a
window is that it is an opening (usually) in a wall. Note in this respect that it is
possible to think of a window without a pane or a frame, but we cannot think of
a window if there is not an opening of some sort. Interestingly enough, when
Langacker (1987: 160) discusses the concept of intrinsicness – which Croft
applies to identify (38) as a metonymy – he cites shape as an example of this
property for physical objects, in contrast to size, since size is understood, but
shape is not, by comparison with other objects. If we follow Langacker's logic,
a window is a physical object with a certain shape and size; while size is an
extrinsic property, shape is an intrinsic property of windows. We may, therefore,
wonder why Croft has reached exactly the opposite conclusion. The source of
the contradiction is perhaps found in that shape may be either an intrinsic or an
extrinsic property of things. Thus, if one uses the word "window" to describe a
physical object in a hardware store room – which is, incidentally, Croft's illustration – its shape is an extrinsic property; but if we think of a window in a wall,
a roof, or the side of a vehicle – the usual places – its shape is an intrinsic
property. Again, we feel that it is centrality as a combination of features that is
the key to identifying metonymies of the target-in-source kind.

Croft also tends to associate domain highlighting with metonymy and other
related polysemy phenomena, but not with metaphor. He contends that domain
mapping occurs with dependent predications and domain highlighting with
autonomous predications, as if both were completely independent phenomena.
Thus, in *He's in love*, "in" is dependent on the rest of the expression and induces

domain mapping. In *He likes to read the* Marquis de Sade, where there is domain highlighting, the object is autonomous relative to the main verb which is dependent on it (see Croft, 1993: 355-358).

These observations are correct but incomplete. First, they tend to avoid discussing metonymy as the result of a mapping process. Thus, Croft tends to place too much emphasis on metonymy as involving a reference shift and domain highlighting. As a consequence, he has not observed, as we have, that some metonymic mappings are not referential, but predicative (e.g. *He's an excellent brain*). Second, domain highlighting and domain mapping are treated as if they were incompatible phenomena. In fact, the situation is rather different since, as may be observed, the mapping process is previous to the highlighting process and domain highlighting also occurs in one-correspondence metaphors. For example, if we take again metaphor (4) above, *Achilles is a lion*, it may be noticed that "courage" is not as central a feature of lions as, for example, their having four legs or the fact that they hunt and eat other animals. Nevertheless, "courage" becomes a relevant feature for the purpose of the metaphor, since it is cued by the conventional mapping PEOPLE ARE ANIMALS, which only allows, as we saw before, behavioral attributes to be mapped from source to target. In this sense, "courage" becomes a primary domain.

Finally, if we compare the metaphor *He's in love* with the metonymy *He likes to read the Marquis de Sade* from the point of view of domain mapping and domain highlighting, we arrive at somewhat different conclusions from the ones pointed out by Croft. In the metonymy, the expression "Marquis de Sade" stands for the literary work. We may agree with Croft that in this metonymy highlighting is induced by the dependent predication. But we may also note that there is a mapping which is induced by the autonomous predication, as with the metaphor *He's in love*. However, in this metaphor there is no domain highlighting since it is not a one-correspondence metaphor but a many-correspondence one where love is conceptualized as a container: the person corresponds to an entity inside a container; the container walls are the impediments the person has in order to get out of the container; the (positive) conditions inside the container map onto positive love feelings; and so on. So there is no highlighting in the sense of making primary a secondary domain, but in the sense that one of the correspondences is cued as central for understanding (i.e. the idea that the person is inside the "love container"). Here, it may be useful to refer back to the diagram for sentence (34) above, where the predicate "read" cues the "reading-guessing" correspondence as central for the metaphoric mapping, while the "mind-thoughts" metonymy raises to primary status its target domain. Note that since the mind is understood metaphorically as a container for ideas, the primary domain for mind would be its "container" qualities, while what is found inside it would become a secondary domain.

From our discussion, it becomes evident that, in metonymy, if we have a case where the target is a subdomain of the source, the target must be a secondary or non-central domain; on the other hand, if we have a source-in-target metonymy, it is immaterial whether the source is deemed to be a primary or a secondary domain. Now, if we combine all the criteria which we have proposed as definitional for metonymy, we may say that a metonymy is a one-correspondence conceptual mapping within a domain where, if the target is part of the source, the target is not a primary or central subdomain of the source (see Ruiz de Mendoza, 1997: 171).

8. Conclusions

We have examined different aspects of metonymy in relation to metaphor and other polysemy phenomena. We have come to the conclusion that metonymic mappings are very similar to mappings for "one-correspondence" metaphors, but they are crucially differentiated from metaphors in that the former involve a domain-internal mapping, whereas in the latter the mapping is carried out across domains. This fact has consequences in that in metonymies the structural relations which hold in the source can hardly be mapped onto the target since source and target stand in an inclusion relationship. This in turn lies at the base of the strong tendency for metonymies to be used referentially. We have also discussed the role of the relationship between a matrix domain and its subdomains in metonymy. We have been able to correlate cases of what we have called source-in-target metonymy with the function of developing a conceptual domain for full interpretation. Cases of target-source inclusion, on the other hand, may only be metonymies if the putative target is a secondary or non-central domain which requires highlighting. We have provided arguments in favor of these two metonymy types by discussing their different roles in several semantic phenomena, including anaphoric reference, predicate conjoining, and conceptual interaction.

Notes

1. Financial support for this research has been provided by the DGES, grant no. PB96-0520. Correspondence to Francisco J. Ruiz de Mendoza, Universidad de La Rioja, Dept. de Filologías Modernas, C/La Cigüeña, 60. 26004 Logroño (La Rioja, Spain); e-mail: franruiz@dfm.unirioja.es; tel. (941) 299433; fax.: (941) 299419. I am grateful to the anonymous reviewers of this article and particularly to the editor, Antonio Barcelona, for a number of very useful comments.

2. The traditional idea that in metonymy parts are associated with parts (see, for example the treatment in Ullmann (1962: 218) has crept into the extant cognitive accounts, as is evident from Lakoff & Turner's (1989: 103) discussion and from Taylor's suggestion that "the essence of metonymy resides in the possibility of establishing connections between entities which co-occur within a given concep-

tual structure" (Taylor, 1995: 123-124).

3. In fact this kind of metonymy is often used either when the speaker cannot clearly describe the referent which he wants the addressee to identify or when, even though he can, he finds it more economical – and still equally effective from the communicative standpoint – not to describe it fully. For example, in *Wall Street is facing changes* it is immaterial to pinpoint accurately what sectors within the Wall Street financial system are going to undergo the changes. From the expression *Apple is selling part of its assets*, we cannot tell who has made the decision or who is in charge of the sale, which does not necessarily mean that the speaker could not have provided the exact information.

4. In the context given, "picture" is profiled in the domain of images rather than in the domain of photographic materials.

5. In this Croft's analysis seems to contradict Langacker's view of shape as intrinsic. We explain away the apparent contradiction below.

References

Barcelona, Antonio
    1997   "Clarifying and applying the notions of metaphor and metonymy within Cognitive Linguistics", *Atlantis*, vol. 19-1, 21-48.
    this volume "On the plausibility of claiming a metonymic motivation for conceptual metaphor."
Croft, William
    1993   "The role of domains in the interpretation of metaphors and metonymies", *Cognitive Linguistics* 4-4: 335-370.
Fauconnier, Gilles – Eve Sweetser (eds.)
    1996   *Spaces, worlds and grammars.* Chicago: University of Chicago Press.
Fauconnier, Gilles – Mark Turner
    1996   "Blending as a central process of grammar", in: Adele Goldberg (ed.), 113-130.
Goldberg, Adele (ed.)
    1996   *Conceptual structure, discourse and language.* Stanford, CA: CSLI Publications.
Goossens, Louis
    1990   "Metaphtonymy: the interaction of metaphor and metonymy in expressions for linguistic action", *Cognitive Linguistics* 1-3: 323-340.
Lakoff, George
    1987   *Women, fire, and dangerous things: What categories reveal about the mind.* Chicago: University of Chicago Press.
    1993   "The contemporary theory of metaphor", in: Andrew Ortony, (ed.), 202-251.
    1996   "The internal structure of the Self", in: Gilles Fauconnier – Eve Sweetser (eds.),
Lakoff, George – Mark Johnson
    1980   *Metaphors we live by.* Chicago & London: The University of Chicago Press.

Lakoff, George – Mark Turner
   1989   *More than cool reason. A field guide to poetic metaphor.* Chicago &
           London: The University of Chicago Press.
Langacker, Ronald W.
   1987   *Foundations of cognitive grammar*, vol. i, *Theoretical prerequisites.*
           Stanford: Stanford University Press.
Nunberg, Geoffrey
   1995   "Transfers of meaning", *Journal of Semantics* 12: 109-132.
Ortony, Andrew (ed.)
   1993   *Metaphor and thought.* (2nd. edition.) Cambridge: Cambridge Univer-
           sity Press.
Ruiz de Mendoza, Francisco
   1997   "Cognitive and pragmatic aspects of metonymy", in: Antonio Barcelona
           (ed.), *Cognitive linguistics in the study of the English language and
           literature in English.* Murcia: University of Murcia. Monograph issue
           of *Cuadernos de Filología Inglesa*, 6.2: 161-178.
   1997   "Metaphor, metonymy, and conceptual interaction", *Atlantis* 19-1,
           281-295.
   1998   "On the nature of blending as a cognitive phenomenon", *Journal of
           Pragmatics* 30/3: 259-274.
Taylor, John R.
   1995   *Linguistic categorization. Prototypes in linguistic theory.* (2nd. edition.)
           Oxford: Clarendon Press.
Turner, Mark – Gilles Fauconnier
   1995   "Conceptual integration and formal expression", *Metaphor and Sym-
           bolic Activity* 10: 183-204.
Ullmann, Stephen
   1962   *Semantics: An introduction to the science of meaning.* Oxford: Basil
           Blackwell.

Metaphor, metonymy, and binding*

Mark Turner and Gilles Fauconnier

Conceptual integration – also known as "blending" or "mental binding" – is a basic mental operation whose uniform structural and dynamic properties apply over many areas of thought and action, including metaphor and metonymy. (Analyses of conceptual integration are given in Coulson 1996 and n.d., Fauconnier & Turner 1994, 1996, 1998, in press, and in preparation; Oakley n.d.; Turner & Fauconnier 1995, in press a, and in press b, Fauconnier 1997, and Turner 1996a and 1996b.

The website is http://www.wam.umd.edu/~mturn/WWW/blending.html.)

Contemporary accounts of metaphor and analogy have focused on structure-mapping from a source (or base) onto a target. Such mappings can exploit existing common schematic structure between domains, or project new structure from the source onto the target. The work on conceptual blending has shown that in addition to such mappings, there are dynamic integration processes which build up new "blended" mental spaces. Such spaces develop emergent structure which is elaborated in the on-line construction of meaning and serves as an important locus of cognitive activity.

1. "If Clinton were the Titanic, ..."

"If Clinton were the Titanic, the iceberg would sink" is a striking conceptual blend that circulated inside the Washington, D.C. Beltway during February, 1998, when the movie "Titanic" was popular and President Clinton seemed to be surviving political damage from yet another alleged sexual scandal. The blend has two input mental spaces – one with the Titanic and the other with President Clinton. There is a partial cross-space mapping between these inputs: Clinton is the counterpart of the Titanic and the scandal is the counterpart of the iceberg. There is a blended space in which Clinton is the Titanic and the scandal is the iceberg. This blend takes much of its organizing frame structure from the Titanic input space – it has a voyage by a ship toward a destination and it has the ship's running into something enormous in the water – but it takes crucial causal structure and event shape structure from the Clinton scenario – Clinton is not ruined but instead survives. There is a generic space that has structure taken to apply to both inputs: one entity that is involved in an activity and is motivated by some purpose encounters another entity that poses an extreme threat to that activity. In the generic space, the outcome of that encounter is not specified.

The cross-space mapping between the inputs is metaphoric, with the Titanic scenario as source and the Clinton scenario as target, but the blend has causal and event shape structure that do not come from the source, indeed are contrary to the source and in some cases impossible for the source, and the central inference of the metaphor cannot be projected from the source. If Clinton is the Titanic and the scandal is the iceberg and we project inferences from the source, then Clinton must lose the presidency. But the contrary inference is the one that is constructed: Clinton will overcome any political difficulty. The blend has emergent structure: in the blend, the Titanic is unsinkable after all, and it is possible for ice to sink, not merely to be submerged.

The source does not provide these inferences to the blend, but neither are they copied into it from the target. In the original target space with Clinton and the scandal, the relative status of the elements and even the nature of their interaction is far from clear. In that target, Clinton merely seems to be surviving the scandal. But these elements take on much sharper and more extreme status in the blend: the scandal-iceberg is the greatest conceivable threat, something that "sinks" even the "unsinkable," and the Clinton-Titanic survives even this greatest conceivable threat. The extreme superiority of Clinton as a force and the extreme status of the scandal as a threat are constructed in the blend, as is their predictive inference that Clinton will survive. This structure, which is not available from the source or the target, is constructed in the blend and projected to the target to reframe it and give it new and clearer inferences.

Further inferencing is possible if we know that the threat to Clinton comes principally from special prosecutor Kenneth Starr's use of the scandal to investigate whether Clinton is guilty of perjury and subornation to perjury. In that case, not only the scandal but also Starr can be projected to the iceberg in the blend. Originally, the antagonism between Clinton and the special prosecutor is understood as asymmetric: the President is at risk, not the special prosecutor. In fact, this asymmetry yields a strong match between the original source and target – just as the iceberg can sink the Titanic but not the other way around, so Starr can ruin Clinton but not conversely. (Technically, the President can fire the special prosecutor, and Nixon did fire a special prosecutor, but firing in this special case is tantamount to beatification.). Accordingly, models that view metaphor or analogy as the retrieval of two concepts and the location of the "strongest" match between them must stop with the inference that Clinton is doomed. But in this case, the sinking of the iceberg by the Titanic emphasizes the ferocious attack on Starr by Clinton and his allies, featuring Hilary Clinton's accusation that Starr is part of a "vast right-wing conspiracy", "trying to overturn the results of two elections." In the blend, but in neither the source nor the target as originally framed, the contest is symmetric. Starr can be ruined, and he will be ruined. You thought that special prosecutors, like icebergs, were unsinkable, but not so. This reframing, constructed in the blend, is projected to the target.

The emergence of meaning and inference in blended spaces was overlooked as a theoretical issue in earlier work on basic metaphor, probably because the focus on abstract mappings at the superordinate level obscured some of the principles of on-line construction of meaning in actual, specific cases. It is uncontroversial that cases like the Clinton-Titanic example involve the basic metaphor PURPOSEFUL ACTIVITY IS TRAVELING ALONG A PATH TOWARD A DESTINA-TION – the traveler projects to the agent, reaching the destination projects to achieving the goal, and so on, as analyzed in Lakoff and Turner (1989, *passim*), Lakoff (1993, *passim*), and Turner (1996b: 88-90). But that metaphor cannot by itself yield the complex inferences outlined above. It is in the blended space that we construct and run the complex counterfactual scenario in which the Titanic sinks the iceberg, and it is that scenario which projects to the input of politics and society to provide the appropriate inferences regarding Clinton, Starr, and the effect of the scandal. This scenario is newsworthy by virtue of what actually happened to the Titanic, and by virtue of the connections from the blend to the current political situation. It would not have been newsworthy before April 14, 1912, given the expectation that "The Wonder Ship," double-bottomed and able to float with as many as four of its sixteen compartments flooded, could not be sunk.

2. Binding, metonymy, and basic metaphors

Actually, it is possible to find in even the most studied of basic metaphors blending and its interaction with metaphor and metonymy. George Lakoff and Zoltán Kövecses provide an impressive analysis of metaphoric understandings of anger in *Women, Fire, and Dangerous Things* (Lakoff 1987: 380-416). This analysis reveals the required mapping between folk models of heat and folk models of anger. In this mapping, a heated container maps to an angry individual, heat maps to anger, smoke/steam (a sign of heat) maps to signs of anger, explosion maps to extreme, uncontrolled, anger. This is reflected in conventional vocabulary: *He was steaming. She was filled with anger. I had reached the boiling point. I was fuming. He exploded. I blew my top.*

Lakoff and Kövecses also note the important basis for this metaphor in the folk theory of the physiological effects of anger: increased body heat, blood pressure, agitation, redness in face. The metonymy linking emotions to their physiological effects allows expressions like the following to refer to anger: *He gets hot under the collar. She was red with anger. I almost burst a blood vessel.*

The metaphor and the metonymy define the following kinds of correspondences:

Table 1. Conceptual correspondences in the ANGER IS HEAT metaphor and in the metonymy linking emotions to physiological effects

SOURCE	TARGET	
"physical events"	"emotions"	"physiology"
container	person	person
heat	anger	body heat
steam	sign of anger	perspiration, redness
explode	show extreme anger	acute shaking, loss of physiological control
boiling point	highest degree of emotion	

The metaphor can be elaborated in various ways:

(1)   *God, he was so mad I could see the smoke coming out of his ears.*

The ears are now mapped onto an orifice of the container in the source. Notice that in this example, and also in the more conventional ones like *He exploded*, the description of the emotion is *presented* as a physiological reaction of the individual. Something is happening to his body, e.g. smoke coming out of the ears. But the *content* of this physiological reaction is *not* obtained through the metonymy in the target. It comes from the *source* (physical events pertaining to heated containers – smoke coming out, explosion, etc.).

The phrase *the smoke coming out of his ears* does not describe anything directly in the source (where smoke comes out of kettles on fire) or in the target (where people's physiology does not include internal combustion). There is selective projection from both inputs, leading to a novel frame in the blend: although there are no ears in the source domain and no smoke in the target domain, the organizing frame of the blend has both and they interact.

In the conceptual integration network model, Lakoff and Kövecses' important observation about the correlation of the physiological reactions with the source domain of heat and fire can be reflected theoretically. "Explosion" cannot be a physiological reaction in the source (where there is no physiology) or in the target (where there is in fact not much heat), but it can in the blend, where a body can explode from anger.

In the blended space, we find the people and their emotions projected from a target input space; we find the corresponding physiological reactions projected either from the source Input of physical heat, explosion, and boiling, or from the target Input of the body physiology linked to the emotions.

The following set of correspondences holds:

Table 2. Correspondences in the ANGER IS HEAT conceptual integration network

SOURCE	BLEND	TARGET	
Input Space 1 "physical events"	*Blended Space*	*Input Space 2* "emotions"	*Input Space 3* "physiology"
container	person/container	person	person
orifice	ears/orifice		ears
heat	heat/anger	anger	body heat
steam/smoke	steam/smoke	sign of anger	perspiration, redness
explode	explode	show extreme anger	acute shaking, loss of physiological control
boiling point	boiling/highest degree of emotion	highest degree of emotion	

If the Blend stood by itself, it could not be interpreted in the real world because anger does not produce smoke or explosion. But in the network model, the Blend remains linked to the Inputs. A sentence like *He was so mad I could see the smoke coming out of his ears* is directly identifying the blend, but inferences in the blend – e.g. smoke is a sign of great anger – are projected back to the Target Input Spaces – he was extremely angry and was showing physiological signs of it. (What these signs actually were is irrelevant.) Of course, the structure of the Blend itself is highly dependent on the conventional metaphorical mapping of heat to anger.

In addition, we find an explanation for the actual grammatical structure of the sentences with mixed vocabulary, like *He exploded, I could see the smoke coming out of his ears*. This analysis explains why the sentence evokes an integrated scene unavailable in either source or target; it applies directly to the Blend. It provides a frame (seeing somebody in an abnormal and dangerous state, with corresponding emotions, etc.) not available in the source or target.

Next, the blend can have a life of its own, not fully determined by the inputs. So, we can say, with some hyperbole:

(2)   *God, was he ever mad. I could see the smoke coming out of his ears – I thought his hat would catch fire!*

It is easy to see how this works: in the blend, the hat on fire is a sign of even greater heat, hence even greater anger, emotions, etc. But there is no counterpart for the hat in the source: the elaboration is in the blend, where the frame of somebody on fire is used (not the boiling kettle anymore), and the existing mapping operates towards the source (greater heat) and towards the target (greater anger, but also greater loss of control, greater social danger, etc.)

The Lakoff – Kövecses analysis underscores the essential role of physiological reaction metonymies in the formation of the metaphorical system for emotions. The metonymic correspondences are in the target – body heat, redness, etc. That maps directly onto the blend, in the sense that in the blend (but not in the target), the physiological reactions are smoke, explosion, etc. This is done by mapping *hot* (in the target, for people with a certain physiology) to *hot* in the source (for containers with quite different physical properties), and then from source to blend, where the new set of physiological reactions is constructed.

3. Metonymy projection in metaphoric blends

The interaction of metaphor, metonymy, and binding is particularly evident in the canonical representation of "death" as "the Grim Reaper," a sinister, skeleton-like character holding a scythe and wearing a cowl (see Turner & Fauconnier 1995). The Grim Reaper arises by blending many spaces: (1) a space with individual human dying; (2) a space with an abstract pattern of causal tautology in which an event of a certain kind is caused by an abstract causal element: e.g., Death causes dying, Sleep causes sleeping, Smell causes smell, Sloth causes laziness, and so on; (3) a space containing a prototypical human killer; and (4) a space with reapers in the scenario of harvest.

This complex blend allows non-counterparts to be combined by virtue of metonymic connections in the inputs. Reapers and skeletons are not counterparts in the cross-space mapping. But Death as a cause is metonymically associated with *skeleton* as an effect. In the blend, the killer-reaper is combined with the skeleton in a way that fits the frame in the blend (people have skeletons). Similarly, Death in the input space of human dying is metonymically associated with priests: priests are stereotypically present at an event of death, and their institution is concerned with death and afterlife. Reapers and priests are not metaphoric counterparts. In the blend, the attire of The Grim Reaper can be the attire of a monk: the metonymy between death and priests in the input is projected to a part-whole relation in the blend. The cowl, for example, pulled over the head of The Grim Reaper at once evokes both religious connotations of death and the impression of Death as mysterious, unknown, solitary, and set apart from norms of human society.

In Fauconnier and Turner (1998), we offer evidence for the following competing optimality principles on integration networks:

Integration:
The blend must constitute a tightly integrated scene that can be manipulated as a unit. More generally, every space in the network should have integration. (Example: a ship hitting something and sinking it is a well-integrated scene, although in this case it is somewhat fantastic for somebody who knows that icebergs cannot sink.)

Web:

Manipulating the blend as a unit must maintain the web of appropriate connections to the input spaces easily and without additional surveillance or computation. (Example: as the Titanic blend gets elaborated, the connections to the inputs are not altered; compare with "If Clinton were the Titanic, the Titanic would be the iceberg.")

Unpacking:

It is optimal for the blend alone to allow reconstruction of the inputs, the cross-space mapping, the generic space, and the network of connections between all these spaces (Example: "I could see the smoke coming out of his ears. He exploded with anger." The literal meaning is impossible, which makes it easy to assign "smoke" and "explode" to the HEAT input, and "he" and "anger" to the EMOTIONS input.)

Topology:

For any input space and any element in that space projected into the blend, it is optimal for the relations of the element in the blend to match the relations of its counterpart. (Example: The Titanic's hitting the iceberg in the TITANIC input matches the Titanic's hitting the iceberg in the blend. The strength and buoyancy of Clinton versus Starr in the POLITICS input matches the strength and buoyancy of the Titanic versus the iceberg in the blend.)

Good reason:

All things being equal, if an element appears in the blend, there will be pressure to find significance for this element. Significance will include relevant links to other spaces and relevant functions in running the blend. (Example: Once the anger-heat blend is launched, we are unlikely to interpret "He was smoking" as purely incidental information about his use of tobacco at the moment.)

Metonymy projection constraint:

When an element is projected from an input to the blend and a second element from that input is projected because of its metonymic link to the first, shorten the metonymic distance between them in the blend. (Example: the skeleton becomes the bodily form of The Grim Reaper.)

We saw above that blending can combine non-counterpart elements from a single input, such as Death, the cowl of the priest, and the skeleton of the person who has died. The metonymic distance is large between abstract death as the general cause of all deaths and the cowl worn by a certain kind of participant in a ritual associated with particular deaths. But in the blend, the metonymic connection is direct: the cowl is the attire of Death. Similarly, the skeleton after decomposition of the body is a distant product of death. But in the blend the skeleton is actually a body part of Death. The fact that metonymy is preserved in such cases can be viewed as a consequence of Topology. The metonymy projection constraint additionally specifies that metonymies get tighter under projection.

Satisfying the metonymic projection constraint is not a matter of blindly projecting metonymic links. The internal integration of the blend provides opportunities for some acceptable metonymies but not for others. Since Death is an active person in the blend, and active persons are known to have skeletons (although they are not normally visible), the part-whole metonymy skeleton-body becomes available as the counterpart of the distant metonymy in the input. Tightening metonymies under projection typically optimizes Integration in the blend, since it helps build a tighter and more easily manipulated unit.

Now consider some additional cases that show how metonymy projection operates. Take the example of a cartoon representing a powerful newspaper company about to succeed in a hostile takeover of a weaker automobile company that will be eliminated by selling off its assets. The cartoon shows a giant printing press smashing a car. This is a metaphorical blend: input one has the stronger and weaker objects; input two has the contest between companies. The cross-space mapping is the basic metaphor that maps stronger objects destroying weaker objects to winning and losing. The strong heavy object is mapped onto the powerful newspaper company; the weaker object is mapped onto the weaker automobile company. But in the blend, we find the printing press as the strong heavy object and the car as the weak object. This is an efficient exploitation of internal connections: the printing press is a salient instrument of producing newspapers, and cars are the salient products of automobile companies. In the input, the printing press is not an instrument of destruction, but it has a force-dynamic function associated with crushing which can be associated with a car-smashing machine of the sort used in recycling automobiles. In the blend, the printing press is fused with both the company and the car-smashing machine.

What is going on here? The blend must achieve three goals. First, given that the cartoon is a visual representation, the blend must be concrete and specific. Second, it must fit the frame of stronger and weaker object. Third, these objects in the blend must be properly connected to the companies in input two. The companies in input two, being abstract, cannot in themselves provide the corresponding concrete elements in the blend. The weaker and stronger objects in input one are concrete but not specific, and so cannot in themselves provide the corresponding specific elements in the blend. But we can exploit internal connections in the inputs to make the elements in the blend adequate. The printing press and the car are concrete, specific objects associated with the companies that can also be fit into the frame of the stronger object destroying the weaker object. They fit this frame in part because the printing press intrinsically has force-dynamic structure capable of destruction and in part because we are familiar with car-smashing machines. In the blend, two elements are simultaneously (1) two concrete, specific objects; (2) a stronger object destroying a weaker object; and (3) two companies.

Clearly, such a blend is creative. Not just any connections will do. There has to be a search for elements that simultaneously satisfy a number of constraints. The printing press and car have topology in the blend (the press crushes and the car is crushed) that their counterparts in Input 2 do not have (the press is an instrument of making newspapers and the car is a salient product of the automobile company). Additionally, the printing press and car in Input 2 have no counterparts in Input 1. Interestingly, the elements that did not project their input-topology (printing press and car) end up being the only objects in the blend. The cartoon of the printing press smashing the car is remarkable because it is a case where Integration and Topology are maximized by recruiting special internal connections in Input 2. Because the topologies of strong and weak object on the one hand and competing companies on the other will match only at a very abstract level, we find that in addition to the companies, objects closely connected to them are projected to the blend in a way that closely matches and elaborates the Input 1 topology of strong and weak objects.

This example emphasizes that conceptual projection is a dynamic process that cannot be adequately represented by a static drawing. Once the conceptual projection is achieved, it may look as if the printing press has always corresponded to the stronger object and the car to the weaker. But in the cross-space mapping, the printing press and the car play no role; they have no counterparts in Input 1. Rather, the cross-space counterparts are stronger object and newspaper company, weaker object and automobile company. Under metonymy projection from Input 2, the printing press *in the blend* becomes the counterpart of the stronger object in Input 1, and the car *in the blend* becomes the counterpart of the weaker object in Input 1.

This example also shows that identity is metonymy of zero distance. The metonymic relation in Input 2 between company and commercial product is transformed into identity in the blend, where the printing press is identically both a printing press and the newspaper company to which it is metonymically related as an instrument (in one of the inputs).

Suppose the cartoon now contains the newspaper magnate operating the printing press to smash the car, which is being driven by the car magnate. Here the blend structure becomes elaborate through the recruitment to the blend of an additional adversaries-with-instruments frame in which adversaries fight with opposing instruments, and in which the winning adversary has the superior instrument. Now the printing press and car in Input 2 have counterparts in the adversaries-with-instruments frame: in input 2, the printing press is a symbol of a capacity for productivity that is an instrument of corporate competition, and the car is a product that is an instrument of corporate competition; these instruments in Input 2 are the counterparts of the instruments in the adversaries-with-instruments frame. Now, the topology of opposing instruments in the blend matches the topology of opposing instruments in the adversaries-with-instruments frame. This frame has the useful property of aligning superiority of instrument with superiority of adversary. In this case, we see that exploiting special internal connections in Input 2 makes it possible to recruit a frame that makes Topology much stronger in the blend structure.

4. Binding in hell

Our last extended example is a literary example, Dante's celebrated portrayal of Bertran de Born in the *Inferno,* canto 28, lines 139-142. While living, Bertran had instigated strife between the King of England and the King's son and heir, tearing father and son apart. When seen in hell, Bertran consists, spectacularly, of two parts: a headless body and its separate head. The body carries its head in its hand, lifting the head manually to talk to Dante as he passes by on his journey through hell. Bertran cites his punishment as the appropriate analogue of his sin:

> Perch'io parti' così giunte persone,
>   partito porto il mio cerebro, lasso!
>   dal suo principio ch'è in questo troncone.
> Così s'osserva in me lo contrapasso.

> 'Because I parted people so joined,
>   I carry my brain, alas, separated
>   from its root, which is in this trunk.
> Thus is to be seen in me the retribution'.

This is an impossible blending, in which a talking human being has an unnaturally divided body. There are many parts to the development of this blend.

First, there is a conventional metaphoric understanding: dividing people socially is understood metaphorically as dividing a joined physical object. This metaphoric projection is not at all novel. We can say conventionally that a homewrecker has "come between" a married couple by creating "distance" between them. "Till death do us *part*" is not a vow to hold hands; "what God has *joined together*, let no man *put asunder*" does not mean that husband and wife are surgically sutured. We can speak of the breaking of a business bond, of a bond of belief, of a bond of loyalty, of a bond of trust. None of this inherently involves the specific information of dividing a head from a body.

In this conventional metaphor, proximity, junction, and separation are projected to an abstract generic space that applies to any number of specific targets, including targets concerned with social and psychological relations.

But in Dante's portrayal of Bertran de Born, the generic space is fleshed out to create a blended space. Dante's blended space takes, from the target, the specific sin and sinner, and, from the source, the source *counterpart* of the sin – the separation of a joined physical object. *In the blended space, the source counterpart of the sin is visited upon the target sinner as punishment.* We can derive a sense of justice in this situation by recognizing figural retribution: the sinner has his own sin visited upon him not literally but figurally; the projection to the sin is traced backward to its source, and this source analogue of the sin is visited upon the sinner. The specific information from the source – physical separation of a joined physical object – is applied impossibly to the target human being in a blended space. The blended space contains something impossible for both source and target: a talking and reasoning human being who carries his detached but articulate head in his hand like a lantern.

In the case of the portrayal of Bertran de Born, the power and even the existence of central inferences of the projection come not from the source space and not from the target space but only from the blended space. This portrayal is often quoted out of context as an example of the kind of horrible punishment found in the *Inferno* – many more people are familiar with this portrayal than have read the *Inferno*. Those familiar with the passage (out of context) typically take it as signifying not merely badness, but badness of a specific description: unnatural, ghastly, violent, destructive of a worthy whole. The bodily division is taken as a sign of profound and specific wrong. A sophisticated reader of this passage in its context may have already concluded that Bertran has sinned, given that he is in hell, and that Bertran has sinned in a particular way, given his location in hell. But even such a reader may derive all the central inferences from the portrayal itself. It is possible to know an abstract definition of a sin while having only the thinnest corresponding conception.

Where are these central inferences constructed? Let us consider the background metaphoric projection. In the source space, there may be nothing wrong with separating a joined physical object, like a nut. In the target space, there may be nothing wrong with setting two people against each other, or, more specifically, in setting son against father (perhaps the father is an evil infidel warrior, for example). The background metaphoric projection does not necessarily carry the inference that division is wrong – "breaking up" can be good. Many readers, informed of the relevant history, would not even agree that Bertran de Born's actions were sinful, much less treacherous. But we all know there is something ghastly and horribly wrong about a decapitated human body that operates as if it were alive. We see the amazing spectacle of Bertran carrying his detached head, and read this division as symbolizing something unnatural, ghastly, violent, inappropriately destructive. The inference is established in the blended space before Bertran de Born begins to tell his story to Dante in hell – which is to say, before we are told the history of the target space.

As we have seen before in metaphor-metonymy interactions, the blend can combine non-counterparts, provided the appropriate metonymic connections are in place. In the metaphoric cross-space mapping, the divided object in the source is the counterpart of the "divided" father and son in the target, not of Bertran de Born in the target. In the target, Bertran de Born is the sinner, the *agent* of the dividing, not the *victim* of the dividing. But Bertran de Born is, in the target, metonymically associated with the divided father and son as the cause of their division. He is projected to the blend as the sinner and the agent of the dividing, but he is also combined there with the divided object itself. It is not that the blend could not have made use of the correspondence between the divided physical object and the father-son. A different blend might have shown de Born pushing father and son apart and suffering some horrible punishment as he does so. But instead, the blend combines the divided physical object with de Born. The blend has exploited metonymies to create a combination of non-counterparts to provide a blended scene that signifies appropriate retribution.

Notes

*   Parts of this article will appear in the article we contributed to the book edited by Klaus-Uwe Panther and Günter Radden (forthcoming) *Metonymy in cognition and language* (Amsterdam: John Benjamins).

References

Coulson, Seana
  1996   "The Menendez brothers virus: Analogical mapping in blended spaces."
            In: Adele Goldberg (ed.), 67-81.
  n.d.   Semantic leaps: The role of frame-shifting and conceptual blending in
            meaning construction. [Unpublished Ph.D. dissertation, UC San Diego.,
            1997.]
Fauconnier, Gilles
  1997   *Mappings in thought and language.* Cambridge: Cambridge University
            Press.
Fauconnier, Gilles and Mark Turner
  1994   "Conceptual projection and middle spaces." [UCSD Cognitive Science
            Technical Report 9401. San Diego.] (Available from the WWW at http:/
            /cogsci.ucsd.edu and at http://www.wam.umd.edu/~mturn.)
  1996   "Blending as a central process of grammar", in: Adele Goldberg (ed.),
            113-129.
  1998   "Conceptual integration networks", *Cognitive Science*, 22: 2, 133-187.
  in press "Principles of conceptual integration", in: Jean Pierre Koenig (ed.)
  in preparation *Making sense.*
Goldberg, Adele (ed.)
  1996   *Conceptual structure, discourse, and language, I.* Stanford: Center for
            the Study of Language and Information.
Koenig, Jean Pierre (ed.)
  in press *Conceptual structure, discourse, and language, II.* Stanford: Center for
            the Study of Language and Information.
Lakoff, George
  1987   *Women, fire, and dangerous things: What categories reveal about the
            mind.* Chicago: University of Chicago Press.
  1993   "The contemporary theory of metaphor", in: Andrew Ortony (ed.),
            Metaphor and thought. (2nd edition.) Cambridge: Cambridge University
            Press, 202-251.

Lakoff, George and Mark Turner
  1989   *More than cool reason: A field guide to poetic metaphor.* Chicago: University of Chicago Press.
Oakley, Todd
  n.d.   Presence: The conceptual basis of rhetorical effect. [Unpublished Ph.D. dissertation, University of Maryland, 1996.]
The Divine Comedy of Dante Alighieri.
  1939   With translation and comment by John. D. Sinclair. New York: Oxford University Press.
Turner, Mark
  1987   *Death is the mother of beauty: mind, metaphor, criticism.* Chicago: University of Chicago Press.
  1989   "Categories and analogies", in: David Helman (ed.), *Analogical reasoning: Perspectives of artificial intelligence, cognitive science, and philosophy.* Dordrecht: Kluwer, 3-24.
  1991   *Reading minds: The study of English in the age of cognitive science.* Princeton: Princeton University Press.
  1996a   "Conceptual blending and counterfactual argument in the social and behavioral sciences," in: Philip Tetlock and Aaron Belkin (eds.), *Counterfactual thought experiments in world politics.* Princeton, N.J.: Princeton University Press, 291-295.
  1996b   *The literary mind.* New York: Oxford University Press.
Turner, Mark and Gilles Fauconnier
  1995   "Conceptual integration and formal expression", *Metaphor and Symbolic Activity,* 10:3, 183-203.
  in press a "Conceptual integration in counterfactuals", in: Jean Pierre Koenig (ed.).
  in press b "A mechanism of creativity", *Poetics Today.*

Metaphor and metonymy in language structure and discourse

Metaphor and metonymy in language structure

Patterns of meaning extension, "parallel chaining", subjectification, and modal shifts

Louis Goossens

1. Introduction[1]

The purpose of this paper is to (re)consider the development of the English modal verbs with respect to the meaning extension patterns recognized by cognitive linguistics (Lakoff 1987, Langacker 1987 and 1991, Sweetser 1990, Hopper – Traugott 1993). More specifically, I would like to argue that neither metaphor nor metonymy provides adequate ways to account for the meaning shifts which the modals exhibit. "Partial sanction", on the other hand, appears to be a better candidate, but then the specificity of the developments under scrutiny requires a specific version of this extension process, which may be referred to as "parallel chaining".

2. Metaphor, metonymy, metaphor from metonymy, partial sanction

Before we consider modal shifts, we first briefly review the meaning extension processes that are foregrounded by cognitive linguistics.

(a) *Metaphor* is an extension process which involves a mapping across domains. In (1) the lower, somewhat projecting part, or base, of the human body is mapped onto the lower, supporting and somewhat projecting part of a mountain.

(1)   *The foot of the mountain.*

(b) In the case of *metonymy*, we get a mapping of one "element" onto another within a single (complex) domain. (2) is Lakoff and Johnson's (1980) classic example, whereby the food ordered by an otherwise unknown customer is mapped onto this person, where the ad hoc complex domain is the snack bar in which this person has just eaten a ham sandwich. Somehow, the ham sandwich is salient enough for both speaker and hearer to identify the person referred to.

(2)   *The ham sandwich is waiting for his check.*

(c) Just as there is a continuum which goes from literal to metonymy, there is not always a clear demarcation between metonymy and metaphor (Goossens 1990,1995; Croft 1993). (3) exemplifies what I have called *metaphor from* *metonymy.*In the metaphorical interpretation, *giggle* means "say lightheartedly"; its prototypical meaning "laugh childishly" is mapped onto a particular subtype of linguistic action (which as such belongs to a different domain). It is, however, also possible to give it a metonymic interpretation, where it applies to a situation in which she says something lightheartedly *while giggling*. In the metaphorical interpretation there may be continued awareness of this metonymic origin.

(3)   *"Oh dear", she giggled, "I'd quite forgotten".*

Figure 1 is a graphic representation of metaphor from metonymy: in the left hand part of the diagram the two domains are intertwined (metonymy), on the right hand side they are separated (metaphor); there is a conceptual link between the two interpretations.

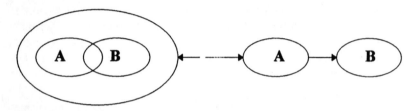

Figure 1. Metaphor from metonymy (from Goossens 1990/1995)

(d) *Partial sanction* is characterized by Langacker as follows (1987:69):

> Often there is some conflict between the specifications of the sanctioning and the target structures, so that the former can be construed as schematic for the latter only with a certain amount of *strain.* When this is so, the relation between the sanctioning and the target structures is one of only *partial schematicity,* and the relation provides only *partial sanction.* Partial sanction can be equated with deviance or ill-formedness, but it should be emphasized that a considerable amount of nonconventionality is tolerated (and often expected) as a normal feature of language use. (original emphasis)

The following figure, borrowed from Langacker, illustrates this for a possible partially sanctioned use of the lexical item *pencil.* In its normal, prototypical use it applies to a cylindrical writing object (depicted on the left hand side); the conic object to the right presents us with a deviation from this canonical form. Still, if this conic object is otherwise like an ordinary pencil, we would have no specific problems if somebody called it a *pencil.* There is, however, only partial sanction. The first time we use *pencil* in this way, we have minimally extended its meaning, even though the cognitive effort needed to interpret this extension is less than in the case of a metonymy, let alone metaphor.

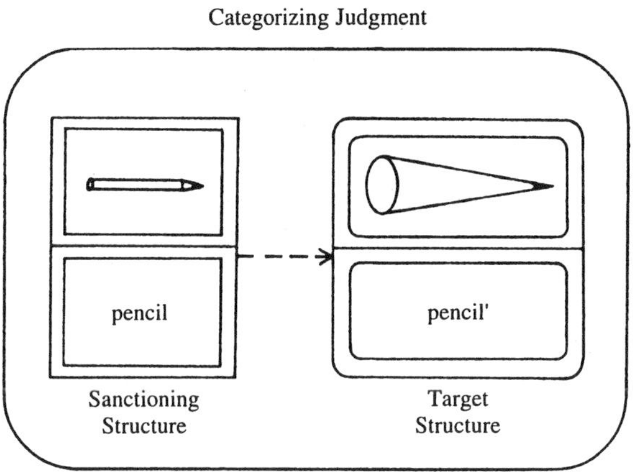

Categorizing Judgment

Figure 2. Partial sanction (= Langacker 1987, fig. 2.2)

3. English modals and modality

In what follows we will be concerned with both synchronic and diachronic meaning extensions in the central modals of English. Although it is not necessary for our purposes to provide an exhaustive discussion of the modals in general, of the semantic space covered by them, or of the semantic shifts which they exhibit, I nevertheless present a brief characterization of the modals to begin with (section 3.1) and, in the wake of van der Auwera and Plungian, of the semantic space of modality (3.2) and of modal shifts in a typological perspective (3.3).

3.1 The central modals of English

The set of central modal verbs in Present-day English is fairly well defined: it includes the items CAN, COULD, MAY, MIGHT, WILL, WOULD, SHALL, SHOULD, MUST.

As their main morphosyntactic properties we may note that they have to be followed by plain infinitives, that they have all lost their non-finite forms, that they take no -s in the third person singular and that they do not require/permit DO-support in the interrogative and negative, in emphasis or in substitution.

Semantically, they largely operate in the semantic space of modality (but what that means precisely depends of course on what we understand by modality, see 3.2). And they have largely become "subjectified" (Traugott 1989), or, to put it in Langacker's (1991: 271) terminology, they have become "grounding predications" (for a critique, see Goossens 1996).

Both from a formal and from a semantic viewpoint, therefore, there are sufficient grounds to take them to be grammaticalized.

3.2 Modality types: modality's semantic space

Defining modality is both a semantic matter and a terminological question. For the purposes of this contribution, I shall take a short cut by adopting the position defended by van der Auwera – Plungian 1998, who propose a typologically workable definition of "modality's semantic space".

The following table is based on their table 1. They restrict modality to the expression of possibility and necessity, with a semantic range going from "subject-internal" to "subject-external" and "epistemic". As will appear from the next subsection, they broaden this somewhat restricted semantic space by considering adjacent semantic spaces which have been found in languages across the world to develop meanings that belong to modality's space as they define it, or that develop out of modality's semantic space.

Table 1. Modality's semantic space (based on van der Auwera – Plungian 1998)

Possibility			
Participant-internal possibility (Dynamic possibility, Ability, Capacity) CAN/COULD	Participant-external possibility		Epistemic possibility (Uncertainty) (COULD) MAY/MIGHT
	(Non-deontic possibility) CAN/COULD (MAY/MIGHT)	Deontic possibility (Permission) CAN/(COULD) MAY/(MIGHT)	
(MUST) Participant-internal necessity (Need)	(MUST) (Non-deontic necessity)	MUST Deontic necessity (Obligation)	MUST Epistemic necessity (Probability)
	Participant-external possibility		
Necessity			

What I have added to van der Auwera – Plungian's table is an indication of how English *can, could, may, might,* and *must* relate to the different modality types. In view of my detailed analysis of a development in Old English *magan*

(Goossens 1987), which covers the span internal possibility-external possibility in a way that is not unlike present-day English *can*, I provide in (4) some examples using the latter modal for part of the possibility range. In (5) necessity is illustrated by examples using present-day *must*, because *must* covers the entire necessity range, and because my main exploration of what extension patterns should be postulated in modal shifts comes from a study of the developments in that modal.

(4) a. *He can lift a hundred kilos.*
         [participant-internal possibility; the possibility resides in the capacity of the subject]
     b. *It can be very hot here in winter.*
         [participant-external possibility: non-deontic; the possibility does not reside in the subject, and is not a matter of social authority or appropriateness]
     c. *You can have one more cookie, but not more.*
         [participant-external possibility: deontic (permission); the possibility does not reside in the subject, but is created by social authority, either the speaker's, or somebody else's (if the speaker merely reports the permission)]

(5) a. *I must see her straight away.*
         [participant-internal necessity; a rather exceptional near-equivalent of *need*]
     b. *Clay pots [...] must have some protection from severe weather.*
         [example from Coates 1983:31; participant-external necessity: non-deontic; rather rare]
     c. *You must do it at once.*
         [participant-external necessity: deontic (obligation)]
     d. *She must have arrived by now.*
         [epistemic; the speaker expresses his judgement and (subjective) certainty that she has arrived]

Note that van der Auwera & Plungian do not explicitly distinguish subjectified from non-subjectified usage, though, of course, deontic uses are often, and epistemic uses are prototypically, subjectified: the speaker is the authority source, or at least strongly associates himself/herself with it in the case of the deontic uses; the epistemic instances typically express the speaker's subjective assessment of a given state of affairs.

3.3 Modal shift: a typological view

Van der Auwera – Plungian (1998) offer blueprints of the semantic map of the grammaticalized expression of modality mainly on the basis of the paths sketched by Bybee – Perkins – Pagliuca (1994).

Figure 3 is borrowed from van der Auwera – Plungian (their figure 14). It sketches the major shifts that take place in modal expressions across the languages of the world.

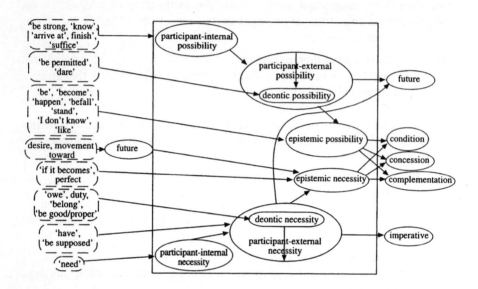

Figure 3. Possibility and necessity paths (= van der Auwera – Plungian 1998, figure 14)

What I want to emphasize here, is that the shift from participant-internal to participant-external modality, and from participant-external to epistemic modality, is witnessed in a great many languages, that there are a number of lexical items that typically feed into modality, and that grammaticalized expressions of modality often develop other grammatical meanings beyond modality as defined above.

Van der Auwera and Plungian are not concerned with the question what/ which extension patterns give rise to these modal shifts. However, in what follows this is exactly the question which I would like to address as regards the modals of English.

4. Characterizing meaning extensions in English modal shifts

Modal shifts in English have been characterized in different ways. We first present the metaphorical and the metonymic view, followed by a metaphor-from-metonymy reinterpretation. We then turn to an exploration of a number of empirical data, which appear to necessitate a partial sanction explanation of the development of Old English *magan* from its participant-internal to a participant-external use. A more detailed investigation of meaning extension in English *must* comes in section 5.

4.1 Metaphor (Sweetser 1990)

Sweetser regards the shift from *deontic* to *epistemic* as involving a mapping from the *socio-physical* domain onto the *epistemic domain*. Epistemic modality is viewed

> as an essentially metaphorical application of our sociophysical concepts to the epistemic world. We have seen that such a unified viewpoint is possible if we analyze modality in terms of general forces and barriers – evidently these are the basic sociophysical concepts in terms of which we understand our mental processes (Sweetser 1990: 68).

In (6) we illustrate this with instances containing *may*.

(6) a. *You may do it.*
       [Speaker creates the possibility for the addressee "to do it"/removes barrier so that the addressee is enabled to "do it"]
     b. *He may have seen her.*
       [Speaker opens a possibility in the epistemic domain for it to have been the case that "he saw her"/removes a knowledge barrier which could have been invoked to claim that he did not see her]

4.2 Metonymy (Hopper – Traugott 1993)

According to Hopper – Traugott shifts giving rise to increased grammaticalization should not be expected to be a matter of metaphor.

> ... since reanalysis, not analogy, has for long been recognized as the major process in grammaticalization, it would be surprising if metaphor, which is analogical, were the prime process at work pragmatically and semantically. ... other processes, which depend on contiguity and reanalysis, also play a major part ... some instances of grammaticalization that have ... been regarded as metaphorical can be seen to arise out of contiguity rather than or as well as out of analogy. ...
> The meaning changes arising out of contiguity in linguistic (including pragmatic) contexts are known as "associative" or conceptual "metonymic" changes. We will use the term "(conceptual) metonymy" here. (Hopper – Traugott 1993:80-81)

Hopper – Traugott illustrate this with the development of English *will*. Although it is somewhat outside the semantic space of modality as delimited by van der Auwera – Plungian, the full-scale volition sense can properly be regarded as a participant-internal (in another terminology a "facultative") modality. Moreover, its development in English includes an epistemic sense, as illustrated in (7a), as well as a deontic sense in contexts where the speaker assumes that the addressee will carry out the predicted action given the authority that he has over this addressee (7b).

(7)   a.   *They will have opened the box by now.*
      b.   *You will do it exactly the way I told you.*

The development with which Hopper and Traugott are concerned involves an intermediary stage between the (prototypical) volition sense of Old English *willan* and the use of *will* as an auxiliary of the future in Present-day English. This development is represented schematically in (8).

(8)   Old English *willan* 'have a desire for some future action' > instances where willingness/intention shade off into a marking of the future > Modern English *will* as marker of a state of affairs as future.

The original "metonymy" persists in Present-day English, as can be illustrated by (9) (instances from Hopper – Traugott: 70).

(9)   a.   *Give them the name of someone who will sign for it and take it in if you are not at home.* [willingness/futurity]
      b.   *I'll put it in the mail today.* [intention/futurity]

4.3 Deontic-to-epistemic as metaphor-from-metonymy

Returning to the shift from deontic to epistemic, which Sweetser interprets as metaphorical, we can also here come across instances that provide us with a "metonymic bridge" between the deontic and the epistemic sense. (10) would be such a metonymic bridge.

(10)   *He may go there at once.*
            [Permission may be taken to shade into an expectation or judgment on the part of the speaker that the state of affairs is possible]

In this view, Sweetser's metaphor may be interpreted as a metaphor from metonymy, and could be represented as in figure 4.

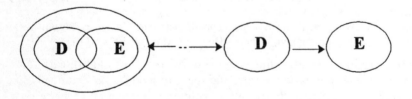

Figure 4. From deontic-to-epistemic as metaphor-from-metonymy
            (= Fig. 2 in Goossens forthcoming)

4.4 Chaining of partial sanction instantiations: The shift of Old English *magan* from participant-internal to participant-external

So far, we have considered interpretations of modal shifts which are cognitively acceptable, but without trying to find out what the details of these developments may have been in actual language use. A consideration of what appears to have happened in the case of the shift of Old English *magan* from its participant-internal sense to a participant-external one, will serve as first indication that this shift happened in a series of minimal steps which can hardly be taken to have involved a clearcut metonymy, let alone a metaphorical "jump".

The analysis which follows is based on Goossens 1987. For the purposes of that contribution I investigated a sample of 100 uses of *magan* from Ælfric, a homilist working around the first millennium. At that stage of the development of English (late Old English, more precisely late West-Saxon) *magan* still had the capacity, or participant-internal, sense as its prototype, but the participant-external sense was well on its way to becoming conventionalized. Table 2 gives the distribution of internal versus external uses, with a sizable group of transitional uses ("internal-external")

Table 2. Magan in sample from Ælfric [N: 100] (= Table 1 in Goossens 1987)

A Internal	B Internal/external	C External
47	28	25

The following instances illustrate the prototype (11) and the participant-external use, (14) and (15). Uses (12) and (13) are transitional between participant-internal and participant-external (or, perhaps more precisely, between subject-internal and subject-external). In line with Langacker (1991: 269-271) we can interpret these instances as illustrating a shift in the "locus of potency".

(11)   [locus of potency subject-internal; "prototype"]

    ne bið he þæra   æhta   hlaford þonne hi   ne   dælan   ne
    not is   he of-the-possessions lord when   them not distribute not
    mæg
    can
    'He isn't the lord of the possessions if he can't distribute them'

(12)   [subject-internal, but with external factor]
    æfter þysum gebede ateowde heofenlic leoht [...]:
    after this   prayer appeared heavenly light

    swa beorhte scinende þæt nanes mannes gesihð
    so   brightly shining   that of-no-man   sight

þæs leohtes leoman sceawian ne mihte
of-the-light rays   behold   not could
'After this prayer there appeared a heavenly light [...] shining so
brightly that no man's sight could behold the rays of the light.'

(13)   [balance between subject-internal and subject-external factors]
nu   synt we ute belocene of   ðam heofenlican leohte:
now are we out locked   from that   heavenly   light
and we ne   magon   on þisum life þæs ecan leohtes   brucan
and we not can/may in this   life of-the-eternal-light enjoy
'Now we are shut out from that heavenly light: and we cannot enjoy
the eternal light in this life.'

(14)   [locus of potency predominantly in the unidentified agent; subject-
external]
hu magon þas   ban beon geedcucade, swilce hi
how can these bones be   revived   as   they
wislice sprecan: ac we cwedað þærtogeanes
wisely speak   but we say   in-opposition-to-this
þæt god is ælmihtig
that God is almighty
'How can/may these bones be revived as they would wisely remark:
but we say to this that God is almighty.'

(15)   [locus of potency in unidentified agent as well as in speaker judg-
ment/permission]
þurh   eastdæl magon beon getacnode þa ðe
through east   may   be   signified those who
on geogoðe to gode bugaþ: for ðan þe on eastdæle is
in youth   to God   turn   because in east   is
dæges   angin
of-the-day beginning
'Through the east may be signified those that turn to God when they
are young: because in the east is the beginning of the day'

In relation to the prototype represented by (11) the other instances exhibit a
gradual shift to the less prototypical uses in (12), (13), (14) and (15). Each of
these instances is only partially sanctioned by the prototype. In (14) and (15),
the "external" uses are partially sanctioned by extended uses of the type represented by (12) and (13). What we get is a sanctioning chain: this can be represented as in figure 5.

(11)	>	(12)	>	(13)	>	(14)	>	(15)
locus of		locus of potency gradually						locus of
potency		shifts away from subject						potency outside
in subject								subject

Figure 5. Partial sanctioning chain for *magan*

The conclusion from this first confrontation with actual usage data would seem to be that, rather than a metaphorical or metonymic shift, we witness a *chaining of partial sanction uses*. Let us now turn to a more detailed investigation of the development of *must*, which, at least by some, is taken to be something of a stronghold for the metaphor-hypothesis.

5. From participant-external to epistemic: A corpus-based account of the development of *must*

5.1 Bybee – Perkins – Pagliuca (1994) versus Traugott – König (1991)

Traugott and König (1991) argue that the change in English *must* from participant-external (deontic) to epistemic was induced from contexts like (16).

(16)   *She must be married.*

> ... *must* in the epistemic sense of "I conclude that" derived from the obligative sense of "ought to" by strengthening of conversational inferences and subjectification. (Traugott – König 1991:209)

In the terminology adopted in this paper, this means that the development would be metonymic or, perhaps, could be treated as an instance of partial sanction. Note, however, that Traugott and König work from a single transitional context, and that their example is a constructed one at that.

Bybee – Perkins – Pagliuca (1994) in general also favor a context-induced pattern of change from "agent-oriented" (= participant-external) to epistemic.

> [It] involves the conventionalization of an implicature, by which the inferences that can be made from the meaning of a particular modal become part of the meaning of that modal. (Bybee – Perkins – Pagliuca 1994:196)

In the specific case of English *must*, however, they are opposed to such an origin.

> Since the epistemic use of *must* arises in contexts with aspectual interpretations distinct from the obligation uses, it appears that metaphor may be at work in this change. (p. 201)

On the basis of our analysis for the gradual shift of internal *magan* to external *magan* (section 4.4), we would not expect the metaphor hypothesis to withstand the confrontation with empirical data. It is this confrontation which comes in sections 5.2, 5.3 and 5.4. Also, we would expect the transition to be too complex to allow us to capture it with a single, constructed contextualization.

5.2 Empirical data from Present-day English

In Goossens (forthcoming) I present an extensive analysis of three present-day samples of contextualized instances of *must* (from the Brown, LOB, and

LondonLund corpora, 296 instances in all). Whereas *must* demonstrates two distinct prototypical cores (a participant-external, deontic use and a subjectified epistemic one), the data also provide us with a number of transitional uses. Two types of "bridges" could be discerned.

(a) Nine instances which may be characterized as "inferential", but which are not subjectified because the inferential ground ["you can't be put on probation unless you're guilty"] is contextually available, as in (17).

(17)   *what Fan didn't realize not being a lawyer #. or a lawyer's wife # –*
        that apparently the wife was put on probation # so that Fan didn't
        realize that # that she must also have been up before court # you can't
        be put on probation # not unless you're guilty. (LondonLund)

(b) Ten uses which are contextually compatible with both a participant-external (deontic) interpretation and a (subjective) epistemic one, as in (18), or at least an inferential one, as in (19).

(18)   *Horatia laughed again. "Well, I cannot say that I approve. You must*
        remember that I am taking your aunt's hospitality, and, if your plans
        go right, on entirely false pretences. [...]"
        [= "I want you to remember" or "I am sure you will remember"]
        (LOB)

(19)   *<A> and conversation. went like this. this sort of conversation ∂m –*
        have you noticed president #. that. ∂m – the boiled eggs # at Sunday
        breakfast – always
        <B> *(laughs)*
        <A> hard – and president said – ah well – the simple truth is that. if
        you're going to boil eggs. communally # they must be hard.

        ["they have to be hard" or "they will necessarily be hard"]
        (LondonLund)

These two present-day "bridges" may be indicative of the paths that led from participant-external to epistemic *must* diachronically, though they do not tell us how exactly the diachronic shift took place. What they do suggest, however, is that more than one path may have been followed. An analysis of data from older language stages in the next subsection should shed light on this. Since we may expect that an increase in subjectification may have played a significant part (cf. Traugott/König 1991 and Langacker 1991), a separate subsection (5.4) will be reserved for that aspect of the development.

5.3 Diachronic stepping stones

The following analysis is based on five successive samples from the Helsinki corpus (ME3 63 instances, ME4 78 instances, EMOE1 88 instances, EMOE2

182 instances, EMOE3 172 instances).[2] (For ampler exemplification and a more detailed discussion see again Goossens forthcoming.)

(a) In all the samples participant-external necessity (but with varying degrees of subjectification, see subsection 5.4) is the single clear prototype. The other uses listed here are in a partial sanction chain relation to this prototype.

(b) From participant-external to "general objective necessity."

A first stepping stone is from participant-external to "general objective necessity" uses. They are amply provided from the earliest samples onwards; (20) is an instance.

(20)   (ME3)
         Wherto and why burieth a man his goodes by his grete avarice, and knoweth wel that nedes moste hy dye? For deeth is the ende of every man [...]
         'For what purpose and why does a man bury his goods because of his great avarice, knowing well that he must necessarily die? For death is the end of every man.'

This usage constitutes a subset of the participant-external type, i.e. the necessity does not reside in the subject's internal urge, and it expresses no obligation (no authority source is involved). On the other hand, though it is not clearly inferential either in that no inference is drawn from implicit or explicit premises, there is an epistemic/inferential ingredient: in instance (20), for example, we have an "epistemic" verb (*knoweth*) in the main clause, and *moste* is accompanied by the adverb *nedes* "necessarily". While coming under the participant-external uses, these "general objective necessity uses" thus provide a bridge to the inferential uses under (c).

(c) Inferential uses

Inferential contextualizations present us with a further extension, partially sanctioned by the usage under (b). They are also well established from the earliest sample onwards (ME3, 1350-1420); (21) is an instance from Chaucer.

(21)   (ME3)
         But I have wel concluded that blisfulnesse and God been the sovereyne good; for which it mote nede be that sovereyne blisfulnes is sovereyn devynite.

         'But I have correctly concluded that blissfulness and God are the supreme good; for which reason it must necessarily be the case that supreme blissfulness is supreme divinity.' [inference drawn objectively]

(d) Towards epistemic necessity: transitional uses

These transitional uses are a further step towards full-scale epistemic uses. They occur from EMOE onwards, but only sparingly (EMOE1: two instances; EMOE2: five; EMOE3: eight). Most of them are rooted in (and partially sanctioned by) the inferential use; this usage is exemplified by (22). Others are complexes of a deontic/epistemic nature, and therefore partially sanctioned by the deontic prototype (23 is an instance).

(d1)

(22)   (EMOE3)
         We were in full discourse of the sad state of our times. And the horrid
         shame brought on the King's service by the just clamours of the poor
         seamen. And that we must be undone in a little time.
         [The sentence with *must* is in semi-indirect speech, i.e. there is sub-
         ordination by means of the conjunction *that*, but person deixis (*we*) is
         as in direct speech; inference derivable from what precedes (sad state
         of our times; horrid shame brought on the King's service) or subjec-
         tive judgment of speaker, paraphrasable by *will*]

(d2)

(23)   (EMOE1)
         A childe shall learne of the better of them, that, which an other daie,
         if he be wise, and cum to iudgment, he must be faine to vnlearne
         againe.
         [paraphrasable by both "will have to/(deontic) must" and "(epistemic)
         will"]

(e) The first clear uses of (subjective) epistemic *must* come in EMOE3 (1640-1710) (seven instances). (24) is an example.

(24)   *That was opposed & spoke against with such vehemency by my L.*
         Clarendon (her owne Unkle) a putt himm by all preferments, which
         must doubtlesse, [{have{] been greate, as could have ben given by
         him.[3]

Figure 6 summarizes the foregoing analysis of the different senses of *must* (or its ancestors) in the five samples in the Helsinki corpus.

Usages (a), (b) and (c) are well established from the earliest sample onwards. Usage (b) is a subset of the participant-external use and is sanctioned by it; (c) receives (partial) sanction from usage (b). The two transitional usages (d1) and (d2) are partially sanctioned by (c) and by the prototype (a) respectively. The fully epistemic use, in turn, is partially sanctioned by uses of type (d1), as well as by uses of type (d2). In other words, it has emerged from our analysis that (at least) *two different parallel partial sanctioning chains* were involved in the development of a (subjective) epistemic sense for *must*.

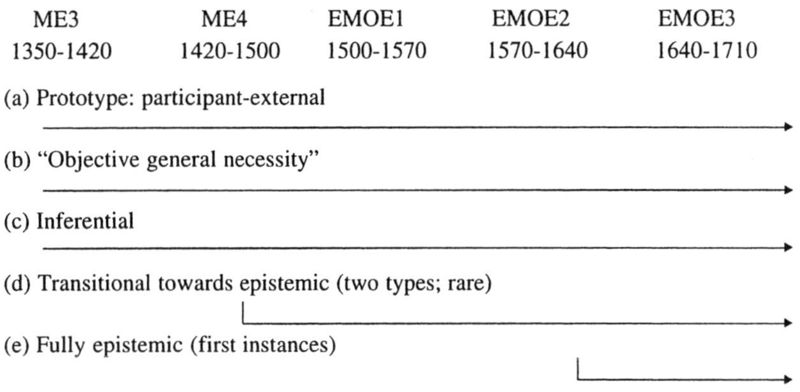

ME3	ME4	EMOE1	EMOE2	EMOE3
1350-1420	1420-1500	1500-1570	1570-1640	1640-1710

(a) Prototype: participant-external

———————————————————————————————————→

(b) "Objective general necessity"

———————————————————————————————————→

(c) Inferential

———————————————————————————————————→

(d) Transitional towards epistemic (two types; rare)

        └——————————————————————————————→

(e) Fully epistemic (first instances)

                         └————————→

Figure 6. Diachronic stepping stones for epistemic *must*

What remains to be done is to define in a more detailed way what role was played in this development by the (suspected) increase in subjectification.

5.4 Subjectification

Subjectification is the tendency for meanings "to become increasingly situated in the speaker's belief or attitude toward the proposition" (Traugott 1989: 31). In the semantic area of necessity, Present-day English usually (though not always) shows an opposition between *must* (subjectified) and *have to*, as is illustrated by (25) vs. (26) for participant-external necessity, and by (27) vs. (28) for inferential/epistemic necessity.

(25)   *"You must play this ten times over" Miss Jarova would say, pointing with relentless fingers to a jumble of crotchets and wavers.*
          (instance from Coates 1983)

(26)   *I have to start as early as 7:33 at my new job.*

(27)   *ooh Jesus – well how would people of the other faith have received Germans from the sea – you must have thought about that.*
          (instance from Coates 1983)

(28)   *If line AB intersects line CD at right angles, and line EF is parallel to CD, AB has to intersect line EF at right angles as well.*

For the purposes of the present diachronic investigation I have examined the present-day samples of section 5.2 (Brown, LOB, LondonLund (LOLU)), as well as the Helsinki samples of section 5.3 (ME3, ME4, EMOE1, EMOE2, EMOE3) in terms of the opposition non-subjectified: subjectified.

Non-subjectified are instances which express an obligation which is not created or not backed by the speaker (29), or a past obligation (30), or a general (non-obligational) necessity as exemplified in instance (20) above. Also inferential instances of the type illustrated by (17) for present-day English and by (21) for the older language stages.

(29)   *[...] For the future therefore I must call Oroonoko Caesar since by that name only he was known in our western world, [...]*
        (EMOE3, CEFICT3B, 322-326)[4]

(30)   *[...] and departed agayne into Galile. And it was so that he must nedes goo thorowe Samaria. Then he came to a cyte of Samaria called Sichar [...]*
        (EMOE1, CENTTEST1, 381-385)

Under subjectified come wishes (a recessive and practically obsolete category found in the Middle English samples only) (31); obligations stemming from the speaker's authority (as illustrated in 25), but also rules and instructions to which the speaker gives his/her support, or which he submits to the hearer on the basis of his expert knowledge (32 and 33 are instances); and, from EMOE3 onwards, the (essentially subjective) epistemic uses, as in (24) or (27).

(31)   *[...] So long sche preyid þat he was clene delyveryd of þe sekenes and leuyd many gerys aftyr & had a wife & a childe, blissyd mote God ben, for he weddyd hys wife in Pruce in Dewchelonde [...]*
        'So long she prayed that he was completely freed from the sickness and lived many years after and had a wife and a child, blessed be the Lord, for he married his wife in Prussia in Germany'
        (ME4, CMKEMPE, 616-620)

(32)   *"[...] And the dethe of thys damesell grevith me sore." "So doth hit me", seyde Balan, "But ye must take the adventure that God woll ordayne you."*
        '"And the death of this young lady grieves me deeply" "It also grieves me", Balan said, "But you must undertake the adventure that God wants you to."'
        (ME4, CMMALORY, 447-151)

(33)   *[...] Whatever particular action you bid him at present doe or forbeare you must be sure to see yourself obeyd*
        (EMOE3, CEEDUC3A, 697-701)

The following charts summarize this non-subjectified vs. subjectified opposition in our data. The percentages were computed taking non-subjectified +subjectified as 100%. For obvious reasons we have not included the "transitional uses" (the bridges to the subjective epistemic discussed under (d) in section 5.3) into the picture.

In chart 1 we see that in the Middle English samples the non-subjectified uses clearly predominate. In the three Present-day English samples (BROWN, LOB and LondonLund) it is the other way around. In the Early Modern stages we witness (at least for these data) that the subjectified and non-subjectified uses are more or less in equilibrium, but also that the subjectified cases begin to outnumber the nonsubjectified ones from EMOE2.

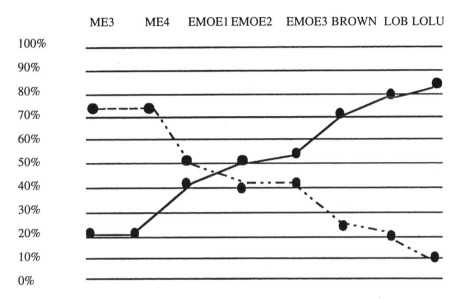

Chart 1. Subjectified vs. non-subjectified participant-external *must*
(Participant-external uses only) [Subjectified —— ; non-subjectified - - -]

Chart 2 shows the rise of the (subjectified) epistemic use. As we found in the preceding section, the first instances come in EMOE3, immediately after the point where the subjectified uses had begun to outnumber the non-subjectified ones. It is clear that the predominance of the subjectified items in EMOE2 must be situated completely in the participant-external, more particularly in the deontic uses (where the speaker is in authority, or can be assumed to give his backing to whatever other authority source may be involved). In other words, the rise in subjectification in the deontic area was an important factor in the rise of the (subjective) epistemic use.

Remember in this context that the (objective) inferential usage partially sanctioned the epistemic use (d1 in section 5.3): the epistemic use can therefore be regarded as the subjectified extension of the nonsubjectified inferential use (at least partially). As far as the other pathway identified in section 5.3 is concerned (d2), subjectification in the deontic area must also have been a factor here to initiate the essentially subjective epistemic use.

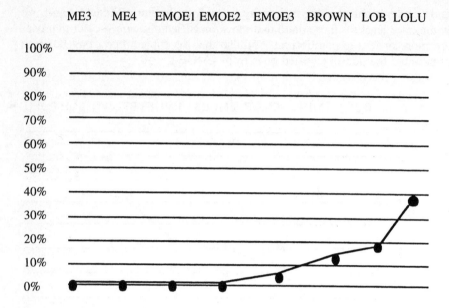

Chart 2. Rise of (subjective) epistemic uses (percentage of total number of uses)

Note, finally, the significant increase of subjectified uses in general (chart 1) and of the epistemic uses in particular (chart 2) in the LondonLund corpus. Whereas BROWN and LOB are written corpora, LondonLund (LOLU) is a spoken data base. In other words, subjectification would seem to be more progressed in the spoken language than in the written medium. What this suggests with respect to our findings on the basis of the Helsinki corpus (which for obvious reasons is a written corpus), is that the spoken language was probably also ahead of the written one as far as subjectification is concerned in the older language stages.

6. Conclusions

(a) An interpretation of the shifts found in the modals in terms of a metaphorical mapping is at best a way to highlight the fact that distinct cognitive domains are involved in the semantic space covered by them.

However, such an interpretation does not do justice to what happened in the development whereby the modals broadened their semantic scope to new domains in (or beyond) modality's semantic space.

I would also like to hypothesize that a metaphorical interpretation does not reflect the cognitive processing of the modals by the speakers of present-day English.

(b) Even a characterization of these changes as metonymic, which presupposes cognitively salient reference points within the same cognitive domain, should not be regarded as an empirically founded account of these modal developments.

Rather, a successive chaining of partially sanctioned uses with respect to some conventionalized (prototypical) use is what appears to have happened. Obviously, over time, this gave rise to shifts in the conventionalized uses from which the new partially sanctioned uses continued to develop.

The best way to conceive of these developments is not to accept that they proceeded along one single path: a multiplicity of paths conspiring to establish a new conventionalized (prototypical) use would appear to be a more adequate way to characterize the linguistic developments that took place. This involves not just the *successive chaining* of partial sanction extensions but also, as we were able to demonstrate with respect to English *must, parallel chaining*.

(c) An overall increase in subjectification was an extra factor in the development of English *must* (and also in the development of the other central modals, except *can* – see Goossens 1996). Judging from what happened in the case of *must*, we can take it that subjectification in the participant-external, more specifically the deontic, area paved the way for the development of the (subjectified) epistemic sense.

(d) Detailed empirical investigations of the type reported on here are a necessary requirement if we are to understand the details of changes in the semantic space of modality. Given the absence of sufficient access to the spoken language of older language stages, however, we cannot hope to reach more than only a partial account of the extension patterns that gave rise to later developments.

(e) The facts of language change (and of language use) are as a rule subtler than the abstractions of linguists. Generalizations are no doubt part of what the art of linguistics is about, but empirical confrontations remain necessary if we wish to understand our own generalizations properly.

Notes

1. As a background to this paper we refer the reader to Goossens (forthcoming), which for sections 5.2 and 5.3 offers a more extensive analysis of the data, but of which this contribution is otherwise an elaboration and a refinement. Parts of it were presented during a workshop at the University of Hamburg (23-24 June 1996), the 5th International Cognitive Linguistics Conference (Amsterdam, 14-19 July 1997) and the 16th Conference of the AESLA (University of La Rioja, Logroño, 22-25 April 1998). Thanks are due to several discussants on each of those occasions, as well as to Johan van der Auwera and Ludo Lejeune for their comments on an earlier version of this paper.

   It is dedicated to the memory of Brygida Rudzka-Ostyn, excellent linguist, and generous friend.

2.   ME3, ME4, EMOE1, EMOE2 and EMOE3 refer to subperiods of Middle English and Early Modern English as they are distinguished in the Helsinki Corpus. For a specification of the temporal segments covered by these sub-periods, see my figure 6.

3.   [{ {] in the Helsinki corpus symbolizes an insertion into the text. Note that a subjective epistemic reading makes sense both with and without this addition. Without it we have to interpret *been* as the equivalent of Present-day *be*.

4.   The abbreviations for the different texts were taken over from the Helsinki Corpus. The sources, in the order of their occurrence in instances (29)-(33), are as follows: CEFICT3B= Behn, Oroonoko; CENTTEST1 = The New Testament, Tyndale; CMKEMPE = Kempe, The Book of Margery Kempe; CMMALORY = Malory, Morte dArthur; CEEDUC3A = Locke, Directions concerning Education. For further details, see Kytö (1993).

References

Bybee, Joan – Revere Perkins – William Pagliuca
    1994   *The evolution of grammar. Tense, aspect and modality in the languages of the world.* Chicago: University of Chicago Press.
Coates, Jennifer
    1983   *The semantics of the modal auxiliaries.* London, Canberra: Croom Helm.
Croft, William
    1993   "The role of domains in the interpretation of metaphors and metonymies", *Cognitive Linguistics* 4:335-370.
Goossens, Louis
    1987   "Modal tracks: the case of MAGAN and MOTAN", in: Anne-Marie Simon-Vandenbergen (ed.), *Studies in honour of René Derolez.* Ghent: Department of English, University of Ghent, 216-236.
    1990   "Metaphtonymy: The interaction of metaphor and metonymy in expressions for linguistic action", *Cognitive Linguistics* 1: 323-340. [Also in: Louis Goossens – Paul Pauwels – Brygida Rudka-Ostyn – Anne-Marie Simon-Vandenbergen – Johan Vanparys (1995), *By word of mouth. Metaphor, metonymy and linguistic action in a cognitive perspective.* Amsterdam, Philadelphia: Benjamins, 159-174.]
    1996   *English modals and functional models: A confrontation.* (Antwerp Papers in Linguistics 86) Antwerp: Department of Linguistics, University of Antwerp. [Preprint monograph.]
    forthcoming "Metonymic bridges in modal shifts", in: Klaus-Uwe Panther – Günther Radden (eds.), *Metonymy in cognition and language.* Amsterdam, Philadelphia: John Benjamins.
Hopper, Paul – Elizabeth C. Traugott
    1993   *Grammaticalization.* Cambridge: Cambridge University Press.
Kytö, Merja
    1993   *Manual to the diachronic part of the Helsinki Corpus of English Texts. Coding conventions and lists of source texts.* (Second edition.) Helsinki: Department of English, University of Helsinki.

Lakoff, George
  1987   *Women, fire, and dangerous things. What categories reveal about the mind.* Chicago: University of Chicago Press.
Lakoff, George – Mark Johnson
  1980   *Metaphors we live by.* Chicago: University of Chicago Press.
Langacker, Ronald W.
  1987   *Foundations of cognitive grammar. Volume I: Theoretical prerequisites.* Stanford: Stanford University Press.
  1991   *Foundations of cognitive grammar. Volume II: Descriptive application.* Stanford: Stanford University Press.
Sweetser, Eve
  1990   *From etymology to pragmatics. Metaphorical and cultural aspects of semantic structure.* Cambridge: Cambridge University Press.
Traugott, Elizabeth Closs
  1989   "On the rise of epistemic meanings in English: an example of subjectification in semantic change", *Language* 65: 31-55.
Traugott, Elizabeth Closs – Ekkehard König
  1991   "The semantics-pragmatics of grammaticalization revisited", in: Elizabeth C. Traugott – Bernd Heine (eds.), *Approaches to grammaticalization. Volume I.* Amsterdam, Philadelphia: Benjamins, 198-218.
van der Auwera, Johan – Vladimir Plungian
  1998   "Modality's semantic map", *Linguistic Typology* 2, 79-124.

Metaphor in semantic change

Verena Haser

1. Introduction

Ever since the early heyday of historical linguistics, the principles governing sense development have been notorious for their elusiveness. Few assessments of the issue are at variance with Blust's verdict that "... the demonstration of semantic relatedness poses far greater problems than the demonstration of phonological relatedness between forms" (Blust 1988: 25). In the eyes of many theorists, uncovering pervasive tendencies amidst the vagaries of lexical change figures as a formidable undertaking. Hock (1986: 308) captures the main thrust of countless complaints about the putative inconsistency of meaning changes: In his parlance, they are typically "... 'fuzzy', highly irregular, and extremely difficult to predict". By the same token, we seem to be a long way from formulating tangible "constraints" as to their direction and outcome.

Following a growing body of research, this paper attempts to challenge the position embraced by traditionally-minded semanticists. The past two decades have witnessed a radical departure from time honored views. Owing to the groundbreaking achievements of eminent linguists such as Traugott, Heine and Sweetser, generalizations on deeply entrenched avenues of development have been brought within the compass of historical semantics (see Wilkins 1996: 266). Unfortunately, the emphasis of most contributions has been on grammaticalization[1] to the exclusion of other types of semantic change. Traugott (1985a: 155) cites some noteworthy findings of the burgeoning discipline: "... aspect → tense (Anderson, 1973); motion verb → preposition (Givón, 1975), and third person pronoun → gender marker → article (Greenberg, 1978)". Thus, the evolution of morphemes encapsulating highly abstract concepts represents the mechanism most extensively explored, while widespread phenomena of comparable import have been upstaged (confer Wilkins 1996: 266-267).

Among the diachronic processes which are commonly dismissed in a cavalier fashion, the emergence of fundamental "lexical" items via recurrent – and possibly universal – pathways looms large as one of the most promising areas of research. In spite of the deplorable scholarly dearth in this field, a few seminal works have paved the way for further discoveries. Notably Williams (1976) Traugott (1985a, 1985b), and Sweetser (1990) provide invaluable inspiration. Though intriguing in their own right, the studies in question are often limited with respect to the range of languages surveyed. Similar to Sweetser (1990), both Williams (1976) and Traugott (1985a) draw on data from Indo-European languages; which they supplement with Japanese examples. Even if comparative analyses along these lines afford revealing insights, they do not permit generalizations on "natural" routes of change. Possibly, the apparent laws which have been singled out are peculiar to one or two cultures and hence of minor interest to linguists attending to "cognitive universals".

Despite recent proposals suggesting overall regularities, attempts at infallible predictions about the evolution of individual words will always be thwarted by the erratic nature of the processes at work. One reason for this truism resides in the possibility of associating (almost?) any two domains via metaphor,[2] which constitutes the foremost agent of semantic change (see below). It is this very type of meaning transformation triggered by metaphoric mappings which will be the focus of my investigation. Its primary objective is to scrutinize cases of metaphorization resulting in lexical changes which are documented (or inferable) in languages around the globe.

The present project hopes to remedy a drawback of certain otherwise stimulating treatments which do not go beyond broad sketches of predominant principles. According to Traugott (1985b: 38), for instance, assertives in Indo-European languages are often

> "...derived from the visual field:
> *argue* < IE *arg-* 'shine, white' ...
> *predict* < IE *deik* - 'show' ...   [or]
> derived from the spatial field:
> *add* < Lat. *ad + dere* ' to + put' < IE *dō-* 'give' ...
> *assert* < Lat. *ad + serere* 'join oneself to' < IE *ser-* 'line up'
> *concede* < Lat. *con + cēdere* 'go away, withdraw'
> *conjecture* < Lat. *con + icere* 'throw together' ...
> *retort* < Lat. *re + torquere* 'bend, twist back' ...
> *state* < Lat. *status* 'standing' ...
> *suggest* < Lat. *sub + gerere* 'under + carry' ..."

The strategy illustrated in Traugott (1985b) should be complemented by careful inquiries into individual donor and recipient expressions.

In fact, many substantial regularities can be phrased in comparatively clear-cut terms. Disparate items (like TO FOLLOW, TO GIVE, TO SEEK, STRAIGHT, CROOKED, etc.) appear to be subject to cross-linguistically recurrent developments bridging neatly specifiable source and target domains (e.g. STRAIGHT → CORRECT).

2. Methodology

The main part of this exposition lays out the essentials underpinning my approach. Before embarking on a discussion of pivotal assumptions, two concepts will be clarified.

2.1 Basic notions defined

2.1.1. Semantic change

I am committed to the definition of semantic change formulated in Werth (1974: 377-378): " ... a lexical item *a*, hitherto associated with a semantic *A*, comes to associate with the new, but related (polysemous) semantic configuration *A'*, which may co-exist with, or replace, *A*".

If necessary, cases of mere polysemy will be tagged lexical change (I), whereas the alternative scenario, i.e. replacement of senses, represents type II developments.

2.1.2. Metaphor

Partly due to the terminological inconsistencies obscuring both traditional and contemporary accounts, the processes governing figurative mappings have to some extent remained arcane. Some scholars opt for a broad definition of metaphor including metonymy as a special subtype. On this view, "metaphor" serves as a generic term for all figures of speech (Eco 1984: 87-91). As a result, a satisfactory elucidation of criterial features is fraught with difficulties. On the other hand, the most mundane expressions are sometimes open to contradictory classifications: To tease apart the differences between metaphor and metonymy has proved an intractable undertaking.[3] Provided the justification of recent theories of metaphor as (typically?) based on metonymy, it may indeed be impossible to neatly disentangle the two notions.

A possible escape hatch might be to view metaphor as a prototype concept. Consequently, the terminology which informs this project is relatively narrow but will nevertheless cover phenomena which may count as instances of metonymy. The label "metaphor" will be reserved for transfer across distinct semantic domains (criterion 1) which is (putatively) based on similarity (criterion 2). Lakoff and Turner (1989: 103) add a third defining characteristic: "In *metaphor*, a whole schematic structure (with two or more entities) is mapped onto another whole schematic structure". Metonymy, on the other hand, refers to " ... a semantic link between two senses of a lexical item that is based on a relationship of contiguity between the referents of the expression in each of those senses" (Geeraerts 1994, 5: 2477). Unfortunately, linguists part company over how to specify the notion of *contiguity*. Space constraints preclude a survey and evaluation of the myriad definitions encountered in pertinent works. Taylor's conception of metonymy as "conceptual cooccurrence" in prototypical situations has gained many advocates: " ... the essence of metonymy resides in the possibility of establishing connections between entities which co-occur within a given conceptual structure (Taylor 1995: 123-124)". It is his notion which will be subscribed to in the following pages.

2.2. Guiding assumptions and implications

2.2.1. Metaphor as a prominent factor in semantic change

A cornerstone of contemporary methodology, metaphoric transfer is widely recognized as a central cause of semantic change. In view of the by now commonplace nature of this insight, further elaboration appears unnecessary. Suffice it to summarize the judgment endorsed by the majority of scholars: "Metaphoric processes have recently been considered to be major, indeed *the* major, factors in semantic change (Traugott 1988: 407)". Hence, probing the former issue frequently implies exploring the latter. The same applies to the present inquiry, which undertakes to pin down pervasive types of metaphoric transfer reflected in lexical developments.

2.2.2. Unidirectionality of semantic change and metaphoric transfer

One of the most far-reaching tenets guiding any assessment of sense developments has been articulated in Kronasser (1952): Given two etymologically related concepts, the more concrete item will typically be antecedent to the more abstract term rather than vice versa (see Traugott 1985a: 159).[4] A correlative observation concerning the directionality of metaphorization has gained ground in historical semantics: As a rule, metaphoric transfer proceeds from basic to abstract domains (see Traugott 1988: 507).[5]

In accordance with what has come to be known as "Kronasser's law", concrete meanings were hypothesized to constitute the sources of complex concepts. For items exhibiting two divergent senses like "straight" and "righteous", the spatial meaning was taken to be prior to the notion of "righteousness".

2.2.3. Interrelatedness of polysemy, semantic change and metaphor

Over the past few years, it has become received wisdom that polysemy relations are diagnostic of semantic change (II):

> Synchronic polysemy and historical change of meaning really supply the same data in many ways. No historical shift of meaning can take place without an intervening stage of polysemy. If a word once meant A and now means B, we can be fairly certain that speakers did not just wake up and switch meanings on June 14, 1066. Rather there was a stage when the word meant both A and B, and the earlier meaning of A eventually was lost. But if an intervening stage of polysemy was involved, then all the historical data, as evidence of past polysemy relations, is an interesting source of information about the reflection of cognitive structure in language. (Sweetser 1990: 9)

In line with this observation, the present project utilizes polysemy as a convenient gauge of incipient change (II).

Originating in the " ... institutionalization ... of originally unconventional uses of a lexeme" (Persson 1990: 171), polysemy in turn is often inextricably linked to figurative transfer.

2.2.4. Cognitive implications

Apart from their intrinsic interest, the cognitive import of sense developments is beyond dispute.

> It is generally agreed that if we could find out which specific subdomains of experience are salient for which subdomains of cognition, we would know a lot about the human mind (cf. Miller and Johnson-Laird, 1976). One way to try to access this information is through psychological experimentation. Another is through the study of child language acquisition. Yet another is to see how meanings change. (Traugott 1985a: 156)

In the first place, it is those metaphors attested across cultures which yield novel insights into the workings of human cognition.

3. Procedure/sampling method

The following inquiry attempts to pinpoint prevailing types of metaphoric mappings involving lexemes such as *to see, hear, seek, count, follow, support, straight, crooked, untie, grasp*, etc. What are recurrent developmental patterns? To indicate the potential omnipresence of natural pathways I gave priority to a general study of numerous source concepts over an in-depth analysis of individual semantic fields. Hence the diversity of items explored. Since I believe that regularities of the type outlined above are not restricted to a few domains, I deliberately chose an apparently random set of source concepts. All of them, however, are part of everyday language. They represent concepts which are frequently used in everyday communication. Technical terms or scientific language were excluded.

In contrast to many contributions, my project has been put on a larger footing. As noted above, its central concern is to adumbrate polysemy relations which may be universal in the sense of attested in genetically and areally remote cultures.

To this end, languages around the world were taken into consideration. Whenever possible, I tried to compile examples from all continents. Occasionally, this endeavor was bound to fail – possibly for entirely circumstantial reasons: For most languages; the word lists available were sparse, at times restricted to citing only a single basic meaning. Add to this the impediment that many reference works did not even contain entries for the items under scrutiny (like *think, count*, etc.). Furthermore, etymological links obscured by morphological alterations usually eluded my notice.

The main sources of reference were ordinary dictionaries, supplemented or replaced by a few etymological works. For some languages, I had the opportunity to interview native speakers.

Given the fulfillment of other vital criteria detailed above, cases of polysemy were ascribed to metaphorical transfer and interpreted as signs of lexical change.

In this way, a number of striking semantic affinities emerged which will be reviewed below.

4. The data

4.1. Perception verbs revisited

Sweetser (1990) attracts attention to a cluster of diachronic processes attributable to the MIND-AS-BODY metaphor (see Sweetser 1990: 28). Three distinct shifts elucidated in her work will be put to the test against the backdrop of a larger sample incorporating non-Indo-European languages:

1) Lexical units denoting physical sight typically expand to the domain of intellection.

2) "Verbs of hearing ... often come to mean 'listen, heed' ... From 'heed' we have a further semantic shift to 'obey' ...". (Sweetser 1990: 35)

3) Several cognates deriving from Indo-European *g'eus- (e.g. Greek *geúomai* 'taste' and Germanic *kusan* 'try') point to a development connecting TASTE and ATTEMPT. Unfortunately, its "... direction ... is not ... clear; the Indo-European root could have meant 'try' rather than 'taste' (Sweetser 1990: 36)".

Intriguingly, the same patterns were found to operate in a great variety of languages. Apropos of vision, research on semantic universals has produced pertinent results: "As in the case of KNOW, THINK is often involved in polysemous relationships with words of perception". Goddard – Wierzbicka 1994: 457)

In a similar vein, we may supply ample evidence of the links between HEAR/OBEY and TASTE/TRY:

1) HEAR – OBEY (English paradigm: *obey* < Latin *oboedire*; *ob-* 'towards' + *audire* 'hear').
Egyptian (*sdm* 'hear'; 'obey'),Ge'ez (*sam'a* 'hear'; 'obey'), Hausa (*ji* 'heard'; 'obeyed'), Finnish (*kuulla* 'hear', 'obey'), Tamil (*kēl* 'hear'; 'obey'), Telugu (*vinu* 'hear'; 'obey'), Manchu (*donjibumbi* 'let someone hear'; 'obey'), Turkish (*dinlemek* 'listen to'; 'hear'; 'obey'), Japanese (*kiku* 'hear', 'obey'), Korean (*tut.ta* 'hears'; 'obeys'), Guugu Yimidhirr (*milga-dhirr* 'obedient' (*milga* 'ear'; *dhirr* COMITATIVE)), Djabugay (*bina warray* 'disobedient' ("ear bad")), Buru (*čaa-n* 'hear'; 'obey'), Kaulong (*hul ßet* literally 'hear under'; 'obey'), Paamese (*loɲe* 'hear'; 'obey'), Kiribati (*oɲo taeka* 'hear the word'; 'obey'), Swahili (*sikia* 'hear'; 'obey'), Zulu (*zwa* 'hear'; 'obey'), Maya/Tzotzil (*'a'ik'op* 'be obedient' ("hear words")), Nahuatl (*caqui* 'hear'; 'obey').

2) TRY, ATTEMPT – TASTE (no English paradigm).
Finnish (*maistaa* 'taste'; 'try'), Japanese (*tamesu* 'try', 'test'; 'taste'), Ponapean (*soɲ* 'try', 'attempt'; 'taste'), Tagalog (*āto* + *-um-/-in, sūbok* 'try', 'test'; 'taste'), Timugon/Murut (*kinam* (*maɲ- -in*) 'taste'; also 'try'), Kilivila (*-yosikola-* 'try'; 'taste'), Malagasy (*manàndrana* 'try'; 'taste'), Swahili (*onja* 'taste'; 'try', 'test'), Nahuatl (*yecoa: tla* 'do something', 'make an effort'; 'try or taste something' (a dish, food)), Quechua (*mali-* 'try', 'test', 'taste'), Maya (*tumtah* 'try'; 'taste').

It will be incumbent on future inquiries to map out the details of the transition from HEAR to OBEY: To determine whether intervening stages have to be posited does not fall within the ambit of this paper.

The foregoing examples raise (at least) two questions to be addressed below.

1. What are alternative pathways undergone by SEE and HEAR?
2. Can we spot some further donor items for INTELLECTION and OBEDIENCE?

4.2. Visual and auditory perception – some alternative developments

Even if the VISION/INTELLECTION metaphor may outweigh other drifts originating in verbs of seeing, large-scale comparison reveals further options: SEE →VISIT; SEE →BEWARE; SEE →TAKE CARE OF/ LOOK AFTER; SEE →WAIT.

3) SEE/LOOK/WATCH → VISIT (English paradigm: *to go and see someone* (for "visit")). Hadiyya (*mo (o) ?-* 'see', 'look (at)'; 'visit'), Ge'ez (*ḥawwaṣa* 'glance', 'look on', 'look after'; 'visit'; 'watch'), Hungarian (*lát* 'see', 'perceive' – *meglát* 'catch sight of' – *meglátogat* 'visit someone'), Ostyak (*wɔpöj-* 'visit', etymon *woppe-* 'see'), Turkish (*görmek* 'see'; 'visit'; 'experience'), North Caucasian (**ʔwerV* 'look', 'sight' – Lezghi **ʔwVr-* 'glance'; 'visit'), Manchu (*tuwambi* 'look'; 'visit'), Korean (*pota* 'perceives', 'sees'; 'visits'), Indonesian (*tilik* 'glance at something'; 'visit someone'), Yoruba (*bèwo* 'visit'; 'look at'), Maya (*il* 'see'; 'visit'), Nahuatl (*iitta* 'visit someone frequently' → frequentative of *itta* 'look at oneself'; 'see something'), Navajo (*-tse'* 'see'; 'visit'), Quechua (*qawayku-* 'visit' – *qawa-* 'watch', 'see').

4) SEE → BEWARE, BE CAREFUL (English paradigm: *watch out!*). Ge'ez (*ṭayyaqa* 'observe', 'look at', 'beware'), Burji (*eeg-ad'-* 'be careful' (*egg-* 'watch')), Hadiyya (*ki-gaga ege'l-* 'your-self watch' + reflexive), Yenisei-Samoyed (*litobiz* 'I am careful' related to an etymon meaning 'see'), Votyak (*ut'-* 'look'; 'be careful'), Hungarian (*vigyáz* 'be careful' from an etymon meaning 'see'), Turkish (*basiretli* 'clear-sighted'; 'far-seeing'; 'cautious', 'circumspect' – *basır* 'who sees'; *basıra* 'eyesight', 'vision'; 'eye'), Mongolian (*charach* 'look (at)'; 'be careful'; 'guard'; 'supervise'; 'look after someone'), Indonesian (*menindjau* 'watch', 'observe' (at a distance); 'look at' – *bertindjau-tindjauan* 'be on one's guard'), Kilivila (*-yamata-* 'have an eye upon'; 'keep an eye on', 'look after' – *Kuyamata!* 'Be careful!'), Proto-Bantu (**-kéb-* 'look'; 'take care'), Swahili (*angalia* 'look at'; 'be careful', 'beware (of)'), Zulu (*beka* 'look'; 'be careful', 'take precautions against'), Maya/Tzotzil (*vik'il sat vinik* 'cautious person'; literally 'open-eyed person'), Nahuatl (*iitzqui in iyollo* 'he is cautious', ultimately derived from *itta* 'look at oneself'; 'see something'), Quechua (*qawa-* 'watch', 'see' – *qawariku-* 'be careful').

5) SEE → TAKE CARE OF/LOOK AFTER (English paradigm: *look after*). Egyptian (*nw* 'see', 'look', 'take care of'; 'look after'), Hausa (*hanga* 'see in distance' – Gude *nəngə* 'watch', 'look after', 'take care of'), Ge'ez (*ḥawwaṣa* 'glance', 'look on', 'look after', 'take care of'), Sumerian (*igi-du + ni* 'look at something'; 'see' – *igi-du-nà-a* 'someone who looks after someone/something'), Kurux (*ērnā (īryas)* 'look', 'see', 'look after'), Finnish (*katsoa* 'look at'; 'take care of', 'look after'), Hungarian (*néz* 'look at'; 'look for'; 'consider' – *utána nez* 'look after' (*utána*

'after')), Turkish (*bakmak* 'look'; 'care for', 'look after', 'tend'), Mongolian (*charach* 'look (at)'; 'guard'; 'supervise'; 'look after someone'), Khmer (*[mə:l]* 'see'; 'take care of'), Vietnamese (*nhìn* 'see'; 'take care of'), Kwamera (*-ata amasan* 'see good'; 'protect', 'look after'), Marshallese (*lale* 'look', 'see'; 'preserve', 'look after'), Yir-Yoront (*mon=karr* 'accompany and look after', 'take care of' (*karr* 'see')), Malagasy (*miàndry* 'expect'; 'take care of' – *miandrànda* 'hope for'; 'look up'), Swahili (*angalia* 'look at'; 'be careful' – *mwangalizi* 'a careful, observant person'; 'caretaker', 'guardian'), Zulu (*beka* 'look'; 'take care of', 'look after'), Nahuatl (*īxōtiā* 'keep watch'; 'take care of something', 'look after something' – *īx-tli* 'face', 'surface', 'eye').

6) SEE → WAIT, EXPECT (English paradigm: *expect* < Latin *exspectare*; *ex-* + *spectare*: 'look at').

Ge'ez (*ta'aqba* 'be watched', 'be cared for', 'wait'), Gedeo (*hekk'-* 'wait (for)', 'watch', 'look after'), Tavgi-Samoyed (*båröd'a* 'wait' from an etymon meaning 'see'), Turkish (*bakmak* 'look'; 'wait (for)'; 'take care of', 'look after' – *-b-nin yoluna bakmak* 'expect someone' (*yol* 'way')), Brahui (*hunning* 'look', 'look at', 'look for', 'wait for'), Kurux (*ērnā (īryas)* 'look', 'see', 'wait for'), Nyawaygi (*ɲa:-G* 'see', 'look at' → *ɲa:gi-∅* (antipassive of *ɲa:-G*) 'wait'), Yir-Yoront (*mel wany* 'keep an eye out for', 'wait and worry'; 'glance' (mutual calque with Kuk-Narr *yel yem* 'looks'; *mel* 'eye'; *wany* 'throw')), Malagasy (*miàndry* 'expect'; 'take care of' – *miandrànda* 'hope for'; 'look up'), Swahili (*tazamia* 'look into'; 'expect' – *tazama* 'look (at)'), Zulu (*beka* 'look'; 'expect', 'wait for'), Proto-Bantu (**-dìnd-* 'wait'; 'watch over'), Nahuatl (*chiya: tla* 'wait for something', 'watch for something'; 'look at something').

That SEE, WATCH, GUARD and WAIT are interrelated is corroborated by further shifts:

7) WAIT/EXPECT – GUARD/TAKE CARE OF (English *to wait* vs. *to wait on* (i.e. "to act as an attendant to"; "to serve") might belong in this group).
Hausa (*dākata* 'wait', 'await' – Bilin *takau* 'guard'), Oromo (*eega* 'wait'; 'watch' (cattle)), Hungarian (*vár-* 'wait', 'expect' – etymon *warʒ-* 'guard'; 'wait'), Turkish (*beklemek* 'wait'; 'guard'; 'keep watch'; 'expect', 'hope for'), Yir-Yoront (*kow* 'take care of', 'care for', 'mind'; 'keep a lookout for (someone in distress)' related to Wik-Mungkan *kuup* 'wait for', Wik-Ngathana *koeoep-* 'care for', 'own'), Zulu (*linda* 'guard', 'keep watch over', 'look after'; 'wait for'; 'expect').

8) SEE → WATCH (i.e. KEEP WATCH, GUARD..) (English paradigm: *watch* (i.e. "look at") – *keep watch*).
Hausa (*dība* 'look at', 'look for' → *bedauye dibi* 'guard', 'watch', 'keep safe'), Sumerian (*igi – ĝál* 'look at'; 'keep watch'), Yurak-Samoyed (*jierā-, jera-* 'guard' – from an etymon meaning 'see'), Ostyak (*wapi-* 'guard' – etymon *woppe* 'see'), Zulu (*beka* 'look', 'watch'; 'supervise'), Mongolian (*charach* 'look (at)'; 'guard'; 'supervise'), Manchu (*tuwambi* 'look'; 'oversee'), Nahuatl (*īxōtiā* 'keep watch'; 'take care of something', 'look after something' – *īx-tli* 'face', 'surface', 'eye').

Comparable to VISION, auditory perception figures as a fundamental vehicle for INTELLECTION (confer Goddard – Wierzbicka 1994: 457).

Capitalizing on the insight that metaphor is " ... primarily a matter of thought and action and only derivatively a matter of language" (Lakoff – Johnson 1980: 153), we might expect the underlying equation to be manifested in different ways. In fact, DEAF →STUPID is modeled on the same paradigm.

9) DEAF → STUPID (no English paradigm).
Ge'ez (*danqawa* 'to be deaf'; 'ignorant', 'stupid'), Sumerian (*idim* 'deaf'; 'stupid'), Hungarian (*süket* 'deaf'; 'stupid' (slang)), Indonesian (*buta tuli* 'blind and deaf'; 'be completely ignorant of something'), Guugu Yimidhirr (*milga-mul* 'deaf', 'stupid' ('ear-PRIVATIVE')), Yir-Yoront (*ngengkeny* 'deaf'; 'stupid and uncontrollably bad-tempered'), Kuuk-Thaayorre (*waal-a* 'hard of hearing', 'silly', 'stupid'), Maung (*galadja* 'deaf person', 'half-wit'), Kilivila (*-nagoa* 'stupid'; 'having a defect of speech'; 'dumb'; 'deaf'), Kayardild (*dunbuwa marralda* 'deaf', 'stupid'), Maya/ Tzotzil (*ton-kokil* 'stupidity' (literally 'stone deafness')), Nahuatl (*atlacaqui* 'deaf', *uel atlacaqui* 'stupid' (*uel* 'very')), Navajo (*t'óójaa' dijolee* 'without understanding' (literally 'with ball-shaped ears')), Quechua (*opa* 'deaf'; 'stupid').

4.3. Obedience and knowledge as target domains

4.3.1. Obedience

HEAR → OBEY (see 4.1) has a match in FOLLOW →OBEY.

10) FOLLOW- OBEY (English paradigm: *follow* (in the sense of "obey")).
Egyptian (*šms* 'follow', 'accompany'; 'obey' (words)), Hausa (*bi* 'follow'; 'obey'), Mongolian (*dagach* 'follow'; 'obey'), Finnish (*seurata* 'follow someone'; 'obey'), Hungarian (*követ* 'follow'; 'obey', 'observe'), Manchu (*dahambi* 'follow'; 'obey'), Korean (*ttaluta* 'follows'; 'obeys'), Japanese (*shitagau* 'follow'; 'obey'), Indonesian (*menuruti (turut)* 'follow'; 'obey'), Buru (*hai* 'follow'; 'obey'), Uma (*tuku²* 'follow'; 'obey'), Malagasy (*manàraka* 'follow'; 'obey').

4.3.2. Knowledge

IE words for physical manipulation (TOUCH, SEPARATE, GRASP, etc.) tend to acquire intellectual senses (confer Sweetser 1990: 38). Obviously, this mechanism transcends the narrow confines of Indo-European:

11) GRASP → UNDERSTAND (English paradigm: *to grasp*).
Hebrew (*[tafas]* 'grasp' (literally); 'understand'), Sumerian (*dab* 'grasp' (literally), 'understand'; 'learn'), Finno-Ugric (**muja-* 'touch' developed into 'know', 'understand'), Hungarian (*felfog* 'gather', 'hold up' (one's skirt); 'grasp', 'comprehend' (i.e. "understand") – *fog* 'hold'; 'seize', 'grasp', *fel* 'up'), Turkish (*kavramak* 'seize'; 'grasp'; 'understand', 'comprehend'), Tamil (*kol* 'seize', 'receive', 'contain', 'learn', 'think', 'regard' –*koluttu* 'cause to hold', 'explain'), North Caucasian (Rutul *l-ä=ḳa-* 'reach' – *χ-a=ḳa-* 'catch', 'hold' – *k-i=ḳa-* 'touch' – *g-i=ḳa-* 'understand'), Korean (*phaak* 'grasping', 'seizing', 'grabbing'; 'understanding'), Indonesian (*menangkap (tangkap)* 'grasp' (literally), 'understand'), Kilivila (*-sau-* 'know'; 'understand'; 'learn'; 'pick'), Djabugay (*dugayi-y* 'comprehend' (i.e. "understand") – *duga-l*

'fetch', 'grab'), Zulu(*bamba* 'catch', 'grip', 'hold', 'grasp'; 'grasp with the intellect', 'understand'), Nahuatl *(aaci* 'reach', 'touch', 'hold', 'come to know something completely'), Navajo (**Øt̯i̯jh* 'handle' – a slender, stiff object; 'show', 'understand').

Manual activity is a central component in a shift reminiscent of GRASP →UNDERSTAND: UNTIE → EXPLAIN.

12) UNTIE/ DISMEMBER → EXPLAIN, "SOLVE" (English paradigm: *to solve* < Latin *solvere* 'loosen').

Egyptian (*wh̯ᶜ* 'unfurl'; 'explain', 'solve', 'loose'), Hausa (*warwar̯ē* 'disentangled'; 'unraveled'; 'unwound (thread) from spool'; 'unfolded' (bundle of thread prepared for weaving); 'explained', 'solved' (problem)), Hungarian (*kibogoz* 'untie', 'unravel', 'undo'; 'solve' (figuratively), 'puzzle out', 'unravel'), Turkish (*çözmek* 'untie'; 'unravel', 'disentangle'; 'solve' (an equation); 'solve' (figuratively: a problem, cipher); 'decipher'), Manchu (*sumbi* 'remove'; 'untie'; 'explain', 'annotate'), Japanese (*toku* 'untie'; 'solve' (a puzzle, equation, difficult question)), Korean (*phulta* 'unties', 'unfastens'; 'pacifies'; 'solves' (a problem...)), Vietnamese (*giai* 'untie'; 'explain', 'solve' (a problem, puzzle)), Khmer (*[sra:y]* 'untie'; 'explain'), Takia (*-filale* 'untie'; 'explain'), Kwamera (*-oseri* 'unroll', 'unwind'; 'solve'; 'explain'), Lango (*gɔŋ̯ɔ* 'untie', 'undress', 'interpret'), Zulu (*qaqa* 'rip up', 'rip open'; 'undo a seam'; 'explain a difficulty'), Swahili (*fundua* 'undo a knot', 'untie'; 'explain a difficulty').

Yet another item which is prone to take a similar course, i.e. COUNT, will be discussed in 4.4.2.

4.4. Polysemy networks

Following the procedure adopted for SEE, this section unravels *clusters* of senses associated with SEARCHING and COUNTING.

4.4.1. COUNT

Linguistic items incorporating the sense of "counting"/ "calculating" frequently encroach upon three semantic fields: UNDERSTANDING, TELLING and READING. The former two drifts are not extraneous to English – witness dictionary entries for *count* ("to reckon", "to consider", "to regard"; "to esteem"; "to tell" (obsolete), "to relate" (obsolete), "to recount" (obsolete)). By contrast, the latter case seems unfamiliar. Within the pale of Indo-European languages, Greek *légein* 'to collect', 'to gather'; 'to count'; 'to speak' – which is related to Latin *legere* 'to gather', 'to read' – might pattern in an analogous way.

(13) COUNT/CALCULATE – CONSIDER; REGARD AS, THINK.
(English paradigm: *to count someone something* (e.g. *He was counted a good parish man*).)
Egyptian (*jp* 'count'; 'pay'; 'consider'; 'be reasonable'), Ge'ez (*hasaba* 'think', 'consider' – *hassaba* 'compute', 'count', 'calculate'), Hausa (*k̯ididdig̯a yan̯ā̱ idid-dig̯a* 'he's reflecting' (*yan̯ā̱* 'he'), 'pondering'; *an̯āk̯ididdig̯ā̱ su* 'they're being

counted' (*su* 'they')), Sumerian (*šár* 'calculate'; 'consider carefully'), Telugu (*ennu* 'count'; 'think', 'esteem'), Kannada (*eṇike* 'counting', 'number', 'thinking'), North Caucasian (*=*īčwĒl* 'count'; 'understand' – Nakhada dialect of Gunzib *=*ēš̌*- 'read'; 'learn'), Estonian (*arvama* 'reckon', 'count'; 'think'; 'consider'), Zyrian (*artal*- 'count', 'calculate'; 'think'), Hungarian (*számol* 'count'; 'take into account/ consideration'), Manchu (*bodombi* 'calculate'; 'plan', 'consider'), Turkish (*saymak* 'count'; 'calculate'; 'assume', 'consider' (figuratively); 'suppose'), Mongolian (*tooloch* 'calculate', 'count'; 'consider'), Indonesian (*menghitung* 'count, calculate' – *memperhitungkan* 'calculate'; 'take into consideration'), Khmer (*[rɔap]* 'count'; consider'), Balinese ((*N-*)*ituŋ* 'calculate', 'think something other', 'weighing up the pros and cons'), Rapanui (*tapa* 'count'; 'consider', 'determine'), Swahili (*hesabu* 'count'; 'consider as'), Zulu (*bala* 'count', 'calculate'; 'take into account'; 'analyze' – *balisa* 'cause to count'; 'ponder over one's troubles'), Yoruba (*kà* 'count', 'regard as'), Nahuatl (*yolpoa* 'think' – *yollotl* 'heart', *poa* 'count').

Incidentally, a related extension which I did not investigate systematically is COUNT → ESTEEM.

14) COUNT – ESTEEM (English paradigm: *to count*, i.e. "esteem").
Ge'ez (*ḥasaba* 'think', 'esteem' – *ḥassaba* 'compute', 'count'), Telugu (*ennu* 'count'; 'think', 'esteem'), Turkish (*saymak* 'count'; 'esteem', 'respect'), Khmer (*[rɔap]* 'count'; 'esteem', 'respect'), Maya (*xok* 'count', 'respect'), Nahuatl (*poa* 'count'; 'respect', 'esteem').

15) COUNT – READ (no English paradigm).
Sumerian (*šid* 'calculate', 'count'; 'read aloud'; 'recite'), Finnish (*luke*- 'calculate', 'count'; 'read'), Estonian (*lugema* 'read'; 'count'; 'consider'), Lappic (*lǫkkâ*- -*g*- 'count'; 'read'; 'bring tidings, news, of'; 'tell'), Cheremis (*luďa* 'count', 'calculate'; 'read'), Hungarian (*olvas*- 'read'; 'count'), North Caucasian (*=*īčwĒl* 'count'; 'understand' – Nakhada dialect of Gunzib *=*ēš̌*- 'read'; 'learn'), Takia (-*siti* 'count'; 'read'), Tolai (*luk* originally only 'count'; 'read'), Motu (*duahi-a* 'read'; 'count'), Mekeo (*e-kuapi (-na)* 'read'; original meaning 'count', 'tell off', 'check off'), Kwamera (-*awsini* 'read'; 'count'), Kiribati (*wareka* 'read'; 'count', 'spell', 'calculate'), Samoan (*faitau* 'count'; 'read'), Dami (*i-wese-ya* 'count'; also now 'read'), Kilivila (-*kalava*- 'count'; 'read'), Lango (*kwànnò, kwân* 'read', 'count'), Proto-Bantu (*-*bediŋg*- 'read', 'count'), Yoruba (*kà* 'count'; 'read'), Maya ((*xok* 'count', 'number'; 'read'), Nahuatl (*tlapōhua* 'count', 'read'), Navajo ('*íńíshta*' 'count'; 'read').

16) COUNT → TELL/ RECOUNT (English paradigm: *tell* < Old English *tellan* akin to Old High German *zellen* 'count', 'tell').
Hebrew (*[mesapér]* 'narrator' – *[mispar]* 'number'), Sumerian (*šiti, šid* 'tell', 'recite'), Malayalam (*ennuka* 'count', 'number', 'esteem', 'relate'), Koḍagu (*ëṇṇ*- 'say', 'tell' – related other Dravidian words meaning 'count'), Estonian (*lugu* 'story'; 'number' – etymon *luke* 'number'; 'count', 'calculate'), Lappic (*lǫkkâ*- -*g*- 'count'; 'read'; 'bring tidings, news, of'; 'tell', 'say'), Hungarian (*számol* 'count'; 'render/ give an account of something' – *beszámol* 'give an account of something', 'relate something'), Zulu (*balisa* 'cause to count'; 'recount the details of one's personal affairs' – *bala* 'count', 'calculate'; 'take into account'), Maya (*xok* 'count' – *u xoka'n*

kuxtal 'account of one's life, thoughts and words'), Nahuatl (*pōhua* 'count something', 'read something', 'recount', 'relate, or give account of something').

4.4.2. SEEK

Dictionary entries for English *seek* display a whole array of polysemous senses, which are – mediately or directly – related to a basic meaning "to search": "to go in search or quest of"; "to look for"; "to ask for", "to demand", "to request"; "to entreat", "to beseech (a person) to do something" (obsolete); "to pursue", "to make an effort", "to try", "to attempt to (do something)", "to aim"; "to examine", "to investigate", "to scrutinize" (obsolete), "to make a search or inquiry", etc.
It is fascinating to find these ostensibly haphazard polysemies paralleled in non-Indo-European languages:

17) LOOK FOR → REQUEST/DEMAND (English paradigm: *to seek* (i.e. "request")).
Egyptian (*wḥ3* 'look for', 'seek'; 'require', 'demand'), Ge'ez (*haśaśa* 'seek', 'look for', 'demand', 'entreat'), Hebrew (*[bikéʃ]* 'look for' – *[bakaʃa]* 'request'), Hausa (*biδa* 'seek' → Tangale *parį* 'look for', 'search' – Dangaleat *bōde* 'reclaim' (a debt)), Finnish (*pyytä-* 'look for'; 'request'), Estonian (*ot'sima* 'look for'; 'request'), Hungarian (*keres* 'look for something', 'seek something'; 'demand (something from someone)'), Turkish (*aramak* 'look for'; 'investigate'; (in certain contexts) 'demand', 'ask for'), Mongolian (*erech* 'look for'; 'ask for'), Manchu (*baimbi* 'seek', 'look for'; 'ask for', 'request'), Indonesian (*cari* 'look for'; *mencari* 'seek', 'look for'; *mencari muka* 'ask a favor' (*muka* 'face', 'front'), Korean (*kwu hata* 'looks for', 'seeks'; 'asks (for)'; 'wants', 'needs'; 'tries'), Japanese (*motomeru* 'demand'; 'request'; 'look for'), ?Maya (*kaxan-nah* 'look for', 'request' – *kaxtah* 'look for'), Nahuatl (*tēmolia: tē-tla* 'ask someone for something' – applicative of *tēmoa: tla* 'seek something').

18) LOOK FOR → TRY/ MAKE AN EFFORT/PURSUE (English paradigm: *to seek* (i.e. "try")).
Ge'ez (*xašaša* 'seek', 'look for'; 'study', 'pursue diligently'), Hausa (*biδa* 'seek' → Tangale *parį* 'look for' – Hadiyya *bu'n* 'taste', 'try'), Sumerian (*kin, kin-kin* 'look for'; 'aim at', 'attempt something'), Tamil (*tēṭu* 'seek', 'search for', 'inquire after', 'try' (as to do a thing)), Hungarian (*keres* 'look for something', 'seek something'; 'demand' (something from someone)), Estonian (*ot'sima* 'look for'; 'try'), Indonesian (*mencari* 'look for'; 'try for'), Vietnamese (*tìm* 'look for'; 'try'), Khmer (*[rɔːk]* 'look for'; 'try'), Korean (*kwu hata* 'looks for', 'seeks'; 'asks (for)'; 'tries'), Japanese (*motomeru* 'try'; 'look for'), ?Hupa (*wûn-* 'pursue or seek something'; 'attempt something by persistent effort').

19) LOOK FOR → INVESTIGATE/ EXAMINE (English paradigm: *to seek* (i.e. "to investigate").
Egyptian (*dᶜr* 'seek out'; 'investigate'),Ge'ez (*ḥatata* 'search', 'search out', 'question', 'ask', 'investigate'), Telugu (*vedaku* 'search', 'explore', 'examine', 'look for'; confer Kannada *bedaku* 'seek', 'look for'), Estonian (*ot'sima* 'look for' – *ära ot'sima* 'investigate'), Hungarian (*kutat* 'try to find', 'look for'; 'be engaged in research'), Turkish (*aramak* 'seek', 'look for'; 'examine', 'investigate'), Manchu (*baimbi* 'look for'; 'investigate'), Japanese (*tansaku* 'search'; 'investigation'), Indonesian (*cari*

'look for'; *mencari* 'seek', 'look for'; *mencari kutu* 'investigate' (*kutu* 'louse')), Khmer (*[rihrɔ:k]* 'look for'; 'investigate'), Zulu (*cinga* 'look for', 'search for'; 'examine'; 'inquire into', 'make research'), Maya (*kaxtah* 'look for' – *kaxlil* 'investigate'), Nahuatl (*itztani* 'someone who searches'; 'someone who examines').

4.5. A preliminary glimpse at the sphere of morality

In English, two words employed to characterize (a)moral behavior, i.e. *straight* and *crooked*, can be traced to complementary spatial terms. As can be gathered from the copious evidence at hand, we are not dealing with a sporadic phenomenon:

20) CROOKED/BENT → DISHONEST (English paradigm: *crooked* (i.e. "bent"; "dishonest")).
Egyptian (*gwš* 'be crooked', 'bent' (wood, oar, heart)),Ge'ez (*ṭawāy* 'crooked', 'bent', 'depraved', 'villain'), Hebrew (*['ivuj]* 'sin'; 'distortion', 'curvature'), ?Sumerian (*kúr* 'foreign'; 'hostile'; 'crooked' – *kúr-lul-tur* 'evil'), Votyak (*ki̠ri̠ž* 'crooked'; 'deceitful'), Tamil (*kōṭu* 'be crooked' – *kōṭṭam* 'bend', 'crookedness' (as of mind)), Turkish (*eğri* 'crooked', 'bent'; 'perverse'; 'devious' – *eğri bakmak* 'look with unkind/evil intentions'), Japanese (*magatta* 'bent'; 'crooked'; 'bad', 'dishonest'), Korean (*(p)pittwul.e cita* 'gets crooked'; 'is crooked' (figuratively)), Khmer (*[vi:ǝc]* 'crooked' (literally and figuratively); 'dishonest', 'deceitful'), Indonesian (*béngkok* 'crooked', 'bent'; 'dishonest'), Guugu Yimidhirr (*gurruunhgurruunh* 'crooked', 'improper'), Kilivila (*dodoga* 'crooked'; 'dishonest'), Malagasy (*mèloka* 'crooked'; 'guilty'), Quechua/Tarma (*wiq-lu-š* 'crooked', 'deformed' (hand) – *wik-su* 'twisted', 'wry', 'unreliable').

21) STRAIGHT – HONEST/SINCERE/TRUE/CORRECT/RIGHT (English paradigm: *straight* (i.e. "free from curves", "honest").
Egyptian (*mt* 'straight'; 'proper'; 'precise'; 'trustworthy'; 'just'), Sumerian (*si-sá* 'straight'; 'just'; 'correct'), Ge'ez (*rat'a* 'be straight'; 'right', 'sincere'), Hebrew ((*[jaʃar]* 'straight', 'upright'; 'honest'), Tamil (*ceppam* 'straightness'; 'correctness'; 'uprightness', 'impartiality'), Finnish (*oikea* 'straight'; 'correct'; 'just'), Hungarian (*egyenes* 'straight' (line); 'honest'; 'straightforward'), North-Caucasian (*=ītV* 'straight' – Avar-Andi *=it-* 'straight'; 'right', 'correct'), Turkish (*doğru* 'straight'; 'right'; 'true'; 'honest', 'faithful'), Manchu (*tob* 'straight', 'upright', 'right', 'just'; *tob tab* 'honest' (*tab* 'upright', 'regular'), Korean (*ōlʰ-palo* 'uprightly', 'straightly'; 'honestly'), Indonesian (*lurus* 'straight'; *lurus (hati)* 'honest'; 'correct' (translation)), Yabem (*kato* 'straight'; 'correct'), Motu (*maoro* 'straight'; 'right', 'correct'), Kayardild (*junku* 'right' (side); 'straight'; 'correct', 'true'), Guugu Yimidhirr (*dhumbuurr-gu* 'straight', 'proper'), Yir-Yoront (*morr-morr* 'straight'; 'true', 'directly' → *wal-morr* 'truth', 'not a lie'; 'proper', 'true'), Malagasy (*mahitsy* 'straight' (path, line), 'straightforward' (character)), Zulu (*-qondile* 'straight', 'direct'; 'righteous'), Maya/Tzotzil (*tojol 'olonton* 'virtuousness', literally 'straight heart' (*tojol* 'straight' (e.g. wall); 'right'))), Nahuatl (*melāhuac* 'something straight'; 'true', 'genuine', 'honest').

4.6. Further results

A keynote permeating this inquiry has been to foster the suspicion that future efforts might enable us to project a system of recurrent semantic affinities for the main portion of the lexicon. Concentrating on "social interaction" as a target scene, I would like to expand on this theme with a view to six etymological connections: SUPPORT →HELP, LEAN ON →RELY ON, GIVE →PERMIT, LEAVE →PERMIT, PAY BACK →REVENGE/PUNISH, FEAR →RESPECT, REVERENCE.

22) SUPPORT / HOLD UP/ CARRY → HELP (English paradigm: *to support* < Late Latin *supportare* 'carry').
Hebrew (*[tamax]* 'support' (literally and figuratively)), Koṇḍa (*ānika* 'support', 'help', 'prop' related to Kannada *ān*, *ānu* 'be upheld', 'rest on', 'support' (as the head)), Lappic (*tår'jō-* 'support' (literally and figuratively)), Hungarian (*támogat* 'support', 'prop up'; 'aid', 'help'), Turkish (*destek* 'support'; 'prop'; 'buttress'; 'aid' (figuratively)), Mongolian (*tulguurtaj* 'involving support' (literally and figuratively)), Manchu (*nikembi* 'lean', 'lean on'; 'rely on'), Indonesian (*menysokong* 'prop up', 'support'; 'aid'), Japanese (*sasaeru* 'support' (literally and figuratively)), Korean (*cici* 'support', 'upholding' (literally and figuratively)), Khmer (*[rɔːŋ]* 'support' (literally and figuratively)), Malagasy (*manòhana* 'support' (literally and figuratively)), Maya (*lat'* 'support with one's hands' – *lat'pach* 'help and favor').

23) LEAN ON → RELY ON (English paradigm: *to lean on* (i.e. "rest supported on something", "rely for support on")).
Egyptian (*rhn* 'lean on'; 'trust (in)', 'rely on'), Gedeo (*irk-at-* 'lean (on)', 'rely on', 'depend on'), Hebrew (*[niʃan]* 'lean on'; 'trust in'), Geʿez (*ʾasmaka* 'rest', 'lean', 'lean upon', 'rely'), Hausa (*dogara* 'lean on'; 'rely on'), Hungarian (*támaszkodik* 'lean on' (the piano, etc.); 'rely on', 'depend on'), Finnish (*nojautua* 'lean on'; 'trust someone'), Turkish (*dayanmak* 'lean on', 'prop oneself up'; 'rely on'; 'confide in'), Malayalam (*cāruka* 'lean against'; 'rely upon'), Manchu (*nikembi* 'lean', 'lean on'; 'depend on', 'rely on'), Malagasy (*miànkina* 'lean on'; 'rely on'), Zulu (*encika* 'lean against'; 'rely upon' (for support, help, or protection)); Swahili (*tegemea* 'lean upon', 'be propped upon'; 'trust (to)', 'rely (upon)').

24) GIVE → PERMIT/ CONSENT (English paradigm: *to give way*).[6]
Egyptian (*dj* 'give'; 'let', 'allow'), Hebrew (*[natan]* 'give'; 'allow'), Kannada (*ī (itt-)* 'give', 'allow', 'permit'), Kui (*sīva (sīt-)* 'give', 'allow'), Tamil (*koṭu* 'give'; 'allow'), Finnish (*antaa* 'give'; 'let'; 'grant', 'permit'), Sumerian (*aš* 'consent'; 'give'; 'agree'), Hausa (*bā* 'give' → Gurage *abä* 'give', 'allow', 'permit'), Indonesian (*beri, memberi(kan)* 'give'; 'permit'), Khmer (*[aːoy]* 'give'; 'permit'), Japanese (*ataeru* 'give'; 'allow', 'permit'), Kilivila (*-kasali-* 'allow'; 'present' (e.g. coconuts); 'distribute' (e.g. yams)), Sawai (*n-po i fiɛ* 'give him well'; 'let', 'permit'), Balinese (*maaŋ (baaŋ)* 'give'; 'let', 'permit'), Woleaian (*faŋa* 'give', 'send'; 'let', 'permit'), Maya/ Tzotzil (*'ak'* 'give'; 'permit'; 'put').

25) LEAVE → PERMIT (English paradigm: *to leave* ("go away from") *vs. to leave* ("allow, permit" (colloquial; chiefly U. S.)).
Hausa (*bari, bar* 'leave'; 'let', 'allow'), Geʿez (*xadaga* 'leave', 'abandon'; 'allow',

'permit'), Kannada (*biḍu* 'let loose'; 'quit' (as work), 'allow', 'permit'; 'go away' – *biḍuhu* 'leaving', etc.), Hungarian (*hagy-* 'let'; 'leave', 'allow', 'permit'; 'leave/ bequeath something someone' – from an etymon meaning 'let', 'leave', 'remain'), Dami (*i-tor-nē-ya* 'let', 'permit', literally 'third-leave-third sing-INF'), Lango (*wèkkò* 'leave'; 'let', 'allow'), Swahili (*acha* 'leave', 'go (part, depart) from'; 'abandon'; 'allow', 'permit'), Proto-Bantu (**-dèk-* 'allow'; 'leave'), Yoruba (*fisílè* 'leave'; 'allow').

26) PAY BACK → REVENGE, PUNISH (English paradigm: *to pay back*).

Ge'ez (*fadaya* 'pay back', 'pay a debt'; *fedā* 'punishment', 'revenge'), Malayalam (*vīṭuka* 'be paid or discharged'; 'be revenged' – *vīṭṭuka* 'discharge what is due', 'repay'), Tulu (*būuni* 'repay', 'give in return', 'avenge'), Finnish (*maksaa takaisin* 'pay back' (literally and figuratively)), ?Indonesian (*balasan* 'repayment', 'compensation'; 'revenge', 'punishment'; 'answer'), Vietnamese (*tra* 'give something back'; 'pay something'; 'revenge on someone'), Kilivila (*-sikweya-* 'revenge'; 'pay back'; 'be of the same size'), Zulu (*enana* 'pay back', 'compensate'; 'retaliate', 'requite'), Swahili (*lipa* 'pay', 'repay' – *lipo* 'payment', 'recompense', 'revenge'), Nahuatl (*cuepiltia* 'revenge'; 'give/pay back', 'pay back a loan'), Maya/ Tzotzil (*tojel* 'payment of debt'; 'punishment'), Navajo (*bich'į̄* *nindex'nishdlé* 'pay him back' (*nindex'nishdlé* 'pay back' (money)).

27) FEAR → RESPECT, REVERENCE, AWE (English paradigm: *to rever* < Latin *revereri*; *re- + vereri* 'fear', 'respect').

Egyptian (*nrj* 'frighten'; 'respect'; *nrw* 'terror', 'fear'; 'awe'),Ge'ez (*farha* 'be afraid'; 'fear' – *farāhi* 'fearful', 'reverent'; *ferhat* 'fear', 'dread', 'awe'), Hausa (*woba* 'misgivings', 'fear' → Arabic *hayba* 'awe', 'reverential fear'), Sumerian (*ní – te* 'be overwhelmed by fear'; 'fear'; 'revere'), Turkish (*perva* 'fear'; 'respect', 'esteem'), Estonian (*pelga-* 'fear'; 'respect' → etymon *pele-* 'fear'), Kurux (*elcnā (ilcyas)* 'fear'; 'have a reverential awe of'; 'have misgivings'), Indonesian (*takut* 'fear'; 'reverence', 'respect'), Marshallese (*lʌɟɡɒŋ* 'fear', 'fright'; 'awe'), Zulu (*ukwesaba* 'fear'; 'reverence'), Nahuatl (*mahui* 'be fearful', 'be afraid'; 'inspire fear or reverence', 'be glorious' – *mahuiztli* 'fear'; 'person worthy of honor'), Maya/ Tzotzil (*xi'* 'be afraid of', 'fear'; 'honor', 'respect', 'revere').

5. A note on image schemata

In the wake of Johnson (1987), Turner (1990) and Lakoff (1990), numerous proposals have been made which seek to explain metaphor by appeal to image schemata. While Lakoff (1990, 1993) and Turner (1990) remain vague as to their nature, Johnson (1987) offers a fully-fledged framework.

The gist of Johnson (1987) is condensed in the following statement:

Basically, what we are interested in is why certain metaphorical mappings exist, that is, why certain source-domains get mapped onto certain target-domains. And we also want to know what constraints govern the nature of the metaphorical mapping. In general, to explain how specific metaphorical projections constrain meaning relations and patterns of inference, we need to explore the structure of the image schemata upon which they are based, and we need to determine why the particular mappings of source-domains onto target-domains occur the way they do. (Johnson 1987: 113)

As Johnson's alternative term for image schema (i.e. "embodied schema") suggests, the constructs under scrutiny are inextricably linked to bodily movement and perception: "This [i.e. focusing on the nature of image schemata] requires an exploration of the way in which our perceptual interactions and bodily movements within our environment generate these schematic structures that make it possible for us to experience, understand, and reason about our world (Johnson 1987: 19)."

Pauwels – Simon-Vandenbergen (1995) provide a neat summary of Johnson's line of thought: "According to Johnson, metaphors are based on our abstract bodily experience of the world, which we translate into basic schemata (Pauwels – Simon-Vandenbergen 1995: 43)."

Johnson (1987: 126) cites a "highly selective" yet ever-recurrent list of image schemata:

CONTAINER	BALANCE	COMPULSION
COUNTERFORCE	RESTRAINT REMOVAL	ENABLEMENT
MASS/COUNT	PATH	LINK
CYCLE	NEAR/FAR	SCALE
MERGING	SPLITTING	FULL/EMPTY
SUPERIMPOSITION	ITERATION	CONTACT
SURFACE	OBJECT	COLLECTION
BLOCKAGE	ATTRACTION	CENTER/PERIPHERY
PART/WHOLE	MATCHING	PROCESS

Some adherents of the Johnsonian theory start out from a more or less fixed inventory of image schemata, relating them to metaphors found in their corpus. Certain refinements of such attempts at establishing the structures underlying metaphoric transfer suggest themselves on two counts.

(1) At times, treatments proceeding from a preconceived inventory of schemata responsible for metaphoric extension are of little explanatory value. Rather than tracing metaphors to a set of abstract models (as is done, for example in Pauwels – Simon-Vandenbergen 1995), we might commend the *reverse* procedure: A *comparative* analysis of similar metaphorization processes may help *discover* relevant "structures" triggering the extensions in the first place. Thus, no item on Johnson's list (see above) will be applicable to notions like STRAIGHT and CROOKED, which prove crucial to the conceptualization of HONESTY and FALSEHOOD.

(2) Whether or not applied in combination, the schemata offered so far are sometimes too general to motivate certain mappings. Consider words corresponding to German *suchen*, English *seek*, etc., which were found to be the starting point of various developments (e.g. SEARCH →TRY). PROCESS (see above)

seems to be the most suitable candidate for a relevant "schema". Yet presumably the bulk of words denoting "processes" do not trigger the metaphorization SEARCH →TRY. Consequently, it would be vacuous to resort to this highly abstract model. Indeed, Johnson's image-schemas are often taken as a starting-point for further elaboration.

The extension from notions like GRASP, HOLD, SEIZE to UNDERSTAND, COMPREHEND is another case in point (cf. 4.3.2.). Reviewing Johnson's list, CONTACT appears to be most closely associated with these notions. However, languages seem to draw on particular manifestations of CONTACT to the exclusion of others. Probably, items like STEP, BLOW, HIT, PAT, or CONTACT as such will generally not give rise to these senses. A more elaborate description of the underlying pattern seems necessary. Above all the manual nature of the contact plays a major role.

Broadly, the level of precision necessary for an adequate representation of schemata triggering metaphoric transfer can be established by suspending features distinctive of individual donor concepts. In other words, image-schemas might be conceived of as a function of similar source domains exploited for similar target domains.

A common metaphor for LIVE is apt to drive home this point most convincingly. Words for LIVING, EXISTING are often derived from etymons meaning "sit", "stand", or "lie". Only a comparative perspective will yield the relevant schema, i.e. POSITION. For these particular recipient units (i.e. LIVE, EXIST, BE), the *mode* of position (LIE, STAND or SIT) is irrelevant. On the other hand, there are liable to be certain metaphors which do exploit a more elaborate image: German *unterliegen* ('under-lie' – 'be defeated') versus *überstehen* ('over-stand' → 'survive') represent near-opposite conceptualizations which seem to preclude an interchange of the source concepts (*liegen* and *stehen*). Hence, uncovering underlying schemata requires a careful look at individual mappings.

6. Conclusion

The foregoing study has advanced some evidence against theories which are blinkered by recitals of the vicissitudes of lexical developments. For a number of core meanings, outlining tendencies of change has turned out a viable task. The more daring assumption that we might be able to prefigure globally recurrent trajectories for most basic senses remains a vague hypothesis to be vindicated or disconfirmed with the help of extensive related investigations. However, the rich gamut of concepts examined indicates that at some stage linguists might be able to chart comprehensive networks of lexical relations. To establish a cognitive topology of this type remains a worthwhile task for further projects.

Notes

1. "Grammaticalization" refers to " ... the routes by which words travel from lexical-content word status to grammatical morpheme status" (Sweetser 1990: 27).
2. Confer Camac – Glucksberg (1984: 450).
3. It would exceed the scope of this paper to elaborate on this problem. Some hints have to suffice: Semantic distance as reflected in domain incongruity is a gradual notion. Hence, whether or not two domains are contiguous or distinct is often a matter of debate. The complexity of domain structure characterizing most lexical items adds to the problem of distinguishing metaphor and metonymy (see Rudzka-Ostyn 1985).
4. Some scholars favor a terminology involving the terms "physical" versus "non-physical" or "emergent" versus "non-emergent" rather than "concrete" versus "abstract".
5. Sweetser (1990: 25) points out that Kronasser's hypothesis has been corroborated by a number of scholars, e.g. Benveniste (1969) and Traugott (1974, 1982).
6. I owe this example to Professor Barcelona.

References

Abraham, R. C.
  1958   *Dictionary of modern Yoruba*. London: University of London Press.
Alpher, Barry
  1991   *Yir-Yoront lexicon: Sketch and dictionary of an Australian language*. Berlin, New York: Mouton de Gruyter.
Anderson, John M.
  1973   *An essay concerning aspect: Some considerations of a general character arising from the Abbé Darrigol's analysis of the Basque verb*. The Hague: Mouton.
Anderson, John M. – Charles Jones (eds.)
  1974   *Historical linguistics I. Syntax, morphology, internal and comparative reconstruction. Proceedings of the first international conference on historical linguistics, Edinburgh 2nd-7th September 1973*. Amsterdam, Oxford: North-Holland.
Ashiwaju, Michael
  1968   *Lehrbuch der Yoruba-Sprache*. Leipzig: Verlag Enzyklopädie.
Barrera Vásquez, Alfredo
  1991   *Diccionario maya: Maya-español, español-maya*. Mexico: Ed. Porrúa. Vols. 1-2. (2nd edition.) Paris: Minuit.
Benveniste, Emile
  1969   *Le vocabulaire des institutions indo-européennes*. Vols. 1-2. Paris: Minuit.
Bergenholtz, Henning – Jürgen Richter-Johanningmeier – Eckehart Olszowski – Volker Zeiss (eds.)
  1991   *Madagassisch-deutsches Wörterbuch*. Moers: Ed. Aragon.
  1994   *Deutsch-madagassisches Wörterbuch*. Moers: Ed. Aragon.

Bierhorst, John
1985   *A Nahuatl-English dictionary and concordance to the CANTARES MEXICANOS: With an analytic transcription and grammatical notes.* Stanford, California: Stanford University Press.
Blust, Robert A.
1988   *Austronesian root theory: An essay on the limits of morphology.* Amsterdam: Benjamins
Burrow, Thomas – Murray B. Emeneau
1984   *A Dravidian etymological dictionary.* (2nd edition.) Oxford: Clarendon Press.
Camac, M. K. – S. Glucksberg
1984   "Metaphors do not use associations between concepts, they are used to create them", *Journal of Psycholinguistic Research* 13-6: 443-455.
Capell, Arthur – H. E. Hinch
1970   *Maung grammar: Texts and vocabulary.* The Hague, Paris: Mouton.
Delitzsch, Friedrich
1914   *Sumerisches Glossar.* Leipzig: Hinrichs'sche Buchhandlung.
[1969]   [Reprinted Leipzig: Zentralantiquariat der DDR.]
Dixon, Robert M. W. – Barry J. Blake (eds.)
1979-1991 *The handbook of Australian languages.* Vols. 1-4. Oxford: Oxford University Press Australia.
Doke, Clement M. – D. M. Malcolm – J. M. A. Sikakana – B. W. Vilakazi
1990   *English-Zulu, Zulu-English dictionary.* Johannesburg: Witwatersrand University Press.
Echols, John M. – Hassan Shadily
1989   *An Indonesian-English dictionary.* (3rd edition.) Ithaca: Cornell University Press.
Eco, Umberto
1984   *Semiotics and the philosophy of language.* Amsterdam: Benjamins.
Evans, Nicholas D.
1995   *A grammar of Kayardild: With historical-comparative notes on Tangkic.* Berlin, New York: Mouton de Gruyter.
Gaudes, Rüdiger
1985   *Wörterbuch Khmer-Deutsch.* Vols.1-2. Leipzig: Verlag Enzyklopädie.
Geeraerts, D.
1994   "Metonymy", in: R. E. Asher (ed.), *The encyclopedia of language and linguistics.* Vol. 5. Oxford: Pergamon, 2477-2478.
Givón, Talmy
1975   "Serial verbs and syntactic change: Niger-Congo", in: C. N. Li (ed.), *Word order and word order change.* Austin: University of Texas Press, 49-112.
Goddard, Cliff – Anna Wierzbicka (eds.)
1994   *Semantic and lexical universals: Theory and empirical findings.* Amsterdam, Philadelphia: Benjamins.
Golla, Victor (ed.)
1991   *The collected works of Edward Sapir VI. American Indian languages 2.* Berlin, New York: Mouton de Gruyter.

Goossens, Louis – Paul Pauwels – Brygida Rudzka-Ostyn – Anne-Marie Simon-Vandenbergen – Johan Vanparys
1995   *By word of mouth: Metaphor, metonymy and linguistic action in a cognitive perspective.* Amsterdam, Philadelphia: Benjamins.
Greenberg, Joseph H.
1978   "How does a language acquire gender markers?" in: Joseph H. Greenberg – Charles A. Ferguson – Edith Moravcsik (eds.), *Universals of human language III: Word structure.* Stanford: Stanford University Press, 47-83.
Guthrie, Malcolm
1967-1971 *Comparative Bantu: An introduction to the comparative linguistics and prehistory of the Bantu languages.* Vols. 1-4. Farnborough: Gregg.
Halász, Elod
1957   *Ungarisch-deutsches Wörterbuch.* Vols. 1-2. Budapest: Akadémiai Kiadó.
Hannig, Rainer
1995   *Großes Handwörterbuch Ägyptisch – Deutsch: Die Sprache der Pharaonen (2800-950 v. Chr.).* Mainz: von Zabern.
Hauer, Erich
1952   *Handwörterbuch der Mandschusprache.* Wiesbaden: Harrassowitz.
Herms, Irmtraud
1992   *Wörterbuch Hausa-Deutsch.* (2nd edition.) Leipzig: Langenscheidt, Verlag Enzyklopädie.
Hirvensalo, Lauri
1963   *Deutsch-Finnisches Wörterbuch.* Porvoo: Söderström Osakeyhtiö.
Hock, Hans Henrich
1986   *Principles of historical linguistics.* Berlin, New York, Amsterdam: Mouton de Gruyter.
Hockings, Paul – Christiane Pilot-Raichoor
1992   *A Badaga-English dictionary.* Berlin, New York: Mouton de Gruyter.
Hony, Henry C. – Fahir İz
1957   *The Oxford Turkish-English dictionary.* (2nd edition.) Oxford: Oxford University Press.
Hübner, Barbara – Albert Reizammer
1985-1986 *Inim kiengi. Sumerisch-deutsches Glossar in zwei Bänden.* Vols. 1-2. Marktredwitz: Selbstverlag A. Reizammer.
Hudson, Grover
1989   *Highland East Cushitic dictionary.* Hamburg: Buske.
Johnson, Frederick
1939   *A standard Swahili-English dictionary.* London: Oxford University Press.
Johnson, Mark
1987   *The body in the mind: The bodily basis of meaning, imagination, and reason.* Chicago, Ill.: University of Chicago Press.
Kahlo, Gerhard – Rosemarie Simon-Bärwinkel
1974   *Wörterbuch Indonesisch-Deutsch.* Leipzig: Verlag Enzyklopädie.

Karow, Otto – Irene Hilgers-Hesse
1978   *Indonesisch-deutsches Wörterbuch.* (2nd edition.) Wiesbaden: Harrassowitz
Karow, Otto
1972   *Vietnamesisch-deutsches Wörterbuch.* Wiesbaden: Harrassowitz.
Karttunen, Frances
1983   *An analytical dictionary of Nahuatl.* Austin: University of Texas Press.
Katara, Pekka
1970   *Finnisch-deutsches Wörterbuch.* (4th edition.) Porvoo, Helsinki: Söderström Osakeyhtiö.
Kimura, Kinji
1965   *Großes japanisch-deutsches Wörterbuch.* Tokyo: Hakuyusha.
Krause, Erich-Dieter
1985   *Wörterbuch Indonesisch-Deutsch.* München: Hueber.
Kronasser, Heinz
1952   *Handbuch der Semasiologie.* Heidelberg: Winter.
Lakoff, George
1990   "The Invariance Hypothesis: Is abstract reason based on image-schemas?", *Cognitive Linguistics* 1-1: 39-74.
1993   "The contemporary theory of metaphor", in: Andrew Ortony (ed.), *Metaphor and thought.* (2nd edition.) Cambridge: Cambridge University Press, 202-251.
Lakoff, George – Mark Johnson
1980   *Metaphors we live by.* Chicago: University of Chicago Press.
Lakoff, George – Mark Turner
1989   *More than cool reason: A field guide to poetic metaphor.* Chicago: University of Chicago Press.
Lambdin, Thomas O.
1978   *Introduction to classical Ethiopic (Ge'ez).* Missoula, Mass.: Scholars Press.
Laughlin, Robert M.
1988   *The great Tzotzil dictionary of Santo Domingo Zinacantán: With grammatical analysis and historical commentary.* Vols. 1-3. Washington, D.C.: Smithsonian Institution Press.
Lavy, Jaacov
1991   *Langenscheidts Handwörterbuch Hebräisch-Deutsch.* (6th edition.) Berlin: Langenscheidt.
Lesko, Leonard H. (ed.)
1982-90   *A dictionary of late Egyptian.* Vols. 1-5. Providence, R.I.: Scribe Publications.
Leslau, Wolf
1987   *Comparative dictionary of Ge'ez (Classical Ethiopic); Ge'ez-English/English-Ge'ez; with an index of the Semitic roots.* Wiesbaden: Harrassowitz.

Liedtke, Stefan
    1991   *Indianersprachen: Sprachvergleich und Klassifizierung; eine ethno-
            linguistische Einführung in die Grundlagen und Methoden.* Hamburg:
            Buske.
Magay, Tamás – László Országh
    1981   *A concise Hungarian-English dictionary.* Oxford: Oxford University
            Press.
Martin, Samuel E. – Yang Ha Lee – Sung-Un Chang
    1967   *A Korean-English dictionary.* New Haven, London: Yale University
            Press.
Miller, George A. – Philip N. Johnson-Laird
    1976   *Language and perception.* Cambridge, Mass.: Belknap Press.
Newman, Roxana Ma.
    1990   *An English-Hausa dictionary.* New Haven: Yale University Press.
Nikolayev, Sergej L. – Sergei A. Starostin
    1994   *A North Caucasian etymological dictionary.* Moscow: Asterisk.
Noonan, Michael
    1992   *A grammar of Lango.* Berlin, New York: Mouton de Gruyter.
Norman, Jerry
    1978   *A concise Manchu-English lexicon.* Seattle, London: University of
            Washington Press.
Paprotté, Wolf – René Dirven (eds.)
    1985   *The ubiquity of metaphor.* Amsterdam: Benjamins.
Parker, Gary John
    1969   *Ayacucho Quechua grammar and dictionary.* The Hague, Paris: Mouton.
Pauwels, Paul – Anne Marie Simon-Vanderbergen
    1995   "Body parts in linguistic action: underlying schemata and value judg-
            ments", in: Goossens, Louis – Paul Pauwels – Brygida Rudzka-Ostyn –
            Anne-MarieSimon Vandenbergen – Johan Vanparys, 35-70.
Persson, Gunnar
    1990   *Meanings and metaphors: A study in lexical semantics in English.* Stock-
            holm: Almqvist & Wiksell International.
Pokorny, Julius
    1959   *Indogermanisches Etymologisches Wörterbuch.* Vol. 1. Bern: Francke.
Rédei, Károly
    1988-91 *Uralisches Etymologisches Wörterbuch.* Vols. 1-3. Wiesbaden: Har-
            rassowitz.
Redhouse, James W.
    1968   *New Redhouse Turkish-English dictionary.* Istanbul: Redhouse Yayi-
            nevi.
Rudzka-Ostyn, Brygida
    1985   "Metaphoric processes in word formation. The case of prefixed verbs",
            in: Wolf Paprotté – René Dirven (eds.), 209-243.
Saagpakk, Paul F.
    1982   *Estonian-English dictionary.* New Haven, Conn.: Yale University Press.

Senft, Gunter
1986   Kilivila: *The language of the Trobriand islanders*. Berlin, New York, Amsterdam: Mouton de Gruyter.
Siméon, Rémi
1885   *Dictionnaire de la langue nahuatl ou mexicaine*. Paris: Imprimerie Nationale.
[1963]   [Reprinted Graz: Akademische Druck- und Verlagsanstalt.]
Skinner, Neil
1996   *Hausa comparative dictionary*. Köln: Köppe.
Steuerwald, Karl
1972   *Türkisch-deutsches Wörterbuch*. Wiesbaden: Harrassowitz.
Sweetser, Eve
1990   *From etymology to pragmatics. Metaphorical and cultural aspects of semantic structure*. Cambridge: Cambridge University Press.
Taylor, John R.
1995   *Linguistic categorization. Prototypes in linguistic theory*. (2nd edition.) Oxford: Clarendon Press.
Traugott, Elizabeth C
1974   "Explorations in linguistic elaboration; language change, language acquisition, and the genesis of spatio-temporal terms", in: John M. Anderson – Charles Jones (eds.), 263-314.
1982   "From propositional to textual and expressive meanings: Some semantic-pragmatic aspects of grammaticalization", in: Winfred P. Lehmann – Yakov Malkiel (eds.), *Perspectives on historical linguistics*. Amsterdam: Benjamins, 245-271.
1985a   "On regularity in semantic change", *Journal of Literary Semantics* 14: 155-173.
1985b   "'Conventional' and 'dead' metaphors revisited", in: Wolf Paprotté – René Dirven (eds.), 17-56.
1988   "Pragmatic strengthening and grammaticalization", *Proceedings of the fourteenth annual meeting of the Berkeley Linguistics Society:* 406-416.
Tryon, Darrell T. (ed.)
1995   *Comparative Austronesian dictionary: An introduction to Austronesian studies*. Vols. 1-4. Berlin, New York: Mouton de Gruyter.
Turner, Mark
1990   "Aspects of the Invariance Hypothesis", *Cognitive Linguistics* 1-2: 247-255.
Vietze, Hans-Peter
1988   *Wörterbuch Mongolisch-Deutsch*. Leipzig: Verlag Enzyklopädie.
Walravens, Hartmut – Martin Gimm
1978   *Deutsch-mandjurisches Wörterverzeichnis (nach H. C. von der Gabelentz' Mandschu-Deutschem Wörterbuch)*. Wiesbaden: Steiner.
Werth, Paul
1974   "Accounting for semantic change in current linguistic theory", in: John M. Anderson – Charles Jones (eds.), 377-415.

Wiedemann, Ferdinand Johann
    1973   *Estnisch-Deutsches Wörterbuch. Nach der von Jakob Hurt redigierten Auflage.* Tallinn: Valgus.
Wilkins, David P.
    1996   "Natural tendencies of semantic change and the search for cognates", in: Mark Durie – Malcolm Ross (eds.), *The comparative method reviewed: Regularity and irregularity in language change.* New York, Oxford: Oxford University Press, 264-304.
Williams, Joseph M.
    1976   "Synaesthetic adjectives: A possible law of semantic change", *Language* 52: 461-478.
Young, Robert W. – William Morgan
    1980   *The Navajo language: A grammar and colloquial dictionary.* Albuquerque: University of New Mexico Press.

Straight from the heart – metonymic and metaphorical explorations

Susanne Niemeier

1. Introduction

Whereas research on metonymies has been rather neglected until quite recently, cognitive linguistics has from its very beginnings been interested in the way metaphors are conceptualized and used. During the last few years, however, the tide has begun to turn (e.g. Croft 1993; Dirven 1993; Goossens 1995; Panther – Radden, forthcoming). Many of the more recent publications on this subject are particularly concerned with the relationship between metaphor and metonymy, both of which represent mental strategies that are considered to facilitate understanding and that carry extra information as opposed to more "neutral" ways of expression.

Dirven (1993), for example, proposes a continuum with metaphor at one end and metonymy at the other and with different interim stages. Goossens (1995) focuses more on the interaction between the two strategies and proposes four different kinds of "metaphtonymies". Both analyses see metaphor and metonymy as strategies of equal importance. In this paper I will argue that this equal ranking is not necessarily a given: it would appear that metonymies antecede metaphors in language development in that many – if not all – metaphors have a metonymic basis, i.e. are dependent on a conceptually prior metonymic conceptualization.

These underlying metonymizations are particularly clear in expressions referring to emotions. I will therefore focus on one particular domain, namely the folk model of the heart as the site of emotions as it exists in the English language. A folk model may be generally defined as both the synthesis and simultaneously as the source of many clusters of metaphors and metonymies and also of many single individual metaphors and metonymies. In this respect, it differs fundamentally from Lakoff's notion of conceptual metaphor which sees one global conceptual domain mapped onto some other domain. A folk model, on the other hand, combines a variety of single and often contradictory metonymic and metaphorical views crystallizing in a more dominant concept. As will be shown, a folk model usually contains various submodels also that complement each other as different facets of the more general folk model.

While the folk model of the heart as the site of emotions does not qualify as a cultural universal,[1] it is nevertheless found in many different cultures. English is particularly rich in both metonymic and metaphorical expressions making use of the concept *heart* to speak of emotional issues, be it in a semasiological or in an onomasiological sense.

The present contribution will briefly discuss cognitive theories of metaphor and metonymy and the relations between them (2.) and then proceed to an analysis of a sample of "heart" expressions taken from a corpus of dictionaries and thesauri: Gadsby (1995), Kirkpatrick (1987), and Rees (1997) (3.). Finally, an attempt will be made at developing a network of meaning of those expressions referring to the folk model of the heart as the site of emotions as it exists in the English language and at showing that the heart metaphors ultimately rely also on a prior metonymic perspectivization of the heart as a source domain for the metaphorical mapping (4.).

2. Metaphor and metonymy from a cognitive point of view

Lakoff & Johnson (1980) were the first to present a cognitive analysis of conceptual metaphors. From a cognitive perspective, metaphors function by mapping the meaning structure of a more concrete source domain onto the as yet dimly seen conceptual structure of a more abstract target domain in order to facilitate understanding of this second domain in some way. Lakoff & Johnson claim that conceptual metaphors in all their complexity, e.g. LIFE IS A JOURNEY, influence not only our linguistic behavior but also our thought processes and our systems of values. Therefore these metaphors appear as very general equations, but they may be specified as more restricted metaphor domains such as LOVE IS A JOURNEY, which in turn can be specified as really existing metaphors as for instance "We have to go our separate ways". New creative metaphors ultimately rely also on conceptual metaphors because they make use of the schemata underlying the latter and extend them in an innovative way by the full lexical or syntactic exploitation of the same principles triggering everyday metaphors (Lakoff – Turner 1989).

As already mentioned above, cognitive theories of metonymy have been quite neglected so far. Although Jakobson, as early as 1956, already differentiated between metonymic and metaphorical principles as the two most basic human abilities to effect conceptualization, his theory has hardly been given any attention in more recent publications on conceptualizations via metaphor and metonymy (Dirven 1993:2-3). In accordance with his post-Saussurean intellectual surroundings, Jakobson formulated his hypothesis as a dichotomy, where metaphors represent the paradigmatic pole because they replace an expression by another expression, and metonymies represent the syntagmatic pole which in a given syntagm, for example the regalia of a monarch, selects an outstanding element, such as the crown, which then evokes the whole syntagm. Dirven (1993) shows how Jakobson's ideas can be made fruitful for cognitive theorizing.

Although the interest in metonymy seems to have been slowly increasing in recent times, scholars are still confronted with a lack of research paradigms and empirical data. Metonymies are often regarded as reference phenomena (Lakoff – Johnson 1980; Lakoff 1987) and the aspect of syntagmatic – or in cognitive terms, "conceptual" – contiguity is stressed. Accepting the view that contiguity is the conceptual basis of metonymy means at the same time accepting it as standing in contrast to the traditionally postulated relation of similarity as a conceptual basis of metaphors (Jakobson 1956; Blank 1993). The conceptual contiguity of metonymy is based on extralinguistic experiences and connotations and is therefore culture-dependent. Most current theories start from the presupposition that metonymies engage in different relations inside a *domain matrix* (Croft 1993), an *ICM (Idealized Cognitive Model*, Lakoff 1987), or a *frame* (Fillmore 1977), whereas metaphors transcend these boundaries.[2]

Dirven (1993) shows that this view is somewhat reductionist because the number of domains involved depends on the process of construal on the language user's part. Furthermore, he shows that metonymies do not have to be limited to one domain but can also contain two different domains. However, these different domains both rest intact and autonomous and no meaning transfer takes place, whereas in metaphor, the target domain always dissolves into the source domain partly or completely. What matters in metaphor, however, is that the two domains are seen as being initially at a conceptual distance. Thus, elaborating on Jakobson's ideas, the relation of similarity which is postulated as the conceptual basis of metaphor can also be conceived of as a relation of opposition.

In any case, both conceptual strategies have been traditionally and predominantly dealt with as stylistic devices in literature studies. Cognitive linguistics, however, is not primarily interested in this creative usage, but in the strategies that underlie both the creative usage and the everyday usage. This everyday usage happens largely subconsciously but is nevertheless able to orientate one's thought processes and at some deeper level reflects the values, attitudes, and norms of the language users, or, in a word, their culture. In this respect, metonymies are even more pervasive than metaphors. They come in all sorts of different shapes, each of them highlighting a further relation between the referent as such and the metonymy denoting it. In contrast to "plain language", these utterances are often endowed with more surprise effects or expressivity insofar as superficially they appear to say similar things as their neutral equivalents but in addition they "color" the utterances with nuances of the language users' inherent worldview.

Thus, both metaphors and metonymies offer a possible inroad into the conceptualization processes underlying them. What is intriguing to analyze then is the process of choice which leads the language user to resort to exactly this way of expressing him-/herself. These processes of choice may have been influenced by a lot of factors outside one's voluntary control, one of these factors being emotions. As emotions correlate quite closely with expressivity, one should be able to find a higher number of metaphorical and metonymic expressions when speaking of emotions or when experiencing a certain emotion. Therefore, choosing expressions which refer to or contain the notion of *heart* seems to be not only a potentially rich but also a heuristically legitimate way of collecting and analyzing a folk-model sample of the language of emotions.

Furthermore, the experience of emotions is very often based on physiological factors (e.g. see Kövecses 1986, 1995 for an analysis of the concept of "anger") which are then taken as metonymies for the emotional experience itself (consider for example the expression "I am boiling with anger", referring to the sensation of increasing heat inside oneself). Such metonymies may themselves be metonymized – the expression "I blew my top", for example, refers to the final moment in the whole scenario of a liquid that boils over. Seen in isolation, "blowing one's top" would not necessarily be considered a metonymy but rather a metaphor. Within the whole folk model of "anger", however, it is connected to other expressions such as "boiling with anger" and "red-hot anger" – insofar as it may be conceived of as the final stage of the "boiling process" – and can thus be presumed to be metonymically linked to these expressions. This kind of linkage seems to work for many other emotion metaphors as well, as will be shown in the analysis below.

Most of the more recent theories stress the fact that metaphor and metonymy are not opposed to each other but rather that they are to be seen in close relation. Already Lévi-Strauss (1976: 205) postulated the interdependence of metaphor and metonymy. This route has been followed by Goossens (1995), who coined the term "metaphtonymy" to globally describe different kinds of relationships between metaphor and metonymy. Pursuing Jakobson's view of metaphor at one extreme and metonymy at the other, it becomes obvious that there have to be certain interim stages. These stages are possible because the boundaries between the two poles and between the domains involved are fuzzy. Goossens differentiates between four different types of interaction between metaphor and metonymy.[3] Dirven (1993) also rejects the view of the two extreme poles of metaphor and metonymy and claims the existence of a continuum of intermediate meaning ascriptions via conceptualization processes between those two poles.[4]

One could even go one step further and wonder if all metaphorical mappings do not require a metonymic perspectivization (Taylor 1995:139). This is asking the question if metaphors are ultimately dependent on a conceptually prior metonymic mapping. There is good evidence that this might indeed be the case, at least concerning the metaphorical and metonymic expressions of emotion. In a wider sense, then, this paper aims at showing that most, or probably all, emotion metaphors have a metonymic basis.

3. Conceptualizations of *heart*

The corpus which serves as the basis for the following analysis stems mainly from Roget's Thesaurus. Some further material comes from dictionaries. The expressions found in the corpus may tentatively be grouped under four different headings. I will discuss separately the examples, their underlying conceptualizations, and the sub-folk models involved for each category.

The categories have been set up because each of them displays a different degree of connection between the metaphors and the metonymies, i.e. the first category (3.1. *Heart* as a metonymy for the person) refers to the most specific level of meaning involved where there is a clear metonymic basis to be found. In the second category (3.2. The *heart* as a LIVING ORGANISM), the metonymic basis is still visible but not as evident as in the first category. Here the heart is considered to be an autonomous entity in a part-for-whole metonymy irrespective of the human being it belongs to. In the third category (3.3. The *heart* as an OBJECT OF VALUE), the metonymic basis is even less obvious, although it is still possible to establish the connection between the metaphors and metonymies. In the fourth category (3.4. The *heart* as a CONTAINER), the metaphors seem at first sight to be unrelated to any prior metonymization, but once the complete folk model is focused upon, the relationship becomes evident. Thus, the four categories mirror the distance between the metonymic and metaphorical conceptualizations of the *heart* expressions under analysis: the first category acts as the underlying basis for all the other categories, but the further away one gets from the first category and moves towards the fourth category, the more metaphorical expressions appear and the relationship of these metaphors to a prior metonymization becomes less obvious.

3.1. *Heart* as a metonymy for the person

On the most specific level of meaning, the *heart* stands metonymically for the whole person. It is the most salient body part in the folk model understanding of emotions. The most prototypical emotion connected with the heart is love, which is at the same time supposed to be a uniquely human sensation. If asked to symbolize love, most people would end up drawing the stereotypical picture of a red heart. This close connection of the feeling of love with the heart can be seen as evidence for the folk model of the heart as being the site of emotions. The heart has traditionally been, and still is, taken as a symbol for love.[5]

However, we do not find one single, clearly delimited folk model, but rather a conglomerate of different submodels, each one focusing on a different aspect, involving different shades of meaning. For instance, if one falls madly in love and is determined to conquer the other person's emotions, metonymically one may be said to

(1)   *set one's heart on somebody.*

The heart is then conceptualized as A MOVABLE OBJECT. In this special case, the heart or – avoiding the metonymy – the person knows only one goal that s/he tries to pursue with perseverance. Conceptualized from the opposite perspective, i.e. from that of a person who inspires love in many other people, a person may

(2)   *set all hearts on fire.*

This example is connected to the saying *who plays with fire gets burned*, which refers to the conceptualization of danger (and love) as heat. Here, two different folk models interact. This results in two interacting metonymies insofar as the *heart* refers to the emotions in a metonymic way (i.e. it is not the heart as an organ that is "on fire"; but the emotions of love, desire etc. considered to be inside the heart are showing strong reactions), and *fire* refers to the heat waves one is experiencing when in love. The notion of *fire* also alludes to its possible consequences, i.e. one's heart may have to suffer, as the expression implicitly entails the notion that the object of one's desire is not available but is only playing around.

A way to conceptualize positive emotions is to imagine an increase in the heart's size or to imagine that it is particularly large in its final state and that it therefore houses a variety of good feelings. In this sub-folk model, the heart is construed as CHANGEABLE IN SIZE:

(3)   *heart-swelling.*
         great heart.
         fullness of the heart.
         have a large heart.
         have a big heart.
         be big-hearted.

In some people, the container is conceptualized as being bigger than normal, meaning that their hearts are especially full of positive emotions, that they are friendly, altruistic, empathetic, and give help generously.

Ironically, the last two expressions with *big heart* can also be used to mean somebody who has sexual affairs with different partners. If these expressions are used in the second sense, the underlying metonymy does not highlight positive feelings in general but is restricted to sexual feelings.

As has already become obvious, there is not only evidence of positive emotions and types of behavior relating to the heart but there is also a multitude of ambivalent or negative emotions metaphorically and metonymically connected to it.

More marginal emotions of this kind may not be what comes to mind immediately when talking about the heart, but as they also belong to the human repertoire of emotions, they are believed to reside in our hearts as well. Characteristic behavior types which are often conceived of in terms of metaphorical *heart* expressions belong to the antonymy of courage versus cowardice (see examples (20) and (22)). In these expressions, people are conceptualized as containers for emotions, i.e. the emotions originate from within people. In this connection, the heart then stands metonymically for the emotions involved as they have a physiological basis in the human body. In addition, the heart is also seen metaphorically as a container for these emotions (see 3.4.). The relevant folk model therefore construes the view of a container (i.e. the heart) within a container (i.e. the person) when speaking of emotions.

Apart from love, the heart is frequently construed as being involved in other less prototypical positive feelings, especially feelings of an altruistic kind. People who like to help others, who display feelings of pity, compassion or benevolence, are said to have a special kind of heart, made from soft materials. The heart is therefore easily indented and impressed, reacting positively and voluntarily to other people's needs:

(4)   *soft heart.*
        tender heart.
        touch the heart.

This results in the sub-folk model of HEART AS A SOLID, which is also present in other conceptualizations, for example in the case of negative emotions, where the heart is conceptualized as consisting of certain materials with which different qualities are associated. In direct contrast to (4), heavy and hard materials are metaphorically connected with an unyielding attitude and "hard" feelings, as in

(5)   *hardness of heart; harden one's heart.*
        heavy-hearted.
        heart of marble.
        heart of iron.
        heart of stone.
        to steel one's heart (against compassion).

Here, the sub-folk model HEART AS A SOLID is even more specified as SOLIDS HAVE WEIGHT and all these seemingly disparate expressions have a certain coherence. In these cases, it may seem as if the heart or, more precisely, the person (here again we encounter the metonymic basis for these expressions) is not easily touched or impressed, and feelings like pity or interest are probably absent whereas feelings like impassivity, cruelty, pitilessness, moral insensibility or inhumanity may predominate. The materials marble, iron, stone and steel are metaphorically endowed with qualities which technically speaking they do not really possess but which are attributed to them due to the qualities that they display, i.e. the hardness of the material is reinterpreted as a hardness in attitude and thus metaphorically mapped onto the domain of the heart. In a further step, these metaphors then are again used metonymically insofar as they pick out one salient detail of a person's disposition which then stands for the whole moral outfit of that person.

The heart may also be conceptualized as being of such a light weight that one could nearly fly away;[6] then one may speak of

(6)   *light-heartedness.*

This feeling of weightlessness rests on a metonymic basis which highlights the effect of being without worries or sorrows, of being "in high spirits".

Similarly, the heart may also be conceptualized as emitting warmth and sympathetic feelings, thereby inviting people to come and warm up. This could be regarded as a metaphor from metonymy, the warmth being simply an indicator of the general warmth a well-meaning, compassionate person is prototypically construed to be spreading, which is then, via the mapping onto the heart, used metaphorically to indicate warm feelings or positive emotions:

(7)   *warm-heartedness.*

Other expressions conceptualize the HEART AS AN ANTHROPOMORPHISIZED ENTITY.[7] This perspective gives rise to expressions such as

(8)   *somebody being one's heart's desire.*

where the heart itself as the most salient entity, and not the human being "connected" to it, is conceptualized as desiring the person in question.

Finally, people without partners who would like to have a love relationship may meet in

(9)   *a lonely hearts club.*

which is the clearest instance of metonymy in the entire corpus. The heart is personified and the emotions are conceptualized as acting autonomously, because the rational side of the people in question might not agree to their emotional desires.

Finally, another sub-folk model visualizes the FULL or WHOLE ENTITY OF THE HEART, which may be only half present, or even totally absent:

(10)   *half-hearted.*
         heartlessness.
         have no heart (for).
         not have one's heart in it.

This sub-folk model is construed as expressing the view that in comparison to the "hard" hearts, where there might still be a glimmer of hope, these persons seemingly cannot be appealed to or be changed. They might not be able to display any positive feelings at all, at least in the context-dependent circumstances. A person with half a heart or without a heart cannot survive, and persons showing the attitudes mentioned in (10) cannot survive morally.

3.2. The *heart* as a LIVING ORGANISM

One of the submodels already hinted at above seems to focus on the fact that the heart may be experienced as an AUTONOMOUS ENTITY. Thus, a love partner may not only instigate a particular emotional stirring inside the other person but he may also be personified in a metonymic way as a

(11)   *heartthrob.*
         all hearts throb for her.

This expression alludes to the heart as an independent entity, indicating that one of the physiological reactions experienced at the sight or the thought of the object of one's desire metonymically stands for the person as such in a cause-effect relationship. When two people are very much in love, one may speak of

(12)   *two hearts that beat as one.*

This expression can be understood as a metonymy for the synchronization and harmonization of the behaviors of two people insofar as the two hearts stand for the two people as a whole. It also indicates a degree of autonomy inasmuch as the two hearts can be understood as acting in their own right. However, the independent or autonomous nature of the respective hearts is ambiguous in that their beating may still be conceptualized as being dependent on or regulated by other bodily organs and physiological processes.

On a more negative note, one's emotions/heart can be hurt or destroyed by various means, and here, we find expressions which at first sight seem to be purely metaphorical, very vividly describing the damage involved. There are even pictorial icons showing some of these metaphors (a broken heart, a bleeding heart). These expressions are primarily used in cases of disappointed love or failed relationships.

In cases where one's emotions are hurt by the behavior of others, one may imagine many different scenarios or attacks on one's heart. This can be expressed neutrally, i.e. one's heart may break, ache, make one melancholic, or bleed, where the cause or the weapon are not mentioned; but it can also be expressed in a more detailed way, i.e. one's heart can burn when set on fire by a strong feeling of jealousy or regret; it can be pierced (by "the sword of hate"), i.e. hurt by a sharp needlelike instrument; and it may be eaten up when experiencing sorrow.

Here as well, we find different sub-folk models focusing on different aspects of the general folk model of the heart as an organism. These submodels can be grouped according to an increase in danger. First of all, the feelings inside the heart may be conceptualized as fire ("the fire of love"), highlighting the intensity of the feeling:

(13)   *heart-burning.*[8]

Another submodel visualizes the heart as a wound, inflicted by different kinds of weapons:

(14)   *make one's heart bleed.*
        pierce the heart.
        something is heartrending.

In yet another way of conceptualization, we have the submodel of illness as in:

(15)   *an aching heart,*
        to be sick at heart; to be heart-sick.

Finally, the heart can be completely destroyed with the consequence that it – and with it the person's life or what the person considers worth living for – vanishes:

(16)   *cry one's heart out*
        to eat one's heart out.

It seems, however, that all these metaphors are based on a prior metonymic understanding: one experiences a certain kind of physiological pain when hurt or disappointed, or when suffering a loss, and subjectively this pain is interpreted as stemming from diverse types of weapons and is thus experienced and expressed differently.

This second category is closely related to the first category. The perspective has narrowed, however, and the heart is no longer considered as part of a person but as a living, autonomous entity in its own right. Consequently, the metonymies involved are less basic ones and often rely on double metonymizations or even appear as metaphors. Nevertheless, the underlying metonymic basis is kept intact.

3.3. The *heart* as an OBJECT OF VALUE

At a more general level of conceptualization, the heart is seen in its totality as a kind of treasure chest containing something of great value to its owner and possibly also to other people. Implicitly, emotions are involved also but they are not named or singled out. Here again, diverse sub-folk models are involved which help to structure this domain of meaning. Thus, the single emotions are not foregrounded here nor is the connection between the heart and the person who possesses it, but in an ever-narrowing perspective the heart is seen as an entity and as an object of value. This level of meaning then is rather culture-specific because the notion of value is a highly culture-determined asset.

Each of the sub-folk models involved takes a different perspective of the *heart* as an object of value. If the heart is seen as a COVETED ENTITY, this entity is not always in one's possession and even if it is, this is by no means a stable situation. On the one hand, one's heart can be conquered or won in a contest or in a war, or it can be given generously, but it cannot just be taken (HEART AS A PRIZE):

(17)   *to win someone's heart.*
         to conquer someone's heart.
         to offer one's heart.

On the other hand, the heart can also be lost and it can even be destroyed. These expressions imply that one no longer wants to be or is no longer able to be in control of one's emotions but lets another person take control. The other person can also take one's heart away without permission (HEART AS BOOTY):

(18)   *to lose one's heart to somebody.*
         to steal every heart.

Furthermore, there are various ways in which the heart can be conceptualized as a MANIPULABLE OBJECT. For example, it may be seen as a fragile object, which is easy to destroy and which must be handled with care:

(19)   *broken heart, heart-broken, broken-hearted.*

Other types of behavior which are associated with the heart are feelings of courage and envy. Thus, people may either show themselves as courageous or they may inspire others to show courage. They may also make a new start with fresh courage. All these expressions refer to active human behavior:

(20)   *to put heart into.*
         to take heart of grace.
         new heart.

Lack of courage can also be expressed by using *heart* expressions but here the perspective taken is one of passivity, i.e. things happen to people which they cannot control or do not want to control. Since the sub-folk model in question sees the heart – and with it one's courage – as a movable and replaceable part, its power can also diminish or even disappear as in

(21)   *to lose heart.*
         faintheartedness.
         his heart sank into his boots.
         not have the heart to do something.

A person who is not courageous may also be said

(22)   *to be chicken-hearted.*

This expression refers to more than just the stereotypical small size of chickens' hearts. Chickens are also renowned for the fact that their small hearts often stop beating when they are frightened or under stress. Thus, a special physiological feature of these animals is first used metonymically to refer to a certain behavior pattern and then it is metaphorically mapped onto human beings who display a similar behavior to that of chickens: they shy away even from the slightest danger and risk and prefer to remain passive and inert.

The feeling of envy may also be conceptualized as being related to the heart. Thus, resenting something or being hurt by somebody may be expressed as

(23)   *to take it to heart,*

which may lead to the idea that the feeling of having been wronged is forcefully kept alive, nurtured, perhaps even strengthened. Taking an opposite perspective, i.e. causing somebody else to feel anger or discontent, can be conceptualized as

(24)   *to dishearten*

this person. A person who has been disheartened has been discouraged from doing something which s/he intended to do or from continuing along a particular path of action. Here again, the question of activity vs. passivity seems to be vital: actively dealing with a situation of envy yields different results, for example energy to overcome the situation rather than just passively enduring it.

It becomes obvious that the majority of the sub-folk models discussed above have positive connotations because they refer to the heart's "value" alluded to in the section title. They do so in different ways, however, depending on the perspective taken. In everyday usage, the sub-folk models are often mixed up and therefore their meanings sometimes get mingled and at times even seem to be incongruous. Nevertheless, these meanings taken on their own are all well-based in the construal of our everyday experiences.

In this third category we still find a conceptual closeness to the nonfigurative understanding of "heart". Even if the metonymic undertones are not always noticeable immediately and not as obvious as in the first two categories, they are still present in the general understanding of the expressions in this category.

3.4. The *heart* as a CONTAINER

One of the first conceptual metaphors identified as underlying the lexical field of communication is the conduit metaphor, as discussed in Reddy (1979). The conduit metaphor focused the attention on the all-pervasive container conceptualization. Both the message and the words in which it is "packed" are seen as containers, which we unpack and out of which we take the contents, i.e. the meaning.[9]

The same applies to the human body and its major parts. Thus, the head, the heart, the chest, or the womb may all be seen as containers. When physiological evidence still was not available, all kinds of folk models for the heart could flourish, which at the same time were specified as different types of containers.

The following examples will show some of the different types of containers which are involved, depending on the aspects focused upon in conceptualization. We will follow these views in a narrowing perspective from the outer qualities of the container including its handlability via its inner qualities to its internal structure.

In a static view, the container is seen as covered by a lid which may be opened or closed. When opened, there is free access to the speaker's emotions. When the heart is conceptualized as closed, there is no entry to the speaker's emotional world. Thus, there are no emotions wasted because the innermost feelings are not touched upon at all. There may also be instances when the heart is full of emotions but one does not wish it to flow over on its own. Then, in order to be able to control where the overflow takes place, one might tell a good friend about one's feelings. In that case the container is conceptualized as being opened and the feelings are flowing out of it just like a liquid:

(25)   *to open one's heart.*
         to close one's heart to something.
         to pour out one's heart to somebody.

The first two examples, which present a more static view of the process involved, highlight the fact that we are thinking in terms of a LID CONTAINER which makes free access to the container's contents more difficult. This fact goes unmentioned in the third example, which carries the extra meaning of personal and willful action and stresses a more dynamic point of view. It also sees the heart as a MANIPULABLE CONTAINER that can be dealt with at one's own will, like a bucket, but in this case the action is less controlled than in the first two instances.

If there are too many feelings involved, the container might be too small to absorb all of them, in which case it might overflow. This is nicely illustrated by the dynamic view of an OPEN CONTAINER FOR LIQUIDS (= positive emotions), as in

(26)   *a heart overflowing (with gratitude).*

where the path of the movement of the liquid from the container is visualized. The opposite kind of movement, namely towards the container, is highlighted in

(27)   *this filled my heart (with joy).*

Thus, the way from feelings to heart is no one-way street but works both ways, as feelings may enter the heart but may also leave it. Another sub-folk model sees the heart as a CONTAINER WITH GREAT DEPTH and as filled with positive emotions. Just like in the conduit metaphor, this type of container is conceptualized as having a bottom representing the location where one's innermost feelings are stored. These feelings are thought to be very intense and sincere:

(28)   *from (the bottom of) one's heart.*

This expression follows the up/down schema (Johnson 1987:126) and implies a dynamic view as movement and direction are involved.

This container may be conceptualized as integrating a further INTERNAL CONTAINER, hosting feelings that are even more intense and thus further accentuated. The same is accomplished by expressions such as *deep down inside* where the heart is not mentioned explicitly but where movement is involved as well:

(29)   *to know something/to believe something in one's heart.*
         in one's heart of hearts.

In this case you are secretly sure of something although you do not admit it. The last example, a Shakespearian coinage for the "deepest and most hidden thoughts and feelings" (Rees 1997:132), may be seen as presenting us with a double metaphorization, but this expression also relies on embodiment because within our folk model of the heart as the site of emotions we experience our emotions as coming from within and presume this place of origin to be the heart. Inside this heart, we metaphorically imagine a center, a "sanctum" containing the most private and hidden emotions (cf. also p. 200-201).

The heart may furthermore be conceptualized as a sort of storehouse where feelings of different kinds are grouped, labeled, stored and found or not found:

(30)   *I could not find it in my heart.*

In this storehouse, not only feelings may be stored, but also opinions and knowledge. Therefore, if one memorizes texts or poems, one puts them into this STOREHOUSE CONTAINER (i.e. learning them *by heart)* in order to be able to take them out again when necessary. This is a very intriguing field of research as the memory is usually seen in connection with the head / the brain – which also acts as a storehouse for information – and not so much with the heart. This may be seen as an indexical sign that learning by heart has to do more with emotions than with "rational behavior".

This notion has a greater degree of specification in the expression:

(31)   *have a place in every heart.*

referring to a person who seems attractive and desirable to many others who reserve some space for her or him in their inner emotional sanctums. Here, the heart is clearly seen as a COMPARTMENTALIZED CONTAINER, able to integrate different types of objects into different slots.

All these different-faceted conceptualizations of the heart as a CONTAINER show that we are not dealing with a one-track conceptualization, but really with a conglomerate of different sub-folk models. Nevertheless, compared to the culture-specific nature of the other categories discussed so far, the container schema seems to be a more universal type of schema. Its higher level of generality is further underlined by the fact that it is not unique to the folk model of the heart but works in lots of different contexts as well (words as containers for meaning, the head as container for rational behavior, etc.). This comes to the fore also in the fact that the image of the heart as a container seems to be much more "metaphtonymically" structured than for example that of the heart as an object of value. As the underlying metonymies are not as obvious as in the other categories, this fourth category seems to be dependent on the existence of the other categories which provide its metonymic basis.

4. Conclusion

In the foregoing sections, some of the main meaning clusters of *heart* expressions have been discussed separately. It is clear, however, that they do not only overlap but that they are also compatible with one another. It should also be noted that the examples quoted do not cover the whole range of possible *heart* expressions but encompass only those that refer to emotions.

On the surface, these different conceptualizations may not seem to have much in common, but actually they are just different facets of the *heart* concept with all its different folk models and sub-folk models as it has traditionally existed in the English language. The different nuances of meaning of the conceptualizations in question are probably due to the fact that these conceptualizations are to be located on different levels of generality.

Moreover, the more general the conceptualizations, the more indirect is the metonymic connection to an underlying concept. Therefore, it is probably not too far-fetched to assume that when it comes to specific conceptualizations, the metonymic basis is clearly designed, whereas the more general conceptualizations have to rely on the more basic concepts acting as some kind of go-betweens.

This is probably due to the fact that we are dealing here with emotion terms – and emotions are concepts everybody has already experienced. In accordance with current folk theories about the site of emotions we have certain ideas about where they might come from.

In general, we know more about the way the heart functions than we know about the brain. The pulse is one of the symptoms of life which can be measured for and by every individual. Here again, we find a metonymic perspectivization in our folk model of the heart. Nobody has been able to precisely locate the site of feelings, and even today with all our neurological and physiological knowledge we run into problems when we have to explain how and where feelings are generated.

Thus, starting with their most basic bodily experiences, people have a heart and they can feel it acting differently according to the emotions they experience: the heartbeat quickens, slows down, stops altogether, etc. Already in ancient times emotions were assumed to reside in the most conspicuous body organ (the only one everybody is able to paint – though physiologically incorrectly) – at least in Western cultures – and the heart was taken as a metonymy for the whole body and thus it stands for the whole person experiencing a specific emotion. It is on the basis of this archetypal metonymy that the other understandings could arise and flourish. This thought was further developed and commonplace experiences strengthened the idea that the heart must be a very valuable and important organ.

Indeed, we are able to experience certain physical sensations connected to our emotions, usually to that of the prototypical emotion of romantic love. As it is not the heart that is in love or loves but the whole person, the metonymic character of these expressions is obvious. The bodily sensations can be used metonymically to refer to the feelings as such and these metonymies may then be used as source domains for either new metonymies or for metaphors. The expressions referring to romantic love seem to be metonymically based, and this is probably true for other emotion concepts as well.

Apart from love, less prototypical instances of emotions, such as compassion, pity, envy, or inhumanity, and types of behavior like courage or cowardice – where one cannot even be sure that they may still be considered to be emotions – are conceptualized as residing in the heart and can also be claimed to be based on metonymic mappings.

One of the most interesting aspects to be encountered in the present analysis is the fact that the broader and the more general the perspective gets, the less metonymies and the more metaphors seem to be involved (and vice versa), although the metonymic basis seems to be kept intact for the metaphors as well.

This leads back to the question already hinted at in the introductory part of this paper, i.e. whether metaphors may indeed have a metonymic basis, a question to which a final answer cannot yet be presented. I hope to have shown, however, that there is evidence for a positive answer to this question concerning expressions that relate to the folk model of romantic love, and this may be true for other emotion expressions as well. Why do emotion expressions seem to play an outstanding role in this respect? Here, we may again want to stress the fact that emotions are one of the earliest embodied experiences of human beings and therefore an intrinsic part of our lives. They are not abstract concepts, and generally we have a very good idea what we are talking about. We therefore do not have to focus on the whole domain of a particular emotion, but it is economical and rational to use a metonymic expression, which in time may lose the obvious connection to its metonymic basis and be considered to be a metaphor at a later stage.

Therefore, I want to propose a functional view of metaphor and metonymy instead of regarding them as fixed concepts. The fact whether the metonymic basis of a metaphor is obvious to a language user or not determines this language user's notion of whether s/he is using or perceiving a metaphor or a metonymy. Scanning the different steps in the development of a metaphorical construction may reveal that all the single steps involve metonymy and that therefore the whole expression may be considered to be a metonymy, but summarizing the development of such an expression by focusing only on the starting-point and the output may lead us to consider it to be a metaphor.

Acknowledgment
I would like to thank René Dirven (Duisburg, Germany) for his valuable comments on a first draft of this paper and Séamus Mac Mathúna (Coleraine, Northern Ireland) for checking my English. All remaining flaws are of course entirely my own responsibility.

Notes

1. There are cultures where the *heart* does not play a role in the conceptualization of emotions, e.g. in Nigerian English the belly is seen as the center of emotions. Thus *gudbele* means 'kind-hearted' and *bedbele* means 'to hate'. Similar observations have been made for other languages, e.g. the Aborigine language Yankunytjatjara (cf. Goddard 1996).

2. These approaches were among those discussed during the *Workshop on Metonymy* (Hamburg, June 1996) organized by Günter Radden (Hamburg), one of the scholars who has inspired the renewed interest in metonymy.

3. Goossens (1995) differentiates between two frequently occurring types (*metaphor from metonymy* and *metonymy within metaphor*) and two types which are more rare because they are more difficult to conceptualize (*demetonymization inside a metaphor* and *metaphor within metonymy*).

4. Dirven (1993) suggests that different types of metonymy are located along a continuum of meaning ascription: he differentiates between linear syntagms (as the most prototypical type of metonymy), conjunctive syntagms and inclusive syntagms, which, in that sequence, bridge the gap to metaphor.

5. On metaphors for love, see also Kövecses 1986, 1988.

6. This meaning may be connected to Lakoff & Johnson's conceptual metaphor HAPPY IS UP (1980) because with a light heart one has shed all one's sorrows and feels happy.

7. This anthropomorphic perspective of the heart is also to be found in other expressions which do not refer to the topic of love, e.g. *to one's heart's content/delight, heart's ease*, etc.

8. This kind of *heart-burning* should not be confused with the medical condition of *heart-burning* which acts in a metonymic way as the passage of a sort of heat from the stomach to the throat.

9. This is closely related to Johnson's image schema of container (1987: 112-138, especially 126).

References

Blank, Andreas
   1993   "Polysemie und semantische Relationen im Lexikon", in: Wolfgang
                Börner – Klaus Vogel (eds.), *Wortschatz und Fremdsprachenerwerb*.
                Bochum: AKS, 22-56.
Croft, William
   1993   "The role of domains in the interpretation of metaphors and meto-
                nymies", *Cognitive Linguistics* 4: 335-370.
Dirven, René
   1993   "Metonymy and metaphor: Different mental strategies of conceptua-
                lisation", *Leuvense Bijdragen* 82: 1-28.
Fillmore, Charles
   1977   "Scenes-and-frames semantics", in: Antonio Zampolli (ed.), *Linguistic
                Structures Processing*. Amsterdam: Benjamins, 55-81.
Gadsby, Adam (ed.)
   1995   *Dictionary of contemporary English* (3rd edition.) London: Langen-
                scheidt-Longman.
Goddard, Cliff
   1996   "Cross-linguistic research on metaphor", *Language & Communication*
                16, No. 2: 145-151.
Goossens, Louis
   1995   "Metaphtonymy: The interaction of metaphor and metonymy in figura-
                tive expressions for linguistic action", in: Goossens, Louis – Paul
                Pauwels – Brygida Rudzka-Ostyn – Anne-Marie Simon-Vandenber-
                gen – Johan Vanparys, *By word of mouth: metaphor, metonymy and
                linguistic action in a cognitive perspective*. Amsterdam: Benjamins,
                175-204.
Jakobson, Roman
   1956   "The metaphoric and metonymic poles", in: Roman Jakobson – Morris
                Halle, *Fundamentals of Language*. (2nd. edition). The Hague-Paris:
                Mouton, 76-82.
Johnson, Mark
   1987   *The body in the mind. The bodily basis of meaning, imagination, and
                reason*. Chicago: Chicago University Press.
Kirkpatrick, Betty (ed.)
   1987   *Roget's thesaurus*. London: Longman.
Kövecses, Zoltán
   1986   *Metaphors of anger, pride, and love: A lexical approach to the structure
                of concepts*. Amsterdam: Benjamins.
   1988   *The language of love*. Lewisburgh: Bucknell University Press.
   1995   "Anger: Its language, conceptualisation, and physiology", in: John R.
                Taylor – Robert E. MacLaury (eds.), *Language and the cognitive
                construal of the world*. Berlin: Mouton de Gruyter, 181-197.
Lakoff, George
   1987   *Women, fire, and dangerous things: What categories reveal about the
                mind*. Chicago: University of Chicago Press.

Lakoff, George – Mark Johnson
  1980   *Metaphors we live by*. Chicago: Chicago University Press.
Lakoff, George – Mark Turner
  1989   *More than cool reason: A field guide to poetic metaphor*. Chicago:
            Chicago University Press.
Lévi-Strauss, Claude
  1976   *The savage mind*. London: Weidenfeld & Nicholas. (1962: *La pensée
            sauvage*. Paris: Plon.)
Niemeier, Susanne – René Dirven (eds.)
  1996   *The language of emotions*. Amsterdam: Benjamins.
Panther, Klaus-Uwe – Günter Radden. (eds.)
  forthcoming *Metonymy in thought and language*. Amsterdam: Benjamins.
Reddy, Michael
  1979   "The conduit metaphor", in: Andrew Ortony (ed.), *Metaphor and
            thought*. Cambridge: Cambridge University Press, 284-324.
Rees, Nigel (ed.)
  1997   *Cassell dictionary of word and phrase origins*. (2nd edition.) London:
            Cassell.
Taylor, John R.
  1995   *Linguistic categorization. Prototypes in linguistic theory*. (2nd edition.)
            Oxford: Clarendon Press.

The EFFECT FOR CAUSE metonymy in English grammar[1]

Klaus-Uwe Panther and Linda Thornburg

1. Introduction

In international U.S. airports, it is not uncommon to encounter at customs locations the following injunctions:

(1)   *Stand behind the yellow line.*
(2)   *Have documents ready.*

These sentences instantiate an apparent grammatical puzzle: they are imperative constructions, yet they contain *stative* verbs, contrary to the requirement for prototypical imperatives to have *action* predicates. The same sentences, when literally translated into German, are ungrammatical, suggesting that German imperative sentences are more restricted as to the range of predicates they admit:

(3)   a.   **Stehen Sie   hinter der gelben Linie.*
                    *Stand you   behind the yellow line

(4)   a.   **Haben Sie   Ihre   Dokumente bereit.*
                    *Have   you   your   documents   ready

An adequate translation of (1) and (2) into German requires choosing a verb denoting *intentional behavior,* as in (3b) and (4b), respectively:

(3)   b.   *Stellen Sie   sich   hinter   die   gelbe   Linie.*
                    Put   you   yourself behind the   yellow line
                    'Put yourself behind the yellow line.'

(4)   b.   *Halten Sie   Ihre   Dokumente bereit.*
                    Hold   you   your   documents   ready
                    'Have your documents ready.'

A traditional solution to account for the "funny" English imperatives in (1) and (2) is to posit (at least) two separate senses for the verbs *stand* and *have*: a stative sense and a second actional sense. We reject this solution because it unnecessarily proliferates meanings. Instead, we propose that one conceptual metonymic principle, namely the RESULT FOR ACTION metonymy, interacts with and accounts for these English imperatives. That is to say, an expression of a *result* may be used in English to stand for the *action* that is presupposed by the result. The grammaticality of (1) and (2) consequently suggests that linguistic form is sensitive to conceptual, i.e. metonymic, structure.[2]

The RESULT FOR ACTION metonymy is a special case of the higher-level EFFECT FOR CAUSE metonymy. The first part of our article focuses on the operation of the RESULT FOR ACTION metonymy in various English grammatical constructions with some contrasts given in German. We show that this conceptual metonymy has a strong impact on grammatical structure in English. The second part of the paper focuses on a single construction which, in some of its senses, exemplifies other subtypes of the EFFECT FOR CAUSE metonymy but without apparent grammatical consequences. Our data lead to important questions about the interface between metonymy and grammar, which we return to in the conclusion.

2. The RESULT FOR ACTION metonymy

Before proceeding we should explain at this point what we mean by the term RESULT: A result often is a STATE but it can also be a RESULTANT EVENT, or even a RESULTANT ACTION. An action resulting from an action can be seen in:

(5)   *Johnny asked the teacher to go to the bathroom.*

The action expressed in the infinitive clause (Johnny's going to the bathroom) is the result of another action not explicit in the sentence, namely the teacher's speech act of giving permission. In this section we focus primarily on resultant states and events.

In order to test the dynamic or action potential of literally stative or other non-actional predications, we use constructions which prototypically require action predicates. We call these test frames *action constructions*:

(6)   Test frames: action constructions
    a.   Imperatives
        e.g. *Wash the dishes!*
    b.   Infinitive complement sentences requiring action verbs
        e.g. *She asked him to wash the dishes. He ordered her to leave town.*
    c.   What about VP_{ing}?
        e.g. *What about washing the dishes?*
    d.   How to VP
        e.g. *How to do things with words.*
    e.   Why not VP?
        e.g. *Why not paint your house purple?*

The constructions in (6a-e) normally exclude stative predicates. For example, as already mentioned, an imperative sentence prototypically requires a predicate that denotes an intentional activity or action. Likewise, the constructions in (6b-e) are preferably used with action predicates.

Examples like (1) and (2) seem inconsistent with the semantics of the test frames in (6). We will however show that they can be elegantly accommodated within a metonymic framework.

2.1. Be + Adj/NP

We assume that the construction *be* + Adj/NP has a prototypical stative meaning as exemplified in sentences such as:

(7)   a.   *Mary is tall.*
       b.   *John is old.*
       c.   *She is an invalid.*

The states expressed by these predicates are not the result of some intentional behavior of some agent. Despite the animacy, and even humanness, of the subjects, the subject argument has no agentivity. According to what people know about the world, height, age, and being an invalid are not under one's control. Therefore, one does not usually say

(8)   a.   *?How to be tall in five weeks.*
       b.   *?What about being old?*
       c.   *?He asked her to be an invalid.*

In contrast, however, there are other adjectives and nominals that occur quite readily in the action frames in (6), such as

(9)   a.   *How to be rich in one week.*
          ("How to act in such a way so as to become rich in one week")
       b.   *What about being quiet.*
          ("What about acting in such a way so as to become quiet")
       c.   *He asked her to be his wife.*
          ("He asked her to act in such a way so as to become his wife")

that are obligatorily interpreted as dynamic. Examples such as these led some generative semanticists in the late 1960s to postulate that these predicate adjectives and nominals are underlying verbs (Bach 1968; Lakoff 1970). In our view, no such assumptions have to be made. Rather, we claim that the action sense comes about through a metonymic process whereby the result expressed by the predicate adjective or nominal is brought about by an unmentioned prior action. The sentences in (9) are thus examples of what we call the RESULT FOR ACTION metonymy. In contrast to the predicates in (8), which are merely STATES, the predicates in (9) are RESULTANT STATES. Because of their metonymic link to actions, RESULTANT STATE predicates can occur in action constructions without semantic anomaly. If such a metonymic link to actions cannot be established, stative predicates are infelicitous in action constructions.

2.2. Passive sentences

Another construction which is usually analyzed as not being action-oriented is the passive. In particular, the human subject of a passive sentence is not regarded as an agent. For example, in

(10)   *She is not deceived by his looks.*

the subject *she* is typically analyzed as the affected patient. Sentence (10) has
a stative meaning. However, passive predicates like those in (10) can often be
used as negative injunctions in imperatives. Consider the following data from
Quirk et al. (1985: 827):

(11) a.   *Don't be deceived by his looks.*
      b.   *Don't be bullied into signing.*
      c.   *Don't be made to look foolish.*
      d.   *Don't be told what to do.*

These negative imperatives only make sense if the passive predicates are
interpreted as results of actions that are themselves not made explicit. Thus the
general meaning of the sentences in (11) is "Do something to the effect that the
PASSIVE STATE/EVENT will not result." For example, (11a) means "Do something
to the effect so that as a result you will not be deceived by his looks." In our
analysis then the RESULTANT STATE/EVENT "You are not deceived by his looks" is
caused by an unspecified intentional self-directed action of the addressee of the
imperative. Analogous readings based on the RESULT FOR ACTION metonymy can
be constructed for (11b-d).

Likewise, the meanings of the positive passive imperatives in (12) can also
be accounted for by the RESULT FOR ACTION metonymy:

(12) a.   *Be guided by what I say.*
      b.   *Be reassured by me.*
      c.   *Hire a Rolls Royce and be driven around by a uniformed
           chauffeur.*

For example, (12a) means "Do something to the effect so that as a result you
are guided by what I say." Again, as in the sentences in (11), it is only the result,
i.e. the RESULTANT EVENT or the RESULTANT STATE that is explicitly expressed in the
sentence. Analogous interpretations hold for sentences (12b-c).

Now notice that the propositional contents verbalized as passive sentences
in (11) and (12) cannot be grammaticalized in the same way in German. Typically in this language, the causative interpretation has to be made explicit through
a verb such as *lassen* 'cause.' Except for (12b) (which translates with *sein* 'be'),
the most natural translations of sentences (11) and (12) would be (13) and (14),
respectively:

(13) a.   *Lassen Sie   sich   nicht von seinem Aussehen   täuschen.*
           Let   you   yourself not of   his   appearance   deceive
           'Don't let yourself be deceived by his appearance.'

      b.   *Lassen Sie   sich   nicht zur   Unterschrift zwingen.*
           Let   you   yourself not   to-the   signature   force
           'Don't let yourself be forced into signing.'

c. *Lassen Sie sich nicht zum Narren halten.*
Let you yourself not to-the fool hold
'Don't let yourself be fooled.'

d. *Lassen Sie sich nicht vorschreiben, was zu tun ist.*
Let you yourself not prescribe what to do is
'Don't let yourself be told what to do.'

(14) a. *Lassen Sie sich davon leiten, was ich sage.*
Let you yourself there-from guide what I say
'Let yourself be guided by what I say.'

b. *Seien Sie beruhigt.*
Be you reassured
'Be reassured.'

c. *Mieten Sie (sich) einen Rolls Royce und lassen Sie*
Hire you (yourself) a Rolls Royce and let you

sich von einem livrierten Fahrer herumfahren.
yourself by a uniformed driver around-drive
'Hire yourself a Rolls Royce and let yourself be driven around by a uniformed chauffeur.'

The possible action interpretation of many English *be* passives is confirmed by their occurrence in other action frames:

(15) a. *She promised not to be deceived by his looks.*
b. *Why not be taught by the best professors?*
c. *How to be admired by one and all.*
d. *What about hiring a car and being driven around by a chauffeur?*

In German, the occurrence of passives in action constructions is much more restricted. Again, in many, though not all, cases the most natural translation of sentences like (15) requires the causative verb *lassen* + *sich* V as in (16):

(16) *Sie versprach, sich nicht von seinem Aussehen täuschen zu lassen.*
She promised herself not by his appearance deceive to let
'She promised not to let herself be deceived by his appearance.'

Let us now turn to state and event passives with non-human subjects as in

(17) *The car was covered with mud.* (state)

At first sight, sentences like (17) look hopelessly stative, having no dynamic potential whatsoever. But surprisingly, in some contexts even a stative sentence like (17) can receive an action interpretation.

(18) a. *They ordered the car to be covered with mud.*
b. *They expected the car to be covered with mud.*

The embedded infinitive clause in (18a), we claim, gets a dynamic interpretation through the RESULT FOR ACTION metonymy: Something is done by some unmentioned agent to the car so that as a result it is covered with mud. The main clause verb *ordered* enforces this metonymic interpretation. In contrast, in (18b), the main clause verb *expected* is open to either a metonymic or non-metonymic interpretation.

Consider now an example of an event passive with a non-human subject as in:

(19)   *The car was hit by a truck.* (event)

The event described in (19) can also be the result of some action performed by an unspecified agent as in

(20)   a.   *The director ordered the car to be hit by a truck.*

in which case the interpretation of the embedded clause comes about through the RESULT FOR ACTION metonymy, whereas in (20b) the embedded clause can be interpreted as a simple event without necessarily involving an agent who causes the event:

(20)   b.   *The director expected the car to be hit by a truck.*

To summarize this section, what we have demonstrated is that state and event passives can occur in constructions that usually require action predicates. We hypothesize that speakers easily process such seemingly anomalous sentences because of the availability of a fundamental cognitive principle, the RESULT FOR ACTION metonymy. Furthermore, we have shown that this metonymic principle has been grammaticalized to greater extent in English than in German.

2.3. Other non-action verbs

In this section we briefly touch upon some verbs that do not denote actions but can, under certain circumstances, be used in action constructions. We consider the achievement verb *win*, the mental state verb *know*, and the emotional state verb *love*.

2.3.1. Win

The verb *win* is not an action verb in the sense that the agent is able to intentionally achieve the desired result. Nevertheless, sentences like the following occur:

(21)   *How to win a million dollars in the lottery.*

The speaker or writer of this sentence suggests that the winning of a million dollars can be intentionally accomplished, for example, through the application of a mathematical system. That there is a factor of intentionality and control in sentences like (21) can also be seen if the propositional content of (21) is embedded under a verb such as *promise* or *ask*:

(22) a. *She promised to win a million dollars in the lottery.*
     b. *She asked him to win a million dollars in the lottery.*

The action interpretations of (21) and the embedded clauses in (22) can easily be accounted for by the RESULT FOR ACTION metonymy: The result (winning a million dollars in the lottery) is brought about by the intervention of a human agent.

2.3.2. Know

It is generally assumed that a mental state verb like *know* is not felicitously used in the imperative. For example, Quirk et al. (1985: 178) claim that "dynamic verb meanings can regularly occur with the imperative, but stative verbs cannot":

(23) a. *Learn how to swim.*
     b. **Know how to swim.*

However, there are communicative situations in which it makes perfect sense to use *know* and even *know how to* in an imperative:

(24) a. *Know thyself!* (this sense dates from c. 1200; see the Oxford English Dictionary).
     b. *Know this chapter by next Tuesday.*
     c. *Know how to format your paper by Tuesday (or you will flunk the course).*

The corresponding sentences in German cannot occur with the literal equivalent of *know*, i.e. *wissen*. Instead, action verbs such as *erkennen* 'recognize' and *lernen* 'learn' have to be used:

(25) a. *Erkenne   dich   selbst!*
        Recognize yourself self
        'Know yourself!'
     b. *Lerne   dieses   Kapitel   bis   nächsten   Dienstag!*
        Learn   this   chapter   by   next   Tuesday
        'Learn this chapter by next Tuesday!'
     c. *Lerne   bis   Dienstag, wie   das   Referat   zu   formatieren ist!*
        Learn   by   Tuesday   how   the   paper   to   format   is
        'Learn by Tuesday how to format the paper!'

Again in English the acceptability of sentences like (24) can be accounted for by the RESULT FOR ACTION metonymy: The mental state of knowledge is caused by the intentional effort of a human agent, in this case by the addressee.

This analysis entails that knowledge states that cannot easily be attributed to an intentional causer are less likely to occur in action constructions:

(26) a. *?Know that John spent the night in jail.*
b. *?She asked him to know that John spent the night in jail.*
c. *?How to know that John spent the night in jail.*

2.3.3. Love and related states

The emotional state verb *love* is also usable in the imperative and in action complement clauses:

(27) a. *Love thy neighbor.*
b. *She promised to love him forever.*

In these contexts the only coherent interpretation is that the addressee is enjoined to or promises to intentionally undertake to do something so that love will result. Sentences like (27), in a nutshell, epitomize theological and folk models of love, respectively. Both sentences implicate that love is an emotional state which can be achieved on the basis of a conscious decision. Sentences (27) can thus be explained on the basis of the RESULT FOR ACTION metonymy. They contrast with other (metaphorically grounded) folk models in which love is conceptualized as a passion that is beyond one's control.

Now note that the more or less synonymous expression *be in love with* is not as happily inserted into action constructions as *love*:

(28) a. *?Be in love with your fiancé.*
b. *?He promised to be in love with her forever.*

The reason for this infelicity seems to be that, when one is in the love "container" one has hardly any control over one's feelings, i.e., one is less likely to be an intentional agent than when one simply *loves*. Nevertheless, in a book-store, one might find a self-help book entitled

(29)   *How to be in Love with Your Mate for the Rest of Your Life.*

The popularized psychological model reflected in such book titles exploits an important aspect of the folk theory of being in love, namely, that being in love is a pleasurable and desirable state that should therefore be prolonged. In contrast to the folk model, which pragmatically regards being in love as a temporary state, i.e. as a stage in the development of a mature relationship, the popularized psychological model suggests that, by mastering learnable techniques, one can perpetuate the state of being in love with one partner. In this marked sense then, being in love can be the result of intentional behavior.

Even lower on the scale of intentional behavior is the idiom *have a crush on someone*, reflected in its infelicity in action constructions:

(30) a. *?Have a crush on your neighbor.*
      b. *?She promised to have a crush on her neighbor.*
      c. *??How to have a crush on someone all your life.*

The idiom *have a crush on someone* prototypically expresses a superficial, temporary and non-reciprocated emotional state of an immature person. "Crushes" are neither under the experiencer's control nor are they sought after. It therefore comes as no surprise that it is even less sensitive to the RESULT FOR ACTION metonymy.

2.4. Negation and metonymy

In this section we consider additional non-actional verbs that typically do not occur in action frames. Yet, when these verbs are negated, their acceptability drastically increases. Consider a verb denoting a non-intentional process like *fall*:

(31) a. *?Fall into the water.*
      b. *?She promised to fall into the water.*
      c. *?How to fall into the water.*
(32) a. *Don't fall into the water.*
      b. *She promised not to fall into the water.*
      c. *How not to fall into the water.*

Falling is prototypically conceptualized as something that happens to a patient, not as intentional behavior. Therefore, a sentence like (31a) is felicitous only under exceptional circumstances such as when a film director instructs an actor to perform a stunt. In contrast, avoiding falling is, to a certain degree, under one's control. In other words, one can achieve the result of not falling through intentional behavior. The sentences in (32) are thus acceptable because they are naturally interpretable as RESULT FOR ACTION metonymies.

Many other verbs, especially those involving "bodily processes" (Levin 1993: 217), evince the same acceptability pattern as *fall*. These include: *belch, blush, burp, flush, hiccup, pant, snore, yawn*, etc.

2.5. Summary

To summarize this first part of the article: We have considered a range of non-actional predicates and constructions in English and have explored their possible acceptability in prototypical action constructions like (6). We have proposed that the non-actional constructions that are grammatical in the test frames "inherit" their actional properties from the underlying RESULT FOR ACTION metonymy.

We suggest that the extent to which a given conceptual metonymy is grammaticalized is a language-specific property and have noted that the RESULT FOR ACTION metonymy appears to be more systematically exploited in English than, for example, in German.

3. The EFFECT FOR CAUSE metonymy in the *What's that N?* construction

In the first part of the paper our methodology was to insert items (predicates, constructions) into other constructions where they would not be expected to "fit". In the next part of the essay, we look at a specific construction, namely, the question *What's that N?*. We investigate its meaning and use, in particular its interaction with the EFFECT FOR CAUSE metonymy.

3.1. The meaning of *What's that N?*

The presence of the interrogative *what* in the *What's that N?* construction suggests that it has a very general meaning, which we paraphrase as the information request "What is a *relevant* property of the noun". What a relevant property is depends on the conceptual domain of the noun and the occasion of use of the construction. We claim that these relevant properties are metonymically inferred. In what follows, we consider two metonymically induced senses: the "taxonomic" sense, and the "causal" sense.

3.1.1. The taxonomic sense

We illustrate the taxonomic sense with

(33)   *What's that bird?*

An appropriate answer to (33) would be (34a) and possibly (34b) but not (34c):

(34) a.   *(It's) a titmouse.*
     b.   *?A fledgling.*
     c.   *?(It's) an animal.*

The questioner in (33) asks for information that specifies the *kind of* bird seen. Thus question (33) metonymically stands for the question

(35)   *What kind of bird is that?*

The answer to questions of type (33) has to contain a noun that is a *hyponym* of the questioned noun, hence our term *taxonomic sense*. Sentence (34c) is infelicitous in the given context because it names a superordinate term. Of course it is not just birds, but a huge class of nouns denoting concrete objects and substances that are used in this sense. This reading of the *What's that N?* construction is grounded in a metonymy that we name GENERIC FOR SPECIFIC.

3.1.2. The causal sense

3.1.2.1. Symptoms

There is another class of nouns that, in this construction, also exhibits the taxonomic sense, but is more likely to be associated with another reading. These nouns are usually, though not necessarily, interpreted as *symptoms* of deeper physiological or psychological *causes*. For example,

(36)   *What's that spot on your cheek?*

may be answered with

(37) a. *A pimple.* (type of object)

or with

(37) b. *(It's) my allergy.* (cause)

In the first reply (37a) the *type* of spot is identified, i.e., the taxonomic meaning holds. In the second reply (37b), it is the *cause* that produced the spot on the cheek that is named. That is, (37b) instantiates the SYMPTOM FOR ITS CAUSE metonymy, which, like the RESULT FOR ACTION metonymy, is a subtype of the EFFECT FOR CAUSE metonymy.

The taxonomic sense is, however, very unlikely in an answer to question (38):

(38)   *What's that bruise?*
(39) a. *?It's a purple bruise.* (type of N)
      b. *I bumped into the desk.* (causing event of N)

As an answer to *What's that bruise?* one would not normally expect to be told about the kind of bruise, as in (39a), but rather to be informed about what caused the injury, as in (39b).

Although the taxonomic sense of the *What's that N?* construction is not systematically excluded with this class of nouns, once the conceptualizer has made the decision to interpret the noun as a symptom, the causal sense is enforced.

3.1.2.2. Sense impressions

Yet another class of nouns that can be inserted into the question *What's that N?* seems to resist the taxonomic sense of the construction, and even more so than symptoms, to enforce a causal meaning. Most sense impressions belong to this class, with the interesting exception of vision, which we will discuss shortly. But first consider cases of auditory perception as in (40):
Hearing

(40)   *What's that noise?*

Natural answers to this question would be:

(41) a.   *(It's) a squirrel.*
      b.   *A burglar.*
      c.   *Rain.*
      d.   *The wind in the willows.*

but not:

(42) a.   *?A loud noise.*
      b.   *?(It's) a shriek.*
      c.   *?A yell.*
      d.   *?A cry.*

The data in (41) and (42) point to the conclusion that question (40) is not about the *kind* of noise. Rather *What's that noise?* is conventionally interpreted as a question about who or what *caused* that noise. The answers (41a-b) provide animate causers of the noise; the answers in (41c-d) refer to causing events. Thus, although (40) literally poses an unspecific question about a perceptual event, it is actually used as a question about the cause of that perceptual event. This is an example of what we call the PERCEPTUAL EVENT FOR ITS CAUSE metonymy. Note, however, that certain kinds of replies with a taxonomic reading such as *purring, barking, roaring, ticking*, etc. are acceptable as answers to (40). This is so because there is an inherent causal metonymic link between the sound of purring and a cat, barking and a dog, ticking and a clock, etc.

Smelling

The same causal analysis holds for other sensory experiences such as smells and tastes:

(43)   *What's that smell?*

Appropriate responses will again refer to *causes* as in:

(44) a.   *Smoke.*
      b.   *The bread in the oven.*

but not to *kinds* of olfactory sensations:

(45) a.   *?An acrid smell.*
      b.   *?A burning smell.*

Tasting

Similarly for tastes, the question

(46)   *What's that taste?*

is more appropriately answered with such responses as

(47) a. *Garlic.*
    b. *Pineapple and mango.*

than

(48) a. *?A salty taste.*
    b. *?A sweet taste.*

The appropriate replies to questions (43) and (46) presume that the questioner is seeking information about the source or cause of the sensory impression, not about its kind. Again, in these cases the expression of the sensory impression is metonymically linked to its cause.

Seeing

For visual perception, however, our analysis regarding hearing, smelling, and tasting does not hold. First, there is no generic visual perception term that can fill the N slot in the *What's that N?* construction:

(49)   *?What's that sight?*

Instead, an interrogative that either does not mention any perceptual term or uses a more specific perceptual term is required:

(50) a. *What's that?*
    b. *What's that streak of light?*

Second, in contrast to the other three sense perceptions, a visual event does not seem to be conceptualized in the folk model as an effect coming from a source or cause. For example, an appropriate answer to (50b) might be

(51)   *A shooting star.*

The question (50b) *What's that streak of light?* does not seem to stand for the question

(52)   *What's the causal source of that streak of light?*

in the same way that the question (40) *What's that noise?* stands for

(53)   *What's the causal source of that noise?*

This analysis is corroborated by other constructions referring to sources or causes. For example, note the greater felicity of (54) over (55):

(54)   *Where is that noise coming from?*
(55)   *?Where is that streak of light coming from?*

and of (56) over (57):

(56) a. *A raccoon* made *that noise.*
    b. *The baking bread* produced *a delicious smell.*
    c. *The garlic* gave *the dressing its special taste.*

(57)   *?A shooting star* made/produced/gave *that streak of light.*

The reason that the EFFECT FOR CAUSE metonymy is not operative in the domain of vision seems to be grounded in the folk belief that vision, in contrast to other senses, provides the most direct and privileged access to knowledge, as reflected in the metaphor KNOWING IS SEEING. In the folk model, the relationship between that streak of light and a shooting star seems to be one of referential identity such that a more appropriate utterance than (57) would be (58):

(58)   *That streak of light is/was a shooting star.*

Feeling/touching

The sense of touch, like vision, lacks a generic term that can be inserted in the N slot of the What's that N? construction:

(59)   *?What's that feel?*

Unlike vision, however, the EFFECT FOR CAUSE metonymy seems to hold in this perceptual domain. Felicitous answers to the question *What's that?*, when referring to a tactile sensation, may be (60), but not (61):

(60)   *(It's) silk.*
(61)   *?It's soft.*

The reply in (60) refers not to a tactile sensation but to a fabric that causes a certain tactile sensation; whereas (61), which names the kind of tactile sensation, seems less appropriate. Also, sentences like

(62) a.   *Silk gives this fabric its softness/its touch.*
      b.   *Where does the softness come from?*

support the EFFECT FOR CAUSE interpretation.

3.2. Remarks on German

We conclude this part by drawing some comparisons with German. Note first that question (33) *What's that bird?* must be rendered in German as the equivalent of "What kind of bird is that?" as in (63):

(63)   *Was   für   ein   Vogel   ist   das?*
        What   for   a   bird   is   that
        'What kind of bird is that?'

This linguistic form is highly motivated to encode the *taxonomic* sense. But surprisingly the causal sense is also conventionally encoded by this construction:

(64)   *Was   ist   das   für   ein   Geräusch?*
        What   is   that   for   a   noise
        'What kind of noise is that?'

Appropriate answers to this question give *causes*:

(65) a. *Ein   Einbrecher!*
    A   burglar
    'A burglar!'

    b. *Die   Katze   von   nebenan.*
      The   cat   from   next-to
      'The cat next door.'

Despite the causal reading of examples like (64) we suggest that, because of the grammatical form of the construction, the taxonomic sense is more basic than the causal sense of the *Was für ein(e) N ist das?* construction. If this assumption is correct, then in the German construction the causal sense must be regarded as a motivated extension of the prototypical taxonomic sense – in contrast to English where the two senses are both derived from a more general constructional meaning.

3.3. Summary

Our discussion of the *What's that N?* construction has shown that its very general sense yields to at least two more specific senses that are metonymically induced, the taxonomic sense and the causal sense. In other words, the two senses are motivated specifications of the general sense "What is a relevant property of that N?" An important question remaining is: How are the two senses related to each other?

We have at least a partial answer to this question. First, there is an interesting structural parallelism between the GENERIC FOR SPECIFIC and the EFFECT FOR CAUSE metonymies. In the GENERIC FOR SPECIFIC metonymy, an *entailed* feature or property stands for an *entailing* property, e.g., the concept of bird is entailed by the concept of titmouse (the entailing entity). Similarly, in the EFFECT FOR CAUSE metonymy, a *triggered* entity (e.g. a perceived sound) stands for a *triggering* entity (e.g. the wind in the willows). However, a crucial difference between the two metonymies is that the GENERIC FOR SPECIFIC metonymy is based on a conceptual inclusion relation whereas the EFFECT FOR CAUSE metonymy is based on real-world contingencies. A robin is necessarily a bird, but the wind in the willows does not necessarily produce a perceptible noise.

4. Conclusion

In this paper we considered two kinds of EFFECT FOR CAUSE metonymies: One that has a strong impact on grammatical structure and others that are conceptually, but not grammatically significant. The RESULT FOR ACTION metonymy is of the first kind: It is systematically grammaticalized in English. We amply documented this, showing that states and events can occur in action constructions if they are interpretable as results of actions. In contrast, for other subtypes of the EFFECT FOR CAUSE metonymy that we analyzed in the second part of the paper, no detectable grammatical consequences emerged. To see this, consider again the metonymy PERCEPTUAL EVENT FOR ITS CAUSE as in:

(66)   a.   *What's that delicious smell?*
        b.   *The bread.*

In a genuine metonymic substitution relation it should be possible to use *that delicious smell* as a metonym for *the bread*. However, this only occurs in playful or creative language use but is not conventionally encoded as shown by the infelicity of (67):

(67)   *?Let's eat some of that delicious smell.*

In conclusion, the systematic investigation of how metonymy and grammar interact is, as we hope to have shown, a fascinating prospect for future research.

Notes

1.   An earlier version of this paper was presented at the *5th International Cognitive Linguistics Conference* in Amsterdam, July 14-19, 1997. We are grateful to the International Exchange Program between Hamburg University and Eötvös Loránd University for financial support of our research.
2.   Our prior empirical research on another general metonymy, the POTENTIALITY FOR ACTUALITY metonymy in English and Hungarian (Panther and Thornburg, forthcoming b), has led to the hypothesis that such cognitive principles are universal, but exploited to different degrees across languages.

References

Bach, Emmon
    1968   "Nouns and noun phrases", in: Emmon Bach – Robert T. Harms (eds.)
            Universals in linguistic theory. New York: Holt, Rinehart and Winston,
            90-122.
Lakoff, George
    1970   *Irregularity in syntax.* New York: Holt, Rinehart and Winston.
Levin, Beth
    1993   *English verb classes and alternations: a preliminary investigation.*
            Chicago and London: The University of Chicago Press.
Panther, Klaus – Linda Thornburg
    forthcoming a "A cognitive approach to inferencing in conversation", *Journal of Prag-
            matics.*

forthcoming b "The POTENTIALITY FOR ACTUALITY metonymy in English and Hungarian",
in: Günter Radden – Klaus Panther (eds.) *Metonymy in cognition and
language.* Amsterdam/Philadelphia: Benjamins.
Quirk, Randolph – Sidney Greenbaum – Geoffrey Leech – Jan Svartvik
1985   *A comprehensive grammar of the English language.* London: Longman.
Thornburg, Linda – Klaus Panther
1997   "Speech act metonymies", in Wolf-Andreas Liebert – Gisela Redeker –
Linda Waugh (eds.) *Discourse and perspectives in cognitive linguistics.*
(Current Issues in linguistic theory 151.) Amsterdam/Philadelphia:
Benjamins, 205-219.

Metaphorical extension of *may* and *must* into the epistemic domain[1]

Péter Pelyvás

1. Introduction

Although the metaphorical extension of the root modal meanings into the epistemic domain is a fascinating topic on its own, this paper has been motivated by more general considerations. My main area of interest is what Langacker's (1987, 1991) cognitive theory calls *epistemic grounding*, defined as a category that relates (the linguistic expression of) a process or a thing (a verb [clause] or a noun) to the situation of its use: speaker/hearer knowledge, and time and place of utterance (the latter being subsumed under the term ground).

In Langacker's theory, epistemic grounding is established by the tense-modal complex. For reasons discussed in detail in Langacker (1991: 240-249), summarized and criticized in Pelyvás (1996: 165-184), grounding in that system can only be established (apart from tense) by the modal auxiliaries,[2] both deontic and epistemic.

One facet of the argumentation given in Pelyvás (1996) is that this analysis does not capture the considerable differences between root (deontic) and epistemic meanings, which are due to *subjectification* in the epistemic meaning, a property of the grounding predication (compare also with Sanders – Spooren 1997: 96-108). In fact, Langacker's version, largely based on Sweetser's (1990) treatment of the metaphorical extension of the modal meanings into the epistemic domain, leaves hardly any room at all for distinguishing the two kinds of meanings (Langacker 1991: 270-271).

Part of the solution to the problems inherent in Langacker's treatment of grounding might result from a reconsideration of Sweetser's system that it relies on. The main point to be considered appears to be whether extension is really as straightforward as is suggested there.

The idea of treating modal meanings in terms of metaphorical extension is intuitively appealing, since in several languages, many of which are totally unrelated (e.g. English and Hungarian),[3] the same set of modal auxiliaries can express both deontic and epistemic meanings, with the latter often felt to be a "superimposition on" or "reinterpretation of" the original deontic (or root) meanings.

Some of Sweetser's analyses, however, prove to be erroneous. Pelyvás (1994: 1-9, 1996: 127-133) reports major problems in her analysis of *may*. In this paper I will give a brief overview of the relevant aspects of that analysis and its critique, and will attempt to point out similar difficulties with, and propose a new analysis for, *must*.

2. A critical survey of Sweetser's analysis of *may*

2.1 Sweetser's analysis

In her analysis of the modal meanings, Sweetser uses Talmy's idea of *force dynamics*, which describes situations (and meanings) in terms of forces and barriers.

For *may*, Sweetser suggests an image-schematic structure with a *potential barrier* that could prevent the occurrence of the situation in question but is *not imposed*:

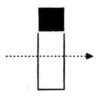

This schema, Sweetser argues, describes root (deontic) *may*, a lexical item pertaining to the socio-physical domain, and can be extended without difficulty to describe the epistemic meaning. As a result,

1. In both the sociophysical and the epistemic worlds, nothing prevents the occurrence of whatever is modally marked with *may*; the chain of events is not obstructed.

In both the sociophysical and epistemic worlds, there is some background understanding that if things were different, something could obstruct the chain of events. For example, permission or other sociophysical conditions could change; and added premises might make the reasoner reach a different conclusion (Sweetser 1990: 60).

In the extension, however, some properties of the source domain will be eliminated owing to the differences between the source and the target (cf. a more detailed discussion of the Invariance Hypothesis below). In Sweetser's view, such properties will include:

– the exact nature of the forces
– the exact nature of the barrier.

In the sociophysical world, the nature of the forces and the kinds of authority may vary: there is an important difference between external and internal forces, etc., which largely accounts for the differences between modals pertaining to that domain, e.g. the differences between *must* and *ought* on the one hand, and *must* and *have to*[4] on the other (Sweetser 1990: 61).

In the epistemic domain, however, "… only premises count as forces or barriers. The only kind of event is a logical conclusion (or the verification of a theory); and it even has to be the speaker's own conclusion, because the force-dynamic structure of other people's reasoning is not readily accessible to us" (Sweetser 1990: 67).[5]

The deontic meaning is paraphrased by Sweetser as

(1)   *John may go.*
        John is not barred (by my or some other) authority (in the socio-physical world) from going.

Metaphorical extension into the epistemic domain will then give:

(2)   *John may be there.*
        I am not barred by my premises from the conclusion that John is there.

2.2 Problems with Sweetser's analysis[6]

Sweetser's version of metaphorical extension does not seem to describe epistemic *may* at all, for reasons connected with her description of the source domain, reinterpretation of its elements in the target domain, and her choice of the exact source of the extension. The problems encountered are as follows:

– The definition of the barrier does not appear to support the meaning of deontic *may*: Example (1) alone describes an epistemically unqualified statement, example (2) a hypothetical one, examples (1) and (2) together seem to describe a situation that is true (but not necessarily true): something is the case, but it could be otherwise – again an epistemically unqualified statement. It appears that example (2) cannot change example (1)'s essential properties and can be regarded as superfluous.[7]

– Because of the difference in the scopes of negation in the deontic and epistemic meanings of *may* (~ *may* vs. *may* ~), one barrier alone cannot describe epistemic *may (not)*. The crucial difference is that whereas deontic *may* and *may not* are contradictory, their epistemic counterparts can be entertained together. We seem to require a system of two barriers: one for *may*, the other for *may not*, both lifted (or imposed?) simultaneously, to account for the fact that (3) and (4) can be entertained simultaneously:

(3)   *He may be there.*
(4)   *He may not be there.*
(3) a.   b.

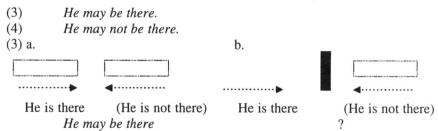

He is there   (He is not there)   He is there   (He is not there)
      He may be there   ?

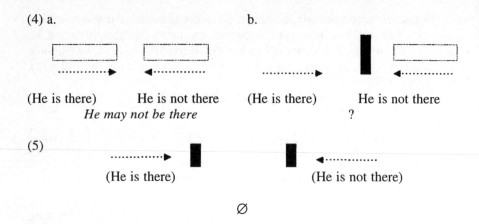

(4) a.   b.

(He is there)   He is not there   (He is there)   He is not there
        He may not be there   ?

(5)

(He is there)   (He is not there)

∅

Both (3) and (4) require the simultaneous lifting of both barriers, as (3a) and (4a) suggest. Imposing one barrier ((3b) and (4b)) does not seem to describe anything excluding the remote possibility that someone should want to describe the "unmodalized" sentences *He is there* or *He is not there* in this roundabout way. Imposing both barriers (as in (5)) leads to a contradiction and cannot be interpreted at all.

– In the extension from the deontic to the epistemic domain doer and speaker roles are confused: the speaker of the deontic domain assumes the doer role in the epistemic domain and the original speaker role is taken by factors that are more or less external to the speaker (or have to be viewed as such by the "logic" of the analysis): premises that lead to a conclusion. This should not be happening since, I would like to maintain, in metaphorical extension of this particular kind, important structural relationships should be preserved.

The Invariance Hypothesis (Lakoff 1990, 1993; Brugman 1990; Sanders – Spooren 1997; Kövecses [in this volume]) states that "all the image-schematic structure of the source domain that is consistent with the image-schematic structure of the target is mapped onto the target" (Kövecses [in this volume]: [84]). One peculiarity of mapping from the socio-physical domain (root meanings) to the epistemic domain is that the domains involved are vastly different, as Sweetser herself observes (cf. 2.1.). Since the more concrete characteristics of the source domain (cf. 2.3.) cannot be mapped onto the target, it is essential that the remaining participants and relationships remain constant, i.e. if a participant can be mapped onto the target, the mapping should not change radically its relationships to other elements of the (target) situation (sources are mapped onto sources, targets onto targets, etc.).

In the metaphorical extension of the modal meanings the speaker/conceptualizer role appears to be such a constant, even though its concrete nature is changed somewhat by what Langacker (1987: 128-131, 1991: 215-217) calls *subjectification.* In this process, certain elements of a situation that have been interpreted objectively are reinterpreted subjectively (are related to the speaker as conceptualizer rather than to any other (objective) element of the situation.

(6)   a.   *An insect crawled across the table.*
       b.   *A famous movie star sat across the table.*

In (6a) the interpretation of the phrase *across the table* is independent of the observer, in (6b) it is clearly not. For this reason, the situation in (6b) is seen as more subjective (and the role of the conceptualizer in it is more objective).

In the deontic meaning of *may*, the permission giver (typically the speaker) is part of the objective scene, whereas the conceptualizer of the epistemic meaning (necessarily the speaker) is not. This also changes the speaker's relationship to other participants somewhat (cf. Sanders – Spooren 1997: 103-104).

If speaker becomes doer in the extension, and his original role is taken by a component not present in the root meaning,[8] then, arguably, all conceived "similarity" between the source and the target is lost and the extension cannot be valid. We will return to this problem in 2.3 and 3.2, in connection with the proposed alternative analyses of both *may* and *must.*

– Diachronic evidence strongly suggests that the deontic sense appeared later than the epistemic sense in the case of *may* (cf. Traugott 1989: 36), which makes extension from that source at least doubtful.

2.3 An alternative analysis for *may*

In order to overcome the problems listed in 2.2, Pelyvás (1994, 1996) proposes a system in which

– counteracting forces of different relative strengths rather than rigid barriers are used;
– both the epistemic and the deontic meanings are extensions of a (now extinct) *ability* meaning of *may* ['be strong enough'].

In the *ability* meaning (Figure 1) the only participant that is highlighted (part of the immediate scope or objective scene (OS)) and so can be endowed with strength is the doer, although it is clear that his/her strength is relative to counteracting forces (seen as relatively weak) that must also be regarded as part of the overall scope: the doer is strong enough to perform some (typically purposeful) action (the latter factor is absent from Sweetser's analysis). The only role of the speaker/conceptualizer in this situation is that of the ground (cf. Langacker's (1987, 1991) epistemic grounding), a role that would be present in the same form in any clause. For this reason such meanings are often not considered to be truly modal at all.

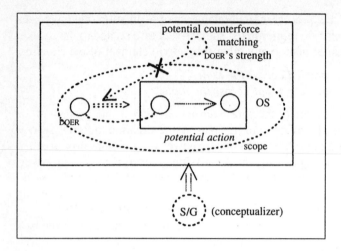

Figure 1. may – ability

In the "prototypical" deontic meaning (Figure 2) the doer intends to perform a purposeful activity (both factors, although clearly part of the deontic sense of *may*, are absent from Sweetser's treatment) and the counterforces take shape in the form of the "permission giver" (typically the speaker). The latter becomes part of the objective scene (cf. Sanders – Spooren 1997: 97).

We can safely assume that the appearance of the speaker in the immediate scope of the predication (OS) (apart from his "normal" role as conceptualizer out of the scope of the predication) is a crucial factor in the development of deontic modal meanings in English.[9]

One innovation of Pelyvás (1996) is the argument that in the deontic sense the speaker (the typical "permission giver") is not strong enough or does not find it necessary to mobilize a force that is strong enough to prevent the action from taking place, i.e., the doer is relatively strong and the permission giver is relatively weak (relinquishes authority).[10]

In the epistemic sense (Figure 3), which also derives from the ability meaning, subjectification has occurred (for a detailed description of the process, compare Langacker 1987: 128-131, 1991: 215-220). The overall effect of the process is the inclusion of the speaker/conceptualizer (the ground) directly (rather than through correspondence, as in the deontic meaning, cf. Figure 2) into the scope of the predication. The relevant relationship now holds between the speaker (conceptualizer) and the situation as a whole. The same relative weakness that was present as an unspecified counterforce in the ability sense (and also reappears at a later date as a force typically associated with the speaker in the deontic sense) now prevents the speaker from becoming fully epistemically committed (cf. Lyons 1995: 254) as to the situation described.

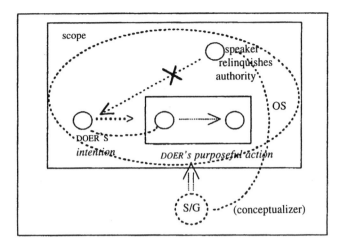

Figure 2. Deontic *may*

The doer is no longer highlighted in the epistemic sense (strength or intention do not play a role and the counterforce has no relation directly to him/her). This is an aspect of the source domain that would not be compatible with the target domain. The situation epistemically qualified by *may* need not be a deliberate action, can be in the progressive and even anterior to the ground. This is further evidence in favor of the view that the speaker cannot simply assume the doer's role.

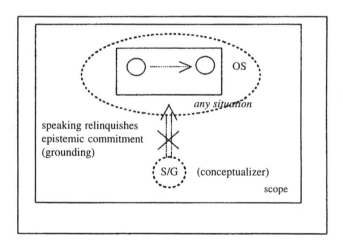

Figure 3. Epistemic *may*

In this analysis

- because of the (relatively weak) counterforce, the sentence containing epistemic *may* is not equivalent to an unqualified statement as Sweetser's analysis would predict;
- the different scopes of negation can be explained. Epistemic *may* and *may not* can be entertained together because negation occurs within the situation that is alone within the objective scene (OS) and does not affect the relationship of the counterforce to any participant of the situation, whereas it makes the speaker (part of OS) strong in the deontic sense;
- the speaker's role remains constant, which means that structural relationships are preserved and invariance criteria are satisfied.

We cannot go here into the details of how Langacker's notion of subjectification plays an essential role in the emergence of the grounding predication, which gives epistemic modals a function that Langacker considers to be unique in the grammatical system of English. The details are described in Langacker (1991: Chapters 5-6) and in Pelyvás (1996: Chapter 9).

3. An analysis of *must*

3.1 Talmy's and Sweetser's suggestions

Talmy's original proposal for *must* is a set of barriers restricting one's domain of action to a single act:

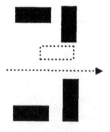

Sweetser abandons this in favor of a compelling force directing the subject towards an act:

Since cognitive grammar allows for the possibility of structuring the same situation in different ways (cf. the subjectivity of different Idealized Cognitive Models), there is nothing intrinsically wrong in postulating that both formulations are equally valid. It can indeed be argued that Talmy's formulation describes the situation from the doer's (imposee's) point of view:

(7)   *I must go there at midnight.* (I have no alternatives.)

whereas Sweetser's describes it from the speaker's (imposer's) point of view:

(8)   *You must go there at midnight.* (I insist that you do.)

Sweetser then states that the deontic meaning can be paraphrased as *"The direct force (of my authority) compels you to go there at midnight"*, which, according to her, can be extended into the epistemic domain as

(9)   *John must be mad.*
        'The available (direct) evidence compels me to the conclusion that John is mad'

3.2 Problems with Talmy's and Sweetser's suggestions

Many of the problems encountered with *may* appear to be repeated here in a similar form:

– Sweetser's solution again confuses speaker and doer roles: the speaker of the deontic meaning again becomes the doer of the epistemic one, with its former slot occupied by "available direct evidence": structural relationships do not appear to be preserved.

Owing to the great differences between the root (deontic in this case) and epistemic domains, which, similarly to the example of *may*, result in the loss of most of the concrete properties of the participants (obligation, purposeful activity, posteriority etc.), the permanence of the speaker role alone and of its relationship to slightly changing but recognizable aspects of the situation appear to be the only factors that hold the metaphor together.

It is also worth mentioning at this point that any such rearrangement of participants would make transitional stages between root and epistemic readings impossible (at least without surface subject-doer identity). It would be impossible to read both meanings into one form without confusion. The example of concessive *may* has been mentioned, and the partially epistemic meaning of *should* is also an obvious case in point. The sentence *They should all be dead by now*, although mostly epistemic, carries definite undertones of a deontic nature.

Such a rearrangement, if it took place, would be likely to involve a rearrangement of syntactic structure as well (symbolicity). The doer appears as subject in the deontic sentence: the same might be expected of the speaker/doer in the epistemic context. In subjectification of the first type (Langacker 1991: 269-273), when the speaker/conceptualizer appears as a reference point (a temporary participant), this happens in the form of a complex clause[11] with the speaker appearing as the subject of a cognitive matrix predicate, as in *I think that John is an idiot* rather than directly becoming the subject of the epistemically qualified clause.

It can be argued that the notion of compulsion that appears to be present in both the deontic and epistemic sense should suffice as a basis for the metaphoric transfer.[12] It is not obvious to me that compulsion is present in the epistemic meaning unless prediction should be considered as such (cf. the alternative to be suggested in 3.3.2). In Sweetser's version the presence of compulsion in the epistemic sense depends on the dubious move "speaker replaces doer", since one can hardly compel third order entities to be true (disregarding the further complications that the permissibility of anteriority would introduce).

– The relationship of negated and non-negated forms is less straightforward with *must* than it was with *may*, where only the scope of negation changed in the transfer. The negation of the lexical item *must* only occurs in the deontic sense (alongside with *need not*, which is traditionally regarded as a negative counterpart to deontic *must*). In the epistemic sense another alternative, *cannot* is used.

There are nevertheless two factors that may justify involving negation in the analysis. One is the example of *may*, where it provides important evidence against Sweetser's analysis and in favor of the alternative proposed. The other is the more general consideration that in studying the extension of grammatical rather than "purely" lexical meanings, disregarding obvious aspects of that grammaticality – negation, grammatical structure, relation of a modal to other elements of the modal scale or to unmodalized statements, which makes this study relevant in the wider perspective outlined in section 1 – would deprive the analyzer of important tools and might render the analysis haphazard, vague or, ultimately, even vacuous.

In the deontic sense, both Talmy's and Sweetser's schemas appear to have some problems with the external negation of *must*.

In Talmy's system external negation (*need not*) can be described as *lifting all barriers*. In my judgment this leads to an unmodalized statement, if not to deontic *may*, with which it is logically compatible. *Need not* would, nevertheless, not be used to grant permission, which suggests a flaw in the analysis. (Internal negation (*must not*) could be *all barriers lifted, only one left imposed* in Talmy's system, which makes it in effect identical with Sweetser's deontic *may not*, an acceptable solution provided that that analysis is correct.)

In Sweetser's system *need not* can be described as removing the compelling force from behind the action, which clearly leaves us with the unacceptable conclusion that it is equivalent to an unmodalized statement. (Internal negation could be seen as a compelling force working against the action, which is in good correspondence with our suggested alternative analysis for deontic *may*.)

Sweetser's paraphrase of epistemic *must* would suggest that it requires internal negation: *"The available (direct) evidence compels me to the conclusion that*

John is *not* mad". The existing form, *cannot*, however, expresses external negation.

– Sweetser's original paraphrases of affirmative *must* (in both senses) suggest that *must* is stronger than the "unmodalized" statement, which is clearly not the case. Being compelled to do so is no guarantee that the doer (or imposee) will carry out the action, just as prohibition is no guarantee that the action will not take place. On the epistemic scale, *must* is weaker than the "unmodalized" statement, although its analysis in terms of possible worlds would predict the opposite (*NP ≡ true in all possible worlds*, cf. Karttunen (1972), Pelyvás (1996), see also Note 7).

All this evidence suggests that neither schema describes deontic *must* satisfactorily, and, necessarily, neither can serve in its present form as a basis for metaphorical extension into the epistemic domain.

3.3 An alternative analysis for *must*

3.3.1 A new force in the deontic sense

I will now suggest that there is one element missing from both Talmy's and Sweetser's conceptual schemas. I will initially call that element, which is to play an important role in metaphorical extension as well, *the doer's reluctance to perform the action*. This factor, which, being a force, could be easily incorporated into Sweetser's schema, is briefly mentioned in her analysis but is not taken into consideration in its formulation.[13]

Deontic *must* typically appears only in dynamic situations marked as agentive (deliberate action). Whenever a deviation occurs, a reinterpretation becomes necessary, as in (10) and (11):

(10)   *You must live there the rest of your life.*
         ≈ You are not permitted to move. [deliberate action]
(11)   *You must be really tall to be able to pick those apples.*

In (11) the generic reinterpretation of the personal pronoun takes place. When that is not possible, the meaning can only be epistemic, as in (12):

(12)   *You must be really tall to have been able to pick those apples.*
         [said to someone the speaker has never actually seen]

That the doer's reluctance is a significant factor in the deontic meaning of *must* is known from experience – sometimes the presence of an obligation makes one reluctant to do something that one would otherwise gladly do. It also plays a crucial role in the linguistic analysis of the difference between *must* and *should*. *Should* is generally regarded as the more polite form, but the source of politeness is usually left unexplained or is simply attributed to its originally being a preterit/non-actual form. I would like to argue, in particular, that the difference is in the different degrees of compliance expected of the addressee (doer), i.e. the different degrees to which his/her reluctance or non-compliance is permitted to play a role. (The essence of politeness is leaving options open to your partner.) Compare the sentences in (13):

(13) a. *You must leave now.*
      b. *You should/ought to leave now.*

		Necessity	Compliance
a.	(MUST)	+	+
b.	(SHOULD/OUGHT)	+	?

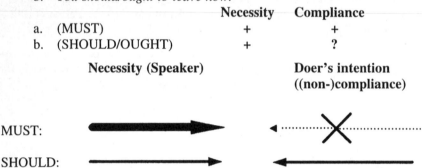

	Necessity (Speaker)	Doer's intention ((non-)compliance)
MUST:		
SHOULD:		

Since inclusion of the new force representing the doer's reluctance only makes sense in Sweetser's model (as it contains only forces), from now on we shall only consider this version. After modification, the rough schema for deontic *must* will be as follows:

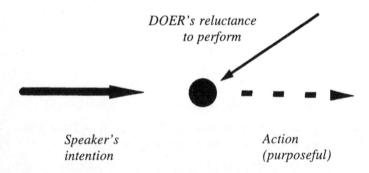

DOER's reluctance to perform

Speaker's intention

Action (purposeful)

The existence of this counterforce explains why deontic *must* is not equivalent to or even stronger than an "unmodalized" statement. It must also be borne in mind that the exact nature and strength of this force is not typically known to the speaker (imposer), a fact that may be seen as the first step in the direction of the epistemic meaning.

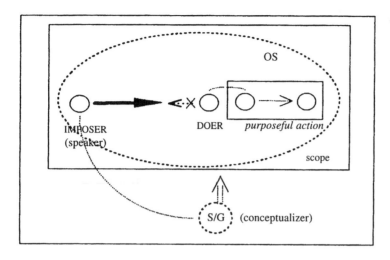

Figure 4. Deontic *must*

The more detailed schema that makes a distinction between scope and immediate scope (objective scene) and also includes the speaker/conceptualizer is given in Figure 4.

As the Figure indicates, the speaker/conceptualizer is again present in a dual role. One is that of the ground, a role that the speaker will take in any clause (cf. 2.3) and is out of the scope of the predication. Similarly to deontic *may*, the speaker also appears as one of the participants (the imposer) in the on-stage relationship (OS) between him and the doer of the purposeful action. This identity is again established through correspondence – which may turn out to be an essential factor in English deontic modals, and perhaps only the prototypical case in Dutch where the imposer can not only be different from the conceptualizer in the deontic sense of *moet* 'must', but can actually appear in the sentence as a prepositional phrase, as in (14)

(14)   *Jan   moet   van   Klaas   thuisblijven.*
        Jan   must   by order of Klaas   home stay
        'Jan must [by order of Klaas] stay at home.'

This example is taken from Sanders – Spooren (1997: 97). It is interesting to note that this option does not appear to be available in the epistemic sense, which can be taken to be evidence that the two roles in that meaning are not separate and speaker involvement is established by means other than correspondence.

3.3.2 Extension of the modified schema into the epistemic domain

Similarly to *may*, the extension of *must* from the sociophysical to the epistemic domain is accompanied by subjectification.

Owing to the great differences between the source and the target domain (cf. 3.2), we argue that it is the forces and interrelationships between these forces that will carry the metaphor.

The objective relationship (one within OS) that used to hold between speaker (through correspondence) and doer is now reinterpreted along the subjective axis (cf. Langacker 1991: 216) and is thus turned into a relationship directly between the speaker as conceptualizer and the situation as a whole.

As with epistemic *may*, the doer loses any role other than the one he has in the embedded situation (of any kind) that replaces the purposeful activity of the deontic sense. His reluctance to perform the act is an aspect of the source that is incompatible with the target domain. Even if the on-stage situation is purposeful action, the doer does not have any obligation in it and, similarly to epistemic *may*, anteriority and progressive forms are possible.

The force that used to represent the doer's reluctance is now reinterpreted as forces of unknown reality that may make the speaker's assessment of the situation imprecise: forces that are unknown to him/her and may ultimately result in a deviation from his prediction of reality (cf. Langacker 1991: 240-249).[14]

The force representing the speaker's intention in the deontic sense now becomes a force rather similar in nature: the force of the speaker's epistemic commitment, his prediction of the likely course of events based on his assessment of known elements of the situation.

Extension into the epistemic domain for *must* can be summarized in the schema given in Figure 5:

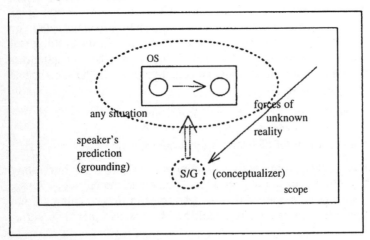

Figure 5. Epistemic *must*

In this solution
- Speaker and doer roles are preserved as in the case of *may*.
- The irregularity of negation can be explained: what is negated with *cannot* in the epistemic sense is a relationship (between conceptualizer and the situation-as-a-whole) that was not highlighted at all (was out of scope) in the deontic sense. Negation is external relative to the situation highlighted in the objective scene.
- Owing to the counterforce that represents factors of unknown reality, the speaker's epistemic commitment is weaker than in an unmodalized statement. There is no such counteracting force highlighted in a statement like *John is mad.*

4. Conclusion

The alternative analyses appear to me to give a more systematic account of the processes underlying the metaphorical extension of modal meanings into the epistemic domain than Sweetser's (1990) version. The proposed alternatives suggest that the differences between root and epistemic meanings are greater than envisaged by Sweetser but can nevertheless be seen as metaphorical extension – of a rather peculiar kind. The nature of the differences are not only compatible with but can be seen as closely related to a modified version of Langacker's notion of subjectification and epistemic grounding.

The essence of this modification is that the target epistemic domain is strongly subjectified through direct involvement of the speaker/conceptualizer in the scope of the predication, whereas the source (sociophysical) domain is only partially so (through correspondences between speaker/conceptualizer and participants more or less objectively construed in the objective scene). From the wider perspective of epistemic grounding this supports my hypothesis that root modals do not function as grounding predications. A root modal could be included in the situation that remains alone in OS with both epistemic modals: root modals can (and must) be epistemically grounded.

In the alternative analyses for the root meanings of both auxiliaries, a relatively weak counterforce was introduced into the situation, ultimately with an aim of preventing the schemas from becoming equivalent to unmodalized statements. The role of these counterforces in the extension can reveal significant aspects of the nature of the epistemic domain.

In the metaphorical extension of *may* this counterforce bears a crucial role: the speaker does not commit himself as to the factuality of the situation described (puts himself in a relatively weak position), which means that this force carries the full weight of the grounding predication.

In the extension of *must*, this force remains in the background: part of the scope of the predication but out of the objective scene: its function is to weaken somewhat the epistemic commitment of the speaker (the force of the grounding predication).

The difference can be seen to be a result of the fact that in *may* the force can be associated with the speaker and thus plays a crucial role in the epistemic sense which, owing to subjectification, highlights the speaker/conceptualizer (if only temporarily – cf. the role of reference point constructions in epistemic grounding, Langacker 1993: 24-26; Pelyvás 1996: 160-163). Association with the speaker may not be necessarily true of the *ability* sense, from which the epistemic meaning is extended in our proposal, but is certainly true of the deontic one, which, although a later development, could nevertheless play a significant role in the even later emergence of the contemporary strongly subjectified epistemic sense of *may* (cf. Traugott 1989: 41-43; Pelyvás 1996: 133-134). In *must* this force cannot be associated with the speaker and so remains secondary in the extension.

Notes

1. A preliminary version of this paper was presented at a Seminar on the cognitive theory of metaphor and metonymy organized by Antonio Barcelona as part of the 4th Conference of the European Society for the Study of English in Debrecen, September, 1997. I wish to express gratitude to Professor Antonio Barcelona and to an unidentified reader of the preliminary version, who, with their remarks contributed a lot to the formulation of this version. I am of course responsible for all the views presented here.
2. Since the grounding predication, owing to its origins in the reference-point construction, profiles the grounded head (the structure to be grounded), and since a grounded predication (on the clause level) profiles a process, the grounded head itself must profile a process. In Langacker's system a non-finite form profiles an atemporal relationship rather than a process. As a consequence, the grounded head cannot be non-finite. The only form (in English) that is neither clearly non-finite nor clearly finite is the bare infinitive, and only modals are followed by that form.
3. Cf. Kálmán et al. (1989), a comprehensive analysis of the Hungarian system of auxiliaries.
4. Sweetser (1990) discusses *have to* among the modal auxiliaries.
5. In what follows we will argue that in addition to the ones mentioned here, other factors, not included in Sweetser's description of the root domain, will also have to be reinterpreted.
6. Since I discuss Sweetser's analysis in detail elsewhere, I will only concentrate here on those aspects of *may* that are relevant to the present discussion of *must*. This is an improved and updated version of Pelyvás (1996: 121-133) but I will not be concerned with all the issues discussed there.
7. The relationship of example (1) and (2) is discussed in Pelyvás (1996: 130) in terms of the necessity and possibility operators in modal logic (relying on Karttunen (1972)). In a system of modal logic, whatever is true is also necessarily true. A

simple "unmodalized" statement, incidentally characterized by Karttunen (1972: 4) as requiring the properties Sweetser assigns to statements involving epistemic *may*, does not seem to have a place in such a system.

8. This is not simply a case of speaker-doer identity, a reading not excluded by the preliminary version of this paper. As both Barcelona and the unnamed reviewer note, this alone would not violate the Invariance Hypothesis. One could even argue, cf. Pelyvás (1996: 150, 166), that identity in such sentences as *I may change my mind* could facilitate the development of the epistemic meaning. But, since the epistemic meaning developed before the deontic one in the case of *may*, the case is not so simple – cf. 2.3.

9. This point deserves further consideration that could lead to the formulation of a theory of *deontic grounding*.

10. It can and has indeed been argued that permission givers are typically strong, or else the speech act could not be successfully performed. We can accept this as mostly true (but bear in mind cases of concessive *may* in such sentences as *All right, he may be a criminal, but he has always been honest with me*, where *may* clearly indicates surrender in an argument and can be argued to bear some epistemic overtones as well) and emphasize the speaker's deliberate relinquishing of authority in situations where (s)he does not find it important (or even desirable) to oppose the doer's deliberate action, thereby putting himself/herself in a weak position. Permission does not force the doer to perform the action; its source can be viewed as relatively weak in this respect as well. In any case, since we propose to derive epistemic *may* from the *ability* meaning where strength can only be attributed to the doer, the deontic meaning is not crucial to the argument.

11. Or what appears to be a complex clause, cf. Pelyvás (1996: 180-184).

12. This observation comes from the unidentified reviewer of the preliminary version.

13. It is difficult to see how it could be incorporated into Talmy's system, which may be a sign of the superiority of Sweetser's version.

14. In 3.3.1. we argued that the (degree of the) doer's reluctance is largely unknown to the imposer in the deontic sense, which is in good correspondence with the proposed reinterpretation.

It can still be argued, as the unidentified reviewer of the preliminary version does, that forces of unknown reality do not necessarily work against, and might even confirm the speaker's assessment of the situation. There is one major objection to this: even if they do, the speaker/conceptualizer is unaware of this and an unknown factor is always a factor of indecision. One of the basic factors in limited resource processing is that the conceptualizer postulates the existence of at least some unknown factors that work against him/her. Factors of unknown reality that may confirm the judgment are thus going to be less "interesting" than factors of known reality that do and than factors of unknown reality that may not. A speaker would not use epistemic *must* unless he believed that there were important factors of this kind (cf. the Gricean maxim of quantity).

References

Brugman, Claudia
  1990   "What is the Invariance Hypothesis?", *Cognitive Linguistics* 1-2: 257-267
Kálmán, C. György – László Kálmán – Ádám Nádasdy – Gábor Prószéky
  1989   "A magyar segédigék rendszere" [The system of Hungarian auxiliaries], in: Zsigmond Telegdi – Ferenc Kiefer (eds.), *Általános Nyelvészeti Tanulmányok* [Studies in general linguistics] XVII. Budapest: Akadémiai, 49-103.
Karttunen, Lauri
  1972   "Possible and Must", in: Kimball, John P. (ed.) *Syntax and Semantics* 1. New York: Academic Press, 1-20.
Kövecses, Zoltan
  this volume   "The scope of metaphor"
Lakoff, George
  1990   "The Invariance Hypothesis: is abstract reason based on image schemas?", *Cognitive Linguistics* 1-1: 39-75.
  1993   "The contemporary theory of metaphor", in: Ortony, Andrew (ed.), *Metaphor and thought.* Cambridge: Cambridge University Press, 202-251.
Langacker, Ronald W.
  1987   *Foundations of cognitive grammar I.* Stanford: Stanford University Press.
  1991   *Foundations of cognitive grammar II.* Stanford: Stanford University Press.
  1993   "Reference-point constructions", *Cognitive Linguistics* 4-1: 1-38.
  1995   "Raising and transparency", *Language* Vol. 71, No.1. 1-61.
Lyons, John
  1995   *Linguistic semantics.* Cambridge: Cambridge University Press.
Pelyvás, Péter
  1994   "Metaphorical extension in MAY", in: Béla Korponay – Péter Pelyvás (eds.) *Studies in linguistics III.* Debrecen: KLTE, 1994, 19-55.
  1996   *Subjectivity in English. Generative grammar versus the cognitive theory of epistemic grounding.* Frankfurt am Main: Peter Lang.
Sanders, José – Spooren, Wilbert
  1997   "Perspective, subjectivity, and modality from a cognitive linguistic point of view", in: Wolf-Andreas Liebert – Gisela Redeker – Linda Waugh (eds.) *Discourse and perspective in cognitive linguistics.* Amsterdam: Benjamins, 85-112.
Sweetser, Eve
  1990   *From etymology to pragmatics. Metaphorical and cultural aspects of semantic structure.* Cambridge: Cambridge University Press.
Traugott, Elizabeth C.
  1989   "On the rise of epistemic meanings in English: An example of subjectification in semantic change", *Language* Vol. 65, No.1: 31-55.

Metaphor and metonymy in discourse

Poetry and the scope of metaphor: Toward a cognitive theory of literature

Margaret H. Freeman

1. Introduction

It is a commonplace of literary criticism that one of the defining characteristics of literature is its ability to generate multiple meanings and interpretations. Literary critics are adept at producing such readings, readings which are often insightful and illuminating. Literary critics, however, on the whole, tend to assume rather than explore the principles and the processes by which such multiplicity occurs. Their readings are shaped by the theoretical stances they take, whether psychological, sociological, historical, or deconstructionist, to name just a few. Readings thus generated of a single literary text exist side by side (a colleague once counted seventy-nine conflicting interpretations of a poem by Emily Dickinson[1]), vying for preferential acceptance with no means independent of the theories being used to determine their validity. Literary criticism, in other words, lacks an adequate theory of literature.

Recent developments in the field of cognitive linguistics have already proven promising and productive in the search for an adequate theory of language. Cognitive theory, for example, has been able to show that meaning does not reside in language so much as it is accessed by it, that language is the product, not of a separate structural system within the brain, but of the general cognitive processes that enable the human mind to conceptualize experience, processes that cognitive linguists call embodied understanding (Johnson 1987). By recognizing the central role played by analogical reasoning which maps elements of one cognitive domain onto another, cognitive linguists have begun to account for a variety of linguistic phenomena occurring in natural languages, such as anaphor or counterfactuals, metaphor or metonymy, that have long eluded logic-oriented theories of meaning (Fauconnier 1997).[2]

If cognitive linguistics can produce an adequate theory of language, it can also serve as the basis for an adequate theory of literature. I therefore propose a theory of literature that is grounded in cognitive linguistic theory: namely, that literary texts are the products of cognizing minds and their interpretations the products of other cognizing minds in the context of the physical and socio-cultural worlds in which they have been created and are read. This is the argument that underlies this paper. The theory I call *cognitive poetics* is a powerful tool for making explicit our reasoning processes and for illuminating the structure and content of literary texts.[3] It provides a theory of literature that is both grounded in the language of literary texts and grounded in the cognitive linguistic strategies readers use to understand them.

The question I raise in this paper is, therefore, "In what ways can cognitive theory as it has been developed in recent years contribute toward a more adequate theory of literature?" To answer this question, I look at Emily Dickinson's poem, "My Cocoon tightens –", to show how the general mapping skills that constitute the cognitive ability to create and interpret metaphor can provide a more coherent theory than the intuitive and ad hoc approaches of traditional criticism. I then look at another Dickinson poem, "My Life had stood – a / Loaded Gun –", to show how a cognitive metaphor approach can illuminate the insights – and the limitations – of traditional literary criticism. Finally, I show how the application of cognitive poetics can identify and evaluate literary style by discussing a poem generally believed to be by Dickinson but which proved to be a forgery, and end by comparing cognitive poetics to other cognitive approaches.

2. Analogical mapping in Dickinson's Cocoon poem

When literary critics analyze literary texts, they apply the same analogical processes of reasoning that enable metaphor construction as the writers do who compose them. The components of these analogical reasoning processes include cognitive mapping skills to create different levels of identification across different domains. Following is a brief discussion of the cognitive theories of analogical mapping, iconicity, and metaphor applied to an analysis of Dickinson's Cocoon poem.

Understanding what it is that human beings do when they make analogies is crucial to understanding what makes us human. In making analogies, we use at least three cognitive skills: perception of similarity between objects, or "attribute mapping", sensitivity to relations between objects, or "relational mapping", and recognition of patterns created by object relations which enables generalization to more abstract structure, or "system mapping". In *Mental leaps* Holyoak and Thagard (1995) compare the cognitive capabilities of a chimpanzee and a child. They conclude that although a chimpanzee is capable of attribute mapping and – with some extensive training – can do relational mapping, only the human child can map at the system level. In Dickinson's Cocoon poem, a reading that depends only on attribute and relational mapping and does not take into consideration system mapping will produce only a partial understanding of the poem.

Charles Sanders Peirce's theory of the complex sign, with its three types – icons, indices, and symbols – approaches these analogical mappings from a somewhat different though compatible perspective. Peirce defines an icon as a sign which represents an object mainly by its similarity to that object; an index as a sign which represents an object by its existential relation to that object; and a symbol as a sign which signifies an object by means of a law or convention (Hoopes 1991). As we shall see, the three subtypes of Peirce's icon – image, diagram, and metaphor – cohere to create iconicity in Dickinson's Cocoon poem.[4]

Cognitive metaphors arise from our embodied understanding, the experience of our physical presence in the world (Johnson 1987). In this "embodied understanding", we as physical objects move in and out of spaces that contain us, as when we come "into" or go "out of" a room. Thus the prepositions "in" and "out" are integrally related to another very basic metaphor in the way we structure our thinking – the CONTAINER metaphor.[5] When we say, for example, that we are "in a good mood" or "in pain", we are seeing ourselves as contained within the mood or pain, instead of perhaps more accurately recognizing that the mood or pain is within us. Likewise, when we say we are "out of sorts", we see ourselves as being *ex*cluded from a state of equilibrium. Just as we ourselves can be contained *in* or *ex*cluded from spaces, our bodies themselves can be containers. We say we are "full of food" or "filled with happiness". Our energies may be "drained" by overwork. Containers can overflow or burst: we brim over with enthusiasm or explode with anger or frustration. The world itself can be contained or is a container. We can see a world in a grain of sand, or the whole world can be our oyster. In fact, there is no way we can conceptualize ourselves and our world without making use of the CONTAINER metaphor.

In composing and reading poetry, poets and readers use the same cognitive principles of embodied understanding. We both create and conceptualize our world through the CONTAINER metaphor, and we do so through the process of analogical mapping, as can be seen in Dickinson's Cocoon poem:

My Cocoon tightens -
Colors tease -
I'm feeling for the Air -
A Dim Capacity for
Wings
+Demeans the Dress I wear -

A power of Butterfly must
be -
The Aptitude to fly
Meadows of Majesty
+concedes
And easy Sweeps of Sky -

So I must baffle at
the Hint
And Cipher at the Sign
And make much blunder

if at last
I take the Clue divine -

+ Degrades   + implies -

Set 6c H 189b, 1150 (J 1099)[6]

From a traditional perspective, the metaphor of the poem seems clear enough. The speaker or persona of the poem is likening herself to a butterfly about to emerge from the container of its cocoon. Literary critics will provide varying interpretations of the poem depending on their choice of the cause and purpose of this analogical mapping. That is, from a feminist perspective, the butterfly may be seen as a woman resisting patriarchal restriction. From a metaliterary point of view, it may represent the power of poetry breaking free from the constraints of prose. From a theological perspective, the butterfly may be a sign of the Resurrection. All these readings are possible. They do not, however, explain what enables the critic to draw such analogies. They are possible because they are all coherent with the poem's prototypical reading, which cognitive analysis reveals.[7] Cognitive poetics may thus be seen as a methodology that constrains literary interpretation.

To see similarity between a person and a butterfly is already to make analogical connections at a higher level. It is easier, for example, to perceive similarity between a cat and a dog than between a butterfly and a person. In the poem as a whole, with attribute mapping, the source domain of the butterfly is mapped onto the target domain of the speaker, the cocoon onto dress, and the development ("dim capacity") of wings onto the speaker wanting to break out. At the relational level, the tightening of the cocoon is mapped onto the speaker's feeling the constraint of enclosure, the teasing of colors onto the attraction of becoming something different, and the "dim capacity for wings" onto the idea that the something that wants to break out is better and more powerful (since it "demeans" or "degrades") than the physical, emotional, or mental constraints binding the person.

It is, however, at the structural, system mapping level that the metaphorical analogy in the poem is created. The first and the last stanzas are related by mappings from the concrete to the abstract. The concrete images of the first stanza – cocoon, colors, wings, dress – are mapped onto the abstract terminology of the last – hint, sign, cipher, clue. As these mappings move from the concrete to the abstract, they work on both structural and semantic dimensions.

Syntactically, the three verbs and their subjects in the first stanza are mapped onto the three verbs and their complements in the last. Thus, "tighten" maps to "baffle" and "cocoon" maps to "hint", "tease" to "cipher" and "colors" to "sign", "demean" (or "degrade") to "blunder" (since to make blunder is to blunder), and "capacity" to "clue". The "'cocoon", in its temporary state, "hints" at its metamorphosis; "colors" are the "sign" of the emergent butterfly; and the "dim capacity for wings" provides a "clue" toward transcendence (fig. 1):

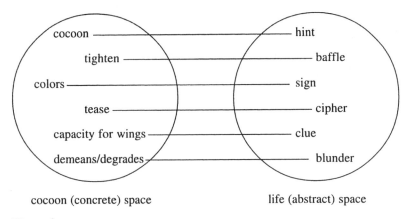

cocoon (concrete) space   life (abstract) space

Figure 1.

On the semantic level, the verbs and noun phrases metaphorically map onto each other, as the poem dynamically progresses from the effect, in the first stanza, of the physical environment represented by the cocoon to the response, in the last, of the human persona to the analogous environment of life. In the process, the focus changes from the constraint of the cocoon itself to the persona struggling within that constraint, and the verbs reflect the transformation. Thus, "tighten" transforms to "baffle", as the speaker struggles ineffectually (the intransitive meaning of the word) with the "hint" of the "cocoon"; "tease" transforms to "cipher", as the sensual, physical idea of "colors" appearing briefly as a glimpse, then hiding, transforms to the intellectual puzzling at the glimpse of the "sign"; and "demean" or "degrade" (the latter word having the specific biological meaning of "to reduce to a lower and less complex organic type" (OED)), caused by the "dim capacity for wings", transforms to making a "blunder" as the persona moves blindly in groping toward the "clue divine".

System mapping connects the semantics of cocooning with the structure of the poem. In drawing the imaginary, overlapping lines that relate the images of the source domain (butterfly) in the first stanza to the abstract terminology of the target domain (person) in the last stanza, a container – a cocoon – has been created around the stanza in the center (fig. 2):

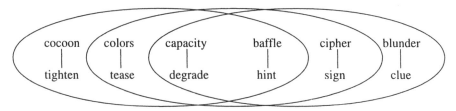

Figure 2.

And what *is* in that stanza but the potentiality of the butterfly itself? Not the caterpillar in its prior state or the pupa within its cocoon, but the fully meta-morphosized form of the butterfly to be, potentially freed from the container of its cocoon to fly in its full power of majesty over meadows and through "easy Sweeps of Sky". The first and last stanzas of the poem surrounding the central stanza thus iconically form a cocoon for the future butterfly it contains. Peirce's image, diagram, and metaphor thus all cohere in the poem's iconicity (fig. 3):

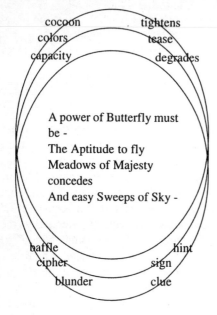

Figure 3.

From a cognitive mapping perspective, however, the poem is incomplete. It is "missing" a fourth stanza, in which, as stanza 1 maps to stanza 3, stanza 2 should map to stanza 4.[8] That is, the cocooning stage (insect: literal) of stanza 1 maps to the cocooning stage (human: metaphor) of stanza 3; the butterfly stage (insect: literal) of stanza 2 should map to the butterfly stage (human: metaphor) of the missing stanza 4. From the perspective of cognitive poetics, the theory predicts that there should be a fourth stanza and explains what would be there if there were one. It shows why the poem works elegantly in not having a fourth stanza, and demonstrates it as an artwork about art reaching beyond the merely representational. The poem as it stands exists at the cocoon stage, the potenti-ality of the butterfly still contained within the frame of the outermost stanzas, its human analog only suggested, not (re)presented. The beauty of Dickinson's poem lies in its incompleteness, the suggestion left in the reader's mind's eye of the "Clue divine" that ends the poem, human life existing in potentiality, not actuality, poetry as possibility – in Dickinson's words, "a fairer House than Prose" (J 657) –, human aspiration toward divine immortality.

In composing and reading poetry, poets and readers share the same cognitive principles of embodied understanding. We both create and conceptualize our world through the CONTAINER metaphor, and we do so through the process of analogical mapping, as we have seen in Dickinson's Cocoon poem. Given the isomorphism created by these structural mappings, we understand the poem according to the purpose and cause of the analogical mapping, as has been noted: for example, in terms of a woman resisting restriction, or the power of poetry, or a symbol of the Resurrection. All these readings (and they are only a few of the possible ones) are consistent with the analogical mapping of the prototypical isomorphic metaphor.

3. Conceptual blending in Dickinson's Loaded Gun poem

Cognitive metaphor illuminates the cognitive principles of embodied understanding that poets and readers use in composing and reading poetry. Unlike the gun persona in Dickinson's Loaded Gun poem, human beings are able to explore the full metaphorical mappings the human mind is capable of. Following is the text of Emily Dickinson's poem: "My Life had stood - a".[9]

My Life had stood - a
Loaded Gun -
In Corners - till a Day
The Owner passed - identified -
And carried Me away -

And now We roam + in
Sovreign Woods -
And now We hunt the Doe -
And every time I speak
for Him
The Mountains straight reply -

And do I smile, such
cordial light
Upon the Valley glow -
It is as a Vesuvian face
Had let its pleasure through -

And when at Night - Our
good Day done -
I guard My Master's head -

'Tis better than the Eider-
Duck's
+ Deep Pillow - to have shared -

To foe of His - I'm deadly
foe -
None + stir the second time -
On whom I lay a Yellow
Eye -
Or An Emphatic Thumb -

Though I than He - may
longer live
He longer must - than I.
For I have but the + power
to kill,
Without - the power to die -

+ the - + low + harm + art

Fascicle 34 H 131, 825 (J 754)

    The poem has puzzled literary critics for years. The problem lies in reconciling the final stanza with the rest of the poem. Attempts at reconciliation seem forced. Most critics give up and conclude that the poem fails or breaks down. It is, of course, self-evident on the literal level that guns can kill but not themselves die. But if the gun is meant to metaphorically represent something else, as the rest of the poem suggests, how are we supposed to understand this final stanza?

    The readings literary critics have produced for this poem tend to map on the one-to-one level of attribute mapping, correlating the gun and its owner with a variety of metaphorical possibilities.[10] Because they adopt a traditional approach to metaphor, they tend to map on the attribute or relational levels without considering the poem on the system mapping level.[11] In my cognitive reading, I will show that the final stanza, far from being an anomaly or an enigma, is the climax of a coherent progression through a complex system of conceptual metaphorical blending that has been building from the very first stanza.

    To take the last stanza first. The speaking persona of the poem – a loaded gun – is comparing itself to its Owner/Master. The gun realizes that it, like its Owner, has the power to kill; it does not, however, as its Owner does, have the power to die. In itself, since inanimate objects can be instruments of death without themselves able to experience it, this does not seem a particularly insightful observation. As Sharon Cameron (1992: 66) has observed, "something further seems intended".

    Something further is intended. A preliminary reading of this poem is straightforward and unproblematic. Its narrative is told from the perspective of a gun –

more specifically a rifle – as the poet metaphorically projects the domain of human experience onto the domain of the gun as it recounts the story of its "life". In contemporary metaphor theory, the image-schematic structure of the target domain "life" constrains which image-schematic structures from the source domain "gun" are mapped onto it (this is the invariance principle of Lakoff (1993) and Turner (1996)). For example, in the LIFE IS A JOURNEY metaphor, the metaphoric path changes as we make our choices in life. As Robert Frost notes in "The Road Not Taken", we can't go back in life and take the other fork. This constrains the mapping of the literal path's fixity, which in real life remains to be taken at some future time, whatever route we take on a particular occasion.

In Dickinson's poem, however, there appears to be a "reversal" in metaphorical mapping constraint: it is the concrete source domain of the physical object "gun" that constrains the way we are invited to interpret the abstract domain of "life". Failure to recognize this constraint is partly why some literary critical analyses go wrong. Rather than mapping those elements of life that are coherent with elements of the gun, it is the elements that are characteristic of the gun that constrain how life in the poem is understood. Because the dominant metaphors in the poem map only those elements of the source domain "gun" that are coherent with the target domain "life", the poem is deeply ironic. Although the gun persona attempts to project itself as a living being, it fails throughout to do so.

Recent research by Fauconnier and Turner (1998) on conceptual integration networks has modified the definition of the invariance principle. With the introduction of a four-space model including a generic and a blended space as well as the original source and target spaces, a richer and more sophisticated account of the invariance principle is made possible. Dickinson's poem is an example of an asymmetric two-sided network, in which topology from both input spaces (gun and life) appear in the blend that is the poem, but the organizing frame of the blend comes from only one input space (the gun space). This constrains the emergent structure in the blend by restricting the activities, events, and participants to those consistent with the gun space.

In one space, we have human life as it is lived, with self-movement, communication with others, emotional feelings that can lead to love and sexual activity, self-protection and hostility that can lead to war, and, finally, the fact of death. In the other space, we have the characteristics of a gun, with its ability to kill a human being, its ability to make noise, its being loaded with cartridges that can fire on being cocked and triggered; its functions as a hunting weapon, a defensive device, an instrument of violence. The generic space abstracts qualities from these two spaces to create the shared concepts of movement, sound, and causation. The poem itself creates a fourth, blended space, which has a new emergent structure shared by neither of the two input spaces. The actions of the gun in the blended space are characteristic neither of the source gun space nor of the target life space, though topological elements from both spaces are projected into the blend. Because the organizing frame of the blend is projected from the source space of the gun and not from the target space of the human, only those topological elements in the human space that are consistent with the organizing frame of the gun space are projected into the blend. In the blended space, the gun persona is trying to project the qualities of human life onto the qualities possessed by a gun. Its language, however, betrays it. Neither of the descriptions in the two input spaces of human life and gun are descriptions of the blended space of the poem (that is, guns don't speak or smile, and people are not literally objects that stand in corners to be picked up; guns don't have thumbs or eyes, and people don't emit a yellow flash).

The apparent paradox of the final stanza that has so puzzled critics results from the emergent structure of the blend, not from a simple attribute or relational mapping between person and gun. As a result, in the blend, the gun appears to act as if it were truly alive as humans are, though (as we shall see in detail below) this construction is illusory. By implicitly comparing the "life" of a gun to human life, Dickinson makes us see how impoverished, unfulfilled, and inadequate the gun's projected "life" actually is, and suggests how impoverished, unfulfilled, and inadequate human life would be if it experienced only those characteristics of life expressed by the gun.

From the first stanza to the last, the gun tries, but fails, to experience life as humans do because it fails to understand the cognitive metaphors that underlie human experience. This failure can be traced in each stanza through the way in which the gun fails to apply the relevant cognitive metaphors to its condition.

George Lakoff has shown how the EVENT STRUCTURE metaphor has two "versions": LOCATION and OBJECT (Lakoff 1993). The difference can be seen in the contrast between "we're coming up on Easter" (Easter as LOCATION) and "Easter is approaching" (Easter as OBJECT). In the first stanza, based on the metaphors ABSTRACTIONS ARE OBJECTS, A PERSON IS A POSSESSED OBJECT, EVENTS ARE ACTIONS, and LIFE IS A JOURNEY, the life of the gun is seen as an object that has come to a standstill, stuck in corners. Now objects in the EVENT STRUCTURE metaphor are self-moving, as in the example just given, "Easter is approaching". But the gun isn't. It must wait for its Owner (who *is* self-moving) to pass, identify, and carry it away. Thus, with respect to the question of self-propulsion and self-motivation, the contrast between the gun's life and its owner's life is laid down in the very first stanza. The gun has managed to get as far as the metaphorical conceptualization of itself as an object in the EVENT STRUCTURE metaphor, but cannot take the human step of being self-moving.

If this were a poem mainly predicated on the LIFE IS A JOURNEY metaphor as is Frost's poem, "The Road Not Taken", it would be unproblematic. However, Dickinson's Loaded Gun poem ranges across a series of complex metaphor systems that interact, as Zoltán Kövecses (1995) has shown, to represent abstract concepts like friendship, love, and life itself. That is to say, the JOURNEY metaphor is not the only source domain for LIFE in this poem: the COMMUNICA-

TION, EMOTION, and BOND metaphors are also active.[12] Thus, in stanza 2, both EMOTION and COMMUNICATION metaphors are activated: AN INSTRUMENT IS A COMPANION in the first two lines (*"We* roam", *"We* hunt"), and a LANGUAGE COMMUNICATION metaphor underlying the gun's attempt to assert autonomy as it "speaks for" its Owner and gets a "reply" from the Mountain. Nevertheless, the gun's "language" is, ironically, not the interactive productive communicative system that characterizes human language. The sound of the gun is merely echoed, not answered. The sound returned to the gun is all noise with no signal, as opposed to the meaningful sounds of human language. Again the gun has failed to experience the kind of life, here of interactive communication, that human beings experience.

From the attempted "companionship" of the second stanza, the gun unsuccessfully attempts to ally itself with its human owner in a progressive movement through the EMOTION metaphor toward the climax of total identification in stanza 5.[13] Briefly, in stanza 3, the metaphor EMOTION IS TEMPERATURE governs the image of cordiality (a word relating to the heart). Related to this metaphor is AFFECTION IS WARMTH, invoked by the "glow" of the gun's "cordial light". As the gun attempts to "enliven", give life to its flash by the metaphor of a smile, it tries to ally itself with the Mountains it failed to communicate with in stanza 2 by comparing itself to Mount Vesuvius. But the "pleasure" of seeming affection is ironically undermined for the reader by the associated threatening image of a volcanic eruption, and the actual function of a gun – death – overrides its attempt to assert its opposite – life. The cordial light of a supposedly human smile is in fact, coming from the gun, volcanic, destructive.

The suggestion of emotion and affection is, in stanza 4, reinforced by the metaphor INTIMACY IS CLOSENESS, as the gun sees its function as protecting its Master. Here, the gun, with its almost defensive assertion that protecting is better than sharing, again fails in its attempt to attain human life, fails to understand the metaphor, THE MORE SHARING THERE IS, THE GREATER THE INTIMACY. The gun betrays its failure in its defensive stance that it is better to guard the head than share the bed.

By the time we reach stanza 5, the metaphor has become THE MORE INTIMACY THERE IS, THE MORE TWO BECOME ONE. But in becoming one, the gun conceives its relationship to its master as one of PROTECTION in the context of WAR (again an image more appropriate to the real function of guns than to what this gun is trying to achieve), instead of the metaphor INTIMACY IN A SEXUAL RELATIONSHIP. The gun's self-deceptive identification with its master is complete; the images of the yellow eye and the emphatic thumb that are mapped onto the sighting and cocking activities the owner employs on the gun's instruments create an ironically sexually suggestive death image. This sexually suggestive image highlights one very obvious fact about this poem that most literary critical analyses overlook – the gun is genderless. Nowhere in the poem does the gun identify itself as a gendered human being. The gun's failure to enjoy a sexual relationship in the human sense poignantly points up its failure to achieve what it aims for: human life.

The gun's tone by now is brash, brazen, confident, a tone that will be totally undermined by the concessionary recognition of the final stanza. Here, the gun faces the truth. The comparison in the final stanza between the human owner and the gun projects back from the blend into the two input spaces to distinguish people who can die from guns that can kill. Although the gun "may" live, have the potentiality it expressed at the beginning of the poem for a rich and fulfilling life, it cannot. Genderless, the gun cannot experience life as humans do. The scope of the metaphor throughout the poem is consistent. Ironically, in its limited understanding of conceptual metaphor as articulated in the story it tells, the genderless gun has failed to understand the level of human metaphor that expresses the full range of life, love, and death that gendered human beings experience. The irony is central to the poem's recognition of what it means to be human: to live and to love, to experience and practice violence, to suffer, ultimately to die.

So, by the final stanza, the argument is revealed as self-evident: the gun's failure to achieve gendered human experience is failure to achieve human life, in all its joys and sufferings; and since it cannot truly be alive, it cannot die: an ironic echo, too, of its inability as a result to "longer live" in immortality. In other words, the gun-persona's failure to achieve gendered human life and all that that implies – the ability to communicate, to love, to cause and to suffer violence, ultimately to die – this failure raises in our minds the overriding question of what it means to be human.

This is the central – or prototypical – reading of the poem. Since we – as humans – do "have the power to die", Dickinson forces us, through the gun-persona's life story, to evaluate our own. And this is where the other possible readings come in. Rather than seeing the gun as a metaphor in traditional terms – the substitution of one thing for another – which leads literary critics to ideas of gun-woman, gun-language, etc., I think that such readings arise indirectly and are given legitimacy from the system of cognitive metaphors that structure the poem. Unlike the gun, we as human beings are able to connect the metaphors of embodied understanding and contrast them with respect to our own life experiences. When we unpack the blend to reconstruct the input spaces, the emergent structure of the blend constrains the way we perceive the target (human) space. To what extent, for example, are women "carried away" by men rather than voluntarily moving on their own? Or how many men (or women) are used as instruments for violence, wielded by a power exerted over them, a power which they find themselves unable to resist? In running the blend of the loaded gun as human potentiality, the poem recognizes the challenge of being human – not only the experience of life, love, suffering, and death, but also the experience of making metaphor – that is the result of embodied human understanding. No wonder the poem is so celebrated – it includes them all.

Under cognitive theory, metaphorical conceptualization is more than a simple one-to-one mapping of attributes or the mapping of metaphorical relations. In Dickinson's Loaded Gun poem, several basic conceptual metaphors systematically cohere. These metaphors are productive in the sense that they enable metaphorical mappings that are multiple and coherent. A reading that is based on a traditional approach to metaphor, that starts, for example, with a one-to-one correlation between gun and woman, is bound to encounter difficulties with the final stanza. It is not the case that the gun is simply a metaphor for a woman, or daemon, for language or Christ, or that the Owner is simply a metaphor for a man or the self, for the mind or God. The poem exists on the more abstract system level of analogical mapping produced by the blend; it may be "about" all these things through the image schemas that represent the various aspects of what it means to experience life, issues such as love and sex, language and power, aggression and violence. A reading that arrives at a more abstract level of metaphorical system mapping, such as the one just given, generates the insightful metaphorical interpretations critics have produced without conflicting with the poem's inner coherence. Because such a reading reveals the structure and identifications of multiple cross-space mappings, it can also expose the incoherent elements of traditional interpretations that fail to account adequately for the literary texts they attempt to describe.

4. Cognitive poetics: Applications

4.1. The limits of forgery: A question of cognitive style

Why should cognitive poetics emerge as an important theory now, and what makes it superior to any other literary theory previously or currently held? First, it is grounded on a theory of meaning as developed by recent research in cognitive linguistics, which enables it to deal with many issues that have troubled literary theory in the past, such as accounting for the capability of a literary text to generate multiple meanings, or explaining what it is literary critics do when they interpret a literary text. Second, it starts with language and not with ideology; it includes cognitive process together with the contextual/cultural dimensions of what Jordan Zlatev (1997) has called "situated embodiment"; and, perhaps most importantly, it can be tested.

As I. A. Richards wisely noted in the era of new criticism, any literary theory should be able to recognize literary style, to be able to distinguish the characteristics of an individual writer. He also noted ruefully that new criticism failed this test when his students were unable to identify beyond any doubt the author of a text he gave them.[14] Even today, current literary theories are unable adequately to identify poetic style, as evidenced by the failure of most literary critics to determine that a poem claimed to be by Dickinson was in fact a forgery.[15] In this section, I discuss the ways in which a cognitive poetics approach can show that Dickinson could not have written the poem.

Cognitive linguistic (CL) theory claims that thoughts are embodied. That is, we conceptualize our ideas about the world and ourselves through our embodied experience of the world and self. That experience is constrained by the physical orientation of our bodies in space, by the constitution of our sense organs, by the repetitive neural synapses of our brains. Abstract ideas, like love, life, and the pursuit of happiness, are understood through the conceptual projection of physical experience. In other words, we cannot think abstractly without thinking metaphorically. Metaphor, according to CL theory, is not a matter of words but a matter of thought.

For example, we cannot experience the notion of time directly. The way we talk about time is conceptually projected from our experience of space, and the expressions we use to describe time are invariably metaphoric. Thus, we say that the past is "behind" us or our future lies "ahead". Time is perceived as a bounded region or container, so that we say we are "in" time or "out of" time. We see moments of time from our own vantage point or deictic center, and we can shift that deictic center when we create a mental space that is different from our current "reality" space. Thus in a sentence like "James plans to leave London to go to Rome tomorrow", a present reality space has been created in which James is making his plans, and a future space in which he will leave his present location to move into another.

How do we understand time? It is commonly understood in two ways, depending on figure-ground orientation. That is, we can perceive time as a figure with respect to some ground, as when we say "Time flies when we're having fun", where time is seen as passing quickly across some given fun-filled space. Or we can perceive time as the ground for the figure, as when we say "The train arrived on time." Both these ways of looking at time come from a very general metaphor in our thought processes: the EVENT STRUCTURE metaphor. When applied to the concept of time, this metaphor produces the dual metaphors of TIME IS AN OBJECT and TIME IS LOCATION. These dual metaphors produce thousands of metaphors in everyday language. For example, TIME IS AN OBJECT: Do you *have* time to go over this paper for me? The time *passed* quickly, Where did all the time *go*? TIME IS LOCATION: *Where* did you pass the time? Did you arrive *in* time? We are almost *out of* time. These last two examples also involve the very common metaphor in our everyday conceptions already discussed: the CONTAINER metaphor.

As may be expected, Emily Dickinson, like any other poet, makes use of the full range of systematic metaphors for time, whether as OBJECT or LOCATION. Time can be *barefoot* (J 717); *weighed* (J 834); *narrow* (J 1100); it can *come and go*; we can be *between* eternity and time (J 644); we can look *back on* time (J 1478), and so on. But, you may argue, so what? All poets make extensive use of metaphor; that's what poetry is; literary criticism is full of metaphor identification in poetry. Just so. But the question is: are these metaphors just strategies for enlivening otherwise prosaic language, for making language fresh through the use of novel metaphors? Or are they indications of a systematic pattern, a marker of the poet's way of thinking about the world, a sign of her conceptual universe (Freeman, Margaret H. 1995)?

Emily Dickinson is a great poet, not only because she is a skillful wielder of words, but because she understands the metaphorical nature of our everyday language and thought. She makes use of that knowledge to create poems that literally take our breath away by disrupting our commonsensical and folk theory ways of thinking about the world.

For example, a very common metaphor for time is TIME IS A HEALER. This metaphor for time depends on the EVENT STRUCTURE metaphor which entails EVENTS ARE ACTIONS, which in turn entails TIME IS AN OBJECT. The EVENT STRUCTURE metaphor is shaped by the notion of causality, in which an agent is understood to bring about an event. Thus we say "Time heals all wounds." But Dickinson rejects this metaphor:

They say that "Time
assuages" -
Time never did assuage -
An actual suffering
strengthens
As sinews do - with Age -

Time is a Test of
Trouble -
But not a Remedy -
If such it prove, it
prove too
There was no Malady -

Fascicle 38, H 163, 942 (J 686)

Dickinson denies the folk theory metaphor that TIME IS A HEALER in order to make the point that true suffering is everlasting. She rejects the idea of time as an agentive figure working against the ground of suffering and replaces it by reversing figure and ground. In the second part of the poem, it is suffering or "trouble" that is perceived as the figure against the ground of time. She replaces THE TIME IS CAUSATION metaphor with one in which time is perceived as a standard, a criterion by which suffering may be judged. The words "test" and "prove" suggest the methodology of science, by which "actual" experience may be empirically verified. What is being suggested in this poem is that some metaphors are better than others in enabling us to understand life's experiences.

Another poem with similar figure-ground configuration sees time as a bounded region in space that pain expands or contracts:

Pain - expands the Time -
Ages + coil within
The minutest Circumference
Of a single Brain -

Pain contracts - the Time -
Occupied with shot
+ Gammuts of Eternities
+ Are as they were not -

+ lurk + Triplets + flit
- show -

Fascicle 40, H 211, 990 (J 967)

In this poem, time is not something objective that exists independent of our
conceptualization. It is contained within the circumference of our brains and can
expand and contract at will. The use of the musical term "Gammuts" (Dickinson's spelling) or, in the variant, "Triplets" relates time to eternities, plural, as
if they were the components of time. The poem ends in a negative hypothetical
space that denies the existence of these eternities. The relation of the concepts
of time and eternity in Dickinson's conceptual universe is difficult to comprehend, unless we are willing to forsake our folk theory notion of eternity as an
object coming somehow "after" time.

In the poems just quoted, Dickinson rejects the idea of time as an agentive
figure working against the ground of suffering or pain. Instead, time is seen as
the ground against which pain and suffering are highlighted. In the following
poem, time is again understood as LOCATION, a bounded region encircling or
containing the speaker.

Time feels so vast that
were it not
For an Eternity -
I fear me this Circum-
ference
Engross my Finity -

To His exclusion, who
prepare
By + Processes of size
For the stupendous
Vision
Of His Diameters -

+ Rudiments / Prefaces of size
for the stupendous Volume -

Fascicle 38 H 162, 938 (J 802)

Within a few lines Dickinson has created in this poem a complex series of alternative mental spaces – epistemic, conditional, causative, hypothetical, counterfactual. Without lines 2-3, the conceptualization is straightforward: the vastness of time results in the speaker's containment within the circumference of her experience. However, lines 2-3 "sore thumb" this straightforward reading. How we interpret the word "for" in line 3 depends on the conceptual mapping we, as readers with our own presupposed cognitive mappings, bring to the poem. If we believe that eternity has an objective existence, exterior to time, we will understand "for" to refer to existence, as in "I didn't want for money", with TIME AS OBJECT, so that in the poem eternity is seen as an agent preventing the speaker from thoughts of annihilation. If, however, we believe that eternity is "in" time, as a component of time, with TIME AS LOCATION, we would read the word "for" as durational, as in "I slept for hours", with the result that the fear of annihilation rests on a conditional state – whether time does or does not last (extend) forever. The difference between the two readings is as vast as the time itself that Dickinson describes in the poem: it is the difference between the security of a safe and comforting belief in an afterlife compared with the existential angst that time itself may not be eternal. Dickinson, characteristically, could not rest with the superficial comfort of the first; she could not accept that eternity somehow "kicks in" after time is over:

Forever - is composed of Nows -
'Tis not a different time -
Except for Infiniteness -
And Latitude of Home -

From this - experienced Here -
Remove the Dates - to These -
Let Months dissolve in + further
Months -   + other -
And Years - exhale in Years -

Without + Debate - or Pause -
Or Celebrated Days - + Certificate -
+ No different Our Years would be
From Anno Dominies -

+ As infinite -

Fascicle 32, H 216, 772 (J 624)

Dickinson rejects the notion that eternity lies in some region somewhere in the future that we are not in yet. Rather, it is a space called "forever" that is composed of "nows". It is not a different time from "now" – it is present, not future. It is "different" though, unlike those nows, in that it is not bounded but boundless, not finite but infinite, and its region or latitude is "home" – where our deictic center is prototypically located. From this vantage point, this deictic center – "here" – we can take away the "dates" we assign to our "nows". The container of time is a vast sea in which months can dissolve; or a body from which years may be "exhaled". The suggested alternative "other" in line 7 reinforces the rejection of time as having some future or "further" existence that is different from now.

The final stanza is practically a poetic version of cognitive theory: it is the conceptualizing processes of our cognizing minds that impose discrete periods on time, that divide one moment from another just as we are separated in argument or "debate", that insert "pauses" or identify particular days for "celebration", like Thanksgiving or Christmas, in the ceaseless "flow" of time. The alternative "certificate" for "debate" suggests the stamping of an individuated identity on an otherwise "undifferentiated" time. It is we who impose divisions and identities on time, with the result that we are trapped in our own metaphorizing of the world in which we live. Cognitive poetics, by identifying the habitual and coherent conceptual metaphors a poet uses, can arrive at an understanding of a poet's conceptual world.

Dickinson's characteristic stance in her poetry is to overturn the stereotypical and superficial metaphors by which we construct our folk theory of the world. What happens in the "Dickinson" poem Mark Hofmann forged?

That God cannot
be understood
Everyone Agrees
We cannot know
His motives nor
Comprehend his
Deeds –

Then why should I
Seek solace in
What I cannot
know?
Better to play
In winter's sun
Than to fear the
snow.

Ignoring other elements of poetic style, where in this poem is the disruption of the commonsensical and the stereotypical? The opening lines assert the very opposite of the Dickinsonian stance (the word "agree" occurs nowhere in Dickinson's poetic lexicon: her stance is to disagree, not to conform). She disrupts the stereotypical through complex inverted syntax and the creation of multiple mental spaces; none exist here. There is no complex metaphorical reversal of figure and ground; the deictic perspective is unrelentingly "ours". The poem ends in the reinforcement of the conventional – the choice of sun over snow. Worst of all are the platitudinous litany of our ignorance in the face of an almighty God and the consequent assertion of an amoral hedonism. Dickinson must have been shuddering in her grave when her readers ascribed this poem to her. Compare the forged poem with the prospectives set up in a poem of similar length which exists in transcript only, no manuscript having yet been found:[16]

That it will never come again
Is what makes life so sweet.
Believing what we don't believe
Does not exhilarate.

That if it be, it be at best
An ablative estate -
This instigates an appetite
Precisely opposite.

(J 1741; no autograph copy)

The negative reversals in this poem are typically Dickinson, including the reversal of the conventional desire for the afterlife to "an appetite / Precisely opposite". Another short poem that also only exists in transcript carries similar marks of authenticity:

God is indeed a jealous God -
He cannot bear to see
+That we had rather not with Him
But with each other play.

+That we desire with ourselves
And not with Him to play.

(J 1719; no autograph copy)

In this poem, Dickinson sets up two mental spaces within the cognitive domain of "play": that is, to play with someone means to be physically in their presence (this before the age of cyberspace). Thus, to play with each other means being within the space of life; to play with God means moving into his space, which we can only do through death (since we "cannot know God and live" – Dickinson knew her Old Testament). In the forged poem, a similar comparison is set up: better to play in the sun of winter than to fear the snow. But for a poet who agonized over the snow of death and the winter of our souls, the certitude of the forged poem does not ring true. The contrasting mental spaces in the forged poem occur within the same cognitive domain of winter, they do not cross domains like the life-death domains of "God is indeed a jealous God". In

Dickinson's poem, the lack of understanding is not ours, it is God who does not understand. It is just this audacity – to jump into God's perspective and then to undermine it – that is characteristically Dickinson. The banality of the forged poem should in itself have raised the suspicions of Dickinson scholars.

But this is just my point. It is not that Dickinson scholars are not sensitive readers or accomplished critics; they are. It is because they don't have an adequate theory of literature that they were unable to determine that the newly discovered poem was a forgery. On the contrary, cognitive poetics provides a very clear means by which we can read and describe and identify a literary text and its style.

4.2. Other theoretical approaches:
A question of cognitive compatibility

Cognitive poetics may be characterized, as I noted at the beginning, by its recognition that meaning does not so much reside in language as that it is accessed by it. That is, we as speakers/readers bring to our understanding of an utterance/text our world knowledge, which includes cultural knowledge, socio-political-economic knowledge, and so forth. All that knowledge, furthermore, is conceptualized through our embodied understanding, our orientation in the physical world. The extent to which we comprehend the meaning of a text depends on the extent of that world knowledge. It is not, however, a one-sided asymmetrical relation: if it were, we would never be able to go beyond the bounds of our own limited experiences. The text can also extend our knowledge. The theory of conceptual integration (Fauconnier – Turner 1998) explains how such extension is possible through conceptual blending and emergent structure. Although all blends are not metaphoric in nature, all metaphor at some stage involves a conceptual blend. That is why metaphor is central to perceptual understanding, scientific discovery, and creativity.

By enabling us to unpack the cognitive layer of a literary text, cognitive poetics provides insight into the conceptualizing framework on which the text is constructed. Although we can never know the particular contexts, impulses, or circumstances that existed for the writer, we can access the cognitive forces that result. We can experience character, emotions, tone, we can discover the causes and comprehend the consequences of events and actions, we can situate our-selves within the world of the text, not because these conform to the actual world, but because the cognitive processes that enable us to conceptualize our own world are identical to those we apply in understanding the worlds of texts. And those worlds become part of our world through such conceptual integration.

Because cognitive poetics is based upon such a powerful theory of concep-tual integration, a theory that is itself compatible with cognitive metaphor, cognitive grammar, and so forth, it incorporates elements of other theories that are nonconflicting. In this section I will compare cognitive poetics to three other cognitive theories by briefly discussing Elena Semino's analysis of a poem by Sylvia Plath. The poem, "The Applicant", was written by Plath just a few days after she had decided to divorce Ted Hughes and exactly four months to the day of her suicide (Semino 1997: 235).

THE APPLICANT

First, are you our sort of a person?
Do you wear
A glass eye, false teeth or a crutch,
A brace or a hook,
Rubber breasts or a rubber crotch,

Stitches to show something's missing? No, no? Then
How can we give you a thing?
Stop crying.
Open your hand.
Empty? Empty. Here is a hand

To fill it and willing
To bring teacups and roll away headaches
And do whatever you tell it.
Will you marry it?
It is guaranteed

To thumb shut your eyes at the end
And dissolve of sorrow.
We make new stock from the salt.
I notice you are stark naked.
How about this suit –

Black and stiff, but not a bad fit.
Will you marry it?
It is waterproof, shatterproof, proof
Against fire, and bombs through the roof.
Believe me, they'll bury you in it.

Now your head, excuse me, is empty.
I have the ticket for that.
Come here, sweetie, out of the closet.
Well, what do you think of that?
Naked as paper to start

But in twenty-five years she'll be silver,
In fifty gold.

A living doll, everywhere you look.
It can sew, it can cook,
It can talk, talk, talk.

It works, there is nothing wrong with it.
You have a hole, it's a poultice.
You have an eye, it's an image.
My boy, it's your last resort.
Will you marry it, marry it, marry it.

Semino discusses "the possibility of describing the poem in three different ways, namely as: a) a situation of discourse involving a speaker, a hearer, and a number of third-person referents within a particular communicative context; b) a state of affairs that are partly impossible if compared with the "real" world; c) a cognitive construct that arises in interaction between the text and the reader's previous knowledge" (4). These correspond to the three cognitive theories Semino discusses: discourse theory, possible worlds theory, and schema theory. Application of each of the theories applies some insight to the poem but also reveals weaknesses in the theories themselves. To what extent does cognitive poetics deal with the weaknesses of the three theories in accounting for the complexities Semino accurately identifies in the poem?

The success of discourse theory in describing the complex and deviant situation of the poem lies in its ability to capture identities, roles, and relations. The identities of the two main participants are problematic. The addressee is presumably male, but why then the "rubber breasts" asks Semino? Is the speaker male or female? Plural or singular? The roles they play shift in the course of the poem. The speaker at first commands but then asks and offers. The addressee at first is an applicant but then seems to have the power to accept or refuse, shifting the balance of power relations between the two participants.

Discourse theory is powerful in being able to "see" these identity, role, and relation dynamics of the poem, but it has no theoretical mechanism to explain how or why these happen. It is, however, compatible with cognitive poetics, since both theories recognize the contextual implications of identification, role, and value that contribute to the conceptual world of the text.

The strength of possible worlds theory, according to Semino, lies in the rigor of its descriptions and categorizations which compare the world of the text to the "real" world. It provides a scale of deviance which can be empirically measured, and highlights the oddity of the world of the poem. As Semino shows in her possible worlds analysis of the poem, the world of the poem is highly deviant; in fact it violates the logical relations of not only the real but all possible worlds. People can't marry suits, for example, suits can't be shatterproof, rubber crotches are anomalous, and so forth. What possible worlds theory fails to do, as Semino points out, is to "account for the fact that … the poem is effective precisely because of the oddly 'mixed' situation it projects" (241).

With its dependence on an objectivist view of reality, possible worlds theory is incompatible with cognitive poetics. It lives in the world of logical relations and truth values and not in the world of conceptual metaphor. Of the three theories Semino discusses, it is the most hostile to cognitive poetics, and cannot therefore legitimately be named a "cognitive" theory as cognitive linguists like Fauconnier, Lakoff, and Turner define the term. In its unproblematized acceptance of the "real" world as one that can be accessed objectively by means of logical reasoning, it has no adequate theory of metaphor, no theory that can successfully account for the conceptualizing power of cognitive processes. It can only evaluate "possible" worlds against the norm of the "real" world; although it succeeds in identifying the extent to which a particular text world deviates from the real world in comparison to other text worlds, it seems to have no way of describing how one may impact on the other, what role the imaginative processes have on "real" world perceptions; what the complex interrelations are between real and possible worlds.

Schema theory, on the contrary, is able to identify the basic schemas or "conceptual frames" operating in the poem. Semino describes the poem's three main schemas as the Interview, Sales Pitch, and Marriage schemas. In her analysis, she recognizes the schema conflicts as well as the schema similarities that appear in the poem. For example, all three schemas "involve a one-to-one or one-to-many verbal interaction aimed at reaching a decision or agreement concerning some form of control over a particular entity" whereas the nakedness of the addressee and the "living doll" conflict with them (248). Semino introduces Cook's (1994) theory of schema refreshment to account for the schema changes that occur in the poem. However, as Semino herself acknowledges, she has to modify the definition of schema refreshment in order to account for the way the different schemas are connected in unusual ways in the poem. She notes that the poem requires readers to "stretch" their schemas in order to accommodate the disturbing extreme situation it presents. The problem is similar to that presented by possible worlds theory: there is still no reference to metaphor resolution or emergent structure in schema theory.

Historically, schema theory represents early formulations that led to cognitive metaphor and conceptual integration theories and thus is most compatible with cognitive poetics. What it lacks is any theoretical mechanism to integrate the three main schemas of the poem. It is precisely this capability that cognitive poetics has, in its ability to apply the principles of cognitive metaphor and conceptual blending to the world of the poem.

A full cognitive poetics analysis of Plath's "The Applicant" merits a chapter of its own. However, I will briefly point to possible strategies for resolution of the problems Semino raises, building on her extensive and beautifully succinct description of the poem. Of the three schemas Semino identifies, the marriage schema appears to be the target space of the elaborate metaphors developed in the poem. That is, the poem addresses the question of how we should understand the marriage state by exploring it in terms of various other scenarios. Because the poem includes multiple source spaces which provide different topologies for the blend, some of which are integrated and some not, the poem is an example of an extremely complex conceptual blend. Each of the three schemas (Interview, Sales Pitch, and Marriage) contribute elements from their own spaces to the blend that is the poem. For example, lines 20-25 invoke the Sales Pitch schema, in which the applicant is being offered a suit to cover his nakedness. In the suit space we have the elements of its color and its fit. In the marriage space we have all the elements of the marriage ceremony and the state of marriage, which include, as Semino notes, the formal attire of the black suit for the groom, providing an appropriate counterpart for cross-space mapping. However, there is a further space in these lines which is also contributing features to the blend. That space I shall call the protective armor space, since it includes the features of protective covering against disasters, disasters like storms, fire, war, and being broken. When these elements are projected into the blend space, the integration appears to be anomalous.

One question that needs to be addressed is whether the multiple spaces form a symmetric or asymmetric network: do they all contribute elements of an organizing frame as well as topological features to the blend that is the poem, or do some spaces contribute organizing frame and some not? Line 25, for example, "Believe me, they'll bury you in it" takes from the suit space the fact that men when they die are dressed for burial in a suit, and from the marriage space the idea that marriage is until "death do us part". The protective armor space too has the feature of possible death if disaster is not prevented. In this line, the organizing frame of the blend is clearly being projected from the suit space, since married partners are not buried with their spouses at death, and the protective armor is supposed to protect against death, not cause it. This raises the question of what topological features of the input spaces get projected to the blend, and are these integrated or not when they do? In the case of lines 20-25, the idea that the applicant is invited to consider the married state as one in which he will be provided with an invincible shield, even to the grave, arises from the emergent structure of the blend and not from any of the input spaces. By projecting the existence of a blend that has emergent structure of its own, the seeming anomaly of marrying a suit can be accommodated.

One thing is clear: cognitive poetics can raise the kind of questions that help to unpack the metaphorical structures of the multiple blended spaces in "The Applicant". It can determine what gets integrated and what does not. By unpacking the cognitive layers of the text, it might even be able to come to an understanding of why the poem appears so incoherent and yet be so effective.

There is a difference between a writer in pain whose writing expresses that pain and a writer in pain whose writing reflects the experience of pain. As readers, we feel the difference because the meaning of the pain is not in the language itself but what we are able to access by means of the language. Conflicted feelings produce conflicted writing. In Dickinson's Loaded Gun poem, the blend works precisely because the gun fails; in Plath's "The Applicant", does the blend fail because the writer is conflicted? Such a question cannot be settled here, but the fact that it can be raised suggests promising avenues for future cognitive poetics research.

5. Conclusion

The kind of analysis cognitive poetics provides opens up the cognitive layers upon which a literary text is built and, in doing so, provides a reading that reveals the frame and structure of meaning that is endemic and central to the text itself. It makes explicit the cognitive skills we apply implicitly when we analyze literary texts. In its explanatory adequacy, cognitive poetics provides the grounding for the demands of a literary theory as follows:

descriptive: accounting for literary characteristics of a text and providing a coherent interpretation of its meaning in its philosophical, historical, cultural, etc. context;

explanatory: accounting for the generation of the text (what is there) and for the multiple ways in which it is understood by readers; showing which readings are valid and why;

theoretical: providing independent justification for interpretation that is grounded in the knowledge of how language works;

predictive: accounting for what is there and why it should be there, and, conversely, what is not;

demonstrative: showing why the text is a work of art in being more than simply representational of meaning;

evaluative: accounting for the aesthetic qualities in a work of art;

elegant: achieving simplicity in its ability to represent all the categories above.

An adequate theory of literature, to my mind, must fulfill all these criteria. A cognitive poetics reading of the few poems discussed in this paper shows just how powerful the theory of cognitive poetics can be in capturing the power, the effect, and the relevance of poetry.

Notes

1. David Porter (personal correspondence) on Dickinson's poem, "My Life had stood – a / Loaded Gun –" (J 754).

2. Analogy is being used here in its most general sense. I am hereby avoiding the precise discriminations of classical rhetoric that resulted in obscuring the common ground of such categories as analogy, metaphor, metonymy, and synecdoche.

3. Cognitive poetics, as I am using the term, is thus related to the call for more rigor in literary studies that has been named the new philology (Freeman, Donald C., forthcoming). Cognitive poetics is more restricted in scope than the new philology in its more exclusive focus on cognitive approaches. The term *cognitive poetics* was first used by Reuven Tsur (1992). However, Tsur's definition of the term specifically excludes the cognitive linguistic research in conceptual integration, blending, and metaphor which I am incorporating in my definition of the term.

4. A discussion of iconicity in syntax may be found in Donald C. Freeman's (1978) analysis of Keats' poem "To Autumn" as a poem about the theory of the imagination.

5. It has become customary in cognitive metaphor research to indicate the image schemas, structural metaphors, and basic conceptual metaphors in small capital letters to indicate an unanalyzed complex structure, much as the Δ is used in transformational grammar. For example, for the purposes of this discussion, I have not opened up the metaphor of AN INSTRUMENT IS A COMPANION, although instrumentality is a significant component in the poem's total metaphorical statement.

6. The texts of Dickinson's poems are taken from Ralph W. Franklin's (1981) manuscript books, and are identified by fascicle or set number, the Houghton Library identification number, marked with H, page location, and T. H. Johnson's (1955) number, marked with J. For ease of reference, poems referred to by line or phrase only are given their Johnson numbers. Texts that occur in transcript only are taken from Johnson's (1955) edition of the poems. Crosses mark the variants that are given at the bottom of or throughout the poem wherever they appear in the original manuscript. Hyphens, rather than dashes, are used to reflect more accurately their nondominating appearance in the manuscript. Line breaks are left as they appear in the manuscript to enable each reader to determine whether to consider them as new lines or runovers. Dickinson's spelling has been kept throughout.

7. Under cognitive theory, readings of a poem may be considered members of a radial category, with some readings being more prototypical, or central, to the category than others. Although a prototypical reading might be close to what literary critics call a "literal" reading, it differs in that it results from the application of a specifically cognitive analysis.

8. I am grateful to Athanasios Kyratzis, Lancaster University, for this insight.

9. An earlier version of this analysis may be found in Freeman, Margaret H. (in press).
10. The following chart outlines the metaphorical correspondences that seven representative critics have drawn for the gun and its owner:

Gun	Self	(Sharon Cameron)
Owner	World force	
Gun	Woman artist	(Albert Gelpi)
Owner	Masculine animus	
Gun	Adolescent girl	(Cristanne Miller)
Owner	"Owner/Master"	
Gun	Dickinson	(Vivian Pollak)
Owner	Male personification of her aggression	
Gun	Language	(David Porter)
Owner	Self	
Gun	Woman poet	(Adrienne Rich)
Owner	Daemon/destructive power	
Gun	Death	(Cynthia Griffin Wolff)
Owner	Christ/God	

All these readings are nonprototypical in that they either map on the basis of similarity (e.g. gun/woman; gun/language) or on the basis of purpose (e.g. feminist/patriarchy; psychological/struggle within the self; linguistic/poetry, language). All are uneasy readings, in the sense that the critics themselves are not entirely satisfied that their readings holistically characterize the poem, and yet all capture essential aspects of the metaphoric domains included in the poem's world.
11. Only Robert Weisbuch's discussion of the poem reflects system mapping in his analysis of the inner analogy and then of the outer analogy or illustrative possibilities. His inner analogy reading, as one would expect, since it is mapping on the basis of the structure of the poem's design, matches my prototypical reading, although his is not presented from the perspective of cognitive metaphor as is mine (Weisbuch 1975). Weisbuch's lengthy discussion of the poem seems to me absolutely correct in its analysis and conclusions. The only distinction between his reading and mine is that in applying cognitive metaphor theory, my reading makes more explicit the conceptual basis on which Weisbuch's reading rests and shows how the poem, like all poetry, adopts the same conceptual metaphorical structures that occur in everyday language.
12. The unanalyzed metaphors in this section are all drawn from Kövecses's (1995) article.
13. See Weisbuch's reading of the poem, especially stanza 3. He proposes that the process of total identification is occurring faster than my analysis suggests: "Unless we see that volcanic face as the owner's (and this would disrupt the physical exactness of the poem, for the face which 'shows through' the gun must be the flash of firing, not the gun's owner and shooter), the life-gun is beginning to speak in relation to itself, as though it can pull its own trigger. Yet from the analogy we

know that no such independence is possible. Instead, the life-gun has equated its purpose so thoroughly with the owner's that it is beginning to perpetuate him; another illusion of selfhood and self-expression" (Weisbusch 1975: 29).

14.   I have been unable to locate the source of this story beyond the fact that we were regaled by it and tested on it as undergraduates at the University of Manchester. Certainly, it is in the spirit of Richards's (1925; 1929) new critical agenda.

15.   The poem that was auctioned by Sotheby's in New York in the summer of 1997 as a new Dickinson manuscript had actually been forged by Mark Hofmann, the so-called "Mormon forger", who is currently serving a life sentence for murder.

16.   I thank Perry Nelson for drawing my attention to this poem.

References

Cameron, Sharon
    1992   *Choosing not choosing: Dickinson's fascicles*. Chicago and London: The University of Chicago Press.
Cook, Guy
    1994   *Discourse and literature: The interplay of form and mind*. Oxford: Oxford University Press.
Fauconnier, Gilles
    1997   *Mappings in thought and language*. Cambridge: Cambridge University Press.
Fauconnier, Gilles – Mark Turner
    1998   "Conceptual integration networks", *Cognitive Science*, 22:2, 133-187.
Franklin, Raplh W. (ed.)
    1981   *The manuscript books of Emily Dickinson*. 2 vols. Cambridge, MA and London, England: The Belknap Press of Harvard University Press.
Freeman, Donald C.
    1978   "Keats's "To Autumn": Poetry as process and pattern", *Language and Style* 11.1: 3-17.
    forthcoming *Shakespearian metaphor: A cognitive approach*.
Freeman, Margaret H.
    1995   "Metaphor making meaning: Dickinson's conceptual universe", *Journal of Pragmatics* 24: 643-666.
    in press   "Metaphors of mind: Troping as poetic strategy", in: Gudrun M. Grabher – Roland Hagenbüchle – Cristanne Miller (eds.) *The Emily Dickinson handbook*. Amherst: The University of Massachusetts Press.
Gelpi, Albert
    1979   "Emily Dickinson and the deerslayer: The dilemma of the woman poet in America", in: Sandra M. Gilbert – Susan Gubar (eds.), 122-134.
Gilbert, Sandra M. – Susan Gubar (eds.)
    1979   *Shakespeare's sisters: feminist essays on women poets*. Bloomington: Indiana University Press
Holyoak, Keith J. – Paul Thagard
    1995   *Mental leaps: Analogy in creative thought*. Cambridge, MA: The MIT Press/Bradford Books.

Hoopes, James (ed.)
1991   *Peirce on signs*. Chapel Hill and London: The University of North Carolina Press.
Johnson, Mark
1987   *The body in the mind: The bodily basis of meaning, imagination, and reason*. Chicago and London: The University of Chicago Press.
Johnson, Thomas H. (ed.)
1955   *The poems of Emily Dickinson: Including variant readings critically compared with all known manuscripts*. 3 vols. Cambridge, MA: The Belknap Press of Harvard University Press.
Kövecses, Zoltán
1995   "American friendship and the scope of metaphor", *Cognitive Linguistics* 6.4: 315-346.
Lakoff, George
1993   "The contemporary theory of metaphor", in: Andrew Ortony (ed.), *Metaphor and thought*. (2nd edition.) Cambridge: Cambridge University Press, 202-251.
Miller, Cristanne
1987   *Emily Dickinson: A poet's grammar*. Cambridge, MA, and London, England: Harvard University Press.
Pollak, Vivian R.
1984   *Dickinson: The anxiety of gender*. Ithaca: Cornell University Press.
Porter, David
1981   *Dickinson: The modern idiom*. Cambridge, MA and London, England: Harvard University Press.
Rich, Adrienne
1979   "Vesuvius at home: The power of Emily Dickinson", in: Sandra M. Gilbert – Susan Gubar (eds.), 99-121.
Richards, I. A.
1925   *Principles of literary criticism*. New York: Harcourt, Brace and Company.
1929   *Practical criticism*. New York: Harcourt, Brace & World, Inc.
Semino, Elena
1997   *Language and world creation in poems and other texts*. London and New York: Longman.
Tsur, Reuven
1992   *Toward a theory of cognitive poetics*. Amsterdam: North-Holland.
Turner, Mark
1996   *The literary mind*. Chicago and London: University of Chicago Press.
Weisbuch, Robert
1975   *Emily Dickinson's poetry*. Chicago and London: The University of Chicago Press.
Wolff, Cynthia Griffin
1986   *Emily Dickinson*. New York: Alfred A. Knopf.
Zlatev, Jordan
1997   *Situated embodiment: Studies in the emergence of spatial meaning*. Stockholm: Gotab.

The cohesive role of cognitive metaphor in discourse and conversation

Diane Ponterotto

1. Introduction

Recent studies in philosophy and linguistics on metaphor have shifted the focus of scientific inquiry from a strictly linguistic plane to a cognitive-based stance, i.e. from the study of metaphor as a purely tropological phenomenon to a reflection on its role in human conceptualization. This epistemological shift has uncovered the centrality of analogical operations, first of all in the structuring of experience, and then as a resultive process, in language (Lakoff – Johnson 1980). In this view, a figurative expression is seen to relate back to a metaphorical perception of reality. The utterance *He is walking on air*, for example, would emerge from the mental association of extreme happiness with the material sensation of rising and weightlessness. It is this "embodied understanding" (Johnson 1987) which informs and directs our way of verbally interacting with society and with the world.

If metaphor has such a central role in the interpretation and expression of human experience, then from a linguistic point of view, it could be hypothesized to be a cohesive force in discourse. Of course, in the history of rhetorics and poetics, metaphor has often been identified as the organizing principle of texts. Recently, however, studies in cognitive poetics have revisited the canon in order to develop cognitive-based descriptive frameworks for the role of metaphor in literary texts (cf. for example, Freeman, this volume).

Within this shift to the cognitive dimension of metaphor, less attention has been paid to its role in conversation. The purpose of this paper is to explore the applicability of cognitive metaphor to analyses of verbal interaction.

As a dynamic, context-specific communicative event (Slama-Cazacu 1969), conversation is universally conditioned by two basic constraints: its development in real-time and as a corollary, the rapidity of the transformation of the psycholinguistic variables which constitute it (speaker, hearer, message, situation, plans and goals, verbal strategies etc.). Although conversations occur in a very short time span, many things happen: problems are presented, topics shift, interlocutor perspectives change, positions are negotiated, goals are achieved and decisions made. Interlocutors must be able to manage an ample set of variables which change continually in split-second succession. This apparently results in faulty information structures, unregulated turns, non-explicated attitudinal positions, fuzzy presuppositions etc. This would imply, therefore, that on the one hand, cohesion of discourse structures is more impelling, but on the other, due precisely to this dynamic-contextual complexity, more difficult to activate. What holds these apparently incomplete verbal segments together? Why is it that such a fluid, precarious, indeterminate communicative event does not get out of hand? What accounts for this cohesion? What accounts for the interlocutors' coherence attribution processes? Why is there no conversation clash or crash?

2. Discourse and cognition

Discourse scholars have always suggested the need to study the role of cognition in discourse organization. In 1977, van Dijk spoke of "cognitive pragmatics" and emphasized the difficulty in understanding the complex relation between contextual analysis and textual analysis, precisely because, when dealing with discourse, we find ourselves in an interdisciplinary camp which involves not only language, but also action, meaning, cognition and social structures.

Recently, discourse scholars have affirmed that in order to account for this complexity, we must demonstrate how text representations are related to deeper conceptual representations. In other words we must be able to describe the link between discourse and cognition, i.e. between discourse/text structure, on the one hand, and mental activities of information processing, storage, and retrieval, on the other. According to Tomlin et al. (1997), this means understanding how speakers construct the conceptual edifice that underlies text representations, and how they guide the listener in accessing this conceptual edifice. We could add here that this also implies accounting for the active role of listeners – how they tune into the speaker's conceptual perspective, as well as how they affect it and how they activate modifications in the speaker's perspective and determine changes in the speaker's discourse strategies.

Now two models have been accredited to explain this conceptualization process: the *conduit model* and the *blueprint model.*

The conduit model is the traditional conception of the relationship between thought and language. The model presents meaning as contained in the mind. Language is the vehicle by which meaning is transferred from one pole, the emitter, to the other, the receiver. This model is inadequate from various points of view. Discourse semantics has demonstrated that meaning is negotiated by speakers (and not carried unilaterally from one to the other). Cognitive linguistics has provided a very virulent criticism of the conduit metaphor of meaning. According to Lakoff & Johnson (1980: 206), the conduit metaphor derives from the objectivist myth in Western linguistics and philosophy which views communication as a conduit where a speaker sends a fixed meaning to a hearer via the linguistic expression associated with that meaning. This model collocates meaning in the words/texts and does not account for the complex nature of human understanding, human experience and verbal interaction.

The blueprint model implies that "the speaker holds a conceptual representation of events or ideas which he intends should be replicated in the mind of the listener" (Tomlin et al. 1997: 64). The text as a blueprint provides the speaker with a stable map for guiding the listener's interpretation. Obviously, a cognitive-pragmatic viewpoint on discourse feels more comfortable with the blueprint model, which, according to Tomlin et al. (1997: 65), must be able to account for two interrelated aspects of information flow:

1. *Knowledge integration,* i.e. how interlocutors integrate the information into a coherent whole. Chafe (1994) has noted that the mind has a large amount of knowledge but focuses on a small amount at any given time. Speakers/ listeners select what to focus on, what to bring to consciousness, what to mentally and verbally activate. How do they do that? How do they incorporate single propositions into textual representations and integrate them to generate final conceptual representations (cf. Tomlin et al. 1997)?

2. *Information management,* i.e. how interlocutors manage the flow of information in dynamic real-time interaction.

The concept of information flow according to Cumming and Ono (1997) and following Chafe (1994) is generally considered to lie within the realm of cognition, referring to the mental states of speakers/listeners during discourse production and reception. Information management refers to how the speaker "directs the listener's efforts to process the information provided through the text. For example, the speaker will help the listener to exploit information held in common as a prelude to or anchor for information the speaker believes will be novel or unexpected for the listener" (Tomlin et al. 1997: 65).

Moreover, Tomlin et al. (1997) following Chafe (1994) note that the efficacy of knowledge integration and information management depends on the speaker's ability to control the information flow on four levels:

- *rhetorical,* i.e. relative to the speaker's goals;
- *referential,* i.e. the speaker's selection of appropriate referents;
- *thematic,* i.e. the speaker's organization of sentence perspective;
- *focus,* i.e. the speaker's highlighting of the right referents at the right time.

The following schema provided by Tomlin et al. (1997) summarizes this process:

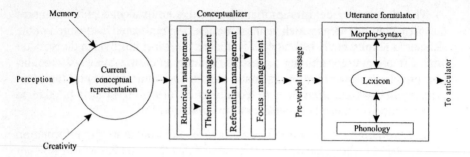

Figure 1. A blueprint for the speaker (regenerated according to the figure in Tomlin et al. 1997: 71)

3. Cohesion in conversation

3.1. Cohesion

What is even more important for our discussion is the point made subsequently that "the coherence of the knowledge held by the listener will be affected by how cohesive the information is that the speaker offers" (Tomlin et al. 1997: 65).

But, what determines degrees of cohesiveness? Cohesion has traditionally been considered a grammatical device signaled by morphosyntactic cues. These are usually identified as reference, ellipsis and substitution, conjunction and word order, etc. However, lexical patterns have also been seen to carry cohesive functions. Lexical reiteration and collocation especially have been demonstrated to structure discourse links (cf. Halliday – Hasan 1976). Relexicalization of basic lexemes in texts permit interlocutors to negotiate topics and shift topic focus without compromising the verbal exchange.

Yet, if the speaker manages so many complex elements simultaneously, there must be some deeper conceptual structure which can account for the integration of all these cognitive and linguistic operations. After all, the output is a unitary linguistic object, a text. What guarantees the "wholeness" of a conversation which occurs not only sequentially but also so rapidly and dynamically?

3.2. Conversation

One of the major problems involved in conversation management is in fact the rapidity of the exchange, which requires language users to make "fast hypotheses with respect to the most plausible structure of the actual and following context states" (van Dijk 1977: 230). If we timed for example the transcript (which is the object of the analysis in section 4.1.), we would note that it occurred within the brief time period of 1 minute 52 seconds – an extremely fast, we could say, "fleeting", verbal exchange.

Now in his research on memory and cognitivism, Eysenck (1986: 60) notes that "it would be extremely difficult to hold a conversation if you were unable to keep in mind what someone else or yourself had just been saying". How do language users hold on to what passes so quickly in conversation? "In similar fashion", he continues, "when thinking about some complicated problem, it is very useful to have a short term system that will store information about part of the problem while you concentrate on other parts of the problem".

4. Cognitive metaphor

What I would like to suggest in this paper is that cognitive metaphor plays a role in memory by somehow aiding the storage and retrieval of information during discourse processing. In other words, cognitive metaphor can contribute in a decisive manner to the cohesive force upon which the text representation depends in order to emerge and be sustained in conversation.

4.1. Example 1: *Scent of a Woman*

The discussion will begin with an illustration of a dialogue segment taken from the film *Scent of a Woman*.[1] The conversation occurs as a sequel to two previous cinematographic scenes: a first scene where a threatening headmaster of Baird, a preparatory high school for the rich tries to convince two students (George and Charles) to squeal on their companions, followed by a second scene, where the headmaster, in the absence of George, tries to bribe Charles. The dialogue follows:

George: What did he say?
Charles: Nothing.
George: What do you mean ... nothing?
Charles: He said the same things he said to both of us, only he said them over to me.
George: You know what he's doing? He's *good cop-bad copping* us. He knows I'm *old guard* and you're *fringe*. He's going to *bear down on me* and *soft soap* you. Did he *soft soap* you, did he?
Charles: No.
George: Chas, I detect a slight *panic pulse* from you. Are you panicking?
Charles: Yeah, a little
George: Come on, you're on scholarship, right?
Charles: Yeah.
George: You're on scholarship from Oregon at Baird. You're a long way from home, Chas.
Charles: What has that got to do with me being on a scholarship?

George: I don't know how it works out there. But how it works here ... we *stick together*. It's us against them, no matter what. We don't *cover our ass*. We don't tell our parents. *Stonewall everybody*. And above all ... never ... never ... never ... *leave* any of us *twisting in the wind* ... And that's it.

Charles: What does that have to do with me being on a scholarship?

George: Just trying to *bring* you *up to speed*, kid, that's it.

Charles: Thanks.

George: Hey are you all right?

Charles: Yeah, I guess so

George: Tell you what. Give me a few hours to *figure out the moves* and call me tonight in Vermont. I'll be at the Sugarbush Lodge. All right?

Charles: All right.

George: You all right?

Charles: Yeah, I guess so.

George: Okay.

4.1.1. Analysis

First of all we would all agree that this segment is a text, structured as in all conversations as a complete verbal interaction containing an opening move, a closing move and the relative intermediate exchanges (see inter alia Sinclair – Coulthard 1975).

Secondly we would probably immediately identify the basic speech act of the segment: George tries to convince Charles not to squeal. On closer scrutiny however, we would all probably agree that this macro speech act comprises three functional substrategies:

a. to persuade Charles to align his perspective with his own: the headmaster is out to trick them.
b. to inform Charles of the students' rule of strong solidarity.
c. to suggest alternative solutions to their problem.

Thirdly, we can notice that this brief segment contains many utterances with an idiomatic expression (IE):

1. He's *good cop-bad copping* us.
2. He knows I'm *old guard* and you're *fringe*.
3. He's going to *bear down on* me and *soft soap* you.
4. Did he try to *soft soap you*? Did he?
5. I detect a slight *panic pulse* there.
6. We *stick together*.
7. We don't *cover our ass*.
8. *Stonewall everybody*.

9. And above all, never ... never ... never ... leave any of us *twisting in the wind.*
10. Just trying to *bring* you *up to speed.*
11. Give me a few hours to *figure out the moves.*

If we tried to map these IEs onto the speech act articulation noted above, we could say that each strategy is targeted by one or more idiomatic expressions; for example:

a. persuading: *He's good cop-soft copping us.*
b. informing: *We stick together.*
c. suggesting: *Give me a few hours to figure out the moves.*

Now according to Lakoff & Johnson (1980) and subsequent research in cognitive linguistics, idiomatic expressions stem from metaphorical ways of conceptualizing experience. Therefore, if we tried to identify the cognitive metaphors behind these IEs we could suggest that:

a. *good cop-bad copping* emerges from the metaphor PERSUASION IS POLICING.
b. *stick together* emerges from the metaphor SOLIDARITY IS CLOSENESS.
c. *figure out the moves* emerges from LIFE IS A GAME.

Thus, we have managed to understand the mapping between speech acts, language forms and cognitive metaphors.

How do these metaphors interrelate? Do they all have the same weight, for example? If not, how are they organized? If the premise of this discussion is that cognitive metaphor has a cohesive role in discourse organization, how does this fit into our cognitive explanation of conversation management?

We could suggest here that the first IE is signaled by the utterance – *Do you know what he's doing?* – which is a typical signal of the intention to tell a story. It seems to be what Labov (1972: 354-396) labels the orientation phase of narration. The first IE (He's *good cop-bad copping* us) then follows, again in Labov's taxonomy, as the first complicating event. As such it states a problem, for which the speaker provides an evaluation. So the first IE, and therefore, the first cognitive metaphor establishes the heuristic frame for the rest of the conversation sequence. Since the word *cop* is a pejorative term for policeman, it activates a negative connotation in the individual's memory, the result of a disparaging stereotype in the collective encyclopedia. *Good cop-bad cop* implies that the strategy used by the police force of being tough one minute, and easy the next, presents a hidden danger for them. In order to achieve the relative rhetorical goals, the speaker's choices of information management will operate within this heuristic frame, expressed by the metaphor PERSUASION IS POLICING. In a sense, this is a social-cognitive metaphor since it emerges from the way members of a community conceptualize the behavior of policing institutions.

The subsequent IEs reiterate the basic cognitive metaphors present in the dialogue or activate what Lakoff & Johnson (1980) label metaphorical entailments. The utterance *He's going to bear down on me and soft soap you* presents two IEs which instantiate metaphors entailed by PERSUASION IS POLICING, that is, PERSUASION IS THREATENING and PERSUASION IS SEDUCING, repeating the binary antonymous concept of *good cop-bad cop.*

Other IEs instantiate entailments of SOLIDARITY IS CLOSENESS, for example SOLIDARITY IS MILITANCY and SOLIDARITY IS RESISTANCE. *I'm old guard* suggests the in-group membership status of tightly structured military organizations, a suggestion reinforced by *Stonewall everybody*, which again adds a socio-political basis to the concept of solidarity. Besides its meaning of steadfast obstruction, the word *Stonewall* also refers to the event which occurred in a New York City gay bar on June 28, 1969, when a group of youths, along with the support of the entire community, compactly resisted a police incursion. This is an example of how encyclopedic knowledge and cultural scenarios become part of what Lakoff (1987) has termed ICMs (Idealized Cultural Models). The word *Stonewall* activates a shared pattern of experience (cf. Radden – Kövecses, forthcoming) in American youth culture. The IE *You're fringe* also instantiates SOLIDARITY IS CLOSENESS through the antonymous entailment NON-SOLIDARITY IS MARGINALITY. The expression *We don't cover our ass* also suggests an antonymous entailment of the Solidarity metaphor: NON-SOLIDARITY IS SELF-PROTECTION. Similarly, the utterance *Never leave any of us twisting in the wind* instantiates SOLIDARITY IS CLOSENESS through the antonymous entailment, NON-SOLIDARITY IS SOLITUDE, which in turn entails NON-SOLIDARITY IS PRECARIOUSNESS. The expression *I detect a panic pulse there* emerges probably from FEAR IS A FAST HEART BEAT, an example of how analogical concepts are grounded in biological processes (Lakoff – Johnson 1980). The utterance *Just trying to bring you up to speed* definitely derives from LEARNING IS FAST MOVEMENT, since there seem to exist many similar idiomatic expressions in the English language.[2]

In this conversation, therefore, we can witness, first of all, what Lakoff and Johnson (1980: 97) call "metaphorical overlaps". "When two metaphors successfully satisfy two purposes, then overlaps in the purposes will correspond to overlaps in the metaphors". Overlaps determine conceptual complexity. Many metaphors may contribute to the structuring of a concept, since we use concepts that are themselves understood in metaphorical terms. We could also suggest viewing this complexity as a kind of dominance hierarchy whereby some metaphors are rewritten as submetaphors of a basic conceptual representation.[3] Furthermore, since metaphor is open-ended (Barcelona, 1997), some also give rise to related metaphors forming a complicated web-like organization (cf. Langacker 1987), characterized by flexibility and multiplicity. We could represent the metaphorical network present in this example as follows:

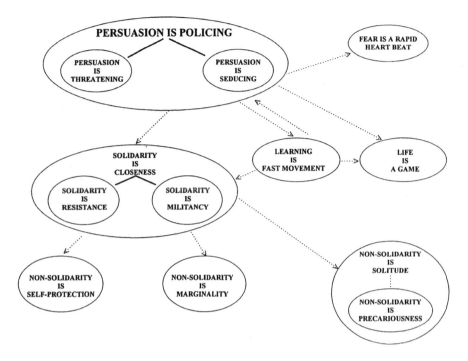

Figure 2. Cognitive metaphor network: dialogue extracted from the film *Scent of a Woman*

4.2. Example 2: Spontaneous conversation

Now although this cinematic dialogue is extremely spontaneous-like, it is none-theless the result of artful creative film-writing. Let us turn to a real-life conversation to see if natural-occurring conversational data can confirm our hypothesis. The following is a segment of a recorded conversation which took place in a London flat in 1994.

B: And Mhmm, I don't know ... even though we had *a big relationship* I can't *see the sense* of getting married.

A: Oh!

B: Sometimes you *go through life* and you're really serious about someone but ... you just don't *keep going* and you have things to do.

A: Six months ago ... I met him, six months later ... he moved to Australia and a month, two months later he got ??? university.[4]

B: Yeah!

A: So he took off thinking "Yeah we see each other in six months back in a month for another two months"

B: [Yeah.

A: so I said, "OK, I'll see you in a couple of months." So three times ... it happened, that separation

B: Mmmm.

A: and it's the fourth time in a month.

B: *It's just so hard* to maintain *a long distance*

A: [Six months ago he used to talk about it

B: *relationship.* Yeah, it's very very difficult.

A: Mhmmm, when you can't *work things out* but six months ago we used to talk about marriage.

B: Yeah.

A: It was really serious, but now it's like, mhmm, *weaving out of it.* But it's easier *to hang on* rather than *let go* ... and that's why I came here ...

4.2.1. Analysis

First of all, we can note that the text displays the general characteristics of natural conversation: overlaps and interruptions, back-channeling and pauses, etc. It demonstrates perfectly the apparently unstructured but nonetheless well-formedness quality of conversations as explained above. Can we identify the cohesive role of cognitive metaphor even here?

The interlocutors in this conversation are discussing problems concerning intimate relationships. The macrospeech act then would be: understanding the problems of love and marriage. The conversation seems to divide into three exchanges where the first and third take shape in an idiomatic manner and the second seems to adhere to a more literal level of expression. It would seem that these speakers use literal language when exchanging information about problems and decisions but resort to more idiomatic expressions when reflecting on opinions and emotions. It would also seem that the opinions/emotions idiomatic segments frame the information segment. If that be so, and if the idiomatic expressions can be said to be organized within a cognitive metaphor framework, then the cohesive role of cognitive metaphor in conversation would again emerge.

In this conversation, the cognitive metaphors are targeted by the sequence of idiomatic expressions as follows:

1. I don't *see the sense* of getting married.
   UNDERSTANDING IS SEEING.
2. Even though we had *a big relationship.*
   SIGNIFICANT IS BIG.
3. Sometimes you *go through life.*
   LIFE IS A JOURNEY.
4. You just don't *keep going.*
   LOVE IS A JOURNEY.

5. *It's so hard.*
   LOVE IS HARD WORK.
6. To maintain *a long distance relationship.*
   LOVE IS CLOSENESS.
7. You can't *work things out.*
   LOVE IS WORK.
8. Now it's sort of like, mhmm, *weaving out of it.*
   LOVE IS A COLLABORATIVE WORK OF ART (knitting or quiltmaking).
9. But then, it's easier *to hang on* than *to let go.*
   LOVE IS A PRECIPICE.

The first major cognitive metaphor UNDERSTANDING IS SEEING introduces the topic (the problem of marriage) which is moreover qualified by the utterance *even though we had a big relationship* (SIGNIFICANT IS BIG). We could therefore consider UNDERSTANDING IS SEEING to be the heuristic frame for the conversation strategies which follow. The interaction is structured around a set of LIFE and LOVE metaphors which exemplify the theorizations found in Lakoff and Johnson (1980), Kövecses (1988, 1990) and Barcelona (1995). A mapping of the metaphor network of this conversation would look like this:

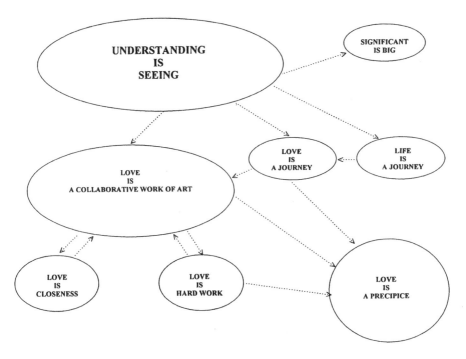

Figure 3. Cognitive metaphor network: spontaneous conversation

At any rate it is this multidimensional aspect of metaphorical structuring which makes possible the organization of experience into a "well-formed whole". "Structuring our experience in terms of such multidimensional gestalts is what makes our experience coherent." (Lakoff – Johnson 1980: 81) In the conversations of this study, the initial cognitive metaphors: PERSUASION IS POLICING of example 1 and UNDERSTANDING IS SEEING of example 2, corresponding to the macrospeech acts, seem to provide the heuristic frame for the ensuing discourse strategies. The cognitive metaphor network then works to structure the mental stance of the interlocutors. It seems to function as the fulcrum of discourse organization, providing thereby a cohesive force to verbal interaction.

4.3. Cognitive metaphor and cohesion

The question now arises as to why metaphor functions so efficiently as a cognitive pivot? First of all, we could cite the point made in Lakoff & Johnson (1980: 97) "...a metaphor works when it satisfies a purpose, namely, understanding an aspect of a concept". I would like to suggest however that it works because it is

1. rapid
2. concise, and
3. vivid

If we go back to our example, *He's good cop-bad copping us* (PERSUASION IS POLICING), we can easily see how the metaphor manages to verbalize a complex content (in only two lexical items) and activate a complicated rhetorical goal (in less than two minutes). However, rapidity and conciseness can jeopardize the permanence of the information in the memory structure of the interlocutors. Research on memory has demonstrated that what limits short-term memory is not a structural constraint (the amount of space available) but a processing one (the possibility of allocation of attention). This is perhaps where vividness comes into play. Chafe (1968: 125) in fact drew attention to the role of vividness in his discussion of idiomaticity. He noted in fact that "it would appear that idioms typically require the occurrence of emphasis with them. Probably, this fact is related to a special vividness associated with the meanings which idioms have". Vividness conveys an emotionally-keyed significance to reported events or states; it provides an ample semantic range for them; it throws a spotlight on a few, selected connotations. Vividness accounts for a rich background and a prominent foreground. It guarantees an adequate allotment of attention to the information thereby focused. Now, according to current research on memory (Eysenck 1986), the efficiency of the memory structure seems to depend on the depth of processing (the meaningfulness of the stimulus), the degree of elaboration of processing (more elaborated, more easily recalled) and on the distinctiveness of processing. This last point has been noted in studies by Bransford et al. (1979) whose experiments demonstrated that analogies are remembered especially when they stand out in some way, i.e. when they are unique and distinctive. We could suggest therefore that speech acts couched in figurative form incorporate precisely these three cognitive qualities. Figurativity lends more significance, greater elaboration and a sense of uniqueness to information structures.

5. Conclusions

Now let us recall the basic questions behind this study: how are conversation strategies related to conceptual representations? What determines the integration of knowledge during such a rapid, complex exchange? What accounts for the coordination of complex information? What explains the movement from the heuristic frame to the rhetorical frame? What defines the matching of referential, thematic and focus functions? What gives cohesion to the utterances thereby formulated? The answer can only be a mental device which, at one and the same time, organizes conceptualization and its transformation into text representations. This is the pivot-like role of cognitive metaphor, which could suggest a revision of the schema in Tomlin et al. (1997) to include the heuristic frame and collocate the cognitive metaphor network, as follows:

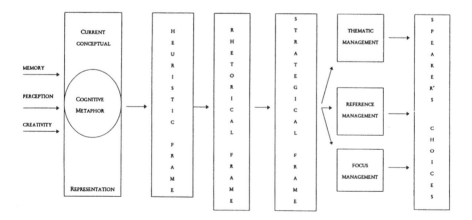

Figure 4. Re-elaboration of Tomlin et al. 1997

Furthermore, if we look more closely at the turntaking alternations of the second conversation, we can note that speakers collaboratively construct the thematic structure of the text, precisely through a negotiation of the metaphorical overlaps. A distribution of metaphors according to the speakers would reveal that speaker B moves from UNDERSTANDING IS SEEING to LIFE IS A JOURNEY to LOVE IS A JOURNEY and finally to LOVE IS HARD WORK, which is then picked up by Speaker A who reiterates LOVE IS HARD WORK, implying its entailment LOVE IS A COLLABORATIVE WORK OF ART, which then triggers the concept of danger, LOVE IS A PRECIPICE.

Therefore, if we sought to understand the role of cognitive metaphor in the interlocutor relations of this exchange, we would note that their conceptual representations meet at the point LOVE IS HARD WORK, which becomes the negotiated agreement of the problem announced at the beginning of the conversation. Keeping within the blueprint model suggested by Tomlin et al. (1997), we could represent the interaction of the interlocutors' metaphorical networks as follows:

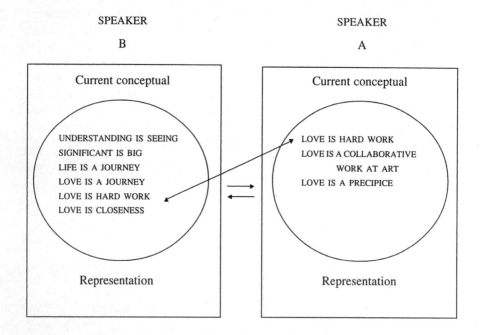

Figure 5. Interaction of interlocutors' metaphorical networks

The cognitive metaphor LOVE IS HARD WORK appears to bind the conceptual perspectives of the two speakers.

It would seem therefore that cognitive metaphor has a role to play in the planning, execution and monitoring of text production. Discourse control is possible only if the basic conceptual representations of the interlocutors are held in storage during processing, so that they can be made readily available in the retrieval and recall of information, and in the reconstruction and reapplication of speech act representations. As illustrated in our dialogue samples, speech acts are negotiated in response to a heuristic frame which emerges from the context-specific conceptual representations of language users who quickly work out a complex text representation without going off track. The role of metaphorization in cognition seems crucial. On the one hand, cognitive metaphor, *brief, concise and vivid*, functions as a pivot which holds everything in place; on the other hand, the cognitive metaphor network, *multiple, open-ended* and *flexible* permits constant reelaboration. Cognitive metaphor therefore guarantees both stability and dynamicity in discourse processes. As a specific discursive form, conversation is a fleeting encounter of multiple perspectives, a fast negotiation of competing goals, a rapid matching of complex positions. Conversation is after all a subtle meeting of minds. Often it is cognitive metaphor which guarantees the cohesion/coherence necessary for successful communication.

Notes

1. I have unsuccessfully tried to obtain permission for this brief quotation from the apparent copyright holders.
2. She *went* through the explanation *very quickly*. He *followed* the lesson *easily*. Her grades are *soaring*. She's *advancing steadily*. She's *a fast learner*. She just *flew through college*. He can't *keep up* with the teacher.
3. As noted by Barcelona (personal communication), many of these metaphors emerge out of metonymic relationships. The decodification of *Stonewall everybody* depends on the stand-for relationship whereby the concrete instance represents all similar instances. However, the connection between the metonymically-based meaning of *stonewall* and the concept of RESISTANCE is metaphorical. As noted by Radden – Kövecses (forthcoming), the metonymy CONCEPT(A) FOR THING/EVENT(A) is not reversible.
4. The question marks indicate an unintelligible voice emission probably decodifiable in this context as "accepted to".

References

Barcelona, Antonio
    1995   "Metaphorical models of romantic love in *Romeo and Juliet*", *Journal of Pragmatics* 24: 667-688.
    1997   "Clarifying and applying the notions of metaphor and metonymy within cognitive linguistics", *Atlantis,* 19-1: 21-48.
Bransford, John D. – Jeffrey J. Franks – Morris C. Donald – Barry S. Stein
    1979   "Some general constraints on learning and memory research", in: Laird S. Cermak – Fergus I.M. Craik (eds.), *Levels of processing in human memory*. Hillsdale, New Jersey: Lawrence Erlbaum, 331-355.
Chafe, Wallace
    1968   "Idiomaticity as an anomaly in the Chomskyan paradigm", *Foundations of Language* 4: 109-127.

1994   *Discourse, consciousness and time.* Chicago: Chicago University Press.
Cumming, Susanna – Tsuyoshi Ono
1997   "Discourse and grammar", in: Teun A. van Dijk (ed.), 112-137.
Eysenck, Michael W.
1986   "Working memory", in: Gillian Cohen – Michael W. Eysenck – Martin E. Le Voi, *Memory: a cognitive approach.* Milton Keynes: Open University Press, 59-102.
Freeman, Margaret H.
this volume "Poetry and the scope of metaphor: Toward a cognitive theory of literature."
Halliday, Michael A.K. – Ruqaiya Hasan
1976   *Cohesion in English.* London: Longman.
Johnson, Mark
1987   *The body in the mind: the bodily basis of meaning, imagination, and reason.* Chicago and London: The University of Chicago Press.
Kövecses, Zoltán
1988   *The language of love.* Lewisburgh: Bucknell University Press.
1990   *Emotion concepts.* New York: Springer.
Labov, William
1972   *Language in the inner city.* Philadelphia: Pennsylvania University Press.
Lakoff, George
1987   *Women, fire and dangerous things: what categories reveal about the mind.* Chicago and New York: Chicago University Press.
Lakoff, George – Mark Johnson
1980   *Metaphors we live by.* Chicago: University of Chicago Press.
Langacker, Ronald
1987   *Foundations of cognitive grammar.* Stanford: Stanford University Press.
Radden, Günter – Zoltán Kövecses
forthcoming "Towards a theory of metonymy", in: Klaus-Uwe Panther – Günter Radden (eds.), *Metonymy in cognition and language.* Amsterdam and Philadelphia: Benjamins.
Sinclair, John – Malcolm Coulthard
1975   *Towards an analysis of discourse.* Oxford: Oxford University Press.
Slama-Cazacu, Tatiana
1969   *Introduzione alla psicolinguistica.* Bologna: Patron Editore.
Tomlin, Russell S. – Linda Forrest – Ming Ming Pu – Myung Hee Kim
1997   "Discourse semantics", in: Teun A. van Dijk (ed.), 63-111.
van Dijk, Teun A.
1977   "Context and cognition: knowledge frames and speech act comprehension", *Journal of Pragmatics* 1: 211-232.
1997   *Discourse as structure and process.* London, Thousand Oaks, New Delhi: Sage.

More metaphorical warfare in the Gulf: Orientalist frames in news coverage

Esra Sandikcioglu

1. Introduction[1]

This paper presents an analysis of the use of metaphor in news coverage of the Persian Gulf War (16 Jan.-Feb. 28 1991). What started out as an extension of the studies by Lakoff (1992) and Pancake (1993), soon developed a life of its own as my own research revealed that neither Lakoff nor Pancake had linked Gulf War metaphors to *Orientalism*,[2] which can initially be defined as the traditional "idealized cognitive model" the West has internalized about *the Orient* and *the Oriental*. In this paper I will argue that the metaphor systems and metaphor categories analyzed by both Lakoff and Pancake merely prove to be part of a much broader conceptual framework, encompassing the West's view of itself as opposed to its view of the East. The use of the two concepts *frames of Self-presentation* and *frames of Other-representation* throughout the study has been primarily inspired by Morgan's "frames of self-presentation" and her application of "idealized cognitive models" to the political reality of the U.S. (1997: 276).

At a more fundamental level, what is meant by Orientalism is what Said (1979: 203) describes as "a school of interpretation whose material happens to be the Orient, its civilizations, peoples, and localities". The argument is that this culture-specific cognitive model helped frame the debate about the Gulf crisis by conceptualizing Iraq as the incarnation of the Orient and thereby justify a specific political and military approach to the conflict which has been symptomatic of the age-old relationship between *the Orient* and *the West*.[3] In spite of various efforts taken to defuse conspiracy theories[4] which claimed that this clash was just another case of *Islam* vs. *the Christian West*, the imagery used by the leaders of the international alliance to depict the enemy as the devil on the one hand, and themselves as the saviors on the other, strengthens these charges.

The debate over the options available to the international community to make Iraq withdraw from Kuwait was characterized by a two-track strategy,[5] an attempt to unite two lines of diplomacy which were at odds with each other, if not mutually exclusive. The first track, the *peace-track*, assumed that Saddam Hussein was a rational enemy, which supported the argument that the military buildup in the Gulf was a show of force designed to back up the sanctions against Iraq. According to the second track, the *war-track*, however, Saddam Hussein was a nonrational enemy, i.e. unsusceptible to logic, and therefore would not be deterred by impending force. While the first track seemed to support the peace effort by stating as the sole objective of the alliance the restoration of the *status ante quo,* the second track could not but lead to war as it raised related issues that revealed *secondary*[6] objectives.

With regard to its internal structure, this paper consists of four main parts. In the first part I will analyze the psychological war waged by the Bush administration and the Pentagon, ably assisted by the news media, against Saddam Hussein and Iraq in order to show that the peace-track was not given a fair chance. Then, in the second part, I will outline the *Orientalist framework*, which provides the larger conceptual structure for Gulf War metaphors, in order to reveal their link to Orientalist patterns of thinking, characteristic not only of the language but also of the actions of the West towards the Orient. In the third part, I will look into the terminological and political dilemma inherent in dichotomous views of *the East* vs. *the West*, and *the Orient* vs. *the West*, particularly in the post-cold-war era. Finally, in the fourth part, I will present examples of Orientalist metaphors in 5 frames[7] to give readers the opportunity to judge for themselves. This analysis will illustrate how – by offering the world culturally preconceived concepts of Iraq and the U.S.-led alliance, i.e. *frames of Self-presentation vs. frames of Other-representation* – each frame helped to convince the public that war was justified.

The focus is on data material collected from *TIME* and *NEWSWEEK*[8] magazines covering the war and the weeks before and after, i.e. July 90-March 91. As the U.S. led the political and military alliance against Iraq, it is the language used by the U.S. government, administration, and military that has shaped Gulf War news coverage throughout the allied media. As this paper eventually hopes to show, the hypothesis I start from is that the West still lives by the images inherent in Orientalist metaphorical conceptualizations, polarizing the world into *the Orient* vs. *the West*, *Us* vs. *Them.*

2. The metaphorical conceptualization of the *Other*

The strategy behind the specific language used with regard to the crisis and the war was referred to by the U.S. media as a *psy war* for "psychological war". The first live television war of our century was fought, not because of metaphor but with the help of metaphor. As metaphors are part of the cognitive process that routinely enables us to understand "[a]bstractions and enormously complex situations", part of which "is devoted to understanding international relations and war", it is "literally vital, to understand just what role metaphorical thought played in bringing us in this war" (Lakoff 1992: 463). What Lakoff says with regard to the use of conceptual metaphors and metaphor systems in the Gulf War, is, on closer inspection of the new data, only a token of a much more general and deeper-rooted "idealized cognitive model", i.e. the Western "Orientalist" mindset. This is the total set of stereotypes built up by the Western mind in its perception and experience of the East. The power of Orientalist metaphors lies in the skillful utilization and application of "the canonical, orthodox coverage of Islam" to the Gulf crisis, presenting the image of Islam the media (in the U.S. in particular) have been shaping for the past two decades: it is a scary image capable of justifying war to protect the Western *way of life* or civilization (see Said 1997: 4; 169). There should be little doubt whose metaphors are more powerful as powerful cultures are more likely to have both the metaphors and the means to justify their position than less powerful cultures. In retrospect, but even as the crisis slowly but resolutely turned into a war, the metaphors of the West proved to be far superior – much like its more lethal weapons – than those of the Iraqis. As Lakoff and Johnson (1980: 157) point out (quoting Charlotte Linde), "people in power get to impose their metaphors."

Particularly in the context of foreign policy, those who act as mediators between the individual and the rest of the world, serve as a filter in the sense that they control both what we perceive – and most importantly – how we perceive it. In Chomsky's terms, the American intelligentsia – in particular the media and the experts – played its traditional role in the Gulf War, that is, "[b]y virtue of their analyses and interpretations, they serve as mediators between the social facts and the mass of the population: they create the ideological justification for social practice." (Chomsky 1979: 4)

The weakness of Chomsky's statement is, however, that he does not link his political analysis of the situation with any linguistics-based approach, which might reveal that the language used in the process is the core of the psychological war. As Lakoff and Johnson established two decades ago, metaphor is not a "matter of mere language" (Lakoff – Johnson 1980: 145), rather they argued (1980: 3), "[o]ur ordinary conceptual system, in terms of which we both think and act, is fundamentally metaphorical in nature. ... Our concepts structure what we perceive, how we get around in the world, and how we relate to other people. Our conceptual system thus plays a central role in defining our everyday realities." In order to structure our conceptual system with regard to what was going on in the Gulf, metaphors had to cover "all aspects of the Persian Gulf War", as Pancake (1993: 281) points out, though within the limits defined by the Pentagon.

As the metaphors conceptualizing Iraqis as prototypical instantiations of the Western concept of Orientals on the one hand, and Americans as Westerners, on the other are systematically related with other metaphors within the Orientalist framework, they can be considered as "metaphors we live by" and as such, they "structure our actions and thoughts" (Lakoff – Johnson 1980: 55). Moreover,

New metaphors, like conventional metaphors, can have the power to define reality. They do this through a coherent network of entailments that highlight some features of reality and hide others. The acceptance of the metaphor, which forces us to focus *only* on those aspects of our experience that it highlights, leads us to view the entailments of the metaphor as being *true*. Such "truths" may be true, of course, only relative to the reality defined by the metaphor. (Lakoff – Johnson 1980: 157-158).

It is therefore necessary to present the opponent's position as wrong or morally inferior. Often, this requires reinterpreting political reality to match the respective images of *Self* and *Other*. And this is where metaphors come into the picture: each of the Orientalist frames with its specific set of metaphors offers a partial explanation for the Iraqi invasion of Kuwait and the West's response to it.

The analysis presented in this paper must be seen in the wider framework of a prejudiced East-West relationship, in which the West can hardly see its own views of the East as distorted or one-sided. It is very difficult, if not impossible, to see the world around us with different eyes, since we are literally products of our cultures. In the light of Western, particularly U.S. relations with Arab nations in the Middle East and with Islamic nations in general, it would be rather short-sighted to ignore the religious dimension involved in conceptualizing certain cultures and nations as fundamentally different from ours. Moreover, it would also serve the interests of those who take pains to disconnect religion from other pressing issues, such as ethnic conflicts in many parts of the world, or the disruptive effect of violent nationalism across geographic borders. The next section will therefore, among other things, discuss the influence of religion in the framing of Orientalist conceptualizations of Iraq, the Iraqis and other Arabs involved in the crisis in the Gulf.

3. The *Orientalist* framework

My use of the term *Orientalist* framework is based predominantly on two sources, in the first place on the work of Said:

> From at least the end of the eighteenth century until our own day, modern Occidental reactions to Islam have been dominated by a radically simplified type of thinking that may still be called Orientalist. The general basis of Orientalist thought is an imaginative and yet drastically polarized geography dividing the world into two unequal parts, the larger, "different" one called the Orient, the other, also known as "our" world, called the Occident or the West. ... Insofar as Islam has always been seen as belonging to the Orient, its particular fate within the general structure of Orientalism has been to be looked at first of all as if it were one monolithic thing, and then with a very special hostility and fear. (Said: 1997: 4-5)

The second source is Martín's concept of the "cultural model" that allows people to:

> ... construct their own and others' sense of self by relying on public resources, as well as on private experiences for self-construction. The concept of self of a given culture is an integral part of the cultural model of person of that culture. It includes the image-

schemata, metaphoric and metonymic mappings, and script-like information with which a culture schematizes cognitive-culturally its members ... (Martín 1997: 59).

The overall structure of the Orientalist framework looks as follows: The Orientalist framework represents the basic level of stereotypical thought in the perceptions of *Self* and *Other*. On the second level, there are a certain number of Orientalist frames, structured as interrelated *frames of Self-presentation* and *Other-representation*. Finally, these *frames of Self-presentation* and *Other-representation* are implemented by conceptual metaphors such as "The Oriental is a student" vs. "The Westerner is a teacher".

The rhetorical effect of using such culture-specific conceptualizations of *Self* and *Other* in the context of international relations is that "[t]he context, framework, setting of any discussion ... [is] limited, indeed frozen, by these ideas" (Said 1994: 295). As Said points out, Islam still serves as a "trigger" for international conflicts, since "[t]here ... seems to have been a strange revival of canonical, though previously discredited, Orientalist ideas about Muslim, generally non-white, people – ideas which achieved a startling prominence at a time when racial or religious misrepresentations of every other cultural group are no longer circulated with such impunity" (Said 1997: xi-xii). Based on a different – less politicized – angle is Hofstede's approach to the nature and origin of "culture-dependent differences in thinking and acting" (Hofstede 1980: 9). Thus, he claims that these values, much like the Orientalist pattern of thinking in the West, are transferred by means of a process he refers to as "collective mental programming" (see Hofstede 1980: 16).

By providing a coherent set of Orientalist frames, which contrast the concept of the *Self* constructed by the U.S. with the concept of the *Other*, i.e. Iraq, the Orientalist framework is basically a "cultural cognitive model" serving two main functions:

(1)   to structure a complex political reality in terms of contrastive concepts of *Self* and *Other* (*Us* vs. *Them*);
(2)   to activate Orientalist conceptualizations of Iraq by using linguistic markers such as metaphor.

Before we look into the framing of the Orientalist conceptualization in the following section, it will be helpful to take a closer look at the relationship between the Orient and the West. By using ideas and images associated with what is thought to be typically Oriental, the Western media conceptualize both Iraq and Muslims in general in terms of a neocolonial relationship. The modern version of the West's colonialist approach to the rest of the world can be summed up by two main characteristics, i.e. *Otherness* and *Inequality*. I have listed the most frequently used categories to outline this asymmetrical relationship in Table 1.

Table 1. Orientalism

Us	Them
Civilization	Barbarism
Power	Weakness
Maturity	Immaturity
Rationality	Emotionality
Stability	Instability

The two *worlds*, *Us* and *Them*, in Table 1 represent mutually exclusive catego-ries, epitomizing the *Us-Them* dichotomy. My argument – supported by Said's extensive work on the subject – is that in the post-communist-era, it is Islam, or rather the threat of Islam, that is conceptualized as a potential rival. In the post-cold-war world order, not only have *East* and *West* ceased to designate two formerly antagonistic ideological systems, but they were also stripped of the traditional historical and geographical limitations long ago. Other factors now determine individual states' membership to either category. In other words, the West has come to be a synonym for the powerful, while the East represents the weak. Therefore, any comprehensive analysis of the war in the Gulf has to take into account the role of Islam in the wider context of East-West relations.

Rather, as the Orientalist examples will hopefully prove, contemporary U.S. foreign policy both on the political, economic and military level is still being shaped by a neocolonial/neohegemonic approach to the Orient and the rest of the world in general.[9]

My use of the term Orientalist framework relies, as I indicated earlier, in part on Martín's understanding of culture as "a complex web of cultural meaning systems which provide its members with schematized versions of the world, motivational forces, belief-systems, evokement potentials, institutional orien-tations, etc." (Martín 1997: 55). The Orientalist framework, no doubt, provides the Westerner with "schematized versions" of the Orient skillfully perpetuating both the perceived and the factual contrast between the Orient and the West. In short, as a "cultural cognitive model", the Orientalist framework "works as a sort of intersubjectively-shared 'simplified', 'schematic' version of experience in the world" (Martín 1997: 60).

This, rather than cultural differences, is what constitutes the seemingly in-surmountable gap between the Orient and the West. According to Said, the systematic study of the Orient by Western scholars – not to mention both fic-tional and semi-fictional accounts by nonprofessional Orientalists – has produced a vast pool of images about both the Orient and the Oriental throughout the peak of British and French colonialism in particular. These images were usually handed on – i.e. by way of "collective mental programming" – either by individuals or institutions related to the colonial enterprise. Moreover, these images resulting from the colonial era, clearly reflect the power asymmetry between former colonial powers and colonized peoples. In other words, the contemporary ethnocentric perspective is probably most evident in the terminology dividing the world into East and West from a Euro-American point of view. Among the Orientalist images[10] most Westerners are familiar with either through schooling or cultural encounters (i.e. literature, theater, cinema, television, travel, migration movements) are those depicting the Orient as a place which is characterized by lack of order (chaos even), a degree of alienness which is not to be mistaken for fascination with the exotic, a sense of being restricted by social control, a subordination and discrimination of women, a social system characterized by kinship networks rather than by meritocratic values.

This image of the Orient has been perpetuated by successive generations of novelists, travelers, film producers, advertisers, news agencies etc., laying the foundation for contemporary news media to use these unchallenged conceptualizations of the Orient to contrast the concepts of *Self* and *Other* respectively in order to win public support for the U.S.-led military action against a threat to "our way of life".

4. Framing images

I have been using the term *Orientalist framework* to refer to the superstructure of the metaphor system. This metaphor system consists of a set of Orientalist frames, each of which is structured by a conceptual metaphor. It is also possible to describe these individual metaphorical conceptualizations (or frames) of the Orient as "schemata which are recognizable" to news recipients as they are "inherently structured" (Wallhead Salway 1997: 66). Wallhead Salway (1997: 66) goes on to say that due to this inherent structuring, "some element in the structuring of one schema will tie in somehow with one or more elements in the other schema or schemata evoked in the reader's mind". Wallhead Salway quotes Cook, according to whom the function of such schemata is to influence the mind in such a way that it is "stimulated either by key linguistic items in the text (often referred to as 'triggers' (see Pitrat 1985/1988)), or by the context, [which] activates a schema, and uses it to make sense of the discourse" (Cook 1994: 11 in: Wallhead Salway 1997: 68). Moreover, as Wallhead Salway (1997: 68) suggests, the schemata are flexible in that they prompt the reader "by a point of reference ... to use his knowledge or imagination to fill in the possible gaps", though "[t]his filling in is not totally arbitrary, but governed by the limits of the schema".

What Wallhead Salway and Cook say, applies also to the functioning of the Orientalist framework. Although metaphors were probably the most powerful means of conceptualizing the enemy in terms of *Orientalism*, they were not the only "linguistic mechanisms"[11] used throughout news coverage of the Gulf War. Thus, there was ample use of formulas as in "the Joker of Baghdad *had more tricks up his sleeve*" (*N*, 4 Feb. 91) to refer to Saddam Hussein's futile attempts to work out some compromise. Also, frequent reference was made to historic figures famous both in the Orient and the West, e.g. King Nebuchadnezzar, Saladin, Adolf Hitler and Mussolini to depict Saddam Hussein, whereas the cadet Schwarzkopf was said to have been a fervent admirer of "Alexander the Great, … Caesar, Hannibal and Napoleon" (*N*, 11 March 91) and Gen. Powell was seen as a "*black Eisenhower*" (*N*, 3 Sept. 90). Among the major metonymies used was "the Ruler-for-State" metonymy" as in "get Saddam out of Kuwait" (Lakoff 1992: 467-468). Another "linguistic mechanism" is the use of informal register to enhance the overall effect of the *frames of Self-presentation* and *frames of Other-representation* respectively. That the war of words was not over when the "smart weapons" had done their job, becomes evident when we look at a nationally televised speech at the end of the war, where President Bush was thanking U.S. troops by saying "Thank you *guys*. Thank you very, very much" (*N*, 18 March 91). Words like these make George Bush come across as a leader who knows that this is not his victory alone, a leader who respects his troops and who is convinced of having made the right decision. Saddam Hussein, on the other hand, is portrayed as a ruthless dictator who is willing to sacrifice his soldiers, using them to increase the "cost" of war for the Americans: "Those guys up front are really *dog meat*," says Ralph Ostrich, an analyst at an American defense-consulting firm (*N*, 11 Feb. 91). The choice of lexical items is equally telling, especially nouns, as in "Baghdad's *Butcher*" (*N*, 24 Sept. 90) or "*a monster, … a madman, … a moron*" (*N*, 11 March 91). The choice of verbs is also not accidental as the following examples illustrate, describing Saddam Hussein as trying "to *worm his way around* the sanctions" (*N*, 24 Sept. 90) nor is the selection of adjectives that ridicule Saddam Hussein as in "*paranoid* thug" (*T*, 19 Nov. 90) or "*loose* cannon" (*T*, 5 Nov. 90). By contrast, President Bush was seen as "strong and steady" when he announced the beginning of the ground war (*N*, 4 March 91).

Having outlined the more general dimension of Orientalism, which is effective without using metaphor, it is now necessary to distinguish between two different kinds of Orientalist frames, as the propaganda value of Orientalist metaphors depends on how convincingly the contrast between *Us* and *Them*, i.e. between the positive self-image and the negative image of the enemy is conveyed to "the watching nation" (*N*, 4 Feb. 91). Thus, while the *frames of Self-presentation* serve to convey a positive image of the U.S. and its allies, the *frames of Other-representation* serve to provide a negative image of the enemy, i.e. Iraq. Most, if not all of the frames and conceptual metaphors collected can be seen as dominated by this dualism. The success of the individual frames depends, on the one hand, on their ability to evoke a strong sense of identification in the reader or audience with what is epitomized in *Us*, while triggering feelings of contempt, bewilderment or even fear with regard to *Them*. Each frame covers a different aspect of the conflict, of the Oriental psyche, of the Western practices of dealing with the Orient etc., thus partially structuring the conflict. Which aspect is covered depends on the metaphors that are held together by the same concept, e.g. "the Westerner is rational"/ "the Oriental is emotional". As the examples will reveal, there are occasional clashes even within individual frames, which is an indication of instances where, as Lakoff would probably put it, President Bush (assisted by his huge administrative staff) "couldn't get his story straight" (Lakoff 1992: 467).

5. Frames of Self-presentation vs. frames of Other-representation

The Orientalist frames contain metaphors that provide "mental representations" – a term used by Cook (1995: 146 in: Wallhead Salway 1997: 68) to characterize schemata as typical instances – of the Orient and the Oriental, of Iraq and the Iraqis as well as of other Arabs. As these are mental images based on "cultural cognitive models", the Orient (and by the same token the Oriental) is a state of mind rather than a physical reality. In its turn, this state of mind or mindset is structured in a number of frames. Morgan's understanding and definition of the term *frames* is partly based on the works of Goffman (1974), and Lakoff (1987). According to Morgan,

> ... each of these 'frames' of self-presentation is a multi-element cognitive model with rich traditional linguistic and cultural components and associations, including presuppositions and entailments or inferences, through which a society views, understands, structures, and conducts itself and its activities. Because of this complexity, these cultural frames are often cognitively linked to each other by the intersection or overlap of some of the elements of their idealized cognitive models (Morgan 1997: 276).

Islam as the core element of Orientalist thinking today is "defined negatively as that with which the West is radically at odds, and this tension establishes a framework radically limiting knowledge of Islam" (Said 1997: 163). In the context of Western thinking patterns characterized by Orientalist metaphors, the function of frames within the "cultural cognitive model" of Orientalism is two-dimensional. It is accomplished with much distinction by the use of *frames of Self-presentation* and *frames of Other-representation* respectively. The first conceptualize the Judeo-Christian West in terms of a civilization or world view that has emerged as the "fittest" (in the Darwinist sense) from a global struggle for survival with rival ideologies (notably, and most recently communism) and civilizations. The second, i.e. the *frames of Other-representation*, conceptualize what has been described as *Orientalism* and *Orientalist* thinking at length. In other words, black-and-white images of *Us* and *Them* were used to explain what had happened in the Middle East and what should happen. And when it became more and more obvious that war was unavoidable, many had come to accept the inevitable or what seemed inevitable, since even the most strident critics of war would identify with *Us* – as presented in these frames – rather than with *Them*.

The function of *framing of images* is to present simplified schemata of a complex cultural and political reality. The polarization inherent in the *frames of Self-presentation* and *Other-representation* reveals the manipulative potential that comes from the conceptual metaphors they depend on. Again, as metaphors allow us to come to terms with a less concrete or inherently vaguer concept such as war by structuring it in terms of more concrete concepts, Orientalist frames serve to focus on those aspects of the Orient that are diametrically opposed to the West, while downplaying or hiding aspects shared by both the Orient and the West (see Lakoff – Johnson 1980: 112; 149). By identifying with what is associated with the West (e.g. freedom, human rights, democracy), the public in the West finds it easier to accept the inevitability of war, as to dissent would mean to identify with the enemy's *way of life*. On the other hand, by identifying Orientals with undemocratic, obsolete political and social systems, the war was characterized as serving another altruistic objective, i.e. the emancipation of the Iraqi people, who would eventually have a chance to get rid of a severely weakened Saddam Hussein. Thus, the success of the war-track diplomacy, which meant the failure of the peace-track, was accomplished by Orientalist metaphors that contrasted the positive self-image of the U.S.-led international alliance with the negative image of Iraq, its leader and its army, as well as of Orientals in general.

I will now present some of the total of 16 frames[12] based on the Orientalist conceptual framework. The source domains for the metaphors presented in the respective frames[13] correlate with the polarized keywords presented in Table 1:

5.1. Frame 1: Civilization vs. Barbarism

This frame consists of the conceptual metaphors "Orientals are barbarians" and "Westerners are civilized" with the subframe "the Oriental is immoral, the Westerner is moral". The most forceful image used in news reports on the Gulf war was the conceptualization of Saddam Hussein as a reincarnation of Hitler. In this light, history proved those who favored war right. Both the invasion and the allies' response to the aggression were cast in terms of an eternal battle between *good* and *evil*. The West used historic figures and references to historic events that were reminiscent of their glorious past in order to enhance its positive image. Saddam Hussein on the other hand was conceptualized as a prototypical immoral, inhuman leader who was driven by the basic instincts of survival, greed, and revenge. By means of the "Ruler-for-State" metonymy, these qualities were extended to include all Iraqis if not all ambitious or independent Arab leaders. Thus, Saddam would be seen as heir to countless Oriental rulers who in ancient times had attempted to defeat or actually succeeded in defeating the Judeo-Christian West, such as the Babylonian King Nebuchadnezzar or the Kurdish warrior Saladin.

- *"They have committed outrageous acts of barbarism,"* he [Bush] charged at a rally in Mashpee, Mass. "Brutality – I don't believe that Adolf Hitler ever participated in anything of that nature," he added, in a bit of verbal overkill. (*N*, 12 Nov. 90)
- Three cheers for *the U.S.* for showing *the tyrant Saddam that the civilized world will not tolerate another Adolf Hitler.* [letter to the editor] (*T*, 10 Sept. 90)
- *Saddam sounds like a ninth-century holy warrior preparing to battle the infidel. ... Saddam borrowed his ghoulish threat to make the Americans "swim in their own blood" word for word from Al-Tabari, the Herodotus of the Arab world who chronicled the jihads of the Abbasid Empire.* (*N*, 21 Jan. 91)
- Knowing that he cannot win the war on the battlefield, *Saddam will sacrifice the lives of his own soldiers in order to kill Americans.* (*N*, 11 Feb. 91)
- *Iraq's leader may be a blood-trenched tyrant,* but for many he is nonetheless a symbol of dignity, unity and self-reliance. (*T*, 28 Jan. 91)
- If tanks move into Saudi Arabia, mocking *Baghdad's butcher* may no longer seem so funny. (*N*, 24 Sept. 90)
- Even in the gulf states, where the vast majority of citizens are grateful for *protection from Saddam's hordes,* there is some bitterness on this point. (*T*, 15 Oct. 90)
- *He may well decide to round up the 6,500 Americans and Britons now in Kuwait* and ship them off to Iraq to serve as pawns in a grotesquely Holy War. (*N*, 27 Aug. 90)
- Some oil-industry analysts questioned how much *the Iraqi leader's strong-arm tactics* would achieve in the long run. (*N*, 6 Aug. 90)
- You could see it at work last week in the swollen faces, glazed eyes and mumbling voices of *the American, British, Italian and Kuwaiti airmen that Saddam Hussein dogmarched through Baghdad and grilled on TV.* (*N*, 4 Feb. 91)
- *Saddam's attempt to "hide behind Western women and children"* was "utterly repulsive"" said Prime Minister Margaret Thatcher. (*T*, 3 Sept. 90)
- If there is a consensus among Kuwaitis about anything, it is this: despite its vast wealth, *Kuwaiti society was sick,* and not merely because of democratic failings or the poor treatment of expatriates. (*T*, 24 Dec. 90)
- According to Scowcroft [National Security Adviser], the gulf crisis poses a crucial question: "Can the U.S. use force – even go to war – for carefully

defined national interests, or do we have to have *a moral crusade* or a galvanizing event like Pearl Harbor?" (*T*, 7 Jan. 91)
- Operation Desert Storm, which started just six weeks before with the launching of the air war, produced a stunning victory for Bush, *a triumph of almost Biblical proportions* – his enemy slain in countless numbers, his own soldiers hardly touched by the battlefield's scouring wind. (*N*, 11 March 91)
- *President Bush* stood in front of the United Nations last week and *offered what seemed like an olive branch to Saddam Hussein.* (*N*, 15 Oct. 90)
- "This is a long, long way from home, but I think *Americans are home wherever their principles are,* " he [James Baker to U.S. troops] said. (*N*, 28 Jan. 91)
- Schwarzkopf: *A Soldier of Conscience.* (*N*, 11 March 91)

5.2. Frame 2: Power vs. Weakness

Here, the relationship between the Orient and the West is conceptualized in terms of an asymmetrical power distribution. As power is always relative, Iraq, too, can be seen as powerful though only as compared to those who are weaker. The subframe "the Oriental is effeminate or emasculated" builds on the conceptualization of power as gender-related both in the Orient and the West. Traditionally, power has been associated with masculinity, while weakness is equated with femininity. Hofstede's extensive cross-cultural study represents valuable research on this issue (1980: 261-311; ch. 6 on "Masculinity"). On the basis of his 40-country-survey on national differences in masculinity and femininity, Hofstede (1980: 278-279) measures these countries' "masculinity" pattern by means of the "MAS" (i.e. "Country Masculinity Index"). The "MAS" (ranging between zero and 100) reflects the degree of importance the respondents attached to occupation-related masculinity and femininity values. As Iraq was not part of the research, the data for Iran will be used here to compare the "MAS" values of the U.S. and Iraq in the context of their power relations. Thus, the U.S. were well above average with a "MAS" of 62, while Iran had a "MAS" of 43, slightly below average. However, even more important are what Hofstede (1980: 288) refers to as the "connotations" of the "MAS Index". For instance, while "Low MAS countries" are characterized by believing in "group decisions", "High MAS countries" are characterized by a "[b]elief in the independent decision maker" (1980: 288). This is just one example of what is conceived of as a culture-specific view related to the process of decision-making in the U.S and Iraq respectively. The difference in "MAS" value for the U.S. and Iraq respectively strengthens the idea underlying conceptualizations of the Orient as weak and therefore feminine or rather emasculated, while the more powerful West is seen as masculine. As Lakoff (1992: 477), too, points out, "it is common for Arabs to conceptualize the colonization and subsequent domination of the Arab world by the West, especially the US as emasculation". At times, the West, which is well aware of the association between political power and masculinity in the Arab world, uses this image to emphasize the power asymmetry between themselves and the Iraqis. However, according to the "just-war scenario", it is Kuwait which is conceptualized as "a weak, defenseless country", "as female", while Iraq is conceptualized as "a strong militarily powerful country", "as male" (Lakoff 1992: 477). Once again, power relationships are always relative. But the power of the conceptual metaphor "Kuwait-as-rape-victim" lies in the strong moral implications, i.e. the utter contempt for the violator and the unconditional sympathy for the victim. Moreover, whoever rescues the victim and punishes the aggressor becomes a hero, a role that the U.S. could easily identify with. Also noteworthy in this context is that the violator is being punished for attacking someone weaker than himself by being emasculated by the more powerful hero or savior. However, as the conceptualization of the U.S. as "a bankrupt, castrated giant" (*N*, 24 Sept. 90) shows, apart from military power, financial power, too, plays a role in determining whether a country is conceived of as masculine or feminine. Thus, health as an indication of national power is expressed in terms of sexual power. The political domination of the Arab world by the West is therefore described as an "Arab malaise" (*N*, 27 Aug. 90).

- Eager to divert attention from *his rape of Kuwait*, the Iraqi leader has tried repeatedly to drag Israel onto center stage in order to convince his fellow Arabs that the enemy is not Iraq but the Zionists and their American backers. (*T*, 22 Oct. 90)
- "*Any time an independent Arab leader looks strong*," he [an old man in Bahrain] boomed, "*the West beats him down.*" (*T*, 15 Oct. 90)
- After all, he would be expected to lose a fight with a superpower, but he might well gain respect for *standing up to the U.S. hard and long*. (*T*, 21 Jan. 91)
- "Preparing the battlefield," the euphemism Schwarzkopf used *for emasculating the Iraqi Army*, had changed the arithmetic. (*N*, 18 March 91)
- One reason for *Iraqi impotence* in the early gulf war was U.S. mastery of the electronic battlefield. (*N*, 28 Jan. 91)
- *Up goes a Scud-like proposal from Kuwait. Down it comes, crushed by a rhetorical Patriot from George Bush.* (*N*, 25 Feb. 91)
- That raised a question: did Dugan knowingly risk his career to put forth the Air Force view that air power is enough *to bring Iraq to its knees*? (*N*, 1 Oct. 90)
- And he [James Baker] privately winced at some *of Bush's macho threats to* "*kick ass*". (*N*, 14 Jan. 91)
- Meanwhile European pundits wrote about the final demise of *both* [this emphasis not mine] superpowers and *buried the United States as a bankrupt, castrated giant*. (*N*, 24 Sept. 90)

5.3. Frame 3: Maturity vs. Immaturity

This frame consists of the conceptual metaphor "the Oriental is a student"/ "the Westerner is a teacher". As in Frame 2, here too, the relationship between the Orient and the West is not one between equals. Rather, one party is in control and the other is controlled. In the case of the student-teacher relationship, the Oriental is conceptualized as someone who is in need of cultural (e.g. women's liberation), political (e.g. political freedom) and economic (e.g. capitalism) education or instruction. This metaphor implies that Orientals, like students, have a lower level of knowledge and experience. The Westerner, on the other hand, is conceptualized as culturally, politically, and economically advanced, i.e. in a position to educate, instruct, and guide. The student is expected to reach the same state through a process of upbringing and education. The teacher on the other hand is expected to be altruistic, his only objective being the healthy mental and physical development of the entrusted student. To accomplish this, teachers have to be patient as the young lack the knowledge and experience which would enable them to make the right decisions.

Also implicit in this conceptualization is that students can become something of a nuisance or problem if they do not fulfill expectations, indulge in provocative behavior or destabilize the rest of the class – or rather, in this context, the "family of nations" – by trying to have it their own way. Thus, the U.S. responded as a responsible teacher to Iraq's invasion of Kuwait. But not only had it become necessary to restore the pre-invasion status and the power balance in the region. In addition, it was said, this was an opportunity to teach a lesson in international politics. After the collapse of the Soviet Union, the U.S. was eager to demonstrate that the idea of two superpowers was not indispensable. Moreover, the superiority of U.S. hightech military equipment and superbly trained personnel could wipe out the Vietnam trauma and restore trust in the U.S. The asymmetry inherent in this relationship is that the "teacher" is allowed to determine everything, i.e. the "teaching methods", the "evaluation" of the performance, and most importantly, the "subjects" (in this context, democracy) to be taught. In the cold-war-era, there had been two main ideologies, not to choose from, but at least to identify with, which gave domination a better face. However, in the post-cold-war era, the "student", here Iraq, is put in a class he/she does not even want to belong to. The *way of life* represented by the U.S. can neither be translated into Iraqi culture and society nor is it desirable. But, as the fashionable phrase "new world order" suggests, it is not for those to question it who have no share in designing it. All they can do is take the place assigned them and try their best to please. Unfortunately, many Arab states are conceptualized as unsuccessful students who have to be disciplined and put back in their place from time to time. The conceptualization of the U.S. as a stern teacher implies the notion that adults sometimes have "to be cruel to be kind", to achieve certain educational objectives. Not rewarding Iraq's aggression by negotiating, which was misrepresented as "compromise", was considered to be the best way to achieve the educational objective, i.e. punish a defiant "student", here Saddam Hussein, and help his country return to the peaceful family of nations, though supervision was considered necessary.

- *Saddam seemed to be playing his familiar role as bully of the Middle East.* (*N*, 6 Aug. 90)
- Much of the talk about a new world order started a year ago, when *Saddam was just another loudmouth bullyboy* who was being paid off by the Gulf Arabs, lethally equipped by the Soviets, as well as the French and Germans, and coddled by the U.S. (*T*, 28 Jan. 91)
- "At one level, for the very first time in Saddam's career *he is exactly where he wants to be – at the center of power, the focus of attention*," says Jerrold Post, a specialist in psychological profiles of world leaders. (*N*, 10 Dec. 90)
- The feckless international response to his muscle flexing during the past decade has nourished his belief that he has little to fear *if he misbehaves.* (*T*, 13 Aug. 90)
- Such a humiliation, they hope, will hasten his overthrow or, at the least, *teach him a lesson.* (*T*, 27 Aug. 90)
- *Saddam has memorized the lesson of Ho Chi Minh*: that no matter how superior America's force in the field, it cannot win without the hearts and minds of the American people. (*N*, 10 Dec. 90)
- *Bush sounds like a high-school football coach on the eve of the Big Game.* ... *The battlefield evoked by Bush has yard markers and goal posts at either end. To Westerners, war has long been seen as rather sporting.* (*N*, 21 Jan. 91)
- *One reason George Bush was so determined to punch this bully in the nose was to deter the other bullies in the schoolyard.* (*N*, 11 March 91)
- *This is a war to punish Saddam*, not the entire Arab world. (*N*, 28 Jan. 91)
- Iraq's ambassador to Britain was summoned to the Foreign Office and *given a 20-minute dressing down.* (*T*, 27 Aug. 90)
- *Jordan has often been praised by the West* for its political realism and moderation. (*N*, 10 Sept. 90)
- *Egypt* – which is sending two mechanized divisions totaling 30,000 personnel to Saudi Arabia and which, in facing up to Saddam, has absorbed economic losses that President Hosni Mubarak estimates at $9 billion – *gets a grade of A+* from Congressman Aspin. Many *others*, however, *deserve a D – or an F.* (*T*, 24 Dec. 90)
- "*We've got a carrot-and-stick policy*," said Baker, "*and the carrot is, if he gets out, he doesn't get the stick.*" (*N*, 17 Dec. 90)
- *Desert Storm was a didactic war, waged to instruct potential aggressors in new rules for the game of nations.* (*N*, 11 March 91)
- *A Textbook Victory.* (*N*, 11 March 91)

- My concern is that in cases of future aggression there will be a temptation *to use Iraq as a model* simply because it worked so well. [American Historian James MacGregor Burns.] (*N*, 11 March 91)
- There is also much talk of maintaining a permanent U.S. presence in Saudi Arabia *to keep Iraq honest*, but most analysts outside the Administration doubt the Arabs would tolerate that for long. (*T*, 10 Sept. 90)

5.4. Frame 4: Rationality vs. Emotionality

This frame depends on two main stereotypes: "Orientals are emotional" and "Westerners are rational". Accordingly, the Orient is conceptualized as ruled by emotionality rather than by rationality and the implication is that this is simply a case of cultural difference, i.e. something that cannot be changed and has to be accepted when dealing with Orientals. This contrast is not only applied to Saddam Hussein and George Bush as the representative adversaries in the crisis, but it is also extended to include on the one hand, the people they represent, and on the other hand, the culture and value system they stand for, i.e. the West and the Orient. A subframe, i.e. "arguments are paths" vs. "arguments are circles" in the West and in the Orient respectively, expands the difference into culture-dependent thinking modes. The Western way of thinking is characterized as linear, as one of rational development (see Lakoff – Johnson 1980: 89-91). The Oriental way of thinking is conceptualized as circular and taken to be true of Saddam Hussein as well as of Orientals at large. From the Western point of view this means that an argument made by an Oriental leads nowhere as it typically returns to the starting point. With regard to the Gulf crisis, this rendered negotiations between the respective leaders meaningless from the very start. However, as rationality may also be interpreted as a lack of compassion, which is a positive kind of emotionality, George Bush, it is occasionally pointed out, had to struggle to remain cool-headed. By establishing this fundamental cognitive contrast between Saddam Hussein and George Bush, between the Orientals and the Westerners, and repeating it over and over again, the Western public gradually came to accept the dismissal of diplomatic efforts in favor of a military option. Another stereotype related to both Frame 3 and Frame 5 conceptualized Orientals as respecting political leaders for pursuing omnipotent (or pan-Arabic) ambitions, while showing less admiration for leaders with diplomatic skills. This stereotype not only questioned the Oriental's political maturity but it also suggested an imbalance between emotionality and rationality in favor of emotionality in the average Oriental. However, an obvious asymmetry remains in the conceptualization of Saddam Hussein as ruled by emotion rather than by logic. Thus, as Lakoff (1992: 466) points out, the Iraqi leader's decisions and political moves are perfectly in line with the "rationality is the maximization of self-interest" metaphor. Another asymmetry is the initial view (as long as the *peace-track* was credibly pursued) that rationality was something that could be "talked into the Iraqis". These two examples are clearly in conflict and even in contradiction with the aura of "emotionality" stamped on the Arab world, as the reasoning here seems to be that neither Saddam Hussein, nor the Iraqis at large, are devoid of rationality. Rather, rationality is viewed as something that can be restored if lost temporarily.

- *Logic in the Arab world is often eclipsed by emotion.* (*T*, 27 Aug. 90)
- And, he adds, "given the unstable political *environment in the region, in which emotions take precedence over rationality*, calculated deterrence may simply not work in the Middle East." (*N*, 2 July 90)
- "*Saddam Hussein thinks in terms of circles*," said Amitzia Baram, a Haifa University expert on Iraq. (*N*, 13 Aug. 90).
- Surely, *Saddam Hussein must have been out of his mind to invade Kuwait* ... (*N*, 1 Oct. 90)
- "I haven't seen *sense or reason from Saddam*," Bush told congressional leaders. (*N*, 10 Sept. 90)
- With sanctions serving only to increase Saddam's belligerence and *the West struggling to fathom his thinking*, war looks more and more inevitable. (*T*, 8 Oct. 90)
- "*King Hussein is running around rather frantically*," Bush was quoted as telling congressional leaders. (*N*, 10 Sept. 90)
- *Bush soberly assessed the costs of conflict.* (*N*, 29 Oct. 90)
- Bush has tried hard *not to be swayed by emotionalism.* (*N*, 3 Sept. 90
- The secretary-general of the United Nations, Javier Pérez de Cuellar, flew to Amman to see if he could *talk some sense into the Iraqis.* (*N*, 10 Sept. 90)

5.5. Frame 5: Stability vs. Instability

This is the category that reveals most clearly that these images of the Orient are detached from physical reality, and they are used to project upon the physically real nation states a conceptualization which has not so much to do with experiences of the Orient but with preconceived ideas about it. For example, oil-rich Arab states such as Kuwait and Saudi Arabia are described as "*built on sand*" (*N*, 13 Aug. 90). The most significant implication here is that the Orient is as unreal and thus as brittle as a fictional place in the political and geographic sense. At this level, the Orient's divergency from the West is either metaphorically conceptualized in terms of natural forces (e.g. the Orient is seen as "volcanic", "out of balance" or "turbulent") or in terms of imagination, or even as a form of deception, as reflected by references to fairytales, stories or wishful thinking. The stability vs. instability frame contains a subframe, i.e. "reality vs. illusion", which is also related to Frame 2 as it establishes power relations between the Orient and the West: as a Western invention, the Orient remains subject to Western reinvention. Thus, in line with its conceptualization as a

fairytale location, the Orient is seen as bound to evaporate (due to disillusion-
ment) or to be destroyed by some kind of outside interference. As a consequence, military or other interventions in the Orient are perceived as less mo-
mentous. The subframe "reality vs. illusion" also illustrates how the average
Oriental's mental and emotional condition is conceptualized as unbalanced,
unpredictable and uncontrollable in analogy to natural forces. Westerners, by
contrast, are conceived of as balanced, reliable and controled. This dichotomy
is indissolubly linked to the Western conception of the superiority of rationality
over emotionality. According to the Western principle of "objective truth" –
discussed at great length and in considerable depth by Lakoff and Johnson
(1980) – emotion is believed to have to be controled by reason and not the other
way round. Therefore, attempts by the West to enforce and maintain a balance
of power in the region are doomed to fail because Saddam Hussein is depicted
as an Oriental leader who "can rock the world" and thus "throw everyone off
balance". Another aspect of the subframe "reality vs. illusion" is implied by the
metaphor conceptualizing Arab leadership as illusory, an act of self-deception.
Thus, Pan-Arabism is conceived of as an *Arabian Dream* that – unlike its
American equivalent – will not come true, as Arabs lack the kind of unity that
would enable them to act as one.

- *He has the army, the arsenal and the audacity to pursue his grand ambition
  to rule the region – or rock the world.* (*T*, 13 Aug. 90)
- They all laughed nervously; *Saddam had thrown everyone off balance.* (*N*,
  28 Jan. 91)
- The bigger problem is that *oil* is not spread randomly: it *is concentrated in
  a region of volcanic politics.* (*N*, 20 Aug. 90)
- Bush's bright hopes for gathering more Republican strength in swelling
  Florida, Texas and California in the election just two months distant are now
  also tied to *the shifting sands of the Middle East.* (*T*, 10 Sept. 90)
- Either way, *if war breaks out, the tremors will shake the entire Arab world.*
  (*N*, 14 Jan. 91)
- As the source of three great religions, *it* [the Middle East] *has always in-
  spired great passions.* (*N*, 28 Jan. 91)
- As war in the gulf looks ever more probable, *the uneasiness and frustration
  of ordinary citizens are beginning to bubble over.* (*T*, 15 Oct. 90)
- *The rising tide of pro-Iraqi sentiment* has caught some by surprise: many of
  the 3 million Egyptian laborers who worked in Iraq before the war brought
  back tales of horror about life in that country. (*N*, 18 Feb. 91)
- *The Kuwaitis thought they would live happily ever after – until Iraq came
  and took Never-Never Land away.* (*N*, 13 Aug. 90)
- I spent five days last week with an Egyptian commando battalion that was
  eyeball to bellybutton with the Iraqi Army *in the center of No Man's Land.*
  [Col. David H. Hackworth] (*N*, 25 Feb. 91)

- In economic terms, the have-nots see little future except as part *of that dream kingdom known as the Arab Nation.* (*T*, 27 Aug. 90)
- *The "Arab Nation" to which they all swore fidelity existed more as a state of mind than as any reality of state.* (*N*, 28 Jan. 91)
- Japan and Germany should share a big chunk of *the financial costs of keeping the world in balance.* [Yasuhiro Nakasone, former Japanese Prime Minister] (*N*, 11 March 91)

6. Conclusion

There is strong evidence that news coverage of the Persian Gulf War made ample use of *Orientalism* or what has been discussed at some length in the second part as the "idealized cognitive model" that dominates Western thought and action with regard to *the Orient.* Since the Orientalist stereotypes had disastrous implications for the way the Iraqi invasion of Kuwait was handled, the analysis of East-West relations against this Orientalist background helps to understand why Iraq – in the post-cold-war era – still finds itself on the other side. It should be clear now that *the West* continues to be used as a label in the aftermath of the cold war to refer to the dominant political, economic, and cultural world system. In other words, it is the "club" that everyone wants to belong to in order to share the prerogatives that come with membership. As the Gulf War has shown, it is the West that determines who qualifies for membership by defining what is "West". My thesis in this study has been that Orientalist metaphors conceptualized the enemy, Iraq, in terms of traditionally rich associations with the Orient, and Islam as an integral part of it, in order to justify the war as a way to protect Western civilization and its way of life.

In order to conceptualize the enemy as a threat to the rest of the world, at least to Western civilization, news coverage relied heavily on the Orientalist framework, characterized by the conceptual metaphors presented in frames 1-5, which are but a fraction of the total picture[14] that emerged from the data analysis. Thus, the Orientalist framework, as the overarching theoretical structure, polarized the world into the Orient and the West, into *Us* and *Them.* For the Iraqis, this meant that they – as part of the Orient and the Islamic world – were associated with images of barbarism, weakness, immaturity, emotionality and instability (see frames 1-5), while the West was equated with the opposite images, i.e. civilization, power, maturity, rationality and stability. These representations of Iraq and the Iraqis served to demonize the enemy, while accumulating in the self-images everything that was worth fighting for. The simplified and schematized conceptualization of Iraq as part of the Orient thus justified a hard-line approach to the Gulf crisis which eventually led to war. Key elements of this simplification and schematization were the "mental representations", the stereotypical ideas and images regarding the Orient which the West has still not been able to give up and probably never will. Despite the negative connotations of the term, this attitude therefore reflects neocolonialism as the dominant cognitive pattern in the West to explain and deal with the cultural and political reality of the Orient.

It seems that as long as the Orient, in particular the Muslim Orient, is used by the West, in particular by the U.S., as a foil, as the embodiment of all that is a threat to "our way of life", international conflicts between the powerful and the weak nations in the world will continue to turn regional conflicts into military showdowns between Islam and the rest of the world.

Notes

1. The argument of this paper was first presented as *More metaphorical warfare in the Gulf* at the 5th International Cognitive Linguistics Conference in Amsterdam (July 1997); I am much indebted to Prof. René Dirven for many valuable criticisms and suggestions. I also benefited from helpful suggestions from the editor.
2. I am greatly indebted to the work of Edward W. Said, whose insights form the cornerstone of my argument in this paper and elsewhere.
3. Said (1997: xix) claims that in discussions of Islam, "[t]he norms of rational sense are suspended." Part of my thesis is devoted to the argument that the suspension of "the norms of rational sense" not only applies to "discussions" of Islam, but even more importantly – as the Gulf War shows – it applies to political interaction with Orientals.
4. *BBC* radio, for instance, listed dozens of songs "unsuitable" for wartime play, including "Everybody Wants to Rule the World", "Give Peace a Chance", "Walk Like an Egyptian", and "We've Got to Get Out of This Place". (see *N*, 4 Feb. 91).
5. This two-track policy has been characteristic of U.S. relationships with the Middle East. A war in the Gulf would definitely help the U.S. facilitate Arab-Israeli peace talks: By reducing Iraq's warmaking capacity, the U.S. could pressure Israel to finally find a solution to the so-called Palestinian problem with the other Arabs. On the other hand, moderate Arab leaders who qualified for negotiations with Israel, had to be helped to gain a strong stand in the Arab world as many Arabs – like many Israelis – do not like the prospect of a negotiated solution, fearing that it will be less advantageous for them than for Israel.
6. By calling these objectives "secondary", I do not mean to diminish their importance, rather I mean that they were not initially stated as official objectives.
7. My use of the term *frame* to refer to what I had hitherto called metaphor *categories* was inspired by Pamela S. Morgan's paper.
8. Throughout my discussion, I abbreviate news magazine names as follows: *NEWSWEEK (N), TIME (T)*.
9. Relatively recent examples of how the U.S. regards sovereign nations as within its sphere of influence are President Reagan's sending U.S. Marines to Beirut in 1982, the invasion of Grenada in 1983, the military aid given to the Nicaraguan contras, the raid on Libya and the overthrow of the U.S.-backed regime of Ferdinand Marcos in the Philippines in 1986. In 1989, the U.S. – under President Bush – invaded Panama using a similarly evocative code-name as in the Gulf War, i.e. *Operation Just Cause*.

10. Among the most popular and widely read sources of "collective mental programming" is, no doubt, *Arabian Nights*, a collection of folktales. And the story of "Ali Baba and the Forty Thieves" can be seen as an epitome of the situation in the Middle East. Among the most obvious parallels between Ali Baba and contemporary Orientals that come to mind are that both Ali Baba and the oil sheiks owe their incredible wealth to sheer luck, both seem to be trusting the wrong people, both are helpless when it comes to defending themselves, both are described as materialistic and fall victim to brotherly envy, both are considered as undemocratic (Ali Baba has several slaves; similarly, the West described the foreign workers in Saudi Arabia and Kuwait as second-class citizens), and both are associated with a fatalistic world view.

11. My use of the term *linguistic mechanisms* is based on Morgan's use of frame-evoking linguistic mechanisms in her analysis of a speech by Newt Gingrich.

12. Some of the Orientalist frames include metaphors that correlate with categories of structural metaphors Pancake presented in her paper, notably her categories "War is a game", "War is entertainment" and "The war zone is the Wild West".

13. The examples in the frames are accompanied by parentheses indicating the source, i.e. either *N* for *NEWSWEEK* or *T* for *TIME*, and the issue. The square brackets give additional information that may not be evident from the sentence context though for the sake of inspection and clarity, some of the full contexts in which the examples occur are quoted in the subsections listing examples of Orientalist metaphors. Italics are used to mark the metaphorical conceptualizations in the examples classified as Orientalist.

14. A more complete picture of *Orientalism* as it appears from the Gulf War news coverage will be presented at the ICLA Conference in Stockholm in 1999.

References

Barcelona, Antonio (ed.)
 1997   *Linguistica cognitiva aplicada al estudio de la lengua inglesa y su literatura / Cognitive Linguistics in the Study of the English Language and Literature in English*. Monograph issue of *Cuadernos de Filologia Inglesa*, 6:2.
Chomsky, Noam
 1979   *Language and responsibility*. Sussex: The Harvester Press.
Cook, Guy
 1994   *Discourse and literature: The interplay of form and mind*. Oxford: Oxford University Press.
Goffman, Erving
 1974   *Frame analysis: An essay on the organization of experience*. Boston: Northeastern University Press.
Hofstede, Geert
 1980   *Culture's consequences: International differences in work-related values*. (Cross cultural research and methodology series 5.) Beverly Hills: Sage Publications.

Lakoff, George
    1987   *Women, fire and dangerous things. What categories reveal about the mind.* Chicago: Chicago University Press.
    1992   "Metaphor and war: The metaphor system used to justify war in the gulf", in: Martin Pütz (ed.), *Thirty years of linguistic evolution: Studies in honour of René Dirven on the occasion of his sixtieth birthday.* Philadelphia – Amsterdam: Benjamins, 463-481.
Lakoff, George – Mark Johnson
    1980   *Metaphors we live by.* Chicago – London: The University of Chicago Press.
Martín, José M.
    1997   "The cultural cognitive model: A programmatic application", in: Antonio Barcelona (ed.), 53-63.
Morgan, Pamela S.
    1997   "Self-presentation in a speech of Newt Gingrich", *Pragmatics,* 7 (3): 275-308.
Pancake, Ann S.
    1993   "Taken by storm: The exploitation of metaphor in the Persian Gulf War", *Metaphor and Symbolic Activity,* 8 (4): 281-295.
Said, Edward W.
    1979   *Orientalism.* New York: Vintage Books.
    1994   *Culture and imperialism.* New York: Vintage Books.
    1997   *Covering Islam: How the media and the experts determine how we see the rest of the world.* (Revised and updated edition.) New York: Vintage Books.
Wallhead Salway, Celia
    1997   "Schema disruption in the re-writing of history: Salman Rushdie's *East, West*", in: Antonio Barcelona (ed.), 65-80.

Muted metaphors and the activation of metonymies in advertising

Friedrich Ungerer

1. Introduction

There are several reasons why advertisements are particularly suitable for an analysis in terms of metonymy and metaphor. The products advertised are never really present in the advert, they are represented by a picture or a brand name, which metonymically stand for the item in question. Similarly, the act of buying, which is the ultimate goal of consumer advertising, is never executed in the advert, but is at best approached by requests like *Buy X. Go and get X right away. Don't wait. Order now. Fill in and post coupon now. Ring our hotline now.* More sophisticated adverts take pains not to address the act of buying or ordering directly and do not verbalize how desirable the purchase of the advertised item should be for the addressee. Yet there can be no doubt that this indirect kind of advertising works, indeed it is often more effective than the cruder, more straightforward variants. The reason is not just that we "know" what the purpose of advertising is (the pragmatic explanation; Nöth 1983, Vestergaard & Schrøder 1985). Taking a cognitive perspective, the link between the advertised product and the arousal of the consumer's desire seems to be established by another powerful conceptual metonymy, the "grabbing metonymy", which will be introduced below.

Turning to metaphors, their role in advertising can hardly be underestimated. No matter whether the advertised item is represented in the advert as a picture or a brand name, it is never presented in isolation, i.e. the conceptualization is never restricted to the concept of the item itself. The "link between the domain of the advertised item and other domains" (if we start out from this very broad definition of metaphor) may be expressed by linguistic means, either by an explicit, but rather ineffective statement like *This lotion is used by Royals and film stars* or, to take the other extreme, by the metaphorical potential inherent in many trade names, such as *Crown,* or *Royal* or *Provence,* or by some intermediate linguistic realization. What is even more important in modern advertising are the links between domains established by the pictorial elements of adverts. From a cognitive stance, these pictorial links can be understood as instantiations of conceptual metaphors just like the linguistic realizations with which they often interact. This is an area which has been explored for some time now, attracting the interest of both semioticians (Barthes 1993[1]) and general linguists interested in metaphor (Forceville 1996).

Compared with the huge range of research goals in the field, the scope of this paper is very restricted. Far from attempting a comprehensive description and evaluation of the role played by metaphors or metonymies in advertising, it tries to show in a very exemplary way how these two conceptual processes interact. The examples used are taken from consumer adverts, mostly from the magazines of British national Sunday papers published between March 30 and April 13, 1997. To keep the material manageable the paper concentrates on adverts with little copy, though the conceptual processes discussed should also be reflected in the bulkier adverts with more text.

As a first step, the basic setup of the GRABBING metonymy and the VALUE metaphor will be introduced in the next section. Further sections will discuss the function of INTEREST metaphors introducing the notion of muted metaphors and showing how they interact with various types of (conventional) metonymies. The final remarks will be devoted to trade names, which promise to offer a nutshell version of the essential conceptual structure of adverts.

2. The basic setup: the grabbing metonymy and the value metaphor

2.1 The GRABBING metonymy

One of the more noticeable occupations of babies and little children is that they tend to get hold of things. In the initial phase this is a matter of clutching the objects offered to them, perhaps a rather reflex-like movement, but later clutching develops into the action of grabbing the things that catch the eye, sparkling or noise-producing objects and the like. In the later stages of our lives this instinctive urge to grab desirable things is more subdued, but it is still active.

How can one claim that grabbing has something to do with the conceptual structure of adverts and how can it be explained in terms of metonymy? If we want to pursue this argument, we have to endorse two claims: First we have to agree with the judgment of psychologists that DESIRE is to be understood as an emotion, even as one of the basic emotions beside ANGER, SADNESS, FEAR and JOY (Johnson-Laird – Oatley 1989, 1992, Ungerer 1995: 187). The second claim we have to accept is that grabbing can be seen as a semi-volitional bodily movement, similar to the jumping up and down movements often accompanying emotions like JOY. This puts the action of grabbing into the range of physiological manifestations of emotions, which are covered by Lakoff and Kövecses' general metonymic principle that PHYSIOLOGICAL EFFECTS OF AN EMOTION STAND FOR THE EMOTION (Lakoff 1987: 382). Figure 1 provides an overview of major physiological metonymies for basic emotions derived from metonymic expressions discussed by Kövecses (1986, 1990a, 1990b, 1991) and empirical data collected by psychologists (Ungerer 1995: 188-190).

Types of physiological phenomena	*Example*
(1) Change in body temperature	drop in body temperature for FEAR
(2) Change in skin color/skin condition	redness in face and neck area for ANGER
(3) Release of sweat, tears, saliva	moist hands for FEAR, tears for SADNESS
(4) Change of respiration and heart rate	quickening of heartbeat for ANGER
(5) Unnatural condition of stomach/bowels	feeling nauseated for DISGUST, FEAR
(6) Bodily tension /release of tension	fists and teeth clenched for ANGER
(7) Specific kinds of physical movements	slow, shuffling movements for SADNESS
	heavy walk, stomping for ANGER
	being startled for FEAR
	jumping up and down for JOY
	touching, hugging, kissing for LOVE
	grabbing for DESIRE
(8) Interference with functioning of senses/speaking, etc.	inability to see properly for LOVE
	inability to speak for FEAR
(9) General agitation	sense of being keyed up for ANGER, JOY

Figure 1. An overview of physiological metonymies for basic emotions
(SADNESS, ANGER, DISGUST/HATE, FEAR, JOY, DESIRE/LOVE)

Looking at Figure 1, it is obvious that physiological metonymies include a wide range of phenomena, reaching from completely nonvolitional, vegetative symptoms like drop of body temperature, redness in the face and neck area or sweating (group 1-3) to the semi-volitional group of movements (group 7) and to borderline cases with psychological reactions such as the inability to speak and the general feeling of being "keyed up" (group 8 and 9). Against this background, the grabbing metonymy is justly placed in group 7, where it seems to hold a middle position, more volitional than being startled (as metonymy for FEAR), but less volitional than hugging and kissing (as metonymies for LOVE).

Establishing grabbing as a physiological metonymy for DESIRE may not appease critics who hold more traditional views about metonymy. Indeed, the notion of a metonymic relationship between emotions and physiological phenomena requires an extension of the classical concept of metonymy. Physiological metonymies differ considerably from the relatively unambiguous relationships involved in part-for-whole (or whole-for-part), place-for-institution/event, or producer-for-product metonymies. The conventional metonymy they come closest to is causation, but even here the similarities are limited because the question whether the physiological phenomena are the effect (as is often assumed; Kövecses – Radden 1998:56) or the cause of the emotion has never really been settled. Considering the various arguments, it may not be beside the point to assume that in this type of metonymy the physiological phenomenon may simultaneously represent cause, effect and, in addition, accompaniment. More modern approaches, like Croft's (1993), which is based on Langacker's notions of domain and domain matrix, will also have their difficulties in pinning down the peculiar relationship involved in physiological metonymies. Yet in spite of the evasiveness and ambiguity of physiological metonymies, the powerful part they play in the conceptualization of emotion concepts is not really disputed. Taking all this into account, it is still worthwhile to understand the grabbing phenomenon as a physiological metonymy, which, in the spirit of Lakoff and Kövecses, can be formulated as GRABBING THE DESIRED OBJECT STANDS FOR DESIRE.

Another advantage of the GRABBING metonymy comes to the fore when we consider that emotions can be seen as scenarios (Kövecses, etc.), as a sequence of stages, discontinuous as this sequence may often be. Yet wherever the notion of scenario has been claimed convincingly, the final stage is some sort of action. This is true of the negative emotions of ANGER and FEAR with their five-stage sequence of "cause-emotion-attempt at control-loss of control-action" (Lakoff 1987: 397-98; Ungerer – Schmid 1996: 141). It seems that this action stage is also a strong option in the case of the positive emotion of DESIRE, much more so than for the emotions of JOY or even LOVE. In other words, DESIRE has the inherent action potential that is proposed as the last element of the well-known AIDA formula (Attention-Interest-Desire-Action), which is not only recommended in practical guidelines for advertising copy writers, but also used in the pragmatic interpretation of adverts (Vestergaard – Schrøder 1985). Needless to say how welcome this action potential of the GRABBING metonymy is in the context of advertising.

Since cognitive linguists are also linguists, it is natural for them to ask questions about the linguistic or at least the communicative realization of conceptual structures, and this includes the GRABBING metonymy. One of the answers is to claim all the verbal imperatives quoted above (*Buy X. Go and get X right away,* etc.) as realizations of the GRABBING metonymy. The problem already touched upon is that these "hard-sell strategies" (Kwanka 1993 ms) are avoided or at least suppressed in the more sophisticated kinds of consumer advertising today. An alternative (though not really a linguistic one) is the visualization of the metonymy, which is probably felt to be less aggressive and may be regarded as a transition from hard-selling to soft-selling strategies. In print advertising the visualization of the GRABBING metonymy is limited to certain actions, especially licking ice-cream or picking a chocolate from a chocolate box, although a photograph of the actual application of a shampoo or toothpaste is also feasible (of course, there are many more possibilities in TV commercials).

The last, and at the same time, most radical option is to concede that often the GRABBING metonymy is not explicitly expressed at all, neither linguistically nor visually, but that it is to be regarded as an underlying, but nevertheless essential, conceptual component of the advert – the "missing conceptual link" that explains why the picture of a chocolate may be sufficient to evoke the desire and even stimulate the action that leads to its acquisition and consumption.

If for the time being we accept this conceptual status of the GRABBING metonymy, we can now proceed to investigate how it might help to explain the effectiveness, and sometimes the failure, of modern consumer advertising.

2.2 The VALUE metaphor and how it is linked to the GRABBING metonymy

What makes the GRABBING metonymy attractive for both advertisers and cognitive linguists is the object that is to be grabbed. For the advertisers the decisive thing is that the object is what they want to present to the customer in the hope of selling it to him or her, and they do so by showing its positive aspects to prove that it is desirable. For the linguist the focus is on how the positive, desirable aspects of the object are represented and put across. This can be done rather explicitly by verbalizing how good, exquisite, prestigious or healthy the advertised object is for the customer.

Sophisticated advertising prefers more indirect strategies, though, and perhaps the most important one among them is to establish a metaphorical link with a domain conventionally representing the desired quality. Precious stones and clothes are used to indicate exquisiteness; castles, royals and jet-set yachts are called up to suggest prestige; a beaming baby signifies health. On the surface these metaphors seem to offer all the advantages a metaphor can provide in terms of conceptual support. One of them is the richness of a well-structured source domain (jewels, castles, yachts) available for mapping onto the target domain (the advertised item) – consider all the details that come to mind when one thinks of jewels, castles, jet-set yachts. This is complemented by the fact that the source domains are – on the whole – prestructured for positive aspects, which can be carried over into the target domain in a seemingly effortless and natural way, i.e. there is no need for interpretive constraints, for anchoring devices and muting strategies, all the aspects that we will come across when we look at other types of metaphors below. Looking for examples, we find that they are more often expressed visually than by linguistic means. Yet conceptually, this does not make any difference. All the metaphorical links mentioned can be subsumed under the metaphor THE DESIRED OBJECT IS A VALUABLE OBJECT.

What we must not forget is that the VALUE metaphor (or any other metaphor involving the advertised item) is just one part of the conceptual setup and must be seen in conjunction with the GRABBING metonymy, with which it seems to interact in two ways, as shown in Figure 2.

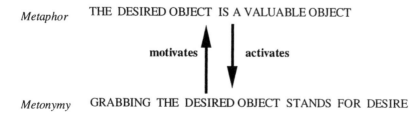

Metaphor   THE DESIRED OBJECT IS A VALUABLE OBJECT

motivates   activates

Metonymy   GRABBING THE DESIRED OBJECT STANDS FOR DESIRE

Figure 2. The interaction of metaphors and metonymies in adverts

On the one hand, the GRABBING metonymy, which stands for our desire to get hold of something, creates the need to justify why the object of the grabbing action is desirable, and this need is met by a VALUE metaphor; in this sense the VALUE metaphor can be said to be conceptually motivated by the GRABBING metonymy (indicated by the upward arrow in Figure 2). On the other hand – and this is probably more important in the advertising context – the VALUE metaphor makes the object in question attractive, and by doing so, it activates the GRABBING metonymy, even where the metonymy is not explicitly expressed (compare the downward arrow).

For the sake of clarity Figure 2 has been simplified. If we go back to the introductory remark that the advertised item is never physically present in the advert, but metonymically represented by a picture or a trade name, it is clear that normally one or several additional metonymies are involved, which mediate between the VALUE metaphor and the GRABBING metonymy, but do not change the basic conceptual operations.

The problem is that this beautifully simple interaction of VALUE metaphor and GRABBING metonymy does not always work as it should, and this is mainly due to the fact that conventional VALUE metaphors are often no longer powerful enough to fulfill their function. As advertisers have found, simple VALUE metaphors increasingly fail to meet the first two criteria of the AIDA formula, i.e. attract the customer's attention and interest. This insight has started off a frantic search for more powerful metaphors.

3. INTEREST metaphors: why they are used and why they are muted

3.1 Some general observations

If we assess the attention-getting potential of VALUE metaphors, these metaphors appear as a special case of a more general metaphor THE DESIRED OBJECT IS AN INTERESTING OBJECT and, we might add, is therefore worth grabbing. Figure 3 gives a first impression of the range of the INTEREST metaphors used in advertising.

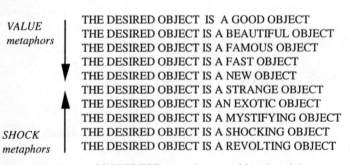

VALUE metaphors

THE DESIRED OBJECT IS A GOOD OBJECT
THE DESIRED OBJECT IS A BEAUTIFUL OBJECT
THE DESIRED OBJECT IS A FAMOUS OBJECT
THE DESIRED OBJECT IS A FAST OBJECT
THE DESIRED OBJECT IS A NEW OBJECT
THE DESIRED OBJECT IS A STRANGE OBJECT
THE DESIRED OBJECT IS AN EXOTIC OBJECT
THE DESIRED OBJECT IS A MYSTIFYING OBJECT
THE DESIRED OBJECT IS A SHOCKING OBJECT
THE DESIRED OBJECT IS A REVOLTING OBJECT

SHOCK metaphors

Figure 3. Types of INTEREST metaphors used in advertising

Figure 3 also shows that the various types can be arranged on a scale which leads us from our conventionalized VALUE metaphors, where the interest is created by the beneficial effects of the object, on to variants where interest is created by the strangeness, mysteriousness and even revoltingness of the metaphor. The extreme case is probably reached by the famous Benetton adverts which try to attract the customer's attention with shocking and cruel pictures of human misery.

The difficulty is that strange, mystifying and revolting source domains may indeed provide more powerful metaphors in terms of attention-getting, but this does not automatically raise their potential to activate the grabbing metonymy. As we travel along the scale from innocuous VALUE metaphors towards more powerful, but also less acceptable variants of the INTEREST metaphor, it becomes increasingly clear that we are less and less inclined to grab the object supported by these metaphors. Even little children intuitively stop grabbing things once they have classified them as revolting. How can this problem be solved?

At this point it seems appropriate to raise the discussion to a more general level and look at the potential of both conventionalized and innovative metaphors. The concept of metaphor which is used as a starting point is essentially cognitive, but tries to pick up major features of the traditional discussion (Leech 1969:148; Black 1993;[2] Goatly 1997:8-9; Forceville 1996:5-12). The concept rests on three parameters: the distance between the source domain (or vehicle, secondary subject) of the metaphor and its target domain (or tenor, topic, primary subject), the conceptual richness of the source domain as mapping potential and finally the constraints imposed on the metaphorical transfer in the mapping process (the cognitive version of the traditional notion of ground). These parameters are visualized in figure 4.

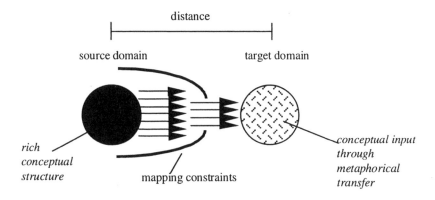

Figure 4. Conceptual factors in metaphor
(distance, conceptual richness, mapping constraints)

While the distance (and linked with it the distinctness) of source and target domains are probably equally valid for all types of metaphors, this seems to be different for the other parameters. Although conventionalized metaphors, as found in everyday language and everyday visual communication (e.g. in traffic signs), benefit from the richness of the source domain in varying degrees, they only function as smoothly as they do because the conceptual transfer emanating from the rich but unordered source domain is channeled by suitable mapping constraints, either in the shape of Lakoff's invariance hypothesis (Lakoff 1990) or as an effect of underlying metonymies (Barcelona, this volume). As a result, a certain balance is maintained between the rich transfer potential of the source domain and the absorption potential of the target domain.

This balance, it appears, is tipped in favor of the richness parameter for innovative or active metaphors (Goatly 1997: 31-35), both in poetic speech (for pictorial metaphors also in art) and in advertising. In all these areas the richness of the source domain is the main concern (together with the undisputed distance from the target domain). Poets need it to capture the reader's imagination, advertisers to rouse the consumer's attention.

However, the difference between the poetic and the advertising use of metaphors emerges when we look at the mapping constraints. Undoubtedly, the transfer in poetic metaphors is also subject to regulation, often determined by poetic or cultural conventions, but the transfer is much freer than with conventionalized metaphors; it leaves room for individual interpretation and makes it possible that additional metaphorical relationships are extracted from the rich source domain with every new reading. This is, of course, what makes poetic metaphor so attractive for imaginative reception. What good poetry does not do is try to impose a certain limited interpretation of its metaphors on the reader.

It is this relative freedom of metaphorical transfer which advertisers cannot permit if they want to achieve their goal of presenting the advertised item in a positive light. Although they depend on innovative source domains to catch the readers' attention, and such "new" domains tend to embrace negative as well as positive attributes, they want to make sure that only the positive attributes are mapped onto the target domain of the advertised item. In other words, the metaphorical process cannot be left unattended (as it largely is in the case of poetic metaphors). The conceptual wealth of the source domain, welcome as it is as an eye-catcher, must be reduced: the metaphor must be "muted" to yield only a positive transfer. Compare Figure 5 for an idealized version of the muting process.

Admittedly, this diagram looks very much like Figure 4, suggesting close parallels between the muting of innovative metaphors in adverts and the mapping constraints of conventionalized metaphors. What is perhaps less obvious is that part of the similarities are above all of a technical nature: in both cases constraints are imposed on the metaphorical transfer. Yet what is the result of a long process which has led to a balance between transfer and absorption

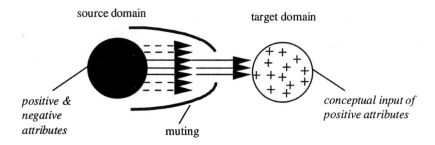

Figure 5. The effect of muting on metaphorical mapping – an idealized view

potential in the case of conventionalized metaphors (see above) is replaced by a carefully master-minded strategy, whose goal is the one-sided selection of positive attributes no matter what the conceptual structure of the source domain may be like. Muting may thus be defined as an attempt to impose artificial mapping constraints on innovative metaphors.

To accomplish the muting task, there are again several options to be considered. The most straightforward muting strategy is to establish an unambiguous link between the positive attributes of the source domain and the target domain, or as Barthes (1993: 1422) puts it in his study of "images" in adverts, "to anchor" the metaphor. In practice this means that a pictorial INTEREST metaphor with a strange, exotic, shocking picture as its source domain is accompanied by an explicit verbal guideline for how the addressee is to interpret the metaphor. An (invented) example would be a picture showing the impact of a hurricane with the verbal message: *No chance for dirt. Our new* CLEANER *has the strength of a hurricane.*

As even this relatively simple example shows, the positive effect of the muting strategy cannot be reliably predicted, but this is a risk present-day advertisers are increasingly prepared to take as long as they can lay hands on an attention-getting picture. In fact explicit anchoring as in our example is much rarer now than it used to be in the 1960s when Barthes investigated adverts (Forceville 1996: 73). One reason is probably that an explicit guideline tends to unmask the advertiser's intentions too quickly for the reader to get involved in the advert at all. To keep the reader fascinated by the source domain picture for as long as possible, muting strategies are now much more indirect and often distributed across several stages of a complex mapping process. This will become clearer when we now look at some examples.

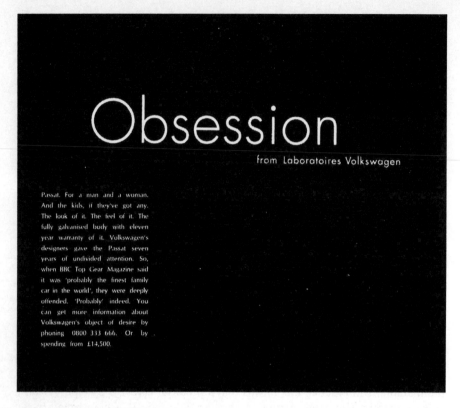

Obsession

from Laboratoires Volkswagen

Passat. For a man and a woman. And the kids, if they've got any. The look of it. The feel of it. The fully galvanised body with eleven year warranty of it. Volkswagen's designers gave the Passat seven years of undivided attention. So, when BBC Top Gear Magazine said it was 'probably the finest family car in the world', they were deeply offended. 'Probably' indeed. You can get more information about Volkswagen's object of desire by phoning 0800 333 666. Or by spending from £14,500.

Figure 6. VW Passat advert

3.2 Muting strategies: some more advanced examples

Our first example is an advert for the Volkswagen Passat (Figure 6), which permits two kinds of interpretation, of which the simpler one will be presented here, while the more sophisticated extensions will be discussed in section 4.

As usual, the INTEREST metaphor is expressed visually, in this case by the picture of the car which is in the process of being examined by five men and a woman wearing white coats and suggesting a scientific laboratory check. Relating the car to the source domain LABORATORY CHECK can be seen as a more specific variant of the metaphor THE DESIRED OBJECT IS A STRANGE OBJECT and there is a good chance that this picture will be more successful in attracting the readers' attention than the picture of the car on the road. Yet however fascinating the idea of a scientific examination may be (which is supported by the message

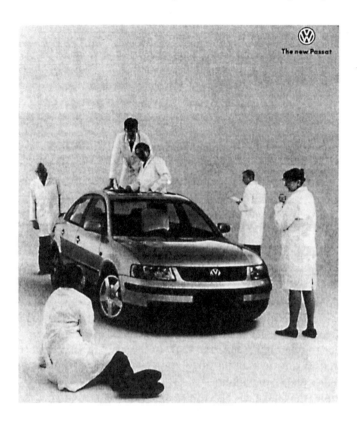

Figure 6 cont. VW Passat advert

"from the Volkswagen laboratoires"), it could also put off people who are somehow afraid of scientific methods and are more interested in getting a manageable and likable car. To filter out these undesirable "scientific" correspondences the metaphor has to be muted, and this is done in an indirect, but nevertheless striking way by prominently placing the word "obsession" on the opposite page of this two-page advert. What this strategy insinuates is that the picture stands for the obsession with which the Volkswagen company has developed the car; the rich source domain of scientific investigation is muted and reduced to the reassuring (and therefore positive) aspects of care and attention that have gone into the design and production of the car. Further support of this strategy comes from a paragraph of small print, which dwells on the topics of attention ("seven years of undivided attention") and reliability ("eleven year warranty"). Compare figure 7, which provides a diagram of the muting process.

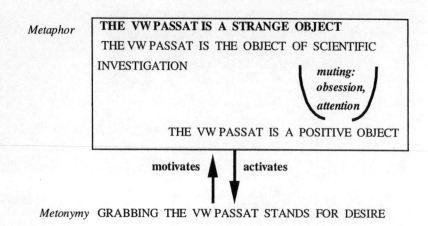

Metaphor

THE VW PASSAT IS A STRANGE OBJECT

THE VW PASSAT IS THE OBJECT OF SCIENTIFIC

INVESTIGATION

muting:
obsession,
attention

THE VW PASSAT IS A POSITIVE OBJECT

motivates   activates

Metonymy GRABBING THE VW PASSAT STANDS FOR DESIRE

Figure 7. The VW Passat advert: First conceptual interpretation

What the figure does not show is that the positive view of the target domain (the VW Passat) is also supported by a second metaphor, this time a VALUE metaphor expressed verbally in the small print: THE CAR IS PEOPLE AND FAMILY. Finally, the references to "the look" and "the feel" of the car can also be seen as attempts to extinguish any remaining misgivings about the scientific approach of the pictorial INTEREST metaphor.

Our second example, the snake advert (figure 8) is more controversial, not only because of its aim (i.e. the promotion of smoking), but also because of the more circumstantial conceptual path it suggests.

This is partly due to the restrictions imposed on this – now doomed? – type of advertising (e.g. that cigarettes must not be shown in the advert, etc.), but these restrictions have certainly favored the development of new and more ingenious advertising strategies. The advert is dominated by the picture of a snake which is obviously digesting its prey. Undoubtedly, the attention-getting potential of this metaphor (which seems to oscillate between the variants THE DESIRED OBJECT IS A STRANGE OBJECT and THE DESIRED OBJECT IS A REVOLTING OBJECT), is formidable, and this potential is heightened by the fact that in the *Sunday Times Magazine* the snake is spread in full length across three pages including a fold-out page. Yet the way in which the snake metaphorically supports the positive qualities of the cigarette is anything but self-evident.

If we go by the strategies observed in the Volkswagen advert, one would expect that the slogan provides a fairly straightforward guideline to ensure the desired positive interpretation of the SNAKE metaphor. Yet what the slogan ("longer than a light snack") suggests is a much more circumstantial conceptual path. True enough, the first element of the statement ("longer") indicates one major correspondence that is to be highlighted, the length shared by the snake

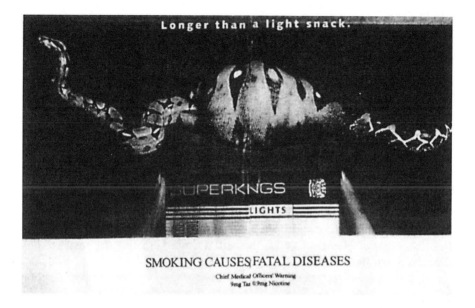

SMOKING CAUSES FATAL DISEASES

Chief Medical Officers' Warning
9mg Tar 0.9mg Nicotine

Figure 8. Superkings cigarette advert

and the kingsize cigarette and the duration of its consumption, and this can be seen as a first muting attempt.

But the comparison made explicit in the slogan concerns the time it takes to eat a light snack, not the time it takes to smoke the cigarette. In terms of metaphor, this means that an additional metaphorical link is introduced, THE SNACK IS THE SNAKE'S PREY, which supports the interpretation that the snake takes longer to digest its prey than the time needed to eat and digest a light snack. Taken at face value, the idea of a snake dealing with its prey will raise negative rather than positive feelings, yet it may nevertheless give rise to associations of a more positive kind. To a certain extent digesting the prey could be interpreted as enjoying its long path through the body, and this may even be supported by reminiscences of the opening passage of Saint-Exupéry's *The Little Prince*, where the prey is the innocent secret of the Little Prince in a non-understanding adult world. More important perhaps, the introduction of the snack, a light harmless meal, brings with it the notion of "no harm" and this may be regarded as a very sophisticated muting strategy indeed. Even the pun created by the juxtaposition of *snack* and *snake* can be seen as supporting the innocent, playful aspects of the metaphor (Goatly 1997: 303). Taken together, it seems that we may already have taken a first step towards a positive interpretation. The second step is provided by the metaphorical link between the snack and the cigarette itself, and here the slogan yields yet another muting device, the attribute "light", which is reflected on the cigarette packet and offers itself as a guideline for the interpretation of the metaphor THE CIGARETTE IS A SNACK. This complex process is illustrated in figure 9.

Compared with the car advert, where muting is a single stage process supported by the catchword and by various other elements, the cigarette advert takes a more risky path. Conceptual processing is divided up into several metaphorical processes, each with its muting component, which may need quite a sizable amount of processing capacity. Whether the addressees are prepared to make the effort to process the metaphors is decisive for the activation of the GRABBING metonymy and whether they have the knowledge to follow the advert into its literary allusions (joining the Little Prince in enjoying an innocent child's secret pleasure, i.e. smoking a cigarette, in a hostile adult, i.e. non-smoking, world) is even more uncertain. Or is there an alternative where the addressee is simply fascinated by the picture and at the same time takes in the brand name more or less as a separate element? And is this still a way of creating the desire to buy the advertised item?

This alternative becomes even more pressing when we think of the Benetton adverts mentioned above as examples of shocking and revolting variants of the INTEREST metaphor. In terms of our simple conceptual mechanisms these adverts involve an INTEREST metaphor like BENETTON IS AIDS and the GRABBING metonymy (GRABBING BENETTON STANDS FOR THE DESIRE TO WEAR BENETTON CLOTHES). But how is the muting accomplished which seems to be desperately needed to support a positive target domain of the metaphor ("Benetton clothes as the desired object")? Undoubtedly, this largely depends on the interpretation of the slogan as a whole: *United colors of Benetton*. If we consider that early adverts of the series showed children of different races, the slogan then suggested a multiracial, humanistic, and therefore positive, interpretation of the term "color" and the metaphor as a whole, thus providing a reliable muting strategy. The question is how the consumers will interpret the slogan in connection with the later pictures of the series (the AIDS patient, etc.), how much of its earlier muting potential will be carried over. Or are the addressees of the adverts prepared to actually honor the daring of the pictures as a positive quality? In other words, will the customers consider Benetton as a desirable object in spite of the shocking effect of the pictures?

Looking back at the three examples it is clear that, driven by the competition for the ultimate visual impact, advertisers have moved a long way from the simple conceptual setup of the VALUE metaphor and the GRABBING metonymy, accepting ever more complex muting strategies. As it appears, an increasing number of advertisers seem prepared to sacrifice the conceptual links inherent in metaphors for the sake of mere eye-catchers, hoping that somehow, even without proper conceptual interaction, there will be a shortcut to imprint the desire for acquiring a certain item.

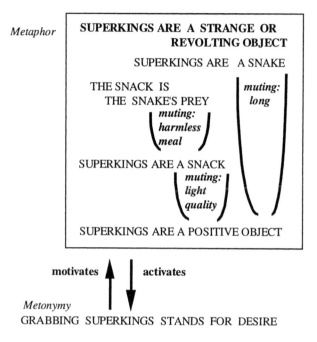

Figure 9. The Superkings advert: Conceptual interpretation

4. The role of "conventional" metonymies

One other thing that has emerged from the discussion of the examples is that the INTEREST metaphor may in fact involve several metaphors. This ties in with our earlier observation that normally several metonymies will be involved in an advert. Some of these metonymies, we have found, arise from the limitations of the medium. Thus the advertised object is never physically present in the advert but replaced by a picture. Food items and liquid items in general are represented by their packages or bottles, an example of the CONTAINER-FOR-CONTAINED metonymy, which is also legally enforced in some other cases, such as tobacco advertising. Another all-pervasive metonymy is THE NAME STANDS FOR THE PRODUCT. In a competitive society, where the majority of products are not monopolized by a single producer, it is, of course, crucial to focus the consumer's desire and action on one's own products and to identify them by using a name.

Yet this is only half the story. There is more than ample evidence that both the CONTAINER-FOR-CONTAINED and the NAME-FOR-PRODUCT metonymies are not just formalities (as we have treated them so far for the sake of simplicity) but have developed into powerful advertising tools which are extensively and consciously used to support the conceptual interaction of the INTEREST metaphor and the GRABBING metonymy. For this purpose bottles of soft and alcoholic drinks, and even more so, the containers in which perfumes are sold, have been shaped in specific and exotic ways and are presented in the advert in unusual surroundings. Compare the perfume advert in Figure 10, where the advert is constructed around the attention-getting force of the container and the trade name *Joop !*

Here it is fairly clear that both the shape of the container and the trade name are used to identify the desired object and thus to activate the GRABBING metonymy. But how does this fit into our concept, and where does the metaphor come in?

Figure 10. Perfume advert.

As shown in Figure 11, the CONTAINER-FOR-CONTAINED metonymy can be seen as an extension of the metonymic component, so that the basic conceptual setup of the advert is not really affected. True, the INTEREST metaphor is not directly motivated by the GRABBING metonymy, but by the intervening container me-

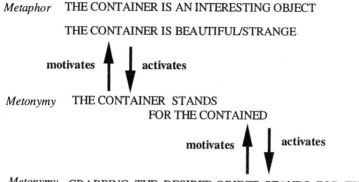

Metaphor   THE CONTAINER IS AN INTERESTING OBJECT

THE CONTAINER IS BEAUTIFUL/STRANGE

motivates ↑ ↓ **activates**

Metonymy   THE CONTAINER STANDS
FOR THE CONTAINED

motivates ↑ ↓ **activates**

Metonymy   GRABBING THE DESIRED OBJECT STANDS FOR THE DESIRE

Figure 11. The interaction of metaphors and metonymies in adverts

tonymy. Nevertheless, it remains unchanged apart from acquiring a slightly different target domain, reflected in the variant: THE CONTAINER (OF THE DESIRABLE OBJECT) IS AN INTERESTING OBJECT. Conversely one might say that the mysterious bottle, and the INTEREST metaphor based on it, activate the container metonymy and, as a consequence, also the GRABBING metonymy. It goes without saying that a parallel process is to be assumed for the NAME-FOR-PRODUCT metonymy, though here the INTEREST metaphor will often appear as a VALUE metaphor based on the reputation of the trade name (The underlying metaphor would be THE NAME (OF THE DESIRED OBJECT) IS A GOOD/FAMOUS NAME).

The sophisticated uses to which the NAME metonymy can be put in conjunction with other metaphors is illustrated by the extended interpretation of the VW Passat advert. If we pursue the allusions connected with the terms *obsession* and *laboratoires,* which in our first simplified interpretation we just took at their (English language) face value, they lead us into the realm of perfumes. As regular readers of Sunday and women's magazines will know, *laboratoires* can be taken to refer to *Laboratoires Garnier,* which stand for a range of perfumes in a PRODUCER-PRODUCT metonymy. *Obsession* also stands for a perfume as a NAME metonymy. Perfumes in turn are well-suited as source domains of VALUE metaphors, and equip the advertised item with additional attractiveness, and this adds its share to the activation of the GRABBING metonymy.

Figure 12 is a attempt to come to grips with the extended interpretation of the Passat advert including the linguistically expressed FAMILY metaphor and the additional hints at "the look" and "the feel" of the car, which were already mentioned above. As with circumstantial muting strategies, it is difficult to decide to what extent this complex interaction of metaphors and metonymies is realized by the average addressee. At least we will have to assume different degrees of conceptual penetration, but if this is a way of satisfying different tastes and different intellectual standards at the same time, advertisers will not be unhappy.

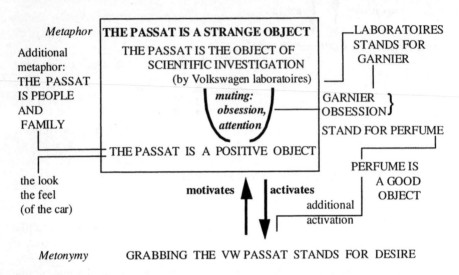

Figure 12. The VW Passat advert. Extended conceptual interpretation

5. Final remarks on metonymies and metaphors in trade names

The names used in the NAME metonymies are very special names, trade names or even registered trade marks, and this is particularly true of brand names. What is more or less excluded, either for legal reasons or because of their low attention potential, are existing common nouns, e.g. calling a new brand of perfume "perfume" or calling a new automobile "car". One of the results is that a large number of trade names rely on a metonymy or metaphor (for other sources see Ungerer 1991: 144). The most common metonymy is probably the PRODUCER-FOR-PRODUCT metonymy based on the name of the inventor or company (which may itself also have a metonymic background). Widely used metaphors involve source domains suggesting prestige such as ROYALTY or DIPLOMATIC SERVICE, natural phenomena like SUN or TIDE or animal concepts.

If we stick to the last-mentioned area and think of names of cars, such as *Jaguar* or *(Ford) Mustang* (Gläser 1973: 229-231), the underlying metaphor could probably be expressed as THE CAR IS A WILD ANIMAL, which could be seen as a variant of the general metaphor THE DESIRED OBJECT IS AN INTERESTING OBJECT. Indeed, one would claim that the coining of a trade name is to be regarded as a nutshell version of the conceptual structure of an advert. Again the starting point (and the goal of the advertiser) is the GRABBING metonymy, which motivates an INTEREST metaphor, and is in turn supposed to be activated by this metaphor. The INTEREST metaphor can be rather tame and ineffective, as with trade names like *Crown, Queen* or *Embassy*. (The underlying metaphor would be THE DESIRED OBJECT IS A PRESTIGIOUS OBJECT.) The more daring metaphor-based trade names like *Jaguar* or *Mustang* raise the same problems as the more provoking type of visual metaphors in the newly-designed adverts discussed above. Since animal concepts like JAGUAR do not only generate positive correspondences, they have to be muted.

As one may assume and should perhaps further investigate, the muting was carried out explicitly when trade names such as *Jaguar* were introduced, but the muted version is now generally accepted and mapping constraints which favor a positive interpretation have been established. This is why analyzing the conceptual background of trade names often gives the impression that one is looking at yesterday's adverts and tomorrow's conventionalized metaphors.

Notes

1. This article was written in 1964.
2. Black's article was first published in 1979, with the first edition of Ortony's book.

References

Barcelona, Antonio
  this volume   "On the plausibility of claiming a metonymic motivation for conceptual metaphor."
Barthes, Roland
  1993   "Rhétorique de l'image", in: Eric Marty (ed.), *Roland Barthes. Oeuvres complètes. Vol 1*. Paris: Editions du Seuil, 1417-1429.
Black, Max
  1993   "More about metaphor", in: Andrew Ortony (ed.), *Metaphor and thought*. (2nd ed.) Cambridge: Cambridge University Press: 19-41.
Croft, William
  1993   "The role of domains in the interpretation of metaphors and metonymies", *Cognitive Linguistics* 4: 335-370.
Forceville, Charles
  1996   *Pictorial metaphor in advertising*. London: Routledge.
Gläser, Rosemarie
  1973   "Zur Namensgebung in der Wirtschaftswerbung: Warenzeichen im britischen und amerikanischen Englisch", in: *Der Name in Sprache und Gesellschaft. Beitraege zur Theorie der Onomastik*. Berlin: 220-239. {No indication of editor or publisher.}

Goatly, Andrew
1997   *The language of metaphors.* London: Routledge.
Johnson-Laird, Philip N. – Keith Oatley
1989   "The language of emotions: analysis of a semantic field", *Cognition and Emotion* 3: 81-123.
1992   "Basic emotions, rationality, and folk theory", *Cognition and Emotion* 6 : 201-223.
Kövecses, Zoltán
1986   *Metaphors of anger, pride and love.* Amsterdam: Benjamins.
1990a   *Emotion concepts.* New York: Springer.
1990b   "Joy – An exercise in the description of emotion concepts", *Grazer Linguistische Studien* 33/34: 153-164.
1991   "Happiness: A definitional effort", *Metaphor and Symbolic Activity* 6: 29-46.
Kövecses, Zoltán – Günter Radden
1998   "Metonymy: Developing a cognitive linguistic view", *Cognitive Linguistics* 9: 37-77.
Kwanka, Bettina
1993   Diskursstruktur und Diskursstrategien in englischen Verkaufs-gesprächen. M.A. thesis, München. [Unpublished MS.]
Lakoff, George
1987   *Women, fire and dangerous things. What categories reveal about the mind.* Chicago: Chicago University Press.
1990   "The Invariance Hypothesis: Is abstract reason based on image schemas?", *Cognitive Linguistics* 1: 39-74.
Leech, Geoffrey
1969   *A Linguistic guide to English Poetry.* London: Longman.
Nöth, Winfried
1983   "Illustrierte Werbetexte: Appell- und Darstellungsstrukturen", *Anglistik und Englischunterricht* 21: 87-102.
Ungerer, Friedrich
1991   "Acronyms, trade names and motivation", *Arbeiten aus Anglistik und Amerikanistik* 16, (1991): 131-158.
1995   "The linguistic and cognitive relevance of basic emotions", in: René Dirven and Johan Vanparys (eds.), *Current approaches to the lexicon,* Frankfurt am Main: Lang, 185-209.
Ungerer, Friedrich – Hans-Jörg Schmid
1996   *An introduction to cognitive linguistics.* London: Longman.
Vestergaard, Torben – Schrøder, Kim
1985   *The language of advertising.* Oxford: Blackwell.

Author Index

Abraham, R.C. 188
Allan, Keith 34, 56
Alpher, Barry 188
Anderson, John M. 171, 188, 193
Apresjan, Valentina 33, 56
Asher, R. E. 189
Ashiwaju, Michael 188

Bach, Emmon 217, 230
Barcelona, Antonio 2, 4-6, 10, 11, 16, 19,
    21, 22, 26, 28, 32, 40, 43, 47, 53, 54, 56,
    91, 106, 107, 121, 131, 132, 249, 290,
    293, 297, 319, 320, 328, 339
Barnden, John A 3, 27
Barrera Vásquez, Alfredo 188
Barry J. Blake 189
Barthes, Roland 321, 329, 339
Belkin, Aaron 145
Benveniste 188
Bergenholtz, Henning 188
Bierhorst, John 189
Black, Max 7, 27, 327, 339
Blank, Andreas 197, 212
Blust, Robert A. 171, 189
Börner, Wolfgang 212
Bransford, John D. 294, 297
Brugman, Claudia 45, 47, 84, 91, 236, 250
Burrow, Thomas 189
Bybee, Joan 153, 159, 168

Camac, M. K. 188, 189
Cameron, Sharon 260, 279, 280
Capell, Arthur 189
Casad, Eugene H. 108
Cermak, Laird S. 297
Chafe, Wallace 285, 294
Chang, Sung-Un 192
Chomsky, Noam 301, 319
Claudi, Ulrike 35, 57, 98, 106, 107
Coates, Jennifer 153, 163, 168
Cohen, Gillian 298
Collins 54
Cook, Guy 275, 280, 305-307, 319
Coulson, Seana 133, 144
Coulthard, Malcolm 288, 298

Cowie, Anthony P. 39, 56
Craik, Fergus I.M. 297
Croft, William 12, 14, 19, 27, 31, 53, 56, 62,
    76, 77, 109, 110, 126-129, 131, 149, 168,
    195, 197, 212, 323, 339
Cumming, Susanna 285, 298

Davidson, Donald 6
Deignan 80, 84, 92
Delitzsch, Friedrich 189
Dirven, René 34, 53, 54, 56, 64, 77, 192,
    193, 195-198, 212, 213, 340
Dixon, Robert M. W. 189
Doke, Clement M. 189
Donald, Morris C. 297
Durie, Mark 194

Echols, John M. 189
Eco, Umberto 35, 173, 189
Edelman, Gerald 2, 27
Emeneau, Murray B. 189
Evans, Nicholas D. 189
Eysenck, Michael W. 287, 294, 298

Fauconnier, Gilles 7, 8, 16, 19, 27, 28, 45,
    55, 56, 58, 69, 77, 78, 113, 124, 131-133,
    144, 145, 253, 261, 272, 275, 280
Ferguson, Charles A. 190
Feyaerts, Kurt 16, 17, 60, 67-69, 76, 77
Fillmore, Charles 197, 212
Forceville, Charles 321, 327, 329, 339
Forrest, Linda 298
Franklin, Ralph W. 278, 280
Franks, Jeffrey J. 297
Freeman, Donald C., 278, 280
Freeman, Margaret 4, 8, 20, 23, 24, 91, 92,
    267, 279, 280, 283, 298

Gadsby, Adam 196, 212
Gaudes, Rüdiger 189
Geeraerts, Dirk 75, 77, 173, 189
Gelpi, Albert 279, 280
Gentner, Dedre 108
Gibbs, Raymond W. jr. 10, 27
Gilbert, Sandra M. 280, 281
Gimm, Martin 193
Givón, Talmy 171, 189

Gläser, Rosemarie 338, 339
Glucksberg, S. 188, 189
Goatly, Andrew 327, 328, 333, 340
Goddard, Cliff 176, 178, 189, 211, 212
Goffman, Erving 307, 319
Goldberg, Adele 131, 144
Golla, Victor 189
Goossens, Louis 10, 11, 16, 20, 22, 27, 31,
    34, 35, 56, 57, 58, 62, 63, 69, 75-77, 121,
    131, 149-151, 153, 156, 157, 159, 161,
    168, 190, 192, 195, 198, 211, 212
Grabher, Gudrun M. 280
Grady, Joseph 16, 51, 57, 91, 92
Greenbaum, Sidney 231
Greenberg, Joseph H. 171, 190
Gregory, Richard 57
Grice, Paul H. 6
Grondelaers, Stefan 75, 77
Gubar, Susan 280, 281
Guthrie, Malcolm 190

Hagenbüchle, Roland 280
Halász, Elod 190
Halle, Morris 212
Halliday, Michael A.K. 286, 298
Hannig, Rainer 190
Harms, Robert T. 230
Hasan, Ruqaiya 286, 298
Haser, Verena 20, 21
Hauer, Erich 190
Heine, Bernd 35, 57, 98, 100, 106, 107, 169,
    171
Helman, David 145
Herms, Irmtraud 190
Hilferty, Joseph 54
Hilgers-Hesse, Irene 191
Hinch, H. E. 189
Hirvensalo, Lauri 190
Hock, Hans Henrich 171, 190
Hockings, Paul 190
Hofstede, Geert 303, 310, 319
Holland, Dorothy 92, 102, 107
Holyoak, Keith J. 3, 27, 254, 280
Hony, Henry C. 190
Hoopes, James 255, 281
Hopper, Paul 149, 155, 156, 168
Hornby, A.S. 38, 57
Hott, Barbara 107
Hübner, Barbara 190

Hudson, Grover 190
Hünnemeyer, Friederike 35, 57, 98, 106, 107
İz, Fahir 190
Jäkel, Olaf 45, 57
Jakobson, Roman 196-198, 212
Johnson, Frederick 190
Johnson, Mark 3, 5, 6, 18, 21, 27, 42, 45, 54,
    57, 58, 61, 76, 77, 79, 82, 92-94, 102,
    107, 109, 110, 113, 131, 149, 169, 179,
    185-187, 190, 191, 196, 197, 211-213,
    253, 255, 281, 283, 284, 289, 290, 293,
    294, 298, 301, 302, 308, 314, 316, 320
Johnson, Thomas H. 278, 281
Johnson-Laird, Philip N. 175, 192, 322, 340
Jones, Charles 188, 193

Kahlo, Gerhard 190
Kálmán, C. György 248, 250
Kálmán, László 250
Karow, Otto 191
Karttunen, Frances 191
Karttunen, Lauri 243, 248, 249, 250
Katara, Pekka 191
Kiefer, Ferenc 250
Kim, Myung Hee 298
Kimball, John P. 250
Kimura, Kinji 191
Kirkpatrick, Betty 196, 212
Koenig, Jean Pierre 144, 145
König, Ekkehard 159, 160, 169
Korponay, Béla 250
Kövecses, Zoltán 4, 6, 8, 10-12, 14-18, 21,
    25-27, 31, 32, 42, 43, 47, 49, 50-53, 57,
    58, 67, 69, 75-80, 84, 89-92, 94, 103, 104,
    106-108, 133, 135, 136, 138, 198, 211,
    212, 236, 250, 262, 279, 281, 290, 293,
    297, 298, 322-324, 340
Krause, Erich-Dieter 191
Kronasser, Heinz 174, 188, 191
Kwanka, Bettina 324, 340
Kytö, Merja 168

Labov, William 289, 298
Lakoff, George 3-7, 10-13, 16-18, 24, 27,
    28, 31, 32, 41-47, 49, 53, 54, 57-59, 61,
    62, 66, 67, 69, 73, 75-79, 82, 84, 92-94,
    98, 100-104, 107, 108, 109, 110-113, 124,
    130-132, 135, 136, 138, 144, 145, 149,
    169, 173, 179, 185, 191, 195-197, 211-

213, 217, 230, 236, 250, 261, 262, 275, 281, 283, 284, 289, 290, 293, 294, 298, 299-302, 306-308, 310, 311, 314, 316, 320, 322, 324, 328, 340
Lambdin, Thomas O. 191
Langacker, Ronald 4, 8, 12, 17, 19, 20, 23, 28, 31, 53, 58, 59, 62, 64, 68, 76, 78, 82, 92, 104, 106, 108, 127, 128, 131, 132, 149-151, 157, 160, 169, 233, 236-238, 240, 241, 246-248, 250, 290, 298, 323
Laughlin, Robert M. 191
Lavy, Jaacov 191
Le Voi, Martin E. 298
Lee, Yang Ha 192
Leech, Geoffrey 231, 327, 340
Lehmann, Winfred P. 193
Lesko, Leonard H. 191
Leslau, Wolf 191
Levin, Beth 223, 230
Lévi-Strauss, Claude 198, 213
Li, Charles N. 189
Liebert, Wolf-Andreas 231, 250
Liedtke, Stefan 192
Linde, Charlotte 301
Lloyd, Barbara B. 2, 28
Lyons, John 238, 250

Mackin, Ronald 56
MacLaury, Robert E. 57, 77, 212
Magay, Tamás 192
Malcolm, D. M. 189
Malkiel, Yakov 193
Martín, José M. 302-304, 320
Martin, Samuel E. 192
Marty, Eric 339
Mathis, Elizabeth 97, 108
McCaig, Ian R. 56
McCloskey, Michael 103, 108
McKechnie, Jean L. 39, 58
Miller, Cristanne 279, 280, 281
Miller, George A. 175, 192
Moravcsik, Edith 190
Morgan, Pamela S. 299, 307, 318-320
Morgan, William 194

Nádasdy, Ádám 250
Newman, Roxana Ma. 192
Nicolle, Steve 106, 108
Niemeier, Susanne 10, 16, 20, 21, 42, 58, 213

Nikolayev, Sergej L. 192
Noonan, Michael 192
Nöth, Winfried 321, 340
Norman, Jerry 192
Nunberg, Geoffrey 19, 117, 118, 119, 120, 132

Oakley, Todd 133, 145
Oatley, Keith 322, 340
Olszowski, Eckehart 188
Ono, Tsuyoshi 285, 298
Országh, László 192
Ortony, Andrew 27, 58, 77, 92, 107, 108, 131, 132, 144, 191, 213, 250, 281, 339

Pagliuca, William 153, 159, 168
Pancake, Ann S. 24, 299, 301, 319, 320
Panther, Klaus-Uwe 20, 58, 77, 78, 108, 144, 168, 195, 213, 230, 231, 298
Paprotté, Wolf 56, 192, 193
Parker, Gary John 192
Pauwels, Paul 27, 34, 57, 58, 77, 168, 186, 190, 192, 212
Peirce, Charles Sanders 254, 255, 258
Pelyvás, Péter 20, 22, 23, 233, 237, 238, 240, 243, 248-250
Perkins, Revere 153, 159, 168
Persson, Gunnar 174, 192
Pilot-Raichoor, Christiane 190
Pitrat 305
Plungian, Vladimir 20, 151, 153-155, 169
Pokorny, Julius 192
Pollak, Vivian R. 279, 281
Ponterotto, Diane 4, 20, 24
Porter, David 278, 279, 281
Prószéky, Gábor 250
Pu, Ming Ming 298
Pütz, Martin 320

Quinn, Naomi 92, 97, 102, 107
Quirk, Randolph 218, 221, 231

Radden, Günter 4, 8, 10-12, 14-16, 18, 19, 22, 25, 27, 31, 32, 42, 43, 49, 50, 51, 53, 55, 57, 76-78, 91, 92, 94, 97, 102, 103, 107, 108, 144, 168, 195, 211, 213, 231, 290, 297, 298, 323, 340
Reddy, Michael 103, 108, 213
Rédei, Károly 192
Redeker, Gisela 231, 250
Redhouse, James W. 192

Rees, Nigel 196, 213
Reizammer, Albert 190
Rhodes, Richard 100
Rich, Adrienne 279, 281
Richards, I. A. 265, 280, 281
Richter-Johanningmeier, Jürgen 188
Rosch, Eleanor 2, 28
Ross, Malcolm 194
Rudzka-Ostyn, Brygida 27, 34, 45, 46, 49, 52, 55, 57, 58, 77, 167, 168, 188, 190, 192, 212
Ruiz de Mendoza, Francisco 6, 8, 13, 16, 18, 19, 21, 22, 28, 31, 53, 55, 58, 112, 117, 124, 130, 132

Saagpakk, Paul F. 192
Said, Edward W. 24, 299, 301-304, 307, 320
Sampson, J.A. 36, 58
Sanders, José 233, 236-238, 245, 250
Sandikcioglu, Esra 20, 24
Schmid, Hans-Jörg 8, 28, 76, 78, 324, 340
Schrøder, Kim 321, 324, 340
Searle, John R. 6, 28
Semino, Elena 273-276, 281
Senft, Gunter 193
Seto, Ken-ichi 106, 108
Shadily, Hassan 189
Sikakana, J. M. A. 189
Siméon, Rémi 193
Simon-Bärwinkel, Rosemarie 190
Simon-Vanderbergen, Anne-Marie 27, 57, 77, 168, 186, 190, 192, 212
Sinclair, John 288, 298
Skinner, B.F. 35
Skinner, Neil 193
Slama-Cazacu, Tatiana 283, 298
Spooren, Wilbert 233, 236, 237, 245, 250
Starostin, Sergei A. 192
Stein, Barry S. 297
Steuerwald, Karl 193
Stevens, Albert R. 108
Svartvik, Jan 231
Sweetser, Eve 22, 23, 98, 131, 149, 155, 169, 171, 174, 176, 179, 188, 193, 233, 234, 236-238, 240-244, 247-250
Szábo, Peter 84, 89, 90, 92

Talmy, Leonard 23, 234, 240-243, 249
Taylor, John R. 2, 6, 8, 10, 14, 15, 16, 28,
31, 34, 35, 39, 41, 53, 57, 58, 77, 94, 108, 130-132, 173, 193, 198, 212, 213
Telegdi, Zsigmond 250
Tetlock, Philip 145
Thagard, Paul 254, 280
Thornburg, Linda 20, 21, 230, 231
Tomlin, Russell S. 24, 284-286, 296, 298
Traugott, Elizabeth Cross 149, 151, 155, 156, 159, 160, 163, 168, 169, 171, 172, 174, 175, 188, 193, 237, 248
Tryon, Darrell T. 193
Tsur, Reuven 278, 281
Turner, Mark 3, 4, 5, 7, 8, 10, 13, 16, 19, 28, 31, 44, 45, 55, 56, 58, 69, 76, 77, 78, 84, 92, 103, 108, 109, 111, 113, 124, 130-133, 135, 138, 144, 145, 173, 185, 191, 193, 196, 213, 261, 272, 275, 280, 281

Ullmann, Stephen 39, 58, 76, 78, 108, 130, 132
Ungerer, Friedrich 2, 16, 20, 25, 28, 43, 58, 322, 324, 338, 340

Van der Auwera, Johan 20, 151-153, 155, 169
van Dijk, Teun A. 284, 286, 298
Vanparys, Johan 27, 57, 77, 168, 190, 192, 212, 340
Vestergaard, Torben 321, 324, 340
Vietze, Hans-Peter 193
Vilakazi, B. W. 189
Vogel, Klaus 212

Wallhead Salway, Celia 305-307, 320
Walravens, Hartmut 193
Warren, Beatrice 69, 78
Waugh, Linda 250
Weiner, E.C.C. 36, 58
Weisbuch, Robert 279-281
Werth, Paul 173, 193
Wiedemann, Ferdinand Johann 194
Wierzbicka, Anna 176, 178, 189
Wildgen, Wolfgang 34, 58
Wilkins, David P. 171, 194
Williams, Joseph M. 171, 194
Wolff, Cynthia Griffin 279, 281

Young, Robert W. 194

Zampolli, Antonio 212
Zeiss, Volker 188
Zlatev, Jordan 265, 281

Subject Index

(The) AIDA formula 324, 326
Analogical mapping 254-5
  attribute mapping 254, 256, 260, 262, 265
  relational mapping 254, 256, 265
  system mapping 254, 256-257, 265; *see also* Cognitive poetics
  metaphor as a kind of analogical mapping 254-259
Analogical reasoning 253; *see also* Analogical mapping

Binding *see* Blending
Blend (*see* Blended space)
Blended space 124-125, 133-144, 261-265
  emergence of independent structure and inferences 133-144, especially 133, 134
  grounded in input spaces 137
  impossible blends 142
  mapped back onto an input space 134, 137
  metonymy in *see* Optimality principles in blending, metonymy projection constraint
Blending 7-8, 124-126, 133-144
  and literary analysis 259-265, 271-272, 275-276; *see also* Cognitive poetics
  as re-framing of source and target 134-135
  cross-space mappings 133, 134, 138, 139, 140, 141, 143
  examples 133-144
  in commercial cartoons 140-141
  input spaces 133, 134, 135, 136-141, 261-265
  interaction with metaphor and metonymy 133-144, especially 133, 134-141
  motivating sentences with mixed vocabulary 137
  notion 133
  overlooked in earlier models of metaphor and metonymy 135
  see also Blended space; Generic space; Metaphorical blends

Central mappings in metaphorical mappings 83-84, 111, 124

central inferences derived from blend only 134, 135
characteristics 83-84
experiential basis 84
in A SITUATION IS FIRE 89
in COMPLEX ABSTRACT SYSTEMS ARE BUILDINGS 83
see also Cohesive role of metaphor in conversation, ... vividness of metaphor
Cognitive linguistics
  main tenets 2-3, 253, 266-267
Cognitive poetics 253-277, especially 253, 265, 270-272
  and literary interpretation (case studies) 253-277
    the *Cocoon* poem 254-259
    the *Loaded Gun* poem 259-265
    the *Applicant* 273-277
  and evaluation of literary style 265-272
  as a foundation for a new theory of literature 253-254, 277
  and other cognitive theories of literature 274-277
    discourse theory 274
    possible worlds theory 274-275
    schema theory 275
Cognitive style 265
Cognitive theory of metaphor and metonymy
  criticism 135, 197
  description 1-15
  outline 196-199
  problems 8-15
Cohesive role of metaphor in conversation 283-297
  case studies 287-294
  efficiency of metaphor in discourse and conversation 290-291, 293-297
  vividness of metaphor 294
  interaction of interlocutors' metaphorical networks 296-297
  metaphor as a heuristic frame in conversation 289-290, 293-297
  pivot-like role of metaphor in conversation 294, 295, 297

role of metaphorical entailments and overlaps 290-291, 293, 295-296
Color 35-39
  scalar construal 36
  see also Metonymic models
Common traits of metaphor and metonymy 5-7
  conventional, unconscious 5, 197
  systematic 5
  culture-specific 6
  cognitive models 6
Concept of metaphor 3-4, 60-62, 109, 149, 173
  a matter of thought, not of words 266
  as a mapping *see* Mapping in metaphor
  as conceptual distance 197, 327-328
  as conceptual similarity 64, 74, 173
  as including metonymy 173
  as a type of blending *see* Metaphorical blends
  cross-domain correspondence as a distinctive property 32, 173; *see* Domains, domain matrices, role in distinguishing metaphor from metonymy
  "domain mapping" *see* Mapping in metaphor, between different domains or domain matrices
  Jakobson's views 196
  systematicity 110
  see also Common traits of metaphor and metonymy; Image schemas; Metonymic basis of metaphor; Metonymy-based metaphors
Concept of metonymy 4-5, 32, 60, 62-65, 109-130,
  as a mapping *see* Mapping in metonymy
  as a stand-for relationship 62, 109, 114-115
  as a type of active-zone phenomenon 12-13, 93
  as a type of blending *see* Blending
  as a type of reference-point construction 12, 33
  as activation 4
  as conceptual contiguity 62, 63-64, 74, 197
    contiguity as co-occurrence in a conceptual structure 173
  as domain highlighting 12-13, 109, 126-130

problems with this notion 127-129
  as involving a conceptual/referential shift 13, 62, 64-65, 74, 129, 173
  referential vs. predicative metonymies 113-115, 129
  as providing mental access to target 12, 32
  broad notion of metonymy 14
  chronologically prior to metaphor 31
  definition 4, 130
  domain-internal correspondence as a distinctive property *see* Domains, domain matrices, role in distinguishing metaphor from metonymy
  doubtful cases 13-14
  pervasiveness 197
  problems 12-15
  see also Common traits of metaphor and metonymy; Domains
Conceptual hierarchies 65-75
  elaboration vs. schematization 65
  elaboration vs. instantiation 65,76 (note 17)
  inheritance hypothesis 59, 66-67
    refinement 59, 73, 75
  metaphoric hierarchies 66-67
  metonymic hierarchies 67-69
    comparison with metaphoric hierarchies 67-69
  metaphtonymic hierarchies 69-74
Conceptual integration *see* Blending
Continuum metaphor-metonymy 10, 93, 94-95, 105, 109,115, 149-150, 195, 198
  metonymy and metaphor as prototype categories 93, 105, 173
  see also Metonymic basis of metaphor; Metonymy-based metaphors
Conventionalization of metonymy *see* General types of metonymy, conventional, factors in conventionalization
Conversation
  and cohesion 286-287, 294-297
  features 283
Conversational implicature 98-101
Cultural models
  of human beings 70
  of love (and metaphor/metonymy) 222-223
  the *Mantafahrer* model 68-69

see also Folk models; Metaphor and cultural frames

Discourse and cognition 284-286
  blue-print model 285-286
  re-elaboration 295
  conduit model 284
Distinction between metaphor and
  metonymy 93, 113-115, 128-130
  criteria 173
  difficulties in distinguishing between
    them 93, 173, 188 (note 3), 197
  similarity (metaphor) vs. contiguity (me-
    tonymy) 63-65
  see also Common traits of metaphor and
    metonymy; Domains, domain matrices,
    role in distinguishing metaphor from
    metonymy
Domain highlighting *see* Concept of metonymy
Domains 60-63, 323
  and subdomains in metonymy 115-121
  primary and secondary domains 126-
    130
  criteria for primary domains 13-14,
    127-128
  matrix domain 112, 116-117, 118, 120,
    121, 130
  domain matrices 323
  role in distinguishing metaphor from
    metonymy 4-5, 197
  problems in ascertaining their bounda-
    ries 8-10, 63
  metaphorically structured domains 67

Embodied understanding 253, 255, 259, 265,
  272
Emotions
  as determining the use of metaphorical
    and metonymic language 197-198
  as scenarios 324
  physiological basis for emotion meta-
    phors 9, 198
  see also Metaphors and submetaphors
    (emotion targets); Physiology-based
    metonymies for emotion
Epistemic grounding 233, 237
  modified notion 247
  see also Subjectification, and epistemic
    meaning

Experiential basis of metaphor *see* Embodied understanding

Folk models
  notion 195
  of the heart 195-211
  vs. conceptual metaphor 195

General types of metaphor
  one-correspondence metaphors 111-113
  many-correspondence metaphors
    110-113
  see also Metonymy-based metaphors
General types of metonymy 33, 115-121
  conventional 14-15, 26 (note 5)
    factors in conventionalization 14-15
  prototypical 26 (note 5)
  schematic 26 (note 5)
  source-in-target 109, 116, 121-124, 125,
    130
  target-in-source 109, 117-118, 121-124,
    125, 126, 128, 130
  typical 14, 26 (note 5)
Generality and metaphorization 42, 208-209
Generic-level metaphors *see* Metaphors and
  submetaphors, COMPLEX ABSTRACT SYSTEMS
  ARE BUILDINGS, (a) SITUATION IS FIRE
Generic space 124-126, 133, 134, 139, 142,
  261
  facilitated by metonymy 125-126
Grammaticalization
  in *be going to* 98
  in predicative possession 100

Image schemas 61, 185-187
  criticism of image schema theory 186-187
  for emotions (sadness) 47-48, 49
  for quantity 48, 49
  for negative states 48, 49
Inheritance Hypothesis *see* Conceptual hierarchies
Interaction between metaphor and
  metonymy 10-12, 59-75, 121-124
  at the purely conceptual level 10-12
  in the same linguistic expression 10, 12,
    69-74
  metaphtonymy 69, 195, 198, 209
  metonymy within the source of a meta-
    phor 121-122

metonymy within the target of a metaphor 122-124
motivation of metaphor by metonymy and
activation of metonymy by metaphor
10-11
motivation of a metonymy by another
metonymy 336, 338
motivation of a metonymy by a metaphor
11-12
see also Metonymic basis of metaphor;
Metonymy-based metaphors; Metaphor
and advertising, interaction of metaphor
and metonymy in advertising; Necessary motivation of metaphor by metonymy (hypothesis)
Invariance principle 4, 44-49, 234, 261, 328
advantages 45
as a consequence of metonymic motivation of metaphor *see* Necessary motivation of metaphor by metonymy (hypothesis)
criticism 236-237
in mapping from deontic onto epistemic
may 236-237
violation in standard metaphorical account of modal shifts 236-237
formulation 45
in Neural Theory of Language 45
modification by many-space model 45,
261
reversal in poetry 261

Literary interpretations 253-254
as radial categories 278 (note 7)
prototypical readings 264, 278 (note 7)
non-prototypical readings 279 (note 10)
see also Cognitive poetics

Main meaning focus in metaphorical mapping 81-89, especially 81-83
dependent on central mappings 50, 83
in A SITUATION IS FIRE 89
in COMPLEX ABSTRACT SYSTEMS ARE BUILD-
INGS 83
vs. invariance 84
see also Central mappings in metaphorical mappings; Necessary motivation of
metaphor by metonymy (hypothesis)
Many-space model *see* Blending

Mapping *see* Analogical mapping; Blending; Central mappings in metaphorical
mappings; Common traits of metaphor
and metonymy; Main meaning focus in
metaphorical mappings; Mapping in
metaphor; Mapping in metonymy; Mapping between metaphor, speech acts and
language forms; Submappings
Mapping between metaphor, speech acts and
language forms 289
Mapping in metaphor 110-113
balance between transfer potential of
source and absorption potential of
target 328
in innovative metaphors 328
between different domains or domain
matrices 3-4, 32, 62-63, 109,110,
129, 173
constraints 327-328; *see also* Invariance
Principle; Muting of innovative metaphor; Metonymic basis of metaphor
domain-internal mapping 62-63
"domain mapping" 109,110, 128-129
from concrete to abstract 174, 188
(note 4)
knowledge (epistemic) submappings 3-4
latent mappings 110-111
mapping potential in terms of conceptual
richness of source 327-328
of a whole schema onto a whole schema
173
ontological, topological, logical
submappings 3-4, 61, 74
open-endedness 4
unidirectional 6-7
see also Central mappings in metaphorical mappings; Metonymic basis of
metaphor; Metonymy-based metaphors; Main meaning focus in metaphorical mappings
Mapping in metonymy 12-13
domain-internal mapping 32-33, 62, 113,
115
one-correspondence mapping 115
see also Metonymic basis of metaphor;
Metonymy-based metaphors; Necessary motivation of metaphor by metonymy (hypothesis)
Mental binding *see* Blending

Mental spaces 124, 270-272
  see Blended space; Blending, input
    spaces; Generic space
Metaphor (general aspects) *see* Concept of
  metaphor; General types of metaphor
Metaphor and advertising
  difference from poetic metaphor 328
  interaction of metaphor and metonymy in
    advertising 325-326, 330-339
  in trade names 338-339
  role of metaphor in advertising 321
  see also Metaphors and submetaphors,
    (the) DESIRED OBJECT IS AN INTERESTING
    OBJECT; Muting of innovative metaphor,
    in advertising
Metaphor and cognition 175
  see also Metaphor and cross-cultural lexi-
    cal semantic shifts
Metaphor and cross-cultural lexical semantic shifts 171-187, especially 176-185
  counting 180-182
    *count*related to *consider, think* 180-181
    count related to *esteem* 181
    count related to *read* 181
    count → *tell, recount* 181-182
  miscellaneous shifts 184-185
    fear → *respect, reverence, awe* 185
    give → *permit* 184
    lean (on) → *rely on* 184
    leave → *permit* 184-185
    pay back -› *revenge, punish* 185
    support → *help* 184
  perception verbs 176-179
    hearing
      deaf → *stupid* 179
      follow related to *obey* 179
      hear → *obey* 176
    taste
      taste related to *try* 176
    vision
      see→ *beware* 177
      see→ *keep watch* 178
      see→ *take care* 177-178
      see→ *understand* 176
      see→ *visit* 177
      see→ *wait expect* (and *wait*, related to
        take care) 178
  physical manipulation 179-180
    dismember→ *explain* 180

grasp→ *understand* 179
  seeking 182-183
    look for → *investigate* 182-183
    look for → *request* 182
    look for → *try* 182
  space mapped onto morality 183
    crooked→ *dishonest* 183
    straight related to *honest* 183
  see *also* Modal shifts; Metaphor and
    polysemy
Metaphor and cultural frames 299-318
  the *Orientalist* conceptual framework
    302-318
  as a cognitive-cultural model 302-303
  "self-presentation" and "other-repre-
    sentation" frames 299, 300, 303, 306,
    307-317
  see also Metaphor and Idealized Cogni-
    tive Models
Metaphor and Idealized Cognitive Models
  299, 300-301, 317
  see also Cultural models; Folk models;
    Metaphor and cultural frames
Metaphor and lexical semantic change *see*
  Metaphor and cross-cultural lexical semantic shifts; Modal shifts; Metaphor and
  polysemy; Semantic change
Metaphor and news coverage 299-318
  the imposition of metaphor 301
Metaphor and non-Indo-European
  languages *see* Metaphor and cross-
  cultural lexical semantic shifts
Metaphor and political discourse 299-318
  in Gulf War crisis 299-318
Metaphor and polysemy 175
Metaphorical blends 124-126, 133-144, especially 133-141
  creative metaphorical blends 140, 142-
    144
  elaboration taking place in the blend 137
Metaphorical entailment 96
  see also Metaphors and submetaphors
Metaphorical explanation of modal shifts
  155
  alternatives to the standard account
    for *may* 237-240
  deontic and epistemic derived from
    ability sense 237-238
  for *must* 243-247

arguments against 149-167, especially
166-167
criticism of the standard account 233-248
for *may* 234-237
for *must* 240-243
see also Invariance Hypothesis, criticism
Metaphors and submetaphors*
ABSTRACTIONS ARE OBJECTS 262
ACTION IS MOTION 50, 96, 102
  SPEED OF ACTION IS SPEED OF MOTION 96
  STARTING AN ACTION IS STARTING ON A PATH
  96
ACTIVE IS ALIVE/INACTIVE IS DEAD 96
AFFECTION IS WARMTH 105, 263
ANIMALS ARE PEOPLE 7
ANGER IS HEAT 104, 135-138
  ANGER IS FIRE 84-86, 90, 104
  ANGER IS THE HEAT OF A FLUID IN A CON-
  TAINER 104; metonymic motivation
  10-11
ANGER IS INSANITY 104
(an) ARGUMENT IS A BUILDING 79, 82
(an) ARGUMENT IS A CONTAINER 79
(an) ARGUMENT IS WAR 79, 110-111
(other) ARGUMENT metaphors 79, 86-88, 90
ATTENTION IS A (MOVING) PHYSICAL
  ENTITY 11
  metonymic motivation 26 (note 4)
(the) BODY IS A CONTAINER FOR EMOTIONS
104
(the) CAR IS PEOPLE AND FAMILY 332, 339
(a) CAREER IS A BUILDING 81
CAUSAL PRECEDENCE IS TEMPORAL PREC-
  EDENCE 99
CHANGES ARE MOVEMENTS OF OBJECTS/
  CHANGE IS MOTION 50, 66, 102
CAUSES OF CHANGES ARE CONTROLLED MOVE-
  MENTS OF OBJECTS 66
CLASSICAL CATEGORIES ARE CONTAINERS 50
(a) COMPANY IS A BUILDING 81
COMMUNICATION IS LINGUISTIC COMMUNICA-
  TION 102

COMPARISON BETWEEN A AND B IS DISTANCE
  BETWEEN A AND B 97
COMPLEX ABSTRACT SYSTEMS ARE BUILDINGS
  82-83
  (ABSTRACT) CREATION IS BUILDING 83
  ABSTRACT STABILITY (OR STRENGTH) IS
    PHYSICAL STRENGTH 83
  ABSTRACT STRUCTURE IS PHYSICAL STRUC-
    TURE 83, 90
  see also (a) CAREER IS A BUILDING, (a) COM-
    PANY IS A BUILDING, (a) LIFE IS A BUILD-
    ING, ECONOMIC SYSTEMS ARE BUILDINGS,
    RELATIONSHIPS ARE BUILDINGS, SOCIAL
    GROUPS ARE BUILDINGS, THEORIES ARE
    BUILDINGS
COMPLEX SYSTEMS ARE PLANTS 84
(the) CONDUIT METAPHOR 103-104
  COMMUNICATION IS TRANSFER 103
  WORDS ARE CONTAINERS FOR MEANING 103
CONFLICT IS FIRE 88, 89, 90
(the) CONTAINER IS AN INTERESTING OBJECT
337
DEATH IS A GRIM REAPER 138-139
(the) DESIRED OBJECT IS AN INTERESTING OB-
  JECT 325-329, 338, especially 325-327
(the) CAR IS A WILD ANIMAL 339
(the) DESIRED OBJECT IS A PRESTIGIOUS
  OBJECT 338
(the) DESIRED OBJECT IS A REVOLTING
  OBJECT 332
(the) DESIRED OBJECT IS A STRANGE OBJECT
332
(the) DESIRED OBJECT IS A VALUABLE OB-
  JECT 325-326
  scale of submetaphors 326
  "SHOCK" metaphors 326
DEVIANT COLORS ARE DEVIANT SOUNDS 36-39
  metonymic motivation 36-39
DOMAINS ARE OBJECTS WITH PARTS 49-50
ECONOMIC SYSTEMS ARE BUILDINGS 81
EMOTION IS HEAT (OF FIRE) 84
  metaphorical entailments 85-86

---

*   Cross-references to other metaphors are to be located within this entry. Metaphors appear in alphabeti-
    cal order on the basis of the words in small capitals; parenthesized low case words such as (the) or (a)
    are ignored for this purpose. The sub-sub-entries under a metaphor are also arranged alphabetically.
    The submetaphors in these sub-sub-entries are only some of the possible submetaphors for the same
    metaphor. Other metaphors which are listed separately could also be regarded as submetaphors of it.
    The same remarks apply to the entry for metonymies and submetonymies.

EMOTION IS TEMPERATURE 263

EMOTIONAL INTIMACY IS PHYSICAL CLOSENESS 97, 105

ENTHUSIASM IS FIRE 86, 90

EVENT STRUCTURE METAPHOR 6, 50, 66-67

   CAUSES ARE FORCES 50, 102

   EVENTS ARE ACTIONS 267

   PURPOSES ARE DESTINATIONS 50, 101

   see also ACTION IS MOTION; CHANGES ARE MOVEMENTS OF OBJECTS; PROPERTIES ARE POSSESSIBLE OBJECTS

EXPERIENCES ARE FOOD 41

   PLEASURABLE MUSIC IS SWEET FOOD 41; metonymic motivation 41

FEAR IS A FAST HEART-BEAT 290

FORCE IS A SUBSTANCE CONTAINED IN AFFECTING CAUSES 103

FORCE IS A SUBSTANCE DIRECTED AT AN AFFECTED PARTY 103

FUNCTIONAL IS UP/DYSFUNCTIONAL IS DOWN 96

GAINING PHYSICAL INTIMACY IS A COMPETITION 105

GENERIC IS SPECIFIC 111,113

(the) GREAT CHAIN METAPHOR 111,113

HAPPINESS IS UP 9, 79, 96

(other) HAPPINESS metaphors 79

(the) HEART IS A CONTAINER 206-209

   (the) HEART IS A CONTAINER FOR EMOTIONS 207-209

(the) HEART IS A LIVING ORGANISM 203-204

(the) HEART IS A LOCUS FOR EMOTIONS 33

(the) HEART IS A MOVABLE OBJECT 200

(the) HEART IS AN AUTONOMOUS ENTITY 203

(the) HEART IS AN OBJECT CHANGEABLE IN SIZE 200

(the) HEART IS AN OBJECT OF VALUE 204-206

   (the)HEART IS A COVETED ENTITY 204-205

(the) HEART IS A SOLID 201

(other) HEART metaphors 199-209

IMAGINATION IS FIRE 88, 90

IMPORTANT IS BIG/UNIMPORTANT IS SMALL 96

(an) INSTRUMENT IS A COMPANION 263

INTENSITY IS HEAT (OF FIRE) 89, 90

INTEREST METAPHORS *see* (the) DESIRED OBJECT IS AN INTERESTING OBJECT

INTIMACY IS CLOSENESS 263

KNOWING IS SEEING 99, 228

LANGUAGE IS COMMUNICATION 263

LEARNING IS FAST MOVEMENT 290

(a) LIFE IS A BUILDING 81

LIFE IS A COCOON 256-259

LIFE IS A GAME 289-291

LIFE IS A JOURNEY 6, 61, 66-67, 196, 261, 262, 292

LINGUISTIC ACTION IS HUMAN SOUND 63

LOVE IS A COLLABORATIVE WORK OF ART 293

LOVE IS A JOURNEY 3-4, 6, 61, 66-67, 112, 196

LOVE IS A PRECIPICE 293

LOVE IS A UNITY 97

LOVE IS CLOSENESS 293

LOVE IS FIRE 85, 90

LOVE IS HARD WORK 293

MARRIAGE IS A DURABLE BOND BETWEEN TWO PEOPLE 97

MEASUREMENT SCALES ARE SPATIAL SCALES 42, 55 (note 21)

   see also SPATIAL MEASUREMENT SCALES ARE PATHS

(the) MIND IS (THE) BODY 97, 176

(the) MIND IS A CONTAINER FOR OBJECTS 104

MORE IS UP/LESS IS DOWN 41-42, 94-95 metonymic motivation 41-42

MORE OF A PRICE IS HIGHER IN A BIRD'S FLIGHT 95

NEGATIVE IS DARK 39-40 metonymic motivation 40

   (a) NEGATIVE EMOTION IS DARK 40

PEOPLE ARE ANIMALS 7, 111-112

   ANGRY BEHAVIOR IS AGGRESSIVE ANIMAL BEHAVIOR 12

PEOPLE ARE MACHINES 112-113

(a) PERSON IS A POSSESSED OBJECT 262

PERSUASION IS POLICING 289-291 metaphorical entailments 290

PITCH SCALES ARE PATHS 41

POSSESSION IS HOLDING 100

PRICES ARE EVENTS 95

PRICES ARE FLYING OBJECTS 95

(a) PROBLEM IS A TANGLE 102

PROPERTIES ARE POSSESSIBLE OBJECTS 66, 70-72

   A DEVIANT PROPERTY IS A DEVIANT CONTENT OF A CONTAINER 71, 72

   A DEVIANT PROPERTY IS A DEVIANT (LOCATED) POSSESSION 71, 72

DEVIANT BEHAVIOR IS QUANTITATIVE DEVI-
ANCE OF A POSSESSION 71-72
PROPERTIES ARE PHYSICAL PROPERTIES 102
(PSYCHIC) HARM IS PHYSICAL INJURY 102
PURPOSEFUL ACTIVITY IS TRAVELING ALONG A
PATH TOWARD A DESTINATION 135
RELATIONSHIPS ARE BUILDINGS 80
SADNESS IS DARK 40
SADNESS IS DOWN 43-44, 47-48
   metaphor, not metonymy 9
   metonymic motivation 9, 10, 43-44
SAYING IS LAUGHING 150
SIGNIFICANT IS BIG 292
SIMILARITY IS CLOSENESS/DIFFERENCE IS RE-
MOTENESS 97-98
(a) SITUATION IS FIRE 89
   metaphorical entailments 87-89
SMELL SCALES ARE PATHS 42
SOCIAL GROUPS ARE BUILDINGS 81
   other metaphors for social groups 142
SOLIDARITY IS CLOSENESS 289-291
   metaphorical entailments 290
SPATIAL MEASUREMENT SCALES ARE PATHS 41,
42, 48, 55 (note 21)
THEORIES ARE BUILDINGS 80
TIME IS A LIMITED RESOURCE 110-111
   TIME IS A VALUABLE COMMODITY 110-111
   TIME IS MONEY 110-111
TIME IS AN AGENT (HEALER) 267
TIME IS AN OBJECT 266
TIME IS LOCATION 266
   TIME IS A CONTAINER 266
TIME IS SPACE 98
UNDERSTANDING IS SEEING 292
VALUE METAPHORS *see* (the) DESIRED OBJECT
IS AN INTERESTING OBJECT, (the) DESIRED
OBJECT IS A VALUABLE OBJECT
WELL-BEING IS WEALTH 99-100
see also Metaphor and cultural frames,
   the *Orientalist* framework, "self-pres-
   entation" and "other representation"
   frames; Synesthesia
Metaphtonymy *see* Conceptual hierarchies,
   metaphtonymic hierarchies; Interaction
   between metaphor and metonymy
Metonymic basis of metaphor 31-53, 93-
   105, 195, 198, 199
   degrees of connection between metonymic basis and metaphors 199-211

in emotion metaphors 43-44, 47-48; *see
   also* Physiology-based metonymies for
   emotion
in metaphors for the heart 195-211, especially 209
"metaphor from metonymy" 149-150
metonymic bridges for metaphor 156, 160
metonymy as underlying the metaphoric
   mapping of non-counterparts 138-141
see also Interaction of metaphor and metonymy; Metaphor and advertising, interaction of metaphor and metonymy in
   advertising; Metonymy-based metaphors; Necessary motivation of metaphor by metonymy (hypothesis)
Metonymic explanation of modal shifts
   155-156
   arguments against 149-167, especially
   166-167
   strengthening of conversational
   implicatures 159
Metonymic links between metaphors 198
Metonymic models
   of darkness 41-42
   of deviant colors 35-39, especially 37-38
   of deviant sounds 35-39, especially 37-38
   of motherhood 13
   of pleasurable experiences (music) 41
   of sadness 43-44, 47
Metonymies and submetonymies
   AUTHOR FOR WORK 13, 14-15, 126
   BODY PART FOR (MANNER OF) FUNCTION 11
   BODY PART FOR PERSON 6
      FACE FOR PERSON 6
   CAUSE FOR EFFECT 40
      see also DARK FOR NEGATIVE STATES
      CAUSED BY DARK
   CONSUMED GOODS FOR CUSTOMER 12, 114-
   115
   CONTAINER FOR CONTAINED 336-337
   DARK FOR NEGATIVE STATES CAUSED BY DARK
   40
   DARK FOR NEGATIVE VALUE JUDGMENT (OF
   DARK) 40
   DEVIANT BEHAVIOR/APPEARANCE/POSSESSION
   FOR STUPIDITY 69
   DEVIANT HEAD FOR DEVIANT MENTAL PROP-
   ERTY 72
   DOWNWARD SPATIAL ORIENTATION FOR DOWN-

WARD BODILY POSTURE 43, 44
EFFECT FOR CAUSE 25, 38 (note 2), 215-230
   PERCEPTUAL EVENT FOR ITS CAUSE 225-229
   RESULT FOR ACTION 215, 216-224
   SYMPTOM FOR ITS CAUSE 225
   see also Necessary motivation of meta-
      phor by metonymy, ... loud color,
      sweet music, high notes on a piano;
      THE PHYSIOLOGICAL EFFECTS OF AN EMO-
      TION STAND FOR THE EMOTION; UP FOR
      MORE
GENERIC FOR SPECIFIC 225, 229
HOLDING FOR POSSESSION 100
IMAGE FOR OBJECT 120-121
NAME FOR PRODUCT 335-338
PART FOR WHOLE 6
PHYSICAL PROPERTY FOR INTERNAL PROPERTY
   71, 72
   DEVIANT PHYSICAL PROPERTY FOR DEVIANT
      INTERNAL PROPERTY 72
PLACE FOR ACTIVITY 101
PRECEDENCE FOR CAUSE 99
PRODUCER FOR PRODUCT 338, 339
(PSYCHIC) HARM FOR PHYSICAL INJURY 102
RULER FOR STATE 306, 308
SALIENT FEATURE FOR CITY 120-121
SALIENT PROPERTY FOR LESS SALIENT PROP-
   ERTY 72
SEEING FOR KNOWING 99
SENSORY PROPERTY FOR MENTAL PROPERTY 71
   DEVIANT SENSORY PROPERTY FOR DEVIANT
      MENTAL PROPERTY 71
THE PHYSIOLOGICAL EFFECTS OF AN EMOTION
   STAND FOR THE EMOTION 11, 322-323
   BEING STARTLED FOR FEAR 323
   BODY HEAT FOR ANGER 104
   DOWNWARD BODILY POSTURE FOR SADNESS
      43-44
   DROP IN BODY TEMPERATURE FOR FEAR 323
   FEELING NAUSEATED FOR DISGUST, FEAR
      323
   FISTS AND TEETH CLENCHED FOR ANGER 323
   GRABBING FOR DESIRE 321, 322-326, 334-
      339; as a conceptual link to action
      324; linguistic realization 324; visu-
      alization 324
   HEART RATE FOR EMOTION 33
   HEAVY WALK, STOMPING FOR ANGER 323
   INABILITY TO SEE PROPERLY FOR LOVE 323
   INABILITY TO SPEAK FOR FEAR 323
   INSANE BEHAVIOR FOR ANGER 104
   JUMPING UP AND DOWN FOR JOY 323
   MOIST HANDS FOR FEAR 323
   QUICKENING OF HEARTBEAT FOR ANGER 323
   REDNESS IN FACE AND NECK AREA FOR AN-
      GER 323
   SENSE OF BEING KEYED UP FOR ANGER,
      JOY 323
   SLOW, SHUFFLING MOVEMENTS FOR SAD-
      NESS 323
   TEARS FOR SADNESS 323
   TOUCHING, HUGGING, KISSING for love
      323
THING FOR ITS REPRESENTATION 95
UP FOR MORE 42, 95
WORD-FORMS FOR CONTENT 103
Metonymy (general aspects) see Concept of
   metonymy; General types of metonymy
Metonymy and advertising 335-339
   in trade names 338-339
   see also Metaphor and advertising, inter-
      action of metaphor and metonymy;
      Metonymies and submetonymies, THE
      PHYSIOLOGICAL EFFECTS OF AN EMOTION
      STAND FOR THE EMOTION, GRABBING FOR
      DESIRE
Metonymy and anaphoric reference with
   conjoined predicates 116-117
Metonymy and deferred reference 117-121
   indexical reference 117-120
   reference with description 119-121
Metonymy and English grammar 215-230
   EFFECT FOR CAUSE in English grammar 215-
      230
   see also The RESULT FOR ACTION me-
      tonymy in English grammar; The
      What's that N? construction
   GENERIC FOR SPECIFIC and English grammar
      see The What's that N? construction
Metonymy and identity 141
Metonymy and predicate transfer 117-119
Metonymy-based metaphors 31-53, 93-105
   definition 93
   source and target related by category
      structure 101-102
   source and target related by cultural mod-
      els 102-105
   in the domain of communication 103

in the domain of ideas and emotions 33-34, 47-48, 104-105
in the domain of pleasant experiences 41
in the domain of physical forces 103
source and target related by implicature 98-101
in sequential events 98-100
in event-result relationships 100-101
in place-activity relationships 101
source and target with a common experiential basis 94-98
based on comparison 97-98
based on complementarity 96-97
based on correlation 40, 42, 46, 48, 51, 95-96
see also Interaction of metaphor and metonymy; Metaphor and advertising, interaction of metaphor and metonymy in advertising; Metonymic basis of metaphor; Motivation, of metaphor; Necessary motivation of metaphor by metonymy (hypothesis)
Modal shifts 149-167
bridges in 156, 160
see also Metonymic basis of metaphor
of *can* and *could* 151-152, 153
of *magan* (Old English) 152-153, 157-159
of *may* and *might* 151-152, 155, 156
deontic to epistemic 234-240
of *must* 152, 153, 159-166
deontic to epistemic 240-247
of *will* and *would* 151-152, 155-156
"partial sanction" explanation *see* Partial sanction, and modal shifts
types
deontic to epistemic 156, 233-248
participant-external to epistemic 159-166
participant-internal to participant-external 157-159
typological perspective 153-154
see also Epistemic grounding; Metaphorical explanation of modal shifts; Metonymic explanation of modal shifts; Modality; Subjectification
Modality
semantic space of modality 152-153
types

deontic (root) 233-248
epistemic 152, 153, 154, 155, 156-167, 233-248
general objective necessity 161, 163
participant-external 152-167
participant-internal 152-159
see also Epistemic grounding; Modal shifts; Subjectification
Modals (central modals)
characterization 151
see also Modal shifts
Motivation
of metaphor 10-11, 93
see also Interaction between metaphor and metonymy; Metonymic basis of metaphor; Metonymy-based metaphors; Necessary motivation of metaphor by metonymy (hypothesis)
of metonymy 11-12, 336, 338, 339
see also Interaction between metaphor and metonymy
Muting of innovative metaphors 321-340, especially 328-339
differences from constraints on conventional metaphors 328-329
in advertising 328-340
specific analyses
Benetton adverts 334
the Joop! advert 336-337
the Superkings cigarette advert 332-334
the VW Passat advert 330-338

Necessary motivation of metaphor by metonymy (hypothesis) 11, 31-53
comparison with notion of main meaning focus (Kövecses) 50-51
comparison with theory of primitive metaphors 51
discussion of apparent counterexamples 35-42
loud color 35-39, 46
black mood, 39-40
sweet music 41, 46
high notes on a piano 41-42
high smell 42
formulation of hypothesis 31
invariance as a consequence of metonymic motivation 44-49, especially 46-49

in emotion metaphors (SADNESS IS DOWN) 47-48
in *loud color* and *sweet music* 45-46
in MORE IS UP 48
in NEGATIVE IS DARK 58
motivation by generalization of a metonymy 42, 47-49; *see also* Generality and metaphorization
in SADNESS IS DOWN 43-44
preservation of source and target roles 44
motivation by metonymic models of target 42, 45-46; *see also* Metonymic models
possible objections 49-50
see also Interaction between metaphor and metonymy, motivation of metaphor by metonymy and activation of metonymy by metaphor; Metonymic basis of metaphor; Metonymy-based metaphors; Motivation, of metaphor

Open-endedness of metaphor *see* Mapping in metaphor
Optimality principles in blending 138-139
metonymy projection constraint 139-141
occurring in the target domain 138
Orientalism *see* Metaphor and cultural frames

Parallel chaining *see* Partial Sanction; Subjectification
Partial sanction 149, 150-151, 157-163, 167
and modal shifts 149-167; *see also* Subjectification
chaining 157-163 *see also* Modal shifts
parallel chaining 149
and modal shifts 149-167, especially 159-163
sanctioning chain 158, 162
notion 150-151
Peirce's theory of the complex sign 254-255
diagram 255, 258
icon 254
image 255, 258
index 254-255
metaphor 255, 258
symbol 255

Presentation of the articles in the volume 15-25
Physiology-based metonymies for emotion 198, 322-324
status as metonymies 323-324

Resultant (action, event, state) 216, 217, 218

Scope of metaphor 79-91, 262-264, especially 80-81
definition 80
of BUILDING 80-81
of FIRE 84-89
selection of aspects of target domain 83, 89
dependent on central knowledge of the source domain 84
see also Main meaning focus in metaphorical mappings; Mapping in metaphor, mapping potential in terms of conceptual richness of source; Metonymic basis of metaphor
Semantic change 171-187, especially 171-185
cognitive universals in 172
direction of change 174
notion 173
see also Metaphor and cross-cultural lexical semantic shifts; Metaphor and polysemy; Modal shifts
Simple vs. compound metaphors 50-51
Sound 35-39
scalar construal 36
see also Metonymic models
Source domain 3
role of source domains in metaphor *see* Scope of metaphor
types of source domains *see* Domains; Metaphors and submetaphors; Metaphor and cross-cultural lexical semantic shifts; Scope of metaphor
Subjectification 159, 160, 161, 163-166
and epistemic meaning 237, 238, 246
modified notion 247
rise in subjectified uses of *must* 165-166
Submappings *see* Mapping in metaphor, knowledge (epistemic) submappings, *and* ontological, topological, logical submappings

Synesthesia 35, 39, 41

Target domain 3
  target domains in metaphor *see* Domains;
  Metaphors and submetaphors; Metaphor and cross-cultural lexical semantic shifts; Scope of metaphor
Test frames for dynamic potential 216
The RESULT FOR ACTION metonymy in English
  grammar 215-224
  be + adj/NP 217
  non-actional verbs (*win, know, love*) 220-
  223
  passive sentences (and comparison with
  German) 217-220

stative imperatives (and comparison with
  German) 215-216
stative verbs with negation 223
see also Test frames for dynamic potential
The *What's that N?* construction 224-230
  and EFFECT FOR CAUSE 224-229
  comparison with German 228-229
  sense impressions 225-229
  symptoms 225
  and GENERIC FOR SPECIFIC 224-225
  senses (taxonomic/causal) 224-225
Theory of literature 253
  see also Cognitive poetics